Socialism, Internationalism, and Development in the Third World

Histories of Internationalism

This book series features cutting-edge research on the history of international cooperation and internationalizing ambitions in the modern world. Providing an intellectual home for research into the many guises of internationalism, its titles draw on methods and insights from political, social, cultural, economic and intellectual history. It showcases a rapidly expanding scholarship which has begun to transform our understanding of internationalism and the modern world.

Cutting across established academic fields such as European, World, International and Global History, the series critically examines historical perceptions of geography, regions, centres, peripheries, borderlands, networks and connections across space in the history of internationalism. It includes both monographs and edited volumes that shed new light on local and global contexts for international projects; the impact of class, race and gender on international aspirations; the roles played by a variety of international organizations and institutions; and the hopes, fears, tensions and conflicts underlying them.

The series is published in association with Birkbeck's Centre for the Study of Internationalism.

Published:

Organizing the 20th-Century World, ed. by Karen Gram-Skjoldager, Haakon Andreas Ikonomou and Torsten Kahlert

Placing Internationalism: International Conferences and the Making of the Modern World, ed. by Stephen Legg, Mike Heffernan, Jake Hodder and Benjamin Thorpe

Inventing the Third World: In Search of Freedom for the Postwar Global South, ed. by Jeremy Adelman and Gyan Prakash

Internationalists in European History: Rethinking the Twentieth Century, ed. by Jessica Reinsich and David Brydan

International Cooperation in Cold War Europe, Daniel Stinsky

Socialist Internationalism and the Gritty Politics of the Particular, ed. by Kristin Roth-Ey

Relief and Rehabilitation for a Postwar World, ed. by Samantha K. Knapton and Katherine Rossy

Dismantling the League of Nations, Jane Mumby

Cosmopolitan Elites and the Making of Globality, Leonie Wolters

Informing Interwar Internationalism, Emil Eiby Seidenfaden

Dam Internationalism, ed. by Vincent Lagendijk and Frederik Schulze

Forthcoming:

International Organizations and the Cold War: Competition, Cooperation and Convergence, ed. by Sandrine Kott, Elisabeth Roehrlich and Eva-Maria Muschik

The War for Anatolia and the Unmaking of International Order: Greece, Turkey and the End of WWI, ed. by Georgios Giannakopoulos, Joseph A. Maiolo and Gonda Van Steen

Student Internationalism and the Global Cold War: The International Union of Students, 1946–1991, Mikuláš Pešta

Poland and the Making of Transnational Social Science: Eastern Europe, the US and the Wilsonian Moment, Olga Linkiewicz

Socialism, Internationalism, and Development in the Third World

Envisioning Modernity in the Era of Decolonization

Edited by Su Lin Lewis and Nana Osei-Opare

BLOOMSBURY ACADEMIC
LONDON • NEW YORK • OXFORD • NEW DELHI • SYDNEY

BLOOMSBURY ACADEMIC
Bloomsbury Publishing Plc
50 Bedford Square, London, WC1B 3DP, UK
1385 Broadway, New York, NY 10018, USA
29 Earlsfort Terrace, Dublin 2, Ireland

BLOOMSBURY, BLOOMSBURY ACADEMIC and the Diana logo are trademarks of Bloomsbury Publishing Plc

First published in Great Britain 2024

Series design by Tjaša Krivec
Cover image © First Afro-Asian Women's Conference, Egypt, 1961. Image courtesy of the Shirley Graham DuBois Papers, Schlesinger Library, Radcliffe Institute, Harvard University

A catalogue record for this book is available from the British Library.

A catalog record for this book is available from the Library of Congress.

ISBN: HB: 978-1-3504-1343-6
ePDF: 978-1-3504-1344-3
eBook: 978-1-3504-1345-0

Typeset by Integra Software Services Pvt. Ltd.

Series: Histories of Internationalism

Contents

Illustrations

List of Contributors

Eric Burton is Assistant Professor of Global History at the University of Innsbruck. For his PhD dissertation on Tanzania's ujamaa and Cold War Germany, he was awarded the Walter Markov Prize from the European Network in Universal and Global History (ENIUGH). He collaborated on the 'Socialism Goes Global' project at the University of Exeter and has published in journals such as the *Journal of Global History*, *Cold War History* and the *Journal of African Cultural Studies*. His ongoing project examines Cairo, Accra and Dar es Salaam as 'hubs of decolonization' for African liberation movements in the late 1950s and 1960s.

Joanna Crow is Professor of Latin American Studies at the University of Bristol. Previously, her work focused on debates about nationalism and nation-building in Chile, with a particular interest in Indigenous-state relations. Her first monograph, *The Mapuche in Modern Chile: A Cultural History*, was published by the University Press of Florida in 2013. Her most recent book, *Itinerant Ideas: Race, Indigeneity and Cross-Border Intellectual Encounters in Latin America* (Palgrave Macmillan, 2022), shifted the focus of analysis from race and nation to transnational race-making, an area she continues to explore in a new project on cities and international congresses.

David C. Engerman is Leitner Professor of History and Global Affairs at Yale and a former president of the Society for Historians of American Foreign Relations. He is the author of three books, most recently *The Price of Aid: The Economic Cold War in India* (Harvard, 2018), and is currently completing a history of international development.

William Figueroa is Assistant Professor of History of International Relations at the University of Groningen. He holds a PhD in History from the University of Pennsylvania and was previously a postdoctoral researcher at the University of Cambridge Centre for Geopolitics. He focuses on historical and contemporary Sino-Iranian relations, as well as China's foreign policy in the Middle East. His dissertation, 'China and the Iranian Left: Transnational Networks of Social, Cultural, and Ideological Exchange, 1905–1979', received the Mehrdad Mashayekhi Dissertation Prize from the Association of Iranian Studies. He is currently working on his first book based on that project.

Su Lin Lewis is Professor in Global and Asian History at the University of Bristol. She is the author of *Cities in Motion: Urban Life and Cosmopolitanism in Southeast Asia 1920–1940* (Cambridge, 2016) and co-editor (with Carolien Stolte) of *The Lives of Cold War Afro-Asianism* (Leiden, 2022). Her current monograph is on socialist internationalism in decolonizing Southeast Asia.

Tehyun Ma is Lecturer in International History at the University of Sheffield. Her research interests include exploring the transnational movement of social policies and ideas in twentieth-century China, as well as state-building and propaganda strategies in China and Taiwan in the 1940s and 1950s. She is currently completing a book manuscript on the Chinese Nationalist mobilization of Taiwan in the early Cold War.

Claudia Martínez Hernández is a PhD candidate at the University of Vienna writing on the circulation of Cuban personnel within the Council for Mutual Economic Assistance (CMEA). She is a collaborator on the research project 'Entanglements Cuba-GDR: Mobilities, exchanges, circulations within the Council for Mutual Economic Assistance'.

Marc Matera is Professor of History at the University of California, Santa Cruz. He is the author of *Black London: The Imperial Metropolis and Decolonization in the Twentieth Century* (University of California Press, 2015). He co-authored *The Global 1930s: The International Decade* (Routledge, 2017) with Susan Kingsley Kent and *The Women's War of 1929: Gender and Violence in Colonial Nigeria* (Palgrave Macmillan, 2012) with Misty L. Bastian and Susan Kingsley Kent.

Kelvin Ng is a PhD candidate at the Department of History at Yale University. He is also a graduate fellow in Women's, Gender, and Sexuality Studies, and in Translation Studies. His dissertation, 'Vernacular Equality: Migration and Resistance in the Indian Ocean, c. 1920–1940', brings together the social history of migration and the intellectual history of internationalism in four linked Indian Ocean spaces: British India, Republican China, British Malaya and the Dutch East Indies. His research interests more broadly include political economy, intellectual history and histories of migration.

Pradipto Niwandhono is Lecturer at the Department of History, Faculty of Humanities, Airlangga University, Surabaya. He published a book stemming from his MA thesis in 2011, entitled *Yang ter(di)lupakan: Kaum Indo dan Benih Nasionalisme Indonesia* [The Forgotten One: The Indos and the Seeds of Indonesian Nationalism]. Since then, his studies have focused on the fields of intellectual history, specifically political ideas and the political culture of Indonesia. He obtained his PhD from the University of Sydney in 2022 with a dissertation entitled 'The Making of Modern Indonesian Intellectuals: The Indonesian Socialist Party (PSI) and Democratic Socialist Ideas, 1930s to mid-1970s'.

Nana Osei-Opare is Assistant Professor in the Department of History and the Center for African and African Studies at Rice University. He is a National Endowment for the Humanities and Ford Foundation Fellow at the Schomburg Center for Research in Black Culture. His monograph, *Socialist De-Colony: Black and Soviet Entanglements in Ghana's Decolonization and Cold War Projects*, is contracted to Cambridge University Press. His work has been published in *Comparative Studies in Society and History*, the *Journal of African History*, the *Journal of West African History*, *The Washington Post* and *Foreign Policy Magazine*.

Taylor C. Sherman works on the history of postcolonial India. She is currently Professor in the School of Humanities and Languages at the University of New South Wales. Her latest book is *Nehru's India: A History in Seven Myths* (Princeton University Press, 2022).

Matthew Shutzer is Assistant Professor of Environmental History at the University of California, Berkeley. His writing has appeared in *The Radical History Review, Past and Present*, and *Comparative Studies in Society and History*, among other venues. His first monograph, forthcoming with Princeton University Press, explores the history of fossil fuels, capitalism, and state development in colonial and post-colonial South Asia.

Berthold Unfried is *Dozent* (Associate Professor) at the Institute for Economic and Social History at the University of Vienna and author of several books in the field of global history. Book publications in print include a comparative history of the development policies of the two German states in the age of 'development' (1960–1990). His current research focus is on policies of 'development' and 'international solidarity' as forms of moral politics and of political economy. His current research project is on Cuba and the German Democratic Republic as developmental actors in the *Council for Mutual Economic Assistance* (https://socialist-entanglements.univie.ac.at/).

Wildan Sena Utama is Lecturer at the Department of History, Universitas Gadjah Mada in Indonesia. He completed his PhD at the University of Bristol on the participation of Indonesian anti-imperialist activists in Afro-Asian movements. He wrote a book on the history of the Bandung Conference in Indonesia titled *Konferensi Asia-Afrika 1955* (2017). He was an associate researcher in the AHRC-funded Afro-Asian Networks Research Network and participated in an AHRC-funded collaborative seminar on Socialist Internationalism in the Afro-Asian World 1950s–1960s. His research interests are in the history of connections between Indonesia and the Afro-Asian world in the twentieth century.

Kevin A. Young teaches Latin American history at the University of Massachusetts Amherst. He is the author of *Blood of the Earth: Resource Nationalism, Revolution, and Empire in Bolivia* (2017) and *Abolishing Fossil Fuels: Lessons from Movements That Won* (2024), and editor of *Making the Revolution: Histories of the Latin American Left* (2019).

Acknowledgements

This volume was generated from a vibrant international conference held at Bristol University in June 2022 called "Development Dreams from the Socialist South". Funding from an AHRC Leadership Fellowship on Socialist Internationalism in the Afro-Asian World (AH/V001205/1) made the event possible. Open Access funding was made possible by UK Research and Innovation (UKRI), as well as a generous grant from Rice University's Creative Ventures Fund: Scholarly and Creative Works Subvention, Rice University's School of Humanities, and Rice University's Office of Research. We would also like to thank the University of Bristol, the Schomburg Center for Research in Black Culture, the Institute for Advanced Studies at Princeton, and Rice University for providing the intellectual spaces for the project's completion. At Bloomsbury, we would like to thank Maddie Holder, our editor, and Megan Harris for seeing this project through to the end, as well as Paige Harris and Hemavathy (Hema) Rammamoorthy for putting this book into production. We thank Jessica Reinisch and David Brydan for their enthusiasm in including the book in their wonderful series.

We thank, in particular, the contributors to the volume, most of whom were participants at our 2022 conference. We were grateful for the valuable discussant comments of Emma Hunter and Christy Thornton. We would also like to thank those whom we contacted after the conference – Kelvin Ng, Kevin Young, and Bill Figueroa - for their enthusiasm in joining this project, and were glad to hear their papers as a group in our ensuing online workshop series. This book is a testament to the fact that global history is at its richest and most exciting when it is a product of generous collaboration between colleagues across geographic, institutional, and intellectual boundaries. We are thankful, too, to our families, including Sean Fox and Vivian Chenxue Lu, whose eyes on the pages and cover design were most useful, and to our children - Juna, Aiyun, Oscar and Osei - for their much-needed levity and patience in permitting us to produce this volume.

Introduction: Development dreams from the socialist South

Su Lin Lewis and Nana Osei-Opare

The inhabitants of post-colonial states were born into worlds of exploitation. They witnessed or suffered the brutalities of forced labour, as their lands were mined, fished and turned into monocrop economies to accumulate greater profits for foreign businessmen, companies and their governments.[1] They were told that they did not have the intellect or 'maturity' to govern themselves and needed the tutelage and the iron fist of those with white skin. The Indian Civil Service Officer H. Fielding Hall referred to the Burmese as 'A People at School', and the murdered anti-apartheid Black South African Black Consciousness leader Steve Biko lamented that colonized people were treated as 'perpetual u/16s' in the colonial system.[2]

The advent of socialism as a state policy in the Soviet Union, with the Bolshevik Revolution in 1917, and the breath-taking speed of the Soviet Union's metamorphosis – under the moniker of socialism – from a rural society to an industrialized one within a generation initially offered hope to many colonized subjects. They believed that they, too, could transform their people's lives within a generation. They dreamt that socialism could and would counteract the negative impact of capitalist development, the extractive export-orientated economy, and European monopoly over their goods. The Comintern's policy of anti-imperialism and outreach to Africa, Asia and Latin America created a new space for political action for intellectuals and activists.[3] But by the 1930s, some, such as the Indian Marxist M. N. Roy and the pan-African intellectual George Padmore, recognized that the Stalinist Soviet model – predicated on extreme violence, a near callousness or disregard of human life and explicit class warfare and alienation – was incompatible with the anti-imperialist goals and political slogans that targeted colonial peoples.[4] Meanwhile, the rise of the Left in America and Europe, particularly amidst the tumultuous aftermath of a global depression, provided models of a welfare state that would protect the rights of workers; yet its wavering commitment to anti-colonialism fell far short of its humanist ideals,[5] leaving many colonized radicals bitterly disappointed that 'leftist' European political parties maintained colonial subjugation and failed to export to the colonies many of the rights and concessions given to those in the metropole.[6]

With the realization of independence, many within this volume were determined to create a more egalitarian world, where states and citizens owned the means of production and would provide for the well-being of all. Socialism – which many had encountered on educational journeys, in translated texts and book clubs, or through burgeoning trade union movements at home – provided a language to articulate these visions.[7] In Africa, Asia and Latin America, socialism was widely understood as the vehicle and ideology through which colonized and formerly colonized states, technocrats and people would employ to 'develop' new societies and new dreams.[8] Development along socialist lines would restore 'human dignity' to the 'darker nations' or '"coloured" peoples' of the world.[9] They would no longer be treated as adolescents but as members, and more importantly, *makers*, of a new international order.

Histories of socialism, development and internationalism from the Global South

The historiography of development, often written from the standpoint of America and Europe, has addressed socialism tangentially; even if it was often Fabian socialists and American New Dealers who were central in advising postwar British and American development policies in Africa and Asia.[10] New histories of the Eastern bloc, meanwhile, examine socialist and development encounters and spaces between the Second and Third World.[11] In African historiography, tales of the African post-colony have long been linked to development discourses and its supposed failures.[12] In recent years, the history of development has paid increased attention to African, Asian and Latin American actors, not as passive recipients, but as individuals who shaped the terms of engagement with European, American and Soviet aid initiatives.[13] Countries in Africa, Asia and Latin America are now becoming part of the origin story of development, with a number of surveys on development giving brief mention to the Meiji restoration or Sun Yat Sen's 1922 *The International Development of China* as examples of development's origins outside the West.[14]

Despite this welcome attention, we still lack an historical perspective on development that focuses explicitly on the Global South.[15] As we argue in this book, development and socialism are impossible to separate within the context of decolonizing states. For many of the leaders and inhabitants of these states, development dreams *were* socialist dreams, or 'freedom dreams'.[16] As Latin American states – who had gained their nominal independence long before countries in Africa and Asia – knew well, colonial freedom did not mean freedom from capitalist exploitation. The demands of an interconnected, global capitalist economy meant that the plunder of a country's resources by foreign business interests continued, prompting many Latin American states to take a leading role in shaping a rules-based multilateral order, even if Latin American communist parties, as Joanna Crow shows us in her study of their 1929 Latin American Communist Parties conference, sought to dismantle it.[17] Indeed, Kevin Young argues that some of the reasons many leftist Latin American leaders and parties failed were because they embraced mixed economies and never truly dispensed with the capitalist system. States that were no longer administered under a British, French, German, Portuguese or Spanish flag were not post-colonies, but 'neo-colonies', still having their economies dictated to by foreign governments and companies.[18] Young's account of the plight of leftist regimes in Cuba and Venezuela underscored the dangers of economic imperialism and colonialism. Likewise, delegates at Cairo's Afro-Asian Women's Conference, as Su Lin Lewis and Wildan Sena Utama show, employed the Ghanaian leader and intellectual Kwame Nkrumah's terminology of 'neocolonialism' to rail against the dominance of American mining companies on the African continent. This was already a contentious issue before Ghana's independence in 1957, as Kelvin Ng shows us: the Indonesian socialist Tan Malaka saw in the development programmes of Indonesia's revolutionary leaders from the 1920s to the 1930s that they operated within the constraints of an export economy rather than state-led industrialization. From Central and South America to Africa to Asia, radicals believed that Western powers and domestic bourgeoisie classes abhorred socialist economic development and worked in concert to stifle this. Socialist development faced strong headwinds internally and externally.

How then to secure economic freedom, social equity and national independence in the vulnerable, early years of the post-colonial state? Where should development be prioritized: urban centres or rural areas, agriculture or heavy industry? Who needed it most: rural labourers or industrial workers, women or men? Was the state to nationalize all industries, some, or none? What, if any, was the role of foreign capital or aid? And, if so, from whom? These questions and tensions preoccupied and haunted the early leaders, technocrats, intellectuals and everyday people of the neo-colonies and within this volume. While attention to 'Socialists' – often read as 'radicals' – in the Global South has focused largely on their revolutionary and anti-colonial visions, what has long been neglected are their plans for economic, social and political development – from Indigenous land reform, examined in Joanna Crow's and Tehyun Ma's chapters, to women's education, in Su Lin Lewis and Wildan Sena Utama's chapter, to overhauling the fishing industry, in Osei-Opare's chapter.[19] Drawing from Frederick Cooper and Randall M. Packard, while the idea of development and the need for concerted government interventions by both poor and wealthy countries were integral to constructing a new, unified conceptual framework between 'industrialized, affluent nations' and 'poor, emerging nations',[20] states and societies differed on the political economic philosophies to drive said development. What unites this volume is our actors' firm commitment to socialist development. While that socialism was contested and differed, they eschewed development from imperial metropoles and Western companies that solely privileged capitalism. Many of the chapters in this volume address how these figures wrestled with different models. They convey how administrators, thinkers, politicians and anti-colonialists in the colonial and post-colonial worlds conjured up and implemented alternative development and socialist visions and policies that suited their own predicaments and societies.

Socialism came in different forms. While the pace of Soviet development prompted many in the decolonizing world to scrutinize those policies, these essays underscore that Soviet socialism was but one of a few visions and ideological currencies of socialism being articulated, circulated and exchanged across the world. While it might have been the largest socialist state by the middle of the twentieth century, the Soviets certainly did not have a monopoly on socialist and development discourses – and neither did

Western leftist circles. The influence of Maoism has long been noted as an inspiration for many leaders and intellectuals in the colonial and post-colonial world, both as an ideology and developmental model.[21] Yasser Nasser has recently shown how both China and Japan offered competing models of development to the Indian economist J.C. Kumarappa.[22] In this volume, Kelvin Ng and Pradipto Niwandhono examine how Indian and Indonesian socialists appropriated and adapted diverse influences from the Asian and European left. Ma explores Sun Yat Sen's legacy for 'socialist' development not in the People's Republic of China, but in Taiwan, particularly in the realm of land reform (that Taiwanese elites could engage with socialism despite its supposed 'alignment' with the United States speaks to the limitations of viewing this period through a bipolar, Cold War perspective). The authors of this volume are also cognizant of how socialism operated across multiple temporal contexts. Working within the historiography of Indian development, Matthew Shutzer focuses on the meanings of socialism in the developmental discourse of the post-colonial state, calling attention to its potential for radical social transformation within three temporal contexts: the emancipatory yearnings of the interwar era, the era of post-colonial state making in the 1950s and the authoritarian politics of the 1970s. Similarly, Eric Burton's study of Kivukoni College in Tanzania provides a microhistory of the continually evolving strategies of socialist state-building. The figures that populate this volume thus employed socialism as a set of practices and vocabulary to fashion a new national identity and society among disparate nationalities and ideologies within the borders of their newfound nation-states.

But as Marc Matera shows in his study of Pan-African federalism and Crow does in her study of the first conference of Latin American Communist Parties, socialism could also be the glue for trans-continental unity and shared development priorities. This speaks to a point that the history of internationalism does not often capture: that regionalisms in the Global South were also internationalisms – with conferences, diplomatic missions, and intellectual and technical exchanges providing opportunities for encounters and re-encounters across continents in the context of decolonization. In many ways, these regional connections were much more emotive and much longer lasting – as evidenced today by continuing presence of regional institutions including the African Union and Association of Southeast Asian Nations, than the Afro-Asian solidarity movements that flourished in the 1950s and 1960s.[23]

This is not to discount the importance of intercontinental movements. For socialists of the decolonizing world, speaking in a collective voice would help secure its interests against the relentless march of capitalism, imperialism and the competing interests of a burgeoning Cold War. Here, we view the interplay of development and socialism within the context of Third World internationalism that began in the early twentieth century with the simultaneous rise of anticolonial movements around the world, connected through new networks of mobility and information. Though scholars are paying increased attention to networks of Afro-Asian solidarity,[24] the circulation of development models and ideas across the Third World remains largely unexamined. While the 1950s and 1960s were an era of aid competition by the Global North, they were also decades of cooperation across the Global South, before, during and after the high-profile diplomacy of the 1955 Bandung conference, the advent of the Non-Aligned movement and the Tricontinental Conference of 1966 in Havana. From Afro-Asian women's conferences to the development legacies of Cuban Tricontinentalism, the chapters show that socialist discourses of development were deeply intertwined with Third World solidarity. The institutions of the United Nations could also serve as platforms for South-South cooperation among socialist states.[25] As Taylor Sherman's paper argues, via the United Nations Educational, Scientific, and Cultural Organization (UNESCO), post-independence India sent its experts across Africa and Asia, particularly to socialist Ghana, to share developmental lessons and technology.

Yet Third World internationalism, too, could not extricate itself from the legacies of colonialism. As Dipesh Chakrabarty has shown, the nations who met at Bandung uncritically subscribed to the tenets of modernization and of 'catching up' to the West, creating a split between 'elite nations and their subaltern counterparts' and 'elites and subalterns within national boundaries'.[26] Despite public claims of solidarity against Western imperialism and racial superiority, some of the papers within this volume also underscore that the legacy of 'progress' – whether the West's stages of civilizational progress or Marxian teleology – was embedded within the minds and policies of our actors, whether they were heads of states, technocrats or intellectual sojourners. They were products of their time. Berthold Unfried and Claudia Martinez Hernandez demonstrate in their chapter that Cuban travellers to Angola, to provide military and civilian assistance, referred to some aspects of Angolan society as 'backward tribal' or Angolan women as 'beasts of burden'. The Cubans also lived within their own enclaves, replicating the model of European officials in the segregated military cantonments of colonial Africa and Asia, or American oil families in the neo-colony.[27] Cubans in Angola ascribed to the idea that Cuban society had progressed up a civilizational ladder while Angolan society had either remained stagnate or declined, whether it was because of the Angolan Civil War, the brutal liberation war against Portugal or Portuguese slavery and colonial rule.[28]

Similarly, William Figueroa's piece on the late nineteenth- and early twentieth-century Afghan thinker, Ahmad Ali Kohzad's thoughts from his trip to China, simultaneously praised China's recent ascent into modernity and criticizes 'the rest of the Eastern lands of Asia' for 'falling into obscurity'. In Osei-Opare's chapter on state-led socialist modernization projects, some members of the Ghanaian socialist government, the fishing corporation and the press constantly referred to the fishing communities as 'backward'. Thus, the paradigm of European ideas of civilizational hierarchies and stages of development influenced the decolonizing world's ideas of development. As Crow shows in her study of the First Conference of Latin American Communist Parties, Soviet socialists, too, could display the same paternalism as European colonizers towards their Latin American socialist counterparts; the latter also presumed to speak for and '*about* rather than *with* Indigenous and Black workers' and debated whether indigenous sovereignty was, in fact, a desirable outcome for Latin American development policies.

This did not prevent non-state actors on the left from challenging the West's record on development and accusing it of under-developing its colonies. As Ng argues, M. N. Roy's central critique of British imperialism in India, following the works of Karl Marx and nineteenth-century Indian economists Dadabai Naoroji and Romesh Chunder Dutt, was its prevention of the introduction of modern machinery following the destruction of domestic craft industries, and the forcible export of its economic surplus. This threw the Indian economy into chaos, resulting in 'exploitation *without* development'. Furthermore, the women who attended Cairo's Afro-Asian Women's Conference pointed to the staggering difference in number of women educated in the Soviet Union and China versus the colonial states. These examples showed that the West was not the sole harbinger of development or modernity.

As the Caribbean Marxist historian Walter Rodney famously captured, the Global North's development was predicated on the material and physical exploitation and enslavement of the people and goods from the colonies,[29] leading actively to their underdevelopment. By engaging with the socialist intellectual cannon on imperialism, as Ng and Niwandhono's chapters show, thinkers and government officials in South and Southeast Asia in the early part of the twentieth century pre-empted some of Rodney's claims.[30] Colonial economics and slavery caused underdevelopment rather than local sociocultural practices or political-economic philosophies. They urge us to rethink 'poverty' as '"aboriginal"' and 'disconnected from the history which gave rise to unequal access to resources'.[31] Such analyses undercut European ideas that administrating their economic policies and ideologies upon the colonized would alleviate underdevelopment. At the same time, as many of these papers show, Third World intellectuals were operating in a new, technocratic world order predicated upon evidence of material progress and modernity, from the number of factories built, of arable land tilled, of children in education and of women in the workforce.

Thus, one of the perpetual struggles of the colonized was to demonstrate through intellectual treatises or policies that they could not only govern themselves but construct developed societies, where the nation's material wealth and resources flowed not only inward to the new state but to their subjects as well. One of the most remarkable aspects of this era was the genuine belief on the part of intellectuals that Third World solidarity, internationalism and interdependency were desirable and important tools towards development and independence from the Global North.[32] Thus, Sherman's paper linking Indian and Ghanaian rural development together, Matera's paper demonstrating how radical thinkers from different parts of the globe envisioned federal unification, Unfried and Martinez's paper on Cuban internationalism in Angola, or Lewis and Utama's essay on Afro-Asian women's internationalism permit us to better historicize and understand these beliefs. They provide multiple angles from different geographic, political and social perspectives on both nation-building and worldmaking from the perspective of the Global South.

Based on extensive archival sources and research from five continents, the chapters in this volume show how socialism, internationalism and development are contentious and unstable categories when viewed from multiple perspectives, from anticolonial intellectuals and everyday people to the leaders, government officials and technocrats who shaped the nation-state. The range of sources in multiple languages on display – political treatises; state corporation documents; travelogues; conference papers and speeches; newspapers, journals, party files and memoranda; school reports, curricula and transcripts; the meeting minutes of government and private entities; colonial records; and private papers and letters, etc. – permit us to peel away at and disentangle the diversity of approaches to socialism, development and internationalism, and to highlight how they intersected and overlapped in various historical and intellectual moments and physical spaces. While we hear from statesmen, intellectuals, journalists, female activists and fishmongers, we do not deny the imbalances of our sources, and also explore problematic questions of representation between socialists and subaltern groups.

Our essays start from the early 1900s to the 1980s and span Africa; Central and Latin America; and South, Southeast and East Asia. While our research articles on Latin America are comparatively fewer than those from Asia and Africa, Young's essay outlines key themes in Latin American historiography where socialism and development converge. Five pieces defy regional categories and focus on the transnational and transcontinental: Sherman's piece connects India and Ghana; Unfried and Hernandez link Cuba and Angola; Lewis's and Wildan Utama focus on sites where African, Asian and Middle Eastern women converged; Matera's piece brings into play ideas and players from the entire African continent; and Figueroa examines encounters between Afghanistan and China. Thus, this volume puts into sharp focus and great scrutiny the interconnectedness of the twentieth-century world outside of Western metropolises. Other pieces such as Burton's story of Kivukoni College in Tanzania, Ma's history of Sun Yat-sen's ideas and their implementation in China and Taiwan, Osei-Opare's account of the fishmongers in Ghana, and Shutzer's story of development and capital in India offer a deep dive into local, national histories, permitting us to understand global historical processes better. In this sense, this volume is truly global in scope. Moreover, by disentangling international and global history as an additive or appendage to socialist Europe, we show that socialist development and internationalism were central to debates amongst and between non-European countries and peoples, the Third World.

Socialism, Internationalism, and Development in the Third World thus connects the history of socialism, development and internationalism in Africa, Asia and Latin America as driving forces for social change. It shows how a belief in a more equitable world order was deeply entwined with dreams of a socialist future. Socialists in these regions sought to undo the damages done by foreign capitalists to colonial economies – and by white supremacist ideology to colonial subjectivities – and aimed to protect newly independent states from a neo-imperialist future. Moving beyond Cold War frameworks, we examine a diversity of socialisms – as articulated by actors in the South – that informed its development dreams.

This book thus complicates and deepens our understanding of the history of development from the perspective of the Third World, bringing together scholars to explore experiences and experiments in revolutionary socialism, socialist internationalism, regional and South-South cooperation. It is countries in the South, under a broad umbrella of socialism, rather than those in the North, that cooperated with each other and provided new models that were shared across the Third World and spoke to new developmental futures. These experiences provide an important counterweight to histories of development focused on institutions and actors based in the Global North that tend to portray Africans and Asians as beneficiaries of aid, rather than as development actors who both shaped and challenged international development norms. We depict Africans, Asians and Latin Americans as drivers of development who employed the visions and vocabulary of socialism both to appeal to the public and to plan for the future. They did so not in isolated national contexts, but as makers of a post-imperial world.[33]

Notes

1 Rosa Luxemburg, *The Accumulation of Capital* (New York: Routledge & Kegan Paul, [1913] 2003).
2 H. Fielding Hall, *A People at School* (New York: Macmillan Co., Limited, 1906); Steve Biko, *I Write What I Like, Selected Writings* (Chicago: The University of Chicago Press, [1978] 2002), 21.
3 See Michele Louro, Carolien Stolte, Heather Streets-Salter and Sana Tannoury-Karam, *The League Against Imperialism: Lives and Afterlives* (Leiden: Leiden University Press, 2020); Tim Harper, *Underground Asia: Global Revolutionaries and the Assault on Empire* (Cambridge, MA: Harvard University Press, 2021).
4 For a synopsis of Black disillusionment of the USSR see Nana Osei-Opare, 'Uneasy Comrades: Postcolonial Statecraft, Race, and Citizenship, Ghana-Soviet Relations, 1957–1966', *Journal of West African History* 5, no. 2 (2019): 90.
5 Geoff Eley, *Forging Democracy: The History of the Left in Europe, 1850–2000* (Oxford: Oxford University Press, 2002); Chris Renwick, *Bread for All: The Origins of the Welfare State* (London: Penguin, 2017); Talbot Imlay, *The Practice of Socialist Internationalism* (Oxford: Oxford University Press, 2017).
6 George Padmore, *Pan-Africanism or Communism* (Garden City: Anchor Books, 1972).
7 See for instance Iskandar Tedjasukmana, *The Political Character of the Indonesian Trade Union Movement* (Ithaca: Cornell SEAP, 1958); Clements Kadalie, *My Life and the ICU: The Autobiography of a Black Trade Unionist in South Africa* (London: Clarke, Doble, and Brendon, Ltd., 1970); Robert Edgar, *The Making of an African Communist: Edwin Thabo Mofutsanyana and the Communist Party of South Africa 1927–1939* (Pretoria: UNISA, 2005); Suchetana Chattopadhyay, 'The Bolshevik Menace: Colonial Surveillance and the Origins of Socialist Politics in Calcutta', *South Asia Research* 26, no. 2 (2006): 165–79; Pierre Brocheux, *Ho Chi Minh: A Biography* (Cambridge: Cambridge University Press, 2007); Marc Matera, *Black London: The Imperial Metropolis and Decolonization in the Twentieth Century* (Oakland: University of California Press, 2014).
8 Alessandro Iandolo, *Arrested Development: The Soviet Union in Ghana, Guinea, and Mali* (Ithaca: Cornell University Press, 2022).
9 Vijay Prashad, *The Darker Nations: A People's History of the Third World* (New York: W.W. Norton & Company, 2007), xv; Leslie Anne Hadfield, *Liberation and Development: Black Consciousness Community Programs in South Africa* (East Lansing: Michigan State Press, 2016), 3; Richard Wright, *The Colour Curtain: A Report on the Bandung Conference* (London: Dennis Dobson Books Ltd., 1956), 9.
10 See for instance Robert L. Tignor, *W. Arthur Lewis and the Birth of Development Economics* (Princeton: Princeton University Press, 2006) and Daniel Immerwahr, *Thinking Small: A History of Community Development* (Princeton: Princeton University Press, 2015).
11 Eric Burton, Anne Dietrich, Immanuel R. Hirsch and Marcia C. Schenck (eds.), *Navigating Socialist Encounters: Moorings and (Dis)Entanglements between Africa and East Germany during the Cold War* (Berlin: De Gruyter Oldenburg, 2021); Lukasz Stanek, *Architecture in Global Socialism: Eastern Europe West Africa, and the*

Middle East in the Cold War (Princeton: Princeton University Press, 2022); Iandolo, *Arrested Development*; James Mark and Paul Betts (eds.), *Socialism Goes Global: The Soviet Union and Eastern Europe in the Age of Decolonisation* (Oxford: Oxford University Press, 2022); Kristin Roth-Ey (ed.), *Socialist Internationalism and the Gritty Politics of the Particular: Second-Third World Spaces in the Cold War* (London: Bloomsbury 2023).

12 See for instance Tony Killick, *Development Economics in Action: A Study of Economic Policies in Ghana* (New York: Routledge, [1978] 2010); P. T. Bauer *Equality, the Third World, and Economic Delusion* (Cambridge: Harvard University Press, 1981); Adebayo Adedeji, *Indigenization of African Economies* (New York: Routledge, [1981] 2023); James Ferguson, *The Anti-Politics Machine: 'Development', Depoliticization and Bureaucratic Power in Lesotho* (New York: Cambridge University Press, 1990); Frederick Cooper and Randall M. Packard (eds.), *International Development and the Social Sciences: Essays on the History and Politics of Knowledge* (Berkeley: University of California Press, 1998); Tignor, *W. Arthur Lewis and the Birth of Development Economics*; Peter J. Bloom, Stephan F. Miescher and Takyiwaa Manuh (eds.), *Modernization as Spectacle in Africa* (Bloomington: Indiana University Press, 2014); Kara Moskowitz, *Seeing Like a Citizen; Decolonization, Development, and the Making of Kenya, 1945–1980* (Athens: Ohio University Press, 2019).

13 Benjamin Zachariah, *Developing India: An Intellectual and Social History, c. 1930–50* (Oxford: Oxford University Press, 2005); Frederick Cooper, 'Writing the History of Development', *Journal of Modern European History* 8, no. 1 (2010): 5–23; David Engerman, *The Price of Aid: The Economic Cold War in India* (Cambridge: Harvard University Press, 2018); Christy Thornton, *Revolution in Development: Mexico and the Governance of the Global Economy* (Berkeley: University of California Press, 2021).

14 Corinna R. Unger, *International Development: A Postwar History* (London: Bloomsbury, 2018); Stephen Macekura and Erez Manela (eds.), *The Development Century: A Global History* (Cambridge: Cambridge University Press, 2018).

15 There are some important exceptions to this. For instance, Priya Lal's fascinating book addresses the question of socialism, development, internationalism and gender within Julius Nyerere's Tanzania. See Priya Lal, *African Socialism in Postcolonial Tanzania: Between the Village and the World* (New York: Cambridge University Press, 2017). Also, Jeffrey Ahlman's masterfully revisitation of life under Nkrumah's socialist Ghana broaches those topics. See Jeffrey Ahlman, *Living with Nkrumahism: Nation, State, and Pan-Africanism* (Athens: Ohio University Press, 2017). We use the term 'Global South', acknowledging the complexity of the term, because of its challenge to deep-seated geopolitical and intellectual frameworks centred in Europe and the United States, and its potential to highlight 'the role alternative regional and global geographies can play in remaking a world order'. See Pamela Gupta, Christopher J. Lee, Marissa J. Moorman and Sandhya Shukla, 'Editor's Introduction', *Radical History Review* 131 (2018): 1–12.

16 Robin D. G. Kelley, *Freedom Dreams: The Black Radical Imagination* (Boston: Beacon Press, 2002). Jeremy Adelman, 'Epilogue: Development Dreams' in *The Development Century: A Global History*, 326–38.

17 J. Luis Rodriguez and Christy Thornton, 'The Liberal International Order and the Global South: A View from Latin America', *Cambridge Review of International Affairs* 35, no. 5 (2022): 626–38; Thornton, *Revolution in Development*.

18 Kwame Nkrumah, *Neocolonialism: The Last Stage of Neocolonialism* (New York: International Publishers, 1964); Kwame Nkrumah, *Handbook of Revolutionary*

Warfare: A Guide to the Armed Phase of the African Revolution (New York: International Publishers, 1968).

19 See also Johanna Bockman, 'Socialist Globalization against Capitalist Neocolonialism: The Economic Ideas behind the New International Economic Order', *Humanity: An International Journal of Human Rights, Humanitarianism, and Development* 6, no. 1 (2015): 109–28.

20 Cooper and Packard, 'Introduction', in *International Development and the Social Sciences*, 1.

21 Most recently, see Priya Lal, 'Maoism in Tanzania: Material Connections and Shared Imaginaries' in AC Cook, *Mao's Little Red Book: A Global History* (Cambridge: Cambridge University Press, 2014): 96–116; Julia Lovell, *Maoism: A Global History* (London: Random House, 2019).

22 See also Yasser Nasser, 'Asia as a Third Way? J.C. Kumarappa and the Problem of Development in Asia' in *The Lives of Cold War Afro-Asianism*, ed. Carolien Stolte and Su Lin Lewis (Leiden: Leiden University Press, 2022): 121–42. We thank Yasser for his contributions to our first workshop.

23 Guy J. Pauker, 'The Rise and Fall of Afro-Asian Solidarity', *Asian Survey* 5, no. 9 (965): 425–32.

24 Carolien Stolte and Su Lin Lewis (eds.), *The Lives of Cold War Afro-Asianism* (Leiden: Leiden University Press, 2022); Shobana Shankar, *An Uneasy Embrace: Africa, India, and the Spectre of Race* (Oxford: Oxford University Press, 2022).

25 Cindy Ewing, '"With a minimum of bitterness": decolonization, the right to self-determination, and the Arab-Asian group', *Journal of Global History* 17, no. 2 (2022): 254–71.

26 Dipesh Chakrabarty, 'The Legacies of Bandung; Decolonization and the Politics of Culture', *Economic and Political Weekly* 40, no. 46 (2005): 4814, quoting Jawaharlal Nehru.

27 See Philippa Levine, *Prostitution, Race, and Politics: Policing Venereal Disease in the British Empire* (Hoboken: Taylor and Francis, 2013), 297–322; Ambe J. Njoh, 'Colonial Philosophies, Urban Space, and Racial Segregation in British and French Colonial Africa', *Journal of Black Studies* 38, no. 4 (2008): 579–99; Hannah Appel, *The Licit Life of Capitalism: US Oil in Equatorial Guinea* (Durham: Duke University Press, 2019), 79–136.

28 Daniel Domingues da Silva, *The Atlantic Slave Trade from West Central Africa, 1780–1867* (New York: Cambridge University Press, 2017); Elizabeth Schmidt, *Foreign Intervention in Africa: From the Cold War to the War on Terror* (Cambridge: Cambridge University Press, 2013), 79–102.

29 Walter Rodney, *How Europe Underdeveloped Africa* (Baltimore: Black Classic Press, [1972] 2011).

30 See for instance Karl Marx, 'The British Rule in India', *New York Daily Tribune*, 25 June 1853, www.marxists.org/archive/marx/works/1853/06/25.htm

31 Cooper and Packard, *International Development and the Social Sciences*, 3.

32 In fact, what is often absent in Global South debt discussions is that many Global South countries lent and owed debt to each other. See Johanna Bockman's fascinating work on this topic – she calls them 'minor creditors'. Also, Bockman, 'Socialist Globalization against Capitalist Neocolonialism'.

33 Christopher J. Lee (ed.), *Making a World after Empire: The Bandung Moment and Its Political Afterlives* (Athens, OH: Ohio University Press, 2010); Adom Getachew, *Worldmaking after Empire: The Rise and Fall of Self-Determination* (Princeton: Princeton University Press, 2019).

1

Development and difference: Alternative genealogies of uneven development, 1920–40

Kelvin Ng

In late 1943, writing in anticipation of India's independence, M. N. Roy authored two statements outlining a broad vision for the country's postwar economic development: the *People's Plan for Economic Development of India* (1943) and the *Draft Constitution of India* (1944). Written in advance of the famous Bombay Plan of 1944 – a proposal advanced by several leading Indian industrialists, which laid the blueprint for the Congress government's later policies for import-substitution industrialization – Roy's two documents remain remarkable for their prescient critique of centralization and the state's prioritization of heavy industry.[1] Emphasizing that any economic programme needs to place 'human freedom' over 'economic benefits', Roy's former proposal advocated for the rationalization of agriculture, the expansion of home industries and the creation of a domestic market for consumer goods.[2] This economic programme found political expression in Roy's draft constitution, which further outlined the case for decentralizing political authority to local people's committees in the form of a federation, which 'implied autonomy on the part of the Constituent units of the Federation'.[3] Despite his several disagreements with both these proposals, Jawaharlal Nehru – who had been acquainted with Roy during his visit to the Soviet Union in 1927, as part of his involvement with the League Against Imperialism – took seriously Roy's arguments around agrarian-centred development, conceding that 'there are some good ideas in the People's Plan of Economic Development'. It was Roy's signal insight – that the infrastructural development of rural industries laid at the heart of any concrete proposal towards India's political independence – that led some other contemporary observers to suggest, even in spite of their ideological divergences, that Nehru 'is likely to find Mr. Roy a valuable and helpful colleague'.[4]

Writing contemporaneously in a markedly different context, Tan Malaka articulated instead a distinct vision of economic policy for post-independence Indonesia in his tract *Rentjana Ekonomi* (*Economic Plan*; 1945). Despite broadly agreeing with Roy on the need to 'match production with consumption', Malaka instead contended that state-led industrialization – rather than a focus on rural development – was necessary to secure Indonesia's political and economic autonomy.[5] Writing in the immediate context of the Second World War, Malaka insisted on the primacy of industry and machinery in economic planning, arguing that the colonial economy of the Dutch East Indies was shot through with sectoral unevenness.[6] Criticizing the Republican government's approach towards *diplomasi* (diplomacy) – whose proponents included Sjahrir, Sukarno and Hatta – Malaka charged that the nationalist leaders of the Republican government were unable to articulate a developmental programme untethered to the domination of foreign capital: 'Engineer Sukarno' and 'Doctor Hatta' both operated within the constraints of bourgeois political economy.[7] Outlining a vision of '100% independence' (*merdeka 100%*), Malaka instead maintained that 'Indonesia's independence in the twentieth century is inseparable from nationalized heavy industry and economic planning' as opposed to continued reliance on rural production and commodity exports.[8]

Understanding the economic and the political as formally separated yet inextricably linked, Roy and Malaka were pivotal figures in the debates around decolonization and development in the mid-twentieth century. Both Roy and Malaka were broadly representative of a left economic critique, retaining important epistemological links to their earlier involvement at the Communist International, and bearing the imprint of Marxist debates around development. Central to their respective economic programmes was the idea of economic unevenness: understanding capitalist development as a global process striated by degrees of social and spatial differentiation, Roy and Malaka interpreted uneven development as the outcome of the contradiction between equalization and differentiation inherent in capitalist production. This article first offers an intellectual history of development – and its necessary correlate, of uneven development – routed through the interwar intellectual networks of socialist internationalism, providing a corrective to the overwhelming focus on such actors as statesmen, economic planners and technocrats in the extant historiography.[9] While their tracts from the 1940s were directly addressed to the immediate conditions of decolonization, the theoretical coordinates for these later contributions were first elaborated across their early works from the 1920s and 1930s. Turning to this corpus of writings, this essay examines the conceptual link Roy and Malaka drew between unevenness and development, highlighting their respective arguments around the relationship between industry, agriculture and the political economy of colonialism. Where both thinkers disagreed with one another, I argue, turned on two lines of contention: first, the nature of the agrarian question; and second, the problem of industrial development. This essay further argues that their respective accounts must be historicized not solely within the context of such debates within the Marxist tradition, but more broadly – and perhaps crucially – within the intellectual coordinates and political-economic conditions of their respective contexts: British India and the Dutch East Indies.

There is an intellectual genealogy of uneven development to be sketched from Marx onwards through the tradition of Marxian economics. Since the late 1990s, the resumed publication of the *Marx-Engels-Gesamtausgabe* has enabled a newfound appreciation of Marx as a thinker attentive to the variegated nature of capitalist development across multiple historical and geographical scales.[10] Addressing the relationship between capitalist development and non-capitalist relations of production, Marx himself had argued in the second volume of *Capital* that the 'capitalist mode of production is conditioned by modes of production lying outside its own stage of development'.[11] This perspective finds further elaboration in his unfinished *Grundrisse*, where Marx further distinguished between the 'formal' subsumption of labour (where preexisting labour processes are subsumed, but unchanged, under capital) and the 'real' subsumption of labour (where the 'methods, means and conditions' of labour are restructured along capitalist lines).[12] This set of ideas would find sustained elaboration among the socialist thinkers of the Second International. In *The Development of Capitalism in Russia* (1889), Vladimir Lenin attempted to theorize the link between the agrarian question and the differentiated rate of capitalist exploitation among the Russian peasantry.[13] Following the First World War, Lenin – influenced by critiques of imperialism launched both by Marxists (Rudolf Hilferding and Nikolai Bukharin) and liberal writers (J. A. Hobson) – articulated a radical theory of global capitalism, understanding financial monopolization and underdevelopment as structurally linked.[14] Engaging with the economic impact of capitalist development in the colonial world, Rosa Luxemburg likewise elaborated a theory of imperialism as the 'political expression' of capitalist competition, borne of constant expansion and subsumption.[15] By the 1920s, the most systematic theory of capitalism's variegated forms came by way of Leon Trotsky's account of 'combined and uneven development', which understood uneven development as 'the most general law of the historic process' revealed 'most sharply and complexly in the destiny of the backward countries'.[16]

The vast Marxist literature on uneven development was surely familiar to both Roy and Malaka, both participants at various World Congresses of the Communist International. While recognizing the important imprint these Marxist debates bore on both these thinkers, this article instead situates their respective theoretical interventions within a different problem-space: one attentive to the divergent political-economic trajectories of British India and the Dutch East Indies. In so doing, it draws on anthropologist David Scott's theorization of a problem-space as an intellectual historical methodology adequate both to the situated nature of intellectual history and to the shifting historical or social contexts in which a particular intervention might be embedded.[17] Understanding Roy and Malaka's political-economic thought in relation to these different problem-spaces, ultimately, enables an appreciation of the radical unevenness undergirding the act of theoretical production itself, offering a mode of reading that links political thought to the historical questions to which texts respond.

* * *

Among the most prominent communist intellectuals of the interwar period, Narendranath Bhattacharya (1887–1954) began his life in politics as a *swadeshi* activist in Bengal, first emerging as an active member in Calcutta's underground networks of revolutionary terrorism, including the Anushilan Samiti and the Jugantar Party.[18] The threat of imprisonment prompted Narendranath to leave India in 1915 on a mission to procure material assistance from Germany and Japan, in what would come to be termed the 'Hindu–German Conspiracy' in British intelligence records. The ensuing years saw him travel to the Dutch East Indies, Japan, China, the United States and

Mexico under an array of pseudonyms before he assumed the name by which he is remembered, Manabendra Nath (M. N.) Roy. He came to be involved in the founding of both the Partido Socialista Obrero (later the Partido Comunista Mexicano, 1917) and the Communist Party of India at Tashkent (1920), and was appointed several leadership positions on the Executive Committee of the Comintern, including the chairmanship of the Eastern Commission, and headed the official delegation to China in 1927.[19] The interwar decades also marked the height of Roy's intellectual career; among the most influential works in his oeuvre of hundreds are *An Indian Communist Manifesto* (1920), *Supplementary Theses on the National And Colonial Question* (1920), *The Future of Indian Politics* (1926) and *Revolution and Counter-Revolution in China* (1930).[20]

Among Roy's most celebrated works was his book-length analysis of the economic history of colonial India, titled *India in Transition* (1922). Printed in English, Russian and German, *India in Transition* drew substantially upon his other works *La India: Su Pasado, Su Presente y Su Porvenir* (*India: Its Past, Its Present, and Its Future*; published in Mexico City, 1918), 'India in a Transition Stage' (published in the *Communist International* periodical, 1921), and *What Do We Want?* (published in Geneva, 1922).[21] Writing amidst the onset of Gandhi's non-cooperation movement, Roy authored the work with a view towards analysing the 'material forces that are pushing the various classes of the Indian people in the present struggle' in conjunction with the 'deep-rooted social character of the present unrest'.[22] Roy's time in Mexico – where socialists had vigorously debated the implications of the Mexican Revolution – bore an indelible imprint on his thinking, as he sought to extend questions of political strategy and agrarian mobilization to the Indian context.[23] The book reached Indian audiences as early as 1922, but was promptly proscribed by the colonial authorities in all three major presidencies.[24] Paraphrased excerpts and reprints of Roy's work nonetheless appeared in several local newspapers, and came to be read and debated by such Indian Marxists as Muzaffar Ahmad, Singaravelu Chettiar and S. A. Dange; arrangements were made for the book's translation into Urdu and Tamil.[25] Elsewhere, British colonial intelligence, evidently alarmed by the text's dissemination along Comintern networks, confiscated copies of *India in Transition* in Sierra Leone and Singapore.[26]

Roy's central argument crucially turns on a structural critique of colonial capitalism: the 'belated growth' and 'backward state' of economic development in British India derived neither from the 'conservatism of her people' nor from the 'shyness of native capital,' but rather due to the fact that the 'abnormal political condition of the country' prevented the introduction of that 'great revolutionary agency': modern machinery.[27] Borrowing from Marx's 'The British Rule in India' (1853), Roy traced the causes of this belated pace of economic development to two characteristics of British rule: first, the 'forcible export' of economic surplus (in Roy's estimation, 'more than 70% of the accumulated wealth of India') remitted to Britain from India; and second, the 'deliberate destruction' of domestic craft industries.[28] For Roy, the disjuncture between the subcontinent's dual role – as a producer of primary products for export, and as a captive market of imported manufactures – further underlined the unequal nature of this exchange. The conjoined effect of both policies – unilateral surplus transfer on one hand and industrial disintegration on the other – arrested the course of economic development in colonial India, while entailing its integration within an emerging global economy as a subsidiary actor: 'India has for a long time been reduced to capitalist exploitation, without receiving the benefits of capitalist development.'[29] This absence of capitalist development, per Roy's description in another work, 'threw the political and economic structure of [Indian] society into an abyss resembling chaos'.[30] Referencing Lenin's argument in *Imperialism, the Highest Stage of Capitalism* (1917), Roy charged that 'while the most highly developed imperialism of today is marked by the export of capital to the colonies, the movement was the reverse in the early days of imperialism', functioning to not only prevent but destroy the growth of industrial capitalism in the colonies. India served as the 'most remarkable example' of how capitalism, despite ostensibly being 'a force of social progress', led instead to 'social stagnation, if not retrogression'.[31]

Roy's central theoretical move is to historicize the nineteenth-century phenomenon of underdevelopment – entailing the decline of domestic manufacturing, growing peasantization, and the institution of a 'dead and uncivilized form of exploitation' in the *zamindari* system – as immanent to the structure of colonial capitalism, rather than extraneous or antecedent to proper capitalist development.[32] The condition of colonial India – one of exploitation *without* development – presents an occasion to grasp the uneven dynamics of capitalism as a global structure: 'the social production and economic life of India today are inseparably interwoven with the structure of world-capitalism'.[33] Roy charged that capitalism is most fundamentally characterized not by the presence of any particular technical markers of development, but rather by the extension of a particular social dynamic over everyday life: the predominance of use value over exchange value.[34] The emergence of such capitalist dynamics gave rise to specific forms of class differentiation, broadly divided into four groups: the landed aristocracy and princely rulers; the urban bourgeoisie and intellectuals; the petty peasantry and small landholders; and the landless peasantry (or 'agricultural proletariat'), comprising the vast majority of the population.[35] Reframing the terms of the agrarian question, Roy argued that this latter group – which he characterized as a 'dead-weight on the rural population of India' – was not symptomatic of the antinomy between a feudal past and capitalist present, but rather came into existence precisely through colonial economic policies geared towards the preservation of 'the monopoly of a foreign capitalist class on the Indian market', necessitating the artificial obstruction of industrial development.[36] The *social* constitution of labour, for Roy, was expressive of the *economic* question of uneven development writ large. The *national* status of British India within a Britain-centred world economy was thus analogous to the *social* position of the agrarian proletariat in colonial Indian society: even as 'the productivity and labor power of India' came to be more tightly articulated within 'the general scheme of capitalist exploitation', it nonetheless remained 'on the outskirts, occupying the place of a reserve force', with 'no great transformation' in the 'form and method of production'.[37]

The two mainstays of Roy's economic analysis of underdevelopment – surplus export on one hand and de-industrialization on the other – closely mirrored the terms of nationalist economic thought in the late nineteenth and early twentieth centuries. From the mid-nineteenth century onwards, several Indian intellectuals critically engaged with several schools of economic thought; drawing variously from classical political economy, the German historical school and Saint-Simonianism – whose canonical texts were translated into such languages as Urdu, Gujarati and Bengali – these thinkers sought to develop a robust *economic* critique of various aspects of imperial policymaking.[38] Invoking the analytical and normative categories of what Manu Goswami terms a 'national developmentalist' model, these nationalist intellectuals began articulating their critique of *colonial* political economy from the standpoint of a *national* economic space.[39] By the first decades of the twentieth century, nationalist critiques of India's underdevelopment came to be organized around the twin arguments of the 'drain of wealth' thesis (associated with the 'Bombay School') and the 'deindustrialization' thesis (associated with the 'Calcutta School').

Advancing a neo-mercantilist critique of British financial domination, Dadabhai Naoroji – among the founding members of the Indian National Congress, the first nonwhite Member of Parliament in the British House of Commons, and onetime member of the Second International – is most closely associated with the former argument on the drain of the nation. Invoking the image of an India 'bled and exploited in every way of their wealth, of their services, of their land, labour and all resources by the foreigners', Naoroji's famous *Poverty and Un-British Rule in India* (1901) characterized the imperial relationship between Britain and India as one of financial domination, a consequence of both government transfers and private transfers made by individual British officials and residents. Drawing on neo-mercantilist precepts, Naoroji criticized this unilateral transfer of surplus on three grounds: that the annual drain of India's national income exceeded receipts, inclusive of bullion inflows; that India did not adequate compensation in return; and that the causes of India's lack of developmental capacity lay in this unilateral and continuous transfer of real income and investible surplus.[40] Naoroji's influential drain theory – which circulated widely among British and Continental socialists – bore an important imprint on Roy's indictment of the 'heavy drain of wealth', which 'exhausted the economic vitality of India for a considerable time', 'disabl[ed] her capitalist class' and prevented it from 'developing machine industry'.[41] The legacy of British rule in India, in Roy's assessment, amounted to a wholesale deprivation of 'the people of all their wealth, all the products of their daily work and of their soil'.[42]

On the other hand, the charge of deindustrialization is linked to the work of economic historian Romesh Chunder Dutt, an important member of the INC. Dutt's influential *Economic History of India* (1904) attributed the decline in standards of living to the deindustrialization of the subcontinent, resulting in the disintegration of crafts industries; this decline was accompanied by a move of labour from manufacture into agriculture, in terms of both real numbers and the total share of employment.[43] Echoing the deindustrialization thesis, Dutt's contemporary, Mahadev Govind Ranade, founding member of the INC and member of the Bombay Legislative Council, extended this argument to frame the question of underdevelopment in terms of India's status as a 'dependent colonial economy'. Influenced by classical political economy and the German historical school, Ranade braided the critique of deindustrialization with that of the drain of wealth, arguing that the mechanisms responsible for the outflow of

Indian surplus – the spread of railways and the removal of import taxes – contributed to the rapid 'decadence of native manufacture and trade'.[44] Ranade moreover charged that colonial India's overdependence on agricultural production – itself subject to the uncertainties of climate and rainfall – 'condemns the poor to grow still poorer', and subjects 'millions to violent or slow death'. This process of 'ruralization' entailed India's 'rustification, i.e., a loss of power, and intelligence, and self-dependence', depriving Indian labourers the benefits of 'art manipulation' or modern technology.[45] These critiques of deindustrialization – particularly by way of Ranade, whose 'social radicalism' Roy appreciatively appraises – bore a clear imprint on *India in Transition*.[46] Indeed, Roy straightforwardly reproduces the very terms of the deindustrialization argument, understanding colonial economic policy as a confrontation between 'foreign mechanofacture' against 'Indian manufacture', resulting in the 'ruthless destruction of the progressive tendencies in production' and the regression of Indian society 'back to the stage of agrarian economy'.[47]

Where Roy crucially diverged from his nationalist predecessors, however, was in their respective formulations of the question of development. Despite their differing analytical priorities, Naoroji, Dutt and Ranade all shared a commitment to industrial and technical development. While the former two remained fundamentally Smithian in their conception of development – with Naoroji's famous exhortation to 'let natural and economic laws have their full and fair play' consonant with a programme of technical improvement, increasing domestic demand and expanding industrial production – the predominant intellectual influence on Ranade was the German historical school of political economy, particularly Friedrich List.[48] Eschewing the analytic individualism of classical political economy, Ranade contended that 'national well-being' inhered not in the 'creation of the highest quantity of wealth measured in exchange value' but rather in the 'full and many-sided development of national productive powers'.[49] If List, in his critique of Smith's 'cosmopolitical economy', had advocated for a protectionist regime to enable weaker economies to develop their productive powers, Ranade would likewise offer a qualified call for industrial protectionism from 'the hostile Competition of Advanced Races'.[50] Ranade advocated for an 'industrial salvation' through the 'due co-ordination of the three-fold forms of industrial activity', i.e. agricultural production, industrial manufacture and commercial circulation.[51] For Ranade, among the most apposite examples of such a system of productive development – involving 'pecuniary assistance in aid of private enterprise' – came by way of the Cultuurstelsel of Dutch Java (1830s–70s), which sought to promote industrial production and export growth through government leases to private individuals, inasmuch as it 'indirectly helped the Netherlands East Indies to attain a high degree of material prosperity'.[52]

For Roy, however, neither Smithian political economy nor Listian national developmentalism provided an adequate resolution to the economic crises immanent in capitalism's structural tendencies. If the practical conditions of economic unevenness had undercut the central conceit of classical political economy – the 'justice and beneficence of the doctrine of Free Trade', now rendered untenable even to the 'Indian adepts of English liberalism' – national developmentalism merely represented a misrecognition of capitalism's globality.[53] Rather, Roy regarded *national* industrial development – i.e. the idea that 'the industrial and commercial development of India will increase the national wealth, and that consequently, the economic conditions of all classes will be improved' – not as a precondition for the overcoming of social inequality, but rather as agent and artefact of those very structures of exploitation.[54] The spectacular 'economic and industrial advancement' on part of the Indian bourgeoisie in the first decades of the twentieth century, for Roy, was not accomplished by 'depriving British capital of the full benefit of Imperial exploitation', but rather attendant with an increase in the 'poverty of the masses'.[55] Observing the 'development of capitalist organization' and the 'improvement of industrial production', Roy argued that these markers of technical progress represented the shifting imperatives of 'the scheme of capitalist exploitation' on part of both the foreign imperialist and the native bourgeoisie; the very outcome of such economic development, however, was the formation and concentration of 'the vast masses of wage-slaves, a fact that 'can no longer be softened by sentiment nor clouded by nationalist preoccupations'.[56] Reinterpreting ongoing nationalist programme for developing 'modern industries with native capital' as a struggle between the 'native middle-class' against the 'economic and political monopoly of the imperialist bourgeoisie', Roy maintained that the aspiration towards economic self-determination ultimately belied the 'revolt of the exploited against the exploiting class, irrespective of nationality'.[57]

Roy's argument turns on his Marxist understanding of the relationship between capital and labour: eschewing the critique of foreign imperialism from the standpoint of the national economy, Roy instead viewed the antinomy between metropolitan Britain and colonial India, between foreign capital and native labour, and between the Indian bourgeoisie and labourers as all structurally analogous. The relationship between British capital and Indian labour transcended their respective national provenance, but rather assumed world-historical significance as 'at once the epitome and bulwark of the capitalistic system' throughout the world, irresolvable within the strictures of a national project.[58] Roy's indictment of national development undertaken by a 'native capitalist class' remains entirely congruent with his earlier position against Lenin's 'Draft Theses on the National and Colonial Questions' at the Second Comintern Congress. If Lenin had accepted the equation between 'bourgeois-democratic' movements in 'oppressed nations' with 'national-revolutionary' significance, Roy instead maintained that the struggle to overthrow foreign domination should be directed towards the creation of workers' and peasants' councils, rather than capitulating to the national aims of the national bourgeoisie. The exploited masses in the colonial world, contended Roy, 'will be brought to communism not by capitalist development but by the development of class consciousness under the leadership of the proletariat of the advanced countries'.[59] In Roy's view, even as the two classes of exploiters – the 'foreign capitalists' on one hand, and the 'native landholder, usurer and trader' on the other – may diverge in their specific economic visions, they remained 'identical in their fundamental social significance – they live and thrive on the labor of the toiler, be he a worker in the factory or cultivator of the soil'.[60] Absent a radical social revolution, national industrial development amounted to nothing more than 'more extensive and intensive exploitation of the labor-power of the working class'.[61] The conceptual import of

Roy's argument, ultimately, lay not merely in its endeavour to apprehend the political economy of empire as structurally analogous to the capital/labour relation, but also in its strikingly original attempt to repudiate the ahistorical naturalization of uneven development shared by Indian economic thinkers in the wake of Smith and List.

* * *

Roy's entanglements with the networks of the Communist International brought him into closer contact with cohorts of Marxist intellectuals from across the colonial world, precipitating a broader internationalist turn in his writings. This conceptual reorientation was best reflected in the title of an essay he published in 1924: 'Europe is not the world.'[62] By the Fourth Comintern Congress, Roy had modified his initial framing of a stark division between the industrialized metropoles and the underdeveloped peripheries. Insisting now that the 'Eastern countries cannot be treated as a politically, economically or socially homogeneous entity', Roy now conceived of the colonial world as three separate categories, ordered by the principle of development: industrialized countries with a 'high level of development' and a 'native capitalism'; semi-feudal countries exhibiting an 'elementary' stage of 'capitalist development'; and 'primitive' countries dominated by 'patriarchal feudalism'.[63] Roy's shift in perspective was occasioned, in part, by his close working relationship with the representatives of the Dutch East Indies at the Comintern – in particular, Henk Sneevliet, the Dutch representative of the Partai Komunis Indonesia – and his engagement with political developments in Java and Sumatra.[64] Citing Luxemberg's *The Accumulation of Capital* (1913), Sneevliet revised Roy's stance on the colonial and national questions on two principles: first, that there exists vast heterogeneity and unevenness within the colonial world, exemplified by the differing economic conditions in the densely populated centres of Java, Sumatra, Bali and Lombok, with the peripheral colonies of Borneo, Celebes and New Guinea; and second, that the emergence of certain mass movements is immanent to the dynamics of capitalist development, and may therefore be 'revolutionary in the sense that Comrade Roy established for British India'.[65] Indeed, if the Dutch East Indies represented, for Sneevliet, the 'foremost' colony 'after British India' and the only colonial space with 'work being carried out in a Marxist spirit', then no other thinker better exemplified this critique of colonial capitalism and social inequalities than Tan Malaka.

A prominent figure in the global networks of the communist underground, Malaka's political itineraries intersected with Roy's many times over. Given the birth name Ibrahim and conferred the Minangkabau title *gelar Datoek*, the Sumatra-born Tan Malaka (1897–1949) received an early education in Haarlem, where he read the works of Nietzsche, Carlyle, Rousseau, as well as the fundaments of communist philosophy: Marx, Engels, Lenin and Kautsky.[66] Following his tenure as a plantation schoolteacher in Deli, Malaka emerged as a prominent political figure upon moving to Java, where he became involved in the Sarekat Islam, the Partai Komunis Indonesia, various labour unions and several left-wing periodicals. Facing threat of arrest under the *exorbitante rechten* ('extraordinary powers') of the Dutch governor-general, Malaka began his decade of exile in the left circles of Europe: first in Amsterdam as a member of the Communist Party of the Netherlands, then in Berlin where he met Roy, and subsequently to Moscow, where he argued for a political consonance between international communism and pan-Islamism at the Fourth Comintern Congress.[67] Delegated as the Comintern agent for Southeast Asia, Malaka was subsequently dispatched to Canton (1923–4), where he met Sun Yat-sen; then Singapore (1924), where he attempted to instigate contact between various anti-colonial groups; and subsequently Manila (1925–27), where he came into contact with the anti-colonial radicals Manuel Quezon and Jose Abad Santos.[68] He eventually returned to Java in the throes of war and revolution in 1942, where he, amidst stints in prison, exerted himself to his philosophical tract *Madilog* (*Materialism, Dialectics, Logic*; 1943) and his autobiography, *Dari Pendjara ke Pendjara* (*From Jail to Jail*; 1948).[69]

Most of Malaka's key arguments, however, had been evident from his early writings in the 1920s. Though mostly written in exile, Malaka's texts from this period thoroughly imbibed the radical spirit of the *pergerakan* ('movement') characteristic of the Dutch East Indies's 'age in motion'.[70] It was in the plantation lines of Deli – where the 'sharp conflict between capital and labor, between colonizer and colonized, was played out' – that Malaka authored his first political tract, *Sovjet atau Parlement?* (*Soviet or Parliament*; 1921).[71] His subsequent writings and pamphlets were composed in the context of exile: *Toendoek kepada Kekoeasaan, Tetapi Tidak Toendoek kepada Kebenaran* (*Abiding by Might, but Not by Right*; 1922), a tract on economic development and class formation, was published in Berlin; *Naar de Republiek Indonesia* (*Towards the Indonesian Republic*; 1925), outlining a programme of revolutionary populism, was composed in Canton, published in Manila and circulated in Sumatra; while his two political pamphlets *Semangat Moeda* (*Young Spirit*; 1926) and *Massa Actie* (*Mass Action*; 1926) were published in Manila and smuggled into the Dutch East Indies by way of Bangkok.[72] As with Roy, the alacrity with which Malaka's 'communistic propaganda' spread across the colonies provoked an elaboration network of surveillance and intelligence exchange among British, French and Dutch colonial officials, who seized copies of his pamphlets in Saigon, Singapore and Amoy.[73]

Malaka was attuned to the profound crisis and contradiction occasioned by Dutch economic policy across the Indonesian archipelago.[74] The most visible manifestation of this crisis, for Malaka, was the increasing structural bifurcation between a sphere of modern industry centred around Sumatra and Java, and a sphere of resource extraction in the outer islands. Capitalism in the Dutch East Indies, Malaka argued, exhibited three major characteristics. First, it remained a 'young' capitalism that exhibited immense unevenness, with comparatively low levels of technological innovation and capital concentration. In his estimation, industrial development in the Indonesian archipelago remained limited to certain agricultural sectors, such as sugar, rubber and tea cultivation, and concentrated on the islands of Java and Sumatra. Yet much of this industrialization and mechanization was firmly geared toward specialized, export-oriented production, resulting in the displacement of earlier economic practices and the deracination of the native Inlanders [*bumiputera*] as 'coolies and laborers'.[75] Consequently, while Java exhibited all the bearings of industrial modernity – commercial agriculture and transportation networks among them – the Outer Islands remained in a state of relative underdevelopment, dependent on subsistence farming and resource extraction.[76] This widening spatial differentiation, argued Malaka, was a consequence of capitalism's intrinsic unevenness: 'Capital separates the city [*kota*] from the village [*desa*]'.[77] The consequence of this uneven development was the incomplete proletarianization of the population across the Dutch East Indies, which saw the coexistence of several distinct labour arrangements: so-called 'free labor' in agriculture and industry in Java, contractual indenture in small-scale industry in southern Sumatra, and peasant cultivation in the rest of the Indonesian archipelago.[78]

Second, in contrast to 'healthy' and 'organic' capitalism in Western Europe, capitalism in the Dutch East Indies was 'deformed' [*verkracht*] and 'artificial' [*kunstamatig*].[79] Capitalist development in the Indies, Malaka argued, was constituted along the regulative interests and principles of foreign domination, through such policies as the dismantling of domestic crafts industries, legal prohibitions on native shipping, and the colonial monopoly on export crops.[80] Yet the nationalist politics of protectionist autonomy – as articulated by the *swadeshi* movement in India – remained inadequate to Indonesia's specific economic conditions. If Roy had noted the emergence of a national bourgeoisie in colonial India, no such class existed in the Dutch East Indies for Malaka; indeed, in contrast to the political assertion of native industrialists, landholders and traders in the Philippines, Egypt and India, 'national capital' [*nasional-kapital*] was entirely absent from Indonesia.[81] Malaka attributed this phenomenon to the specific historical form of imperialism assumed in the Dutch context. Mapping the political structure of imperialism to the economic formation of capitalism, Malaka distinguished between four conceptions of empire: *barbaric imperialism*, corresponding with Spanish and Portuguese mercantilism; *autocratic imperialism*, associated with Company monopoly in the Dutch East Indies; *semi-liberal imperialism*, exemplified by dyarchy in post-1919 British India; and *liberal imperialism*, embodied by free trade in the American Philippines.[82] The Amsterdam-centred system of entrepôt trade and government protection, argued Malaka, was reliant on commercial supremacy at the expense of industrial expansion; its goal remained one of 'monopoly'. Whereas the demand for industrial autonomy advanced by the *swadeshi* movement in India and the Ilustrado leadership of the Philippines was plausible in their respective contexts, buoyed by the British and American rhetoric of 'free trade, liberalism and constitutionalism', no equivalent existed in the Indonesian context for Malaka.[83]

Third, and most consequentially for his argument, capitalism in the Dutch East Indies was 'international' in the truest sense of the word.[84] Malaka maintained that the context of the Dutch East Indies was unique in the unprecedented degree of penetration of foreign capital, beyond national and imperial lines: 'The Indies is the economic home of world capitalism.'[85] In Malaka's account, the relative weakness of Dutch industry and the breakup of the VOC's quasi-absolute commercial monopoly forced the colonial state to adopt a policy of deregulation in the Indies, enabling the influx of foreign capital. By the 1920s, then, the Dutch East Indies had been thoroughly suffused by 'Dutch, Swiss, American, British, Chinese, Japanese, etc. capital'.[86] This development was further conditioned by the Indonesian archipelago's prized location at the point of confluence between the Indian Ocean and the China Sea: eastward, the Sunda and Malacca Straits served as the 'door to the continents of China, Japan and the Americas';

westward, one finds 'the continents of Hindustan and Europe'.[87] Malaka surmised that as much as 44.7 per cent of the capital invested in the agricultural industry in Sumatra was non-Dutch in origin, divided between British, French/Belgian, Japanese and German firms; foreign ownership of the rubber plantations in Sumatra was as high as 42.2 per cent, with the British enjoying an unquestioned monopoly. Britain and her colonies, moreover, had surpassed the Netherlands as both the largest export market (42.55 per cent) and the largest import source (40.4 per cent) of the Dutch East Indies, enabling it to significantly channel and regulate the terms of economic activity beyond its state territories.[88]

As an outcome of Indonesia's export dependence, popular anxieties over the structural effects of market fluctuations and economic upheaval came to be displaced onto the figure of the Foreign Oriental [*Vreemde Oosterlingen*], and specifically the Chinese. The rhetorical inflation of the excesses of foreign capital – captured in the sentiment that 'Europeans, Chinese and Arabs control all trade, big, medium and small' – compounded local resentment toward 'Chinese and Arab loan sharks'.[89] Dutch imperialism, argued Malaka, used Chinese capital to 'separate the Indonesian people from the Dutch', such that popular agitation against 'foreign capital' (as in the Sarekat Islam) manifested itself as opposition towards the 'Chinese merchant' [*saudagar bangsa Cina*]; the Chinese were furthermore viewed as a comprador class whose influx contributed to the disintegration of 'all national socioeconomic and technical instruments'.[90] If, for Roy, Indian emigration to British Malaya typified the excesses of 'native traders who found it profitable to speculate in human labor', so too did Tan Malaka regard unrestricted labour migration as the clearest expression of a generalized crisis in social relations: 'Wretched indeed, that the natives on the Malay Peninsula cannot defend themselves from the flood of Indians and Chinese who continue to flow there.'[91] Malaka's argument, here, mirrored a broader resurgent nativism reverberating across colonial Southeast Asia in the 1930s. It bore, on one hand, echoes of the anti-Chinese rhetoric of the Sarekat Islam, vocalized by merchants in the *batik* industry; elsewhere, the economic pressures wrought by the economic depression fed directly into anxieties around 'Indian domination' among Burmese nationalists, or sharp attacks on 'foreigners' among Malay nationalists.[92]

Malaka's argument around capitalist unevenness was responsive to the prevailing themes guiding economic thought in the late colonial Dutch empire. Unlike India, critiques of financial drainage – such as those raised by N. P. van den Berg, president of the Javasche Bank and the Nederlandsche Bank, or engineer H. H. van Kol, member of the Social Democratic Workers' Party – lost currency with the institution of the Dutch Ethical Policy in the early twentieth century.[93] Neither did arguments around deindustrialization gain significant traction among Indonesian nationalists, in light of the archipelago's reliance on commodity extraction.[94] Rather, the debate around economic policy in the late colonial Dutch East Indies turned on the question of development: to what extent might liberal economic principles – private property, free labour and individual interests – be apposite to Indonesian society? The debate set the liberal proponents of the Utrecht School, who sought to introduce a unified, capitalist-oriented legal system, with the scholars affiliated with the Leiden School of Law, including Dutch *adatrecht* (customary law) scholar Cornelis van Vollenhoven and Dutch Indologist A. D. A. de Kat Angelino, who appealed to an idea of a collectivist, 'organic' indigenous society.[95] These debates shaped the parameters for economic thought among a generation of Dutch and Indonesian thinkers, including Julius Herman Boeke. Advisor to the Credit Service and professor of tropical colonial economics at Leiden, Boeke is best associated with the critique of 'economic dualism': the economy of the Netherlands Indies, so the argument goes, is bifurcated into a subsistence economy characterized by limited needs in rural society, and a market economy governed by capitalist laws in the commercial centres.[96] Maintaining that capitalism was an 'inevitable stage of transition' in Indonesia's development as a 'truly independent state', Boeke proposed a programme geared towards encouraging native enterprise – what sociologist W. F. Wertheim later termed 'betting on the strong' – to mount a challenge to European and Chinese economic dominance.[97] Ultimately, it was industrial and agricultural development undertaken with local initiative – rather than state-led industrialization or 'welfare socialism' – that conjured the promise of material progress for Boeke.

However contentious, the legacy of Boeke's theory of economic dualism in public policy and historical scholarship remains undisputed. The Dutch long-wave economist Jacob van Gelderen, who served as director of the Central Office for Statistics and assumed leadership of the Indies Social Democratic Association (ISDV), drew on Boeke's dualist perspective in arguing for the relationship between cheap labour and high productivity in the sugar industry of Java.[98] Decades later, American anthropologist Clifford Geertz would come to be best associated with his thesis of agricultural involution, likewise founded upon a division between the *sawah* system of densely populated Java and the swidden systems of the Outer Islands.[99] Among Boeke's contemporaries, however, it was John S. Furnivall, the Rangoon-based British scholar, administrator and Fabian socialist, who most thoroughly engaged with the implications of Boeke's argument. Furnivall, who possessed firsthand experience of the Burmese system and studied colonial administration in 1930s Java, argued that the uneven development of the Netherlands Indies economy derived from the fact that the Dutch colonial authorities 'omitted to cultivate the development of economic activities among the people', such that the 'motive power of labor was compulsion and not profit', with the outcome that 'economic sense grew feebler even than it had been under native rule'.[100] For Furnivall, moreover, the contradiction 'between town and country, industry and agriculture, capital and labour' assumed the racialized appearance of an alien social form – Indian and Chinese middlemen in Burma, Chinese merchants in Indonesia, and Indian moneylenders in Indochina – in such plural societies.[101] Yet it was precisely his observations of colonial Java that reinforced his Fabian political commitments, based on a deep faith of an administrative elite (or 'social engineers' in Dutch parlance) to reintegrate the various constituent groups and 'enable [subject peoples] to leave the Empire'.[102] Furnivall's vision of 'progress, welfare and autonomy', ultimately, inhered in a programme of social and economic integration with the 'growing industrialization of the tropics', the 'economic advancement of tropical peoples' and the 'direction and conduct of private enterprise by natives.'[103]

At the core of Malaka's political vision, in that respect, was a normative claim about the general utility of developmental policies, not dissimilar to Furnivall's arguments, rooted in political investment in material development. Malaka's economic and political programme, outlined over the course of the three pamphlets *Naar de Republiek Indonesia*, *Semangat Moeda* and *Massa Actie*, bears testament to his commitment to developmentalism, laying emphasis not simply on the state-led development of new industries or the modernization of extant infrastructure, but also on the establishment of an educational system 'based directly on the existing or future industrial needs' with new vocational, agricultural and trade schools.[104] The import of industrial development lay in the present 'sluggishness of industry and commerce', a deliberate outcome of Dutch colonial policy with an aim towards relegating the Indies as 'agrarian country' [*landbowland*] rather than a 'commercial' or 'industrial' one.[105] It was colonial capitalism, for Malaka, that stood as *anti*-development; a socialist economic programme, in contrast, would provide the necessary corrective to draw Indonesia 'into the age of modern industry'.[106] It was incumbent on socialist development, for Malaka, to serve as an equalizing force, with the establishment of state enterprises enabling the triumph of 'technical expertise, common property and cooperation' across disparate classes.[107] Development, in this view, stood as the political and economic antithesis to the ills of colonial capitalism: urban-rural polarization, class and regional inequalities, and the existence of contending social formations.

* * *

The onset of political decolonization and the inauguration of the 'Third World' project during the Bandung era provided intellectual and political impetus for the emergence of renewed critiques of the dominant paradigms of development.[108] Among such critiques, the *dependencia* theorists of the 1960s drew on the context of Latin America to argue that international specialization along the lines of comparative advantage has excluded developing economies from the benefits of industrial technical progress, higher productivity or improved terms of trade.[109] Yet others associated with the world systems school, most prominently Egyptian economist Samir Amin, located the structural cause of underdevelopment in the divergent tendencies of the global accumulation of capital, organized along the lines of 'autocentric' central development and 'dependent' peripheral development.[110] Yet, if the ascendance of these postwar critiques of underdevelopment rendered the questions of political self-determination and economic autonomy commensurate with one another, it was during the crisis-ridden interwar moment that the debate around uneven development first became attuned to the experiential contradictions of colonialism, necessitating political responses attuned to local specificity. Relegating these critiques to a single 'Marxist' perspective alone ignores the heterogeneous origins of the category 'uneven development', and elides the regional contexts through which they were reworked and translated.

Even as they articulated divergent critiques around the nature of colonial capitalism, the relative importance of production and commerce, and the applicability of developmentalist solutions, the political-economic thought articulated by Roy and Malaka nonetheless cohered around particular recurring problematics: the vexing question of rural economics and agrarian development, and the pertinence of infrastructure as a site of political struggle. For both Roy and Malaka, the pressing questions of class inequality, uneven development and the still-ongoing task of ending colonialism run square through questions of rural infrastructure. In important ways, this preoccupation reflected the central importance the 'agrarian question' came to assume to larger debates around freedom, sovereignty and class struggle in British India and the Dutch East Indies: in both colonies, the overwhelming export orientation of agriculture precipitated a form of labour-intensive capital accumulation, where large masses of peasants came to be engaged in production for the global market under conditions of extra-economic control, coupled with a structural disincentive to invest in technological change or improve the productive capacities of land. The divergent critiques of development articulated by Roy and Malaka, in the final instance, represented their varied attempts at mapping their political thought onto the fractious terrain of rural development.

Notes

1 Purushottamdas Thakurdas (ed.), *A Brief Memorandum Outlining a Plan of Economic Development for India* (London: Penguin, 1945). See also Vivek Chibber, *Locked in Place: State-building and Late Industrialization in India* (Princeton: Princeton University Press, 2003).

2 B. N. Banerjee, G. D. Parikh and V. M. Tarkunde, *People's Plan for Economic Development of India*, 1944, BL/IOR/Mss Eur F235/639.

3 M. N. Roy, *Constitution of Free India: A Draft* (Delhi: Radical Democratic Party, 1945). See also M. N. Roy, 'New Federal Scheme for India', *Independent India*, 9 March 1941.

4 M. N. Roy, *Jawaharlal Nehru* (Delhi: Radical Democratic Party, 1945). For the relationship between Roy and Nehru, see also M. N. Roy, 'Jawaharlal Nehru, An Enigma or a Tragedy?' and Philip Spratt, 'Roy and Nehru', in *Jawaharlal Nehru: A Critical Tribute*, ed. A. B. Shah (Bombay: Manataklas, 1965), 37–47.

5 Tan Malaka, *Rentjana Ekonomi* (Surakarta: Badan Penerbit Indonesia Soerakarta, 1945), 76.

6 Malaka, *Rentjana*, 76.

7 Tan Malaka, *From Jail to Jail*, Vol. 2 (Athens: Ohio University Press, 1991), 154; Tan Malaka, *From Jail to Jail*, Vol. 3 (Athens: Ohio University Press, 1991), 75–8.

8 Tan Malaka, 'Politik', in *Muslihat, Politik, & Rencana Ekonomi Berjuang* (Yogyakarta: Penerbit Narasi, 2014).

9 See, for example, Jens Steffek, *International Organization as Technocratic Utopia* (Oxford: Oxford University Press, 2021); Michele Luoro, *Comrades Against Imperialism: Nehru, India, and Interwar Internationalism* (Cambridge: Cambridge University Press, 2018); Glenda Sluga and Patricia Clavin (eds.), *Internationalisms: A Twentieth-Century History* (Cambridge: Cambridge University Press, 2017); Patricia Clavin, *Securing the World Economy: The Reinvention of the League of Nations, 1920–1946* (Oxford: Oxford University Press, 2013).

10 For theoretical works representative of this critical reappraisal of Marx, see Jairus Banaji, *Theory as History: Essays on Modes of Production and Exploitation*

(Chicago: Haymarket Books, 2010); Lucia Pradella, *Globalization and the Critique of Political Economy* (London: Routledge, 2014); and Kevin Anderson, *Marx at the Margins: Nationalism, Ethnicity, and Non-Western Societies* (Chicago: University of Chicago Press, 2010).

11 Karl Marx, *Capital: A Critique of Political Economy*, Vol. 2 (London: Penguin, 1978), 193.

12 Karl Marx, *Grundrisse: Foundations of the Critique of Political Economy* (London: Penguin, 1973), 513; 645.

13 Vladimir Illich Lenin, *The Development of Capitalism in Russia* (Moscow: Progress Publishers, 1967).

14 Vladimir Illich Lenin, *Imperialism: The Highest Stage of Capitalism* (Moscow: Progress Publishers, 1970).

15 Rosa Luxemburg, *The Accumulation of Capital* (London: Routledge, 2003), 345–6.

16 Leon Trotsky, *History of the Russian Revolution*, Vol. 1 (London: Sphere Books, 1965), 23.

17 David Scott, *Conscripts of Modernity: The Tragedy of Colonial Enlightenment* (Durham: Duke University Press, 2004), 4. See also Omnia El Shakry, 'Rethinking Arab Intellectual History: Epistemology, Historicism, Secularism', *Modern Intellectual History* 18, no. 2 (2021): 547–72.

18 Durba Ghosh, *Gentlemanly Terrorists: Political Violence and the Colonial State in India, 1919–1947* (Cambridge: Cambridge University Press, 2017).

19 For fuller biographical accounts of M. N. Roy's political trajectory, see M. N. Roy, *Memoirs* (Delhi: Ajanta, 1984); Kris Manjapra, *M. N. Roy: Marxism and Colonial Cosmopolitanism* (New York: Routledge, 2010); John P. Haithcox, *Communism and Nationalism in India: M.N. Roy and Comintern Policy, 1920–1939* (Princeton: Princeton University Press, 1971); Samaren Roy, *The Restless Brahman: Early Life of M. N. Roy* (Bombay: Allied Publishers, 1970); and Sibnarayan Ray, *In Freedom's Quest: A Study of the Life and Works of M. N. Roy, 1887–1954* (Calcutta: Minerva Associates, 1998).

20 M. N. Roy, *An Indian Communist Manifesto* (1920), *Supplementary Theses on the National and Colonial Question* (1920), *The Future of Indian Politics* (1926) and *Revolution and Counter-Revolution in China* (1930).

21 M. N. Roy, *La India: Su Pasado, Su Presente y Su Porvenir* (Mexico City: n.p., 1918), M. N. Roy, 'India in a Transition Stage', *Communist International*, no. 19 (December 1921): 429–36; and *What Do We Want?* (Geneva: Edition De La Librarie J. B. Target, 1922).

22 M. N. Roy, *India in Transition* (Geneva: Edition De La Librarie J. B. Target, 1922), 12–13.

23 Michael Goebel, 'Geopolitics, Transnational Solidarity or Diaspora Nationalism? The Global Career of M. N. Roy, 1915–1930', *European Review of History* 21, no. 4 (2014): 485–99.

24 Prohibition from Entry into India under the Sea Customs Act of the Book entitled *India in Transition* by M. N. Roy, NAI, Home (Political) Department, No. 939, September 1922; Communism: Propaganda and Smuggling of Arms, TNSA, Under Secretary's Safe Files, No. 403, March 1924; Indian Communist Party, BL/IOR/L/PJ/12/52, September 1923.

25 Letter from G. M. Husain, Lahore, to Singaravelu Chetti, Madras dated January 1923, NAI, Home (Political) Department, No. 261, 1924; Muzaffar Ahmad, *Myself and the Communist Party of India* (Calcutta: National Book Agency, 1970), 221–3; Interview

with G. Adhikari, Nehru Memorial Museum and Library, Oral History Project (NMML-OHP), Acc. No. 378, 51–3; Interview with S. A. Dange, NMML-OHP, Acc. No. 823, 72–3; Interview with Shaukat Usmani, NMML-OHP, Acc. No. 307, 20–2.

26 Indian Communist Party, BL/IOR/L/PJ/12/52; *Malayan Bulletin of Political Intelligence* No. 7 (September 1922), BL/IOR/L/PJ/12/103.

27 Roy, *India in Transition*, 89–90.

28 Ibid., 17–18; 101–2.

29 Ibid., 80.

30 Roy, *La India*, 88.

31 Roy, *India in Transition*, 92–3.

32 Ibid., 84.

33 Ibid., 102.

34 Ibid., 97–8; 77.

35 Ibid., 18–25.

36 Ibid., 53.

37 Ibid., 93.

38 See Andrew Sartori, 'Global Intellectual History and Political Economy', in *Global Intellectual History*, ed. Samuel Moyn and Andrew Sartori (New York: Columbia University Press, 2013), 110–33; Osama Siddiqui, 'Narrating Economic History and the History of Economic Thought in Urdu', *Journal of Urdu Studies*, 3, no. 1/2 (2023): 1–39; Michael O'Sullivan, *No Birds of Passage: A History of Gujarati Muslim Business Communities, 1800–1975* (Cambridge: Harvard University Press, 2023).

39 Manu Goswami, *Producing India: From Colonial Economy to National Space* (Chicago: University of Chicago Press, 2003). See also Ajit Dasgupta, *A History of Indian Economic Thought* (London: Routledge, 1993); V. B. Singh, *From Naoroji to Nehru: Six Essays in Indian Economic Thought* (Delhi: Macmillan, 1975); and Joseph Spengler, *Indian Economic Thought* (Durham: Duke University Press, 1971).

40 Dadabhai Naoroji, *Poverty and Un-British Rule in India* (London: S. Sonnenschein & Co., 1901), 338–40. See also B. N. Ganguli, *Dadabhai Naoroji and the Drain Theory* (New York: Asia Publishing House, 1965). For precursors, J. V. Naik, 'Forerunners of Dadabhai Naoroji's Drain Theory', *Economic and Political Weekly* 36, no. 46/47 (2001): 4428–32.

41 Ibid., 101–2; See also Marx, *Capital*: Volume 3, 699–726.

42 Roy, *La India*, 71.

43 Romesh Dutt, *The Economic History of India under Early British Rule* (London: Kegan Paul, Trench, Trübner & Co., 1906). For a concise statement, see Amiya Bagchi, *The Political Economy of Underdevelopment* (Cambridge: Cambridge University Press, 1982), 78–82. Also see Morris D. Morris, 'Towards a Reinterpretation of Nineteenth-Century Indian Economic History', *Journal of Economic History* 23, no. 4 (1963): 606–18; Frank Perlin, 'Proto-Industrialization and Pre-Colonial South Asia', *Past and Present* 98, no. 1 (1983): 30–95; Tirthankar Roy, 'De-Industrialisation: Alternative View', *Economic and Political Weekly* 35, no. 17 (2000): 1442–7.

44 Mahadev Govind Ranade, *Ranade's Economic Writings*, ed. Bipan Chandra Pal (Delhi: Gian, 1990), 322–49; 411–12.

45 Mahadev Govind Ranade, *Essays on Indian Economics: A Collection of Essays and Speeches* (Madras: G.A. Natesan & Co., 1906), 27–9; 127.

46 Ibid., 177–8; 182.

47 Ibid., 100; 160.

48 Naoroji, *Poverty and Un-British Rule*, 216.
49 Ranade, *Essays on Indian Economics*, 20–1.
50 Friedrich List, *The National System of Political Economy* (London: Longmans, Green and Co., 1941); Ranade, *Essays on Indian Economics*, 128. See also Thomas Hopkins, 'The Limits of "Cosmopolitical Economy": Smith, List, and the Paradox of Peace through Trade', in *Paradoxes of Peace in Nineteenth Century Europe*, ed. Thomas Hippler and Miloš Vec (Oxford: Oxford University Press, 2015), 77–91.
51 Ranade, *Essays on Indian Economics*, 28–42; 126–7.
52 Ibid., 72–3, 83–5, 98.
53 Roy, *India in Transition*, 181.
54 Roy, *What Do We Want*, 19.
55 Roy, *India in Transition*, 37–9.
56 Ibid., 118; 135–43.
57 Ibid., 204.
58 M. N. Roy, 'Hunger and Revolution in India', *The Call*, 25 September 1919, 5, Nehru Memorial Museum and Library: M. N. Roy Private Papers.
59 M. N. Roy, 'Supplementary Theses on the National and Colonial Questions', in *Liberate the Colonies: Communism and Colonial Freedom, 1917–1924*, ed. John Riddell, Vijay Prashad and Nazeef Molla (Delhi: LeftWord Books, 2009), 43–5.
60 Roy, *India in Transition*, 86–7.
61 Roy, *What Do We Want*, 20.
62 M.N. Roy, 'Europe Is Not the World', *Inprecor* 4.90, 31 December 1924: 1045–6.
63 M. N. Roy, 'Speech at Fourth Congress of the Communist International', in *Liberate the Colonies*, 191–8.
64 See, for example, M. N. Roy, Letter to Henk Sneevliet, International Institute of Social History (IISH): Henk Sneevliet Papers, inv.nr.362, December 1926. In his memoirs, Roy would describe Sneevliet as 'the only European Communist who had actually lived in the East Indies, acquired first-hand knowledge of the nationalist movement, and actively helped the development of the labour movement and a Socialist Party', possessing 'unique experience and a thorough understanding of Marxism'. See Roy, *Memoirs*, 381.
65 'Session 5, July 28: National and Colonial Questions', in John Riddell (ed.), *Workers of the World and Oppressed Peoples, Unite!* Vol. 1 (New York: Pathfinder Press, 1991), 254–60.
66 Malaka, *From Jail to Jail*, Vol. 1, 26–8.
67 On the links between M. N. Roy and Tan Malaka, see Indian Communist Party: SIS Reports on Manabendra Nath Roy's Berlin-based activities (1921–22), BL/IOR/L/PJ/12/46; and *Malayan Bulletin of Political Intelligence* No. 9 (November 1922), BL/IOR/L/PJ/12/103.
68 R. Onraet, *Report Showing the Connection between Chinese and Non-Chinese Concerned in Communist Activities in Malaya*, TNA, CO 273/564/10, April 1930; *Malayan Bulletin of Political Intelligence* No. 34 (Dec 1925), TNA, CO 273/534/1; *Malayan Bulletin of Political Intelligence* No. 35 (Jan 1926), TNA, CO 273/534/4.
69 For biographies of Tan Malaka, see Syaifudin, *Tan Malaka: Merajut Masyarakat dan Pendidikan Indonesia yang Sosialistis* (Yogyakarta: Ar-Ruzz Media, 2012).
70 Takashi Shiraishi, *An Age in Motion: Popular Radicalism in Java, 1912–1926* (Ithaca: Cornell University Press, 1990).

71 See Ann Laura Stoler, *Capitalism and Confrontation in Sumatra's Plantation Belt, 1870–1979* (Ann Arbor: University of Michigan Press, 1995); Malaka, *From Jail to Jail*, Vol. 1, 43.
72 Helen Jarvis, 'Partai Republik Indonesia (PARI): Was It "the Sole Golden Bridge to the Republic of Indonesia"?' *Occasional Paper* 11 (Townsville: James Cook University of North Queensland, 1981): 13; Helen Jarvis, 'Tan Malaka: Revolutionary or Renegade?' *Bulletin of Concerned Asian Scholars* 19, no. 1 (1987): 41–54.
73 Netherlands East Indies Native Movements, TNA, CO 273/558/23; *Malayan Bulletin of Political Intelligence* No. 43 (October 1926) and No. 45 (December 1926), TNA, CO 273/535/11. See also Heather Streets-Salter, 'The Noulens Affair in East and Southeast Asia: International Communism in the Interwar Period', *Journal of American-East Asian Relations* 21, no. 4 (2014): 394–414.
74 Tan Malaka, *Semangat Moeda* (Tokyo: n.p., 1926), 40–4.
75 Tan Malaka, *Toendoek kepada kekoeasaan* (Berlin: n.p., 1922), 10; 53–4.
76 Malaka, *Semangat Moeda*, 39–40; Tan Malaka, *Aksi Massa* (Yogyakarta: Penerbit Nararsi, 2013), 39–41.
77 Malaka, *Aksi Massa*, 40.
78 Ibid., 57–9.
79 Malaka, *Semangat Moeda*, 32.
80 Tan Malaka, *Naar de Republiek 'Indonesia'* (Jakarta: Badak Merah Semesta, 2015), 16–17; *Semangat Moeda*, 33; *Aksi Massa*, 41.
81 Malaka, *Semangat Moeda*, 44–9; *Naar de Republiek*, 15–16.
82 Malaka, *Aksi Massa*, 27–8.
83 Ibid., 29; 38.
84 Ibid., 43.
85 'Hindia ini adalah sebagian dari rumah ekonominya Kapitalisme dunia'. Tan Malaka, *Parlemen atau Sovjet* (Jakarta: Yayasan Massa, 1987), 125–6.
86 Malaka, *Parlemen atau Sovjet*, 110.
87 Ibid., 126.
88 Malaka, *Aksi Massa*, 43–6.
89 Ibid., 8; 48.
90 Malaka, *Naar de Republiek*, 16; Malaka, *Parlemen atau Sovjet*, 93; Malaka, *Aksi Massa*, 43.
91 Roy, *India in Transition*, 56–7; Malaka, *Aksi Massa*, 112.
92 Azyumardi Azra, 'The Indies Chinese and the Sarekat Islam: An Account of the Anti-Chinese Riots in Colonial Indonesia', *Studia Islamika* 1, no. 1 (1994): 25–53; Siddarth Chandra, 'Race, Inequality, and Anti-Chinese Violence in The Netherlands Indies', *Explorations in Economic History* 39, no. 1 (2002): 88–112; James R. Rush, *Opium to Java: Revenue Farming and Chinese Enterprise in Colonial Indonesia, 1860–1910* (Ithaca: Cornell University Press, 1990); Sunil S. Amrith, *Crossing the Bay of Bengal* (Cambridge: Harvard University Press, 2013); Anthony Milner, *The Invention of Politics in Colonial Malaya* (Cambridge: Cambridge University Press, 1995).
93 N. P. van den Berg, *Munt-Crediet-En Bankwezen, Handel En Scheepvaart in Nederlandsch Indië: Historisch-Statistische Bijdragen: Historisch-Statistische Bijdragen* (The Hague: Martinus Nijhoff, 1907); N. P. van den Berg, *Uit de dagen der Compagnie: Geschiedkundige Schetsen* (Haarlem: H. D. Tjeenk Willink & Zoon, 1904); H. H. van Kol, *Het imperialisme van Nederland* (Rotterdam: Masereeuw & Bouten, 1901).

94 H. W. Dick, V. J. H. Houben, J. Th. Lindblad and Thee Kian Wie, *The Emergence of a National Economy: An Economic History of Indonesia, 1800–2000* (Leiden: Brill, 2002).

95 Suzanne Moon, *Technology and Ethical Idealism: A History of Development in the Netherlands East Indies* (Leiden: CNWS Publications, 2007); Peter Burns, *The Leiden Legacy: Concepts of Law in Indonesia* (Leiden: KITLV Press, 2004); David Bourchier, *Illiberal Democracy in Indonesia: The Ideology of the Family State* (New York: Routledge, 2014).

96 Julius Herman Boeke, *Economics and Economic Policies of Dual Societies as Exemplified by Indonesia* (New York: Institute of Pacific Relations, 1953).

97 J. H. Boeke, 'Economic Conditions for Indonesian Independence', *Pacific Affairs* 19 (1946): 399–401. See also W. F. Wertheim, 'Betting on the Strong', in *East-West Parallels: Sociological Approaches to Modern Asia* (The Hague: W. van Hoeve, 1964), 259–77. On the legacy of Boeke, see Sebastiaan Broere, 'Auto-activity: Decolonization and the Politics of Knowledge in Early Postwar Indonesia, ca. 1920–1955', *Lembaran Sejarah* 16, no. 2 (2021): 143–64.

98 J. van Gelderen, 'Western Enterprise and the Density of the Population in the Netherlands Indies', in B. J. O. Schrieke ed., *The Effect of Western Influence on Native Civilisations in the Malay Archipelago* (Batavia: G. Kolff, 1928), 85–102. See also Ulme Bosma, 'Cane Sugar and Unlimited Supplies of Labor in the 1930s: New Thinking and the Origin of Development Economics', in *Working on Labor: Essays in Honor of Jan Lucassen*, ed. Marcel van der Linden and Leo Lucassen (Leiden: Brill, 2012), 371–91.

99 Clifford Geertz, *Agricultural Involution: The Processes of Ecological Change in Indonesia* (Berkeley: University of California Press, 1969).

100 J. S. Furnivall, *Netherlands India: A Study of Plural Economy* (Cambridge: Cambridge University Press, 2010), 454–6.

101 Ibid., 311.

102 Julie Pham, 'J. S. Furnivall and Fabianism: Reinterpreting the "Plural Society" in Burma', *Modern Asian Studies* 39, no. 2 (2005): 321–48; Rudolf Mrazek, *Engineers of Happy Land: Technology and Nationalism in a Colony* (Princeton: Princeton University Press, 2002).

103 John S. Furnivall, *Colonial Policy and Practice: A Comparative Study of Burma and Netherlands India* (Cambridge: Cambridge University Press, 1948), 482–4.

104 Malaka, *Aksi Massa*, 120–3; Malaka, *Naar de Republiek*, 22–4; Malaka, *Semangat Moeda*, 58–62.

105 Malaka, *Semangat Moeda*, 35–6; Malaka, *Parlemen atau Sovjet*, 105.

106 Malaka, *Semangat Moeda*, 53–5; Malaka, *Naar de Republiek*, 21.

107 Malaka, *Naar de Republiek*, 27.

108 See Carolien Stolte and Su Lin Lewis (eds.), *The Lives of Cold War Afro-Asianism* (Amsterdam: Amsterdam University Press, 2022); Gyan Prakash and Jeremy Adelman (eds.), *Inventing the Third World: In Search of Freedom for the Postwar Global South* (London: Bloomsbury, 2022); and Christopher Lee (ed.), *Making a World after Empire The Bandung Moment and Its Political Afterlives* (Athens: Ohio University Press, 2010).

109 Raul Prebisch, 'The Economic Development of Latin America and Its Principal Problems', *Economic Bulletin for Latin America* 7, no. 1 (1962): 1–22; H. W. Singer, 'U.S. Foreign Investment in Underdeveloped Areas: The Distribution of Gains

between Investing and Borrowing Countries', *American Economic Review, Papers and Proceedings* 40 (1950): 473–85; Fernando Henrique Cardoso and Ernesto Faletto, *Dependency and Development in Latin America* (Berkeley: University of California Press, 1979); and Theotônio Dos Santos, 'The Structure of Dependence', *American Economic Review* 60, no. 2 (1978): 231–6. For an overview, see Cristobel Kay, *Latin America Theories of Development and Underdevelopment* (London: Routledge, 1993).

110 Samir Amin, *Accumulation on a World Scale* (Sussex: Harvester Press, 1974); Samir Amin, 'Accumulation and Development: A Theoretical Model', *Review of African Political Economy* 1, no. 1 (1974): 9–26; and Samir Amin, *Delinking towards a Polycentric World* (London: Zed Books, 1990).

2

Debating development and race from the Latin American South: Buenos Aires, 1929

Joanna Crow

Introduction

Between 1 and 12 June 1929, approximately forty-five delegates met in Buenos Aires, Argentina, for the First Conference of Latin American Communist Parties. These delegates mainly hailed from formally independent but economically marginal nations, and their discussions focused on how to best lead the workers in the struggle for socialist revolution, which they envisaged would bring an end to the imperialist-capitalist system, and enable a more equal, just, and independent development of national economies. In contrast to post-Second World War Eastern Europe, discussed by James Mark in *Socialism Goes Global*, there had been no 'consolidation of Communist power' in late 1920s Latin America.[1] The Communist Parties (or communist-affiliated parties) represented in Buenos Aires were nowhere close to getting into power, let alone consolidating it. In many countries, they were banned, persecuted and operating underground.

The dream of a different world existed, though, and in the conference proceedings and subsequent reports published in *La Correspondencia Sudamericana* (the official mouthpiece of the South American Secretariat of the Communist International), we can detect a certain determination and energy, and concerns and fears about how to transform the dream into reality. This was an unprecedented transnational meeting in at least two different ways. It was the first time that Latin American Communist Parties had come together to address their own problems as opposed to being present at, but relegated to the side-lines of, global forums, like the World Congresses of the Communist International (Comintern). It was also – as Peruvian delegate Hugo Pesce commented – 'the first time an International Congress of Communist Parties has focused in such a wide-ranging and detailed manner on the racial problem in Latin America'.[2]

In dialogue with Kevin Young's chapter in this volume, my chapter uses the First Conference of Latin American Communist Parties as a window into debates about economic development in the region during the early twentieth century. It underscores the centrality of 'race' to these debates. It shows how the language of race served as a means of rooting critiques of capitalism and explaining under-development in Latin America. It also explores how race became a lens through which to envisage and enact a future anti-capitalist revolution, especially with regard to land ownership. In doing this, my analysis draws on, contributes to and expands several different bodies of scholarship, not least exciting new collective and global histories of development and leftist internationalism.[3] It brings Latin America more fully into these histories, and thereby complements the work of scholars such as Christy Thornton, who shows, through an examination of post-revolutionary Mexico, that development as an international project was birthed earlier than the (oft-cited) post-Second World War period and not only as a US initiative.[4]

I take us further south, to Argentina, and emphasize the importance of South-South conversations as well as South-North (or North-South) exchanges.[5] Some individual interventions at the Conference of Communist Parties in Buenos Aires – for instance those of José Carlos Mariátegui (Peru) and Sandalio Junco (Cuba) – have already been well-summarized, as has the complex relationship developing between the Comintern and Latin America during this period.[6] I bring this scholarship together to probe in more depth how regional visions of economic development and world revolution took shape during the early twentieth century, sometimes in line with Soviet visions, but also against them. The first section of the chapter explores the significance of where the conference was held (not least the host country's renown for 'whitening' its population), emphasizing that rather than one centre and one periphery, there are many different centres and peripheries, and that these are relational and therefore always in motion. The second section reinforces this complex picture of diversity and movement by investigating the cast of characters speaking at the conference, who they were representing, the organization of the discussion sessions, and how the 'race problem' got on to the agenda. Delegates' multi-directional exchanges about race point to the manifold socialisms and imperialisms vying for supremacy in the 1920s. From the *where* and *who*, the final section moves on to interrogate exactly *what* communists said about race in Buenos Aires. In the context of the Comintern's announcement of its 'Third Period' and 'class against class strategy', and Latin Americans' discussions about the relationship between foreign economic dependency and racist domestic oppression, we get a clear sense of just how contested and unstable the category of race was. More specifically, I scrutinize what happened when the so-called 'Indigenous Question' was put in dialogue with the 'Black Question', as part of a broader Comintern debate about the 'National Question'. Some delegates conceived Indigeneity primarily in relation to land (pre-conquest, collective ownership of the land), whilst Blackness was largely equated with imported, industrial labour. Others disputed such distinctions, however, and sought to bring the two together, as part of a cross-racial class struggle.

Setting the scene: How 'South' was this Latin American South?

The First Conference of Latin American Communist parties took place in the second southernmost capital in the region and the fourth southernmost capital in the world. Nowadays, both Buenos Aires and the country of which it is part are routinely viewed as part of the 'developing world', 'Third World' or 'Global South'.[7] But if we go back to June 1929, Argentina ranked among the ten richest economies in the world and did not fit such 'dualistic hierarchies of development'.[8] With sustained mass immigration from Italy and Spain since the mid-nineteenth century, Buenos Aires was one of the fastest-growing urban centres on both sides of Atlantic and showed myriad signs of impressive infrastructural development: an underground metro, a municipal sewage and water system, and a newly expanded and modernized port. It also boasted scores of monumental civic buildings and a globally acclaimed opera house, the Teatro Colón. In the eyes of British traveller James Bryce, who visited in the 1910s, Buenos Aires was 'something between Paris and New York'.[9] Nowhere, he said, 'does one get a stronger impression of exuberant wealth and extravagance'.[10] Shifting the focus from socio-economic performance to intellectual and political activity, Mexican educator and philosopher José Vasconcelos described early 1920s Buenos Aires as 'the centre' of Ibero-American thought.[11] In 1929, Peruvian political activist Julián Petrovick similarly designated it '*the* cosmopolis of South America' and Chilean poet Pablo Neruda pronounced it a veritable literary 'paradise'.[12]

Figure 1 Calle Reconquista, Buenos Aires, *c.* 1929.[13]

Such acclamations were not universal, however. Writing the same year as Petrovick and Neruda, Swiss-French architect Charles-Edouard Jeanneret (known as Le Corbusier) proclaimed Buenos Aires 'the most inhuman city' he had ever known.[14] For Jules Humbert-Droz – founder of the Swiss Communist Party, member of the Communist International's Executive Committee and a prominent voice at the 1929 conference – it was typical of the 'big parasitic cities' where 'the great masses live, not from [their own] wealth-creating labour, but from the exploitation of others'.[15] Representatives of the Communist Party of Argentina (PCA) painted an analogous picture: Paulino González Alberdi claimed that the inhabitants of Buenos Aires were entirely ignorant 'of life in the countryside and the slave-like conditions imposed on the peons of the imperialist companies of the North'.[16] The city was easily 'as big and as populated' as European cities, which suggested 'the existence of an advanced capitalist country' but, in front of conference delegates, he insisted on a different reality – for this economist, like Humbert-Droz, the Argentine capital was 'exemplary of parasitism, caused by imperialism and its landowning allies'.[17] Whilst possibly proud to welcome their comrades to Buenos Aires, González Alberdi and other PCA representatives were keen to expose what they saw as its deceptive façade of successful modernization.

They were also keen to connect their country's economic history to that of the broader region. Countering the image of Argentina as an exceptional socio-economic success story in Latin America, PCA delegates cast it as exemplary of the continent's long-standing lack of independent development, with its national economy markedly 'deformed' by imperialism.[18] Argentina had been officially independent since the early nineteenth century but in practice lived a 'colonial or semi-colonial' existence.[19] Like its neighbours, this Southern Cone country depended 'on one or two [extractive] industries either directly owned or whose market [was] controlled by imperialist powers'.[20] During conference discussions, Pedro Romo lamented how the only rural regions in Argentina experiencing any progress – by being plugged into the rail network for example – were those that could 'provide [enough] grain and meat to satisfy the needs of England'.[21] Despite the wide variety of possibilities, he explained that nothing else was being produced on an industrial scale in his country; what's more, he claimed only 7 per cent of the land was being used and yet the cost of buying or renting land was extortionate.[22] Argentina, in brief, had a wheat and meat crisis, and this looked very similar to Mexico's oil and copper crisis, Chile's nitrate crisis, Cuba's sugar crisis, Colombia's coffee crisis, and so on.[23] Reporting back on the conference to readers of *The Communist* (the official journal of the Communist Party of the United States) in August 1929 – a couple of months before the Wall Street crash – William Simons remarked that such national crises were part of a world crisis but asserted that this was playing out particularly intensely in Latin America because the region had become 'one of the most important battlegrounds of English and American imperialisms'.[24] Not for nothing had Latin Americans tried to claim a voice at the First International Congress Against Colonialism and Imperialism in Brussels in 1927. In some ways, this meeting paved the way for and helps us make sense of the power dynamics on display at the 1929 conference in Buenos Aires.

As commented by Michael Goebel, less than 10 per cent of the delegates in Brussels in February 1927 came from Latin America, but they had 'a discernible presence' nonetheless and enabled the development of a theory of imperialism, following Lenin's treatise of 1917, that 'went beyond the customary understanding of formal colonial political control'.[25] Italian-born Argentine Victorio Codovilla, member of the PCA and head of the Comintern's South American Secretariat (SSA) – and therefore an instrumental figure in the organization of the 1929 conference in Buenos Aires – attended this global forum in Belgium's Egmont Palace together with the Uruguayans Carlos Quijano and Carlos Deambrosis Martins, Cubans Luis Casabona and Julio Antonio Mella, Peruvians Eudocio Ravines, César Falcon and Víctor Raúl Haya de la Torre, and the aforementioned José Vasconcelos from Mexico. Addressing the congress on the opening day, Vasconcelos denounced the dangers of US capitalist investment in his country.[26] His and other Latin American participants' target of protest was thus a different imperial power to that of Asian and African delegates, but – as noted above – British imperialism was still considered a major threat in Latin America in the late 1920s. This recognition of US imperialism, together with the fact that several Latin Americans in Brussels were not communists, suggests that in 1927, when it sponsored the founding congress of the Anti-Imperialist League, the Communist International was promoting a relatively inclusive revolutionary project of solidarity with 'oppressed nations' throughout the world. As Goebel tells us, however, Comintern policies towards non-communist allies became increasingly implacable from 1928 onwards.[27] Such rigidity was asserted – but also energetically contested – in Buenos Aires in 1929.

Despite this 'discernible presence' in Brussels in 1927, Moscow viewed Latin America as 'geo-strategically unimportant and [...] distinctly unpromising'.[28] By 1929, Latin America was on the Comintern's map at least, with the latter agreeing, for the first time, to organize a conference *in* the region that was focused on the specific needs of its own communist parties. Latin American activists, meanwhile, had shown that they wanted to participate in and shape global projects of anti-imperialist development. And Buenos Aires, as an important hub of continental intellectual and political networks, seemed an ideal place to bring people together to debate these projects. It is not insignificant that this *centre* was often seen as 'whiter' or 'more European' than other cities in the region. In the early twentieth century, Argentina and particularly Buenos Aires were widely imagined as a thriving 'melting pot'. Costa Rican writer Rafael Cardona, for example, celebrated the country as a 'purifying furnace, wherein diverse races gestate'.[29] And yet, as happened with myths of Argentine economic exceptionalism, myths of Argentine racial democracy and whiteness were hotly disputed in Buenos Aires.[30] For one thing, representatives of the PCA, such as Romo, were emphatic that rural Argentina was still home to many Indigenous people and that they suffered disproportionately the horrors of dispossession and slave-like labour conditions imposed by imperialist powers together with local landowners. Argentina, like elsewhere, Romo said, had massacred untold numbers of Indigenous people in the name of 'civilization' and 'progress'.[31]

The PCA was the oldest, largest and most 'theoretically advanced' Communist Party in Latin America.[32] Created in 1918, it closely followed the dictates of the Soviet Union and suffered many internal disputes and splits as a result.[33] Given this demonstration of allegiance to Moscow, the PCA's (comparative) strength in numbers, theoretical capacity, and institutional longevity, and the fact that the Comintern's South American

Secretariat (SSA) was based here, Argentina was the obvious choice to host the First Conference of Latin American Communist Parties.[34] The country was also living the last months of its 'Radical Period' (1916–30) under Hipólito Irigoyen, leader of the Radical Civic Union (UCR). Irigoyen was the first Argentine president to be elected democratically (through a secret and mandatory male vote) and was often referred to as 'father of the poor' because he passed a series of popular social reforms (extending social security benefits, for example, and increasing state investment in education).[35] This is not to say that his government endorsed the conference or that the PCA had any power. Far from it, but Communism was at least semi-legal here, in contrast to many other countries where the revolutionary left (and sometimes even moderate left) was being systematically and violently repressed.[36]

If Argentina was the obvious host nation for the conference, Buenos Aires was the obvious host city. It was the country's largest city, chief port and capital. It was also home to the headquarters of the SSA, which organized the conference. These headquarters were located relatively centrally, on the south side of Avenida Independencia, a working-class area with a history of labour uprisings (quite different to the Buenos Aires of luxury motor cars and top hats captured in Figure 1) – a good option, symbolically speaking, for the venue of a conference that aimed to come up with a strategic plan for leading 'the working masses to struggle and victory'.[37] This was *not* the venue that the organizers chose, however. According to Victor Jeifets and Lazar Jeifets, delegates stayed in hotels all over the city but the formal discussion sessions took place in the premises of the PCA's Avellaneda district committee.[38] Avellaneda was an industrial suburb of Buenos Aires – more suitable than a central, public location, if the anonymity of envoys from Moscow and delegates of illegal organizations and parties in Latin American needed to be protected. It was also equally representative of working-class Buenos Aires, and – with several football clubs and a thriving periodical press – served as an exciting showcase of what could be achieved through popular mobilization.[39] In a sense, then, the stage for the discussions under scrutiny here was simultaneously peripheral and central: an important, vibrant *barrio* on the outskirts of a city of capital and inequality.

The cast: Representing multiple socialisms and imperialisms

Who spoke for those being 'developed' at this First Conference of Latin American Communist Parties? The conference proceedings record the attendance of thirty-eight delegates from fourteen different countries in Latin America (Argentina, Bolivia, Brazil, Colombia, Cuba, Ecuador, El Salvador, Guatemala, Mexico, Panama, Paraguay, Peru, Uruguay and Venezuela). Only thirty-four, though, were documented as having spoken. They often appear in the records under an alias, but thanks to the efforts of Victor and Lazar Jeifets, we know many of their full (real) names.[40] All are male names.[41]

Some of these men – such as those from Argentina, Brazil and Uruguay – belonged to well-established Communist Parties, but many did not. A significant number of participating countries did not yet have a Communist Party in 1929.[42] Hugo Pesce and

Julio Portocarrero of Peru, for example, were members of the Socialist Party. Ecuador also had a Socialist (instead of a Communist) Party, and Colombian delegates travelled to Buenos Aires on behalf of their country's Revolutionary Socialist Party. Bolivia, like Panama, had a Labour Party. As commented by one of the Bolivian representatives in Buenos Aires, it had been impossible to publicly label their party 'Communist' because this scared off the workers they were trying to recruit.[43] In the case of Cuba, both delegates – Sandalio Junco and Alejandro Barreiro – were renowned trade union leaders, and were living in exile in Mexico at the time. This brief description of nine delegations indicates the many institutional variations of socialism represented in Buenos Aires. Some saw such diversity as a major obstacle to organizing internationally across the continent.[44]

Added into this complex mosaic were several attendees from the 'North': William Simons of the Communist Party of the United States, for example; Octave Rabate of the French Communist Party; and the aforementioned Swiss Communist Jules Humbert-Droz, representing the Comintern's Executive Committee. According to *La Correspondencia Sudamericana*, party *apparatchiks* like Humbert-Droz constituted almost 20 per cent of the delegates in Buenos Aires.[45] Perhaps predictably, Comintern or Comintern-affiliated agents directed most of the discussion sessions, which were organized around ten main themes. Codovilla, leader of the SSA, acted as 'informant' (i.e. gave an introductory report) for two themes. Orestes Tomás Ghioldi, responsible for the SSA of the Communist Youth International, did the same for another three, and presided over a fourth. Humbert-Droz chaired one session. Only three topics of debate were introduced by Latin Americans who did not belong to the Comintern bureaucracy: 'The Trade Union Question', 'The Peasant Question' and 'The Problem of Race in Latin America'.

The report on this last 'problem' was delivered by Peruvian Hugo Pesce, but was mainly authored by his compatriot Mariátegui (who could not attend due to ill health). Marc Becker claims that Codovilla prompted Mariátegui to prepare this report, with instructions to consider the 'possibility of forming an Indian Republic in South America' (an adaptation of the Black Belt and Native Republic Thesis, which I'll discuss in more detail shortly). Codovilla, in turn, had been urged by Humbert-Droz to put the race question on the agenda in Buenos Aires.[46] To Humbert-Droz's mind, there was a marked racial dimension to the class struggle underway in Latin America, but its Communist Parties had been reluctant to address this issue: 'many comrades have denied that the racial problem exists in Latin America, asserting that Blacks, Indians and mestizos have the same rights [as whites]'.[47] In particular, he said, Latin American comrades liked to distinguish their part of the world from the United States and its system of legalized racial segregation. Such assertions came across loud and clear in Brussels in 1927, specifically in the congress's 'Joint Resolution on the Negro Question', which claimed that 'in Latin America the Negroes do not have to lament any race prejudice'.[48] In Buenos Aires, Humbert-Droz turned delegates' attention to the 'Indigenous Question':

> It is true that the laws do not establish differences between the races but let us look at the facts. Who are the poorest and most exploited of the agricultural workers?

> Who are the peasants dispossessed of their lands by the large estate owners and foreign companies? The Indians. Who are the large landowners and estate managers that exploit them? For the main part, [they are] whites and mestizos.[49]

It is possible to read the intervention of Swiss Communist Humbert-Droz as an outside imposition – an assertion that he somehow understood the Latin American reality better than the comrades who lived and worked there. This links with Comintern bureaucrats' criticisms of Latin American communists' 'ideological deviations' and 'dangerously erroneous political positions'.[50] Humbert-Droz, for instance, took advantage of his platform in Buenos Aires to flag 'the completely mistaken ideas' of Colombia's Revolutionary Socialist Party (PSR).[51] French Communist Rabate similarly accused the PSR of lacking the 'necessary understanding of Marxism'.[52] Such comments suggest European Communists had, in Klaus Meschkat's words, 'come not to learn but to teach true Bolshevik principles that could be applied to any country in the world'.[53] Colombian delegate in Buenos Aires, Moises Prieto, kicked back against this, and what he saw as Moscow's arrogance and ignorance, protesting that Humbert-Droz did not know or comprehend the Colombian 'map'.[54]

At least a year before Buenos Aires, Mariátegui had famously proclaimed 'we must give life to an Indo-American Socialism reflecting our own reality and in our own language'.[55] As commented by Mahler, this Peruvian Marxist had been 'celebrated for his innovative ideas on land reform and economic justice for Indigenous communities and for theorizing a rural, peasant-based movement that sought to adapt Marxist theories to the concrete realities of Peru rather than to follow the Comintern's centralized attempts to export revolutionary models'.[56] And yet it was precisely Mariátegui that Codovilla (prompted by Humbert-Droz) approached to put together a paper on 'The Race Problem'. Why ask him for his views about the possibility of creating an Indian Republic in South America if the Comintern was not willing to expand their understanding of the local situation? Why ask Mariátegui to talk about the issue when he had already published views (stressing the limitations of such racialized self-determination projects) which ran counter to official Comintern policy? The tabled session itself, moreover, was chaired, introduced and concluded exclusively by Latin Americans. The Brazilian Communist Party's representative Mario Grazini presided over the discussion. Pesce (Peru), Junco (Cuba) and Leoncio Bausbaum (Brazil) delivered the introductory reports. And Ricardo Martínez of Venezuela had the last intervention (following the longest and most inclusive discussion at the conference). Perhaps, then, the story of Comintern agents trying to control socialist internationalism does not fully work here.

The proposal to form an 'Indian Republic' in the Andean region was an extension of the Comintern's proclaimed commitment to Black and Native rights to self-determination in Africa, the United States and the Caribbean. That Comintern requested input from the Latin America 'South' makes sense if we look back to how such revolutionary rhetoric came about in the first place. It emerged at the Fourth Congress of the Communist International in 1922, when delegates' deliberated about Lenin's 'Theses on the National and Colonial Questions' and acknowledged that people 'of African descent had been the victims of a particular form of racist oppression'.[57] As commented by Hakim Adi,

Claude McKay and Otto Huiswoud – Afro-Caribbean migrants to the United States – took on 'a key role in drafting the Thesis on the Negro Question'.[58] These proposals were developed further at the Sixth Congress of the Communist International in 1928, which resolved that African Americans in the southern states and Afro-descendants in the easternmost region of Cuba (as a majority of the population) constituted a special type of nation with the right to independence (the 'Black Belt' thesis). The other race-focused resolution focused on South Africa, where the plan was to fight for Black majority rule (making the country a Native or Black Republic). Again, Black communists – namely James La Guma, James Ford and Harry Haywood – 'played a leading part in drafting and advocating' the adoption of both theses.[59] In sum, instead of simply adhering to Comintern policy on the matter, African, African-American and Afro-Caribbean activists were the driving force behind it.[60]

Focusing on mid-twentieth-century Eastern Europe, James Mark claims that 'Communist elites sought to close-down "excessive" race talk which undermined a politics of class-based proletarian revolution'.[61] The opposite seems to have happened in Buenos Aires. Rather than shutting down 'race talk', Comintern officials were opening it up. They were highlighting a hitherto wilful blindness to the concept of race. And they did so among Latin American activists who, whilst in many cases working class (*La Correspondencia Sudamericana* categorized 51 per cent of attendees as 'workers' and 11 per cent as 'peasants'), were in the main part urban and white (or *mestizo*).[62] According to Becker, none of the delegates 'considered consulting with Indians as to their views on establishing an independent native republic or even bringing them into the discussion'.[63] In this sense, *internal* colonialism was as prominently exhibited in Buenos Aires as attacks on *external* imperialist powers. I partially concur with Becker's assessment.

We certainly see in Mariátegui's thinking some elements of the 'paternalist civilising discourses of socialist anti-colonialism' scrutinized by Mark.[64] Via Pesce, the leader of the Peruvian Socialist Party stressed the 'ignorance and backwardness' of Indigenous people, even if this was framed as a legacy of the racist capitalist colonial system.[65] For him, revolution was only possible if Indigenous peasants joined the struggle. They were the power behind the revolution, but this was a latent power that needed to be ignited by 'national communist parties'. As narrated by Mariátegui, Indigenous communities' land claims were 'deep rooted and instinctive'. This was their strength and would lead to the kind of collective, egalitarian, independent and sustainable economic development that the left wanted to see in Latin America. However, such claims lacked 'a coordinated, systematic, defined character', and Mariátegui saw it as the task of communist parties to provide this.[66] Several delegates concurred, in some cases dismissing Indigenous agency more vehemently than Mariátegui.[67]

Now withstanding this Peruvian Marxist's patronizing statements and his decidedly urban reality (he lived most of his life in the capital city, and only rarely visited other regions of Peru), I suggest that Mariátegui was not speaking from an *exclusively* white space. Several scholars such as Ricardo Melgar Bao have highlighted Mariátegui's close and sustained collaborations with many Indigenous activists in Peru: Hipólito Salazar, Francisco Chuqiwanka Ayulo, Mariano Larico Yujra, Julián Ayar Quispe and Manuel Camacho Alqa, to name just a few.[68] Salazar was a leader of the Peruvian Indigenous

Workers Federation (FIORP) founded in 1924. By 1926, he was informing the SSA in Buenos Aires that in 'Cuzco and Puno alone there are more than 200 indigenous federations and all of them sympathise with Communism'.[69] In documents that take us beyond the conference, then, we see direct communications between Indigenous organizations and the Comintern. In the case of Chuquiwanka Ayulo we don't need to go beyond the conference; he was cited in the published proceedings. Pesce informed delegates that this Quechua linguist and lawyer had lost his post as a public prosecutor for speaking out against the use of slavery in Amazonian Peru and the dispossession of Indigenous lands.[70] Chuqiwanka was not physically present in Buenos Aires. He did not get to speak for himself in this transnational forum. But he was evoked as an example of both Indigenous political activism and government repression of such activism. What's more, Mariátegui had published some of Chuqiwanka's letters in his avant-garde magazine *Amauta*; here Chuqiwanka was telling readers directly about the exploitation of Peru's Indigenous workers.[71] And whilst delegates were meeting in Buenos Aires, Mariátegui was in contact with Moisés Arroyo Posadas, an organizer from Jauja, about allocating a page of *Labor* (his other major print periodical) to news items authored by local Indigenous people, and setting up a new magazine entitled *El Ayllu*, which would be entirely dedicated to the 'indigenous peasantry' of Peru.[72] So, with the platform he had, Mariátegui might have spoken *over* Indigenous voices, but he was not evading or quashing them.

There are some resonant correlations and parallels to be drawn with the Ecuadorian Socialist Ricardo Paredes here. In his chapter in this volume, Young spotlights Paredes' important interventions in the 1928 Comintern Congress in Moscow about the 'intermediary forms' of foreign subjugation (as opposed to formal colonial rule) lived by Latin American countries. Paredes also, apparently, made use of his time in Moscow to press the urgency of addressing Latin America's 'Indigenous Question'; it was, Tony Wood asserts, 'thanks to Paredes' that Communists in Buenos Aires 'included "the problem of race" on their agendas at all', meaning that the previously outlined Humbert-Droz > Codovilla > Mariátegui conversation started with Paredes.[73] In other words, this agenda item was not externally imposed. More significantly, Paredes' interest in the 'Indigenous Question' derived from his long-standing collaboration with Indigenous organizer – and fellow founding member of Ecuadorian Socialist Party – Jesús Gualavisí.[74] Like Mariátegui, Paredes was unable to go to Buenos Aires, but he helped to shape the discussions that took place there, having been shaped himself by Indigenous leftist activism and discourse.

There are two other people who help to confound the picture of the Buenos Aires conference as a wholly white or *mestizo* conversation about the future of socialist revolution in Latin America. One of these was Raúl Mahecha, an ex-army captain, and labour organizer and co-founder of Colombia's Revolutionary Socialist Party.[75] Mahecha was keen to distinguish himself from the other Colombian delegates in Buenos Aires. He described himself as a 'pure blooded Indian' who put himself on the frontline in the banana workers' strikes of 1928, in contrast to party bureaucrats, like Prieto (mentioned above), who tried to 'organise the workers from [behind] desks in Bogotá'.[76] As Mahecha lamented, this was the reason for the failure of the 1928 strike: the indecision of, and lack of solidarity from, city-based leaders.

Afro-Cuban trade union leader Sandalio Junco was the other exception to the rule. A 'powerful orator with a magnetic personality', he had already addressed the Latin American Trade Union Confederation in Montevideo in May 1929 and would soon to be invited to speak at the First International Congress of Negro Workers, which was due to take place in London (but ended up taking place in Hamburg) in 1930.[77] I will return to his interventions below because he was one of the informants for the session on 'The Problem of Race' and, in this capacity, directly engaged with (and contested some of) Mariátegui's views. For the moment, though, I mention Junco merely to reiterate the range of socialisms present at the Buenos Aires conference. This transnational encounter brought together (pro- and less-pro Moscow) Communist Parties, (diverse) Socialist Parties, trade union representatives, rural organizers, urban bureaucrats, Indigenous and Afro-Latin American revolutionary projects, 'white' or *mestizo* articulations of leftist internationalism, and alternative imaginaries of development from both the Global North *and* the Global South.

Racist development policies and anti-racist revolutionary dreams

Delegates' discussion of 'The Problem of Race in Latin America' started with – and largely revolved around responses to – a report delivered by Peruvian physician Hugo Pesce.[78] As noted above, this report was based for the main part on Mariátegui's paper. Its focus was the 'Indigenous Question', but Mariátegui started with a broader overview of race in the region, and made this concept central to Marxist critiques of capitalist development. As presented here, capitalism was fundamentally racist. People of Indigenous and African descent were the most obvious victims of this economic system in Latin America. Elites justified the exploitation of Indigenous and Black labour and the expropriation of Indigenous lands on the basis of the supposed racial inferiority of these people, an idea, Mariátegui said, that was 'too widely discredited to merit the honour of [further] refutation'.[79] The white race's economic and political power – which both sustained and was sustained by the imperialist capitalist (or in Latin America's rural areas still semi-'feudal') system – *depended* on the notion that the Indigenous and Black proletariat were the proletariat because they were racially inferior. In short, racial hierarchies were *invented* to support imperialist capitalism. As outlined by Mariátegui and Pesce, and corroborated by other delegates in Buenos Aires, this system was the problem *not* Indigenous or Afro-Latin American people themselves; their lack of development – their illiteracy, poor health and poverty – was not intrinsic to their 'culture', as racist elites asserted, but a result of the system imposed on them, first by the Spanish colonial state and, afterwards, by independent, neo-colonial republican states.

Viewed from a slightly different angle, though, 'race' became part of the solution to the problem as well as the root cause of it. Indigenous and Afro-descendant people suffered discrimination and marginalization on the basis of their ascribed (inferior) racial status, but, for many delegates in Buenos Aires, their political mobilization specifically as Indigenous and Black (i.e. around their racial identities) was crucial to a successful revolution and the installation of an alternative, socialist development model; the revolution could not happen *without* this race-based consciousness.[80] In the case of Indigenous peoples, moreover, Mariátegui insisted not just on how they would benefit from socialism (because of the redistribution of land that socialist governance would enact) and on their status as the driving force behind the revolution (once 'ignited' by the party vanguard), but also on the idea that socialism was inspired by their 'collectivist spirit'.[81] It did not originate in Europe. It had existed – albeit in a more 'primitive' form – 'among the Inca Indians' (of Peru, Ecuador, Bolivia, Chile and Argentina) since pre-Columbian times.[82] More significantly, this autonomous form of development continued through to the present day, as demonstrated by Indigenous people's collective ownership of land, their communitarian social organization (the *ayllu*) and the 'secular custom of *minka*' (relations of reciprocity and obligation, the rituals of asking for and acknowledging help).[83]

And yet, this continued racial affiliation – understood as intimately linked to cultural heritage and the socio-economic system – was also perceived as a significant obstacle to communist parties' endeavours to recruit Indigenous (and Black) workers. Race could be a mobilizing factor, but it could just as easily divide the proletariat and impede class struggle. This was the subject of much discussion in Buenos Aires. Mariátegui's paper underscored the fact, for example, that many Indigenous people only spoke their native languages, which made it difficult to spread the 'message' of revolution. The point was not to denigrate or invalidate such linguistic pluralism, or to insist on teaching Spanish. Instead, his report suggested – and the conference concluded – that communist parties needed to prioritize the publication of political magazines and pamphlets in Quechua, Aymara and other Indigenous languages.[84] It also stressed the urgent need for more 'Indian propagandists'.[85] A related problem, as commented by several delegates, was Indigenous communities' understandable distrust of 'anyone who isn't of the same race'.[86] To try to get Indigenous people to '*solidarizarse*' with 'the whites' (regardless of their leftist and pro-Indigenous credentials) was a difficult task when the latter were so closely associated with colonialism and its legacies.[87]

One particularly interesting thread of conversation was the distinctions and parallels drawn between the situation of Indigenous and Black workers. In that context, the 'race problem' was presented as an internally diverse one, or in some cases, a problem that concerned one 'race' more than another. Mariátegui emphasized that Afro-descendants in Latin America lived the same 'harsh exploitation' as Indigenous people.[88] But he also talked of their frequent appointment as overseers or supervisors of Indigenous labourers, which meant assuming a colonialist function and reinforcing the oppression of the Indigenous 'race'. Additionally, he claimed Black workers in Latin America did not have their 'own' languages (speaking instead the language of the colonizer); they 'almost do not have their own traditions', he said – an intriguing claim that ran counter to many ideas of Black culture in the 'New World' at the time.[89] To Mariátegui's mind, all of this signalled that Afro-Latin Americans did not think of themselves distinctively as 'Black', and that theirs was more a class-based than race-based struggle.[90]

For Mariátegui, the 'race problem' was fundamentally connected to land (and, vice versa, the land question was a race question, because elites justified dispossession by asserting Indigenous people's racial inferiority).[91] The only way to solve the Indigenous question was to break up the large estates [*haciendas*] and redistribute the land to those who worked it and, especially, to those who had owned it 'since time immemorial'. Agrarian reform – which Tehyun Ma talks about later in this volume, focusing on mid-twentieth-century Taiwan – was a key component of delegates' dreams for a more equitable form of economic development in Latin America: it was central to the manifestos of Communist and Socialist Parties across the region and it was reiterated as a goal to work towards in the conference resolutions.[92] Quite obviously, it underpinned conference discussions not just about 'The Problem of Race' but also 'The Peasant Question'. As summarized by *La Correspondencia Sudamericana* afterwards, *campesinos* [rural workers] had a right to land – and should be acknowledged as owners of the land – because they toiled it and made it productive; for Indigenous *campesinos*, there was the additional claim of the restitution of ancestral lands that had been stolen from them. The conference resolutions also stressed Indigenous traditions of collective land ownership and agricultural production, meaning Indigenous communities required more lands than individual (non-Indigenous) farmers.[93] The Peruvian delegation in Buenos Aires intimated that such redistributive policies, designed to eliminate rural poverty, were not as applicable to Afro-descendants because they mainly worked in the industrial sector.[94] Furthermore, as the colonizers had imported their ancestors from Africa, Mariátegui asserted Black workers in Latin America could not lay claim to the same 'originary' status as Indigenous workers; they had no land to claim *back*. Neither could they, he implied – indicating much ignorance of African history – appropriate the pre-Columbian Inca tradition of collective labour that formed the blueprint for socialist utopias.[95]

Afro-Cuban Sandalio Junco agreed that Black workers' relationship to the land differed to that of Indigenous workers, but countered the narrative presented by Mariátegui on several different fronts. In his report to delegates in Buenos Aires, Junco maintained that many Black people worked in agriculture (as well as in the industrial sector).[96] More importantly, he negated Mariátegui's (and others') assertions that the 'Black problem' was not really a 'race problem'.[97] He insisted that anti-Black racism was very real throughout the Americas, and that this racism needed to be looked at together with anti-Indigenous racism, for they were intimately connected through colonialism and imperialism; they built on and reinforced each other, as Black slave labour had been brought in to replace Indigenous slave labour.[98] He also contended that there was a strong racial consciousness amongst Black workers – evidenced in their resistance against discriminatory laws (for instance, the 1912 law in Cuba that prohibited Black people from running for president) and their creation of race-based cultural and political organizations.[99] For Junco, such initiatives demonstrated that the 'Black race' *did* have their 'own' traditions. He also noted how commentators referred to their rebellion against the 1912 law specifically as a 'race war'.[100] Pre-empting and countering Brazilian delegate Bausbaum's report, this Cuban activist alluded to anti-Black racism among workers as well as elites.[101] Lastly, and critically, he stressed the importance of considering migrant labourers as part of the 'race problem', for instance the large number of Black Haitians and Jamaicans working on Cuban sugar plantations.[102] This was taken forward as part of a broader discussion about the need for solidarity with migrant workers.[103] Calling out xenophobic discrimination against

Chinese and non-national Black labourers, several delegates promoted the urgency of reaching out to and mobilizing migrants as part of a fundamentally transnational struggle for the abolition of capitalism.[104]

Ruling Communist Parties in mid-twentieth-century Eastern Europe 'claimed that Communism rendered racism structurally irreproducible' and that they therefore did not need to formally investigate genocidal acts committed during the Second World War.[105] Their priority was to create and sustain a unified national proletariat. Class cohesion was also a priority for Junco and Mariátegui but neither believed that Communism *necessarily* 'rendered racism structurally irreproducible'. Junco denied that to be Communist or to be a class-conscious proletarian signified an automatic adherence to racial equality. For him, race consciousness and race-based organizing – and specifically the conception of and identification with a *transnational* Black community – were essential for equitable economic development and full liberation from oppression.[106] By the same token, Mariátegui only saw socialist revolution as the solution to racism if it was rooted in the Indo-American reality, which in Peru – with a majority rural population – was a reality of Indigenous communal land ownership and collective social organization. For him, racism could only be eradicated if socialism was inspired by and responded to this reality, not least by securing the return of Indigenous ancestral lands.

This did not, however, equate with establishing an autonomous (Aymara or Quechua) Indigenous nation (à la Native Republic thesis). Mahler argues that, in rejecting 'Comintern's project for Indigenous nationalism and self-determination', Mariátegui dismissed 'the viability of any ethnicity-based organizing for Indigenous communities'.[107] In Mariátegui's words (delivered by Pesce), it was only by fighting in 'close alliance with the white and *mestizo* proletariat' that the 'Indian race' could overthrow the capitalist-imperialist system and 'develop freely'; to fight separately, as an Indigenous republic or 'nation', was to divide the proletariat, and thereby hinder the struggle for socialist revolution.[108]

We certainly sense at least a hint of 'white' or *mestizo* fear of Indigenous sovereignty – and a desire to channel and contain the potency of Indigenous rebellion – in the anti-colonial socialist discourse of Mariátegui and his followers in Buenos Aires. However, several delegates, such as Martínez of Venezuela, Siquieros of Mexico and Muñoz of Argentina, challenged the Peruvian delegation's stance, affirming Indigenous people's right to national self-determination and the significance of their cultural differences with non-Indigenous workers.[109] Publicly declared fear of Indigenous sovereignty was thus far from unanimous at this Conference of Latin American Communist Parties. And Mariátegui himself, as noted above, explicitly celebrated Indigenous communities' independent social organization. Furthermore, this Marxist philosopher asserted that, with capitalism's overthrow, there was the potential for broader cooperation between Indigenous people of different countries and a subsequent 'political autonomy of the race'.[110] So, it was plausibly more a question of what *kind* or *level* of Indigenous autonomy best coincided with socialist revolution (and of whether autonomy or revolution came first), than a clear-cut rejection of 'ethnicity-based organizing for indigenous communities', as Mahler argues.

There were, to be sure, many fault-lines in the Latin American left's assertions of anti-racism in the early twentieth century but we also see frank and open attempts to reveal and debate racism. To a certain extent, even just the revelation of racism and the racial dimensions of the global class struggle (and Latin America's place in it) constituted a revolution at this time. In the context of widespread Indigenous rebellions in defence of community lands, Indigenous voices were incorporated into discussions in Buenos Aires, albeit only indirectly and fleetingly. And it is surely significant that Junco – a Black communist who denounced the racism of elites and workers alike, and underscored the dangers of impressing Moscow-created Marxist theories on Latin America – was one of three delegates chosen to head up a 'Majority Commission on the Racial Problem' after the conference.[111] In his own paper, Junco did not explicitly support Black self-determination, either in Cuba or elsewhere. In fact, according to the published proceedings, he did not *mention* the Black or Native Republic Thesis.[112] Instead, he focused on making sure Communist Parties acknowledged the realities of anti-Black as well as anti-Indigenous racism in Latin America, and the equal importance of radicalizing Black and Indigenous – and crucially, national and migrant – workers, if they were to be successful in their bid to overthrow imperialist capitalism.

Conclusion

The above analysis shows how difficult it is to categorize one person's thinking let alone a divided collective of more than forty activist intellectuals. Communist delegates in Buenos Aires failed to reach a definitive conclusion on the 'Problem of Race' and its role in the revolutionary struggle for an alternative form of economic development, leaving us with many questions, not least about the conspicuous silence of Raúl Mahecha (the only delegate on record to self-identify as Indigenous) in the discussions about this question. Some delegates believed that Indigenous and Black populations constituted oppressed nations, and should organize and be supported as such; some argued against their national status. Some endorsed Indigenous but not Black nationhood. Among those that advocated for Indigenous self-determination, there were disagreements as to what this meant – just recognition of cultural autonomy or separate self-government? This lack of consensus was recognized in the resolutions published shortly after the conference.[113] But there *was* a consensus that 'race' constituted a problem and that it was intimately tied to development, or indeed the region's lack of development: failed industrialization, increasing rural poverty and continued dependency on imperialist powers through mono-crop economies. 'Race' was also deemed part of the solution. Delegates largely agreed that the revolutionary class struggle would only be successful if it was a race-conscious one. This applied particularly to the agrarian or *campesino* question (and the urgent need for a radical overhaul of the land tenure system), but was relevant to the urban sphere too. Finally, there was a consensus that the region's Communist Parties needed to continue studying and debating the issue of race.

Discussions about race and alternative development models *did* continue after 1929. The multiple socialisms that came into view in Buenos Aires continued to interact with each other and to engage with the possibility of Indigenous and Black cultural and political autonomy well beyond this critical moment of encounter. An analysis of where the conversations go *from* Buenos Aires, though, is beyond the remit of this chapter. They are part of a larger work in progress, which traces the interventions of Indigenous and Afro-descendant men and women in various transnational forums in twentieth-century Latin America. The point of this chapter has been to zoom in on the location, cast and content of twelve days of intense (South-South and South-North/North-South) dialogues about revolutionary socialism. By probing the racial dimensions of leftist delegates' hopes and fears for the future, I have reaffirmed race as a malleable, unresolved category, and underscored the complex power dynamics at play in international debates about development.

Notes

1 James Mark, 'Race', in *Socialism Goes Global*, ed. James Mark and Paul Betts (Oxford: Oxford University Press, 2022), 221–54.

2 South American Secretariat of the Communist International (SSA), *El Movimiento Revolucionario Latino Americano: Versiones de la Primera Conferencia Comunista Latino Americana* (Buenos Aires: La Correspondencia Sudamericana, 1929), 263.

3 For example, Mark and Betts (eds.), *Socialism Goes Global*; Stephen Macekura and Erez Manela (eds.), *The Development Century: A Global History* (Cambridge: Cambridge University Press, 2018); Norman Naimark, Silvio Pons and Sophie Quinn Judge (eds.), *The Cambridge History of Communism* (Cambridge: Cambridge University Press, 2017); Marcel van der Linden (ed.), *The Cambridge History of Socialism* (Cambridge: Cambridge University Press, 2022); Celia Donert (ed.), 'Women's Rights and Global Socialism: Gendering Socialist Internationalism during the Cold War', special issue of *International Review of Social History* 67 (2022); Michael Louro, Carolien Stolte, Heather Street-Salter and Sana Tannoury-Karam (eds.), *The League Against Imperialism: Lives and Afterlives* (Leiden: Leiden University Press, 2020).

4 Christy Thornton, *Revolution in Development: Mexico and the Governance of the Global Economy* (Berkeley: University of California Press, 2021).

5 Here I build on the excellent new volume *Transnational Communism across the Americas*, ed. Marc Becker, Margaret Power, Tony Wood and Jacob Zumoff (Champaign, IL: University of Illinois Press, 2023).

6 Marc Becker, 'Mariátegui, the Comintern, and the Indigenous Question in Latin America', *Science and Society* 70, no. 4 (2006): 450–79; Anne Garland Mahler, 'The Red and the Black in Latin America: Sandalio Junco and the "Negro Question" from an Afro-Latin American Perspective', *American Communist History* 17, no. 1 (2018): 16–32; Victor Jeifets and Lazar Jeifets, *América Latina en la Internacional Comunista, 1919–1943: Diccionario biográfico* (Santiago: Ariadna Ediciones, 2015); Jeifets and Jeifets, 'The Comintern, Soviet Diplomacy, and Latin America (1919–1941)', in *A New Struggle for Independence in Modern Latin America*, ed. Pablo Baissoti (New York: Routledge, 2021); Mariana Massó and Manuel Quiroga, 'Building a Continental Policy: The South American Secretariat of the Communist International', *Historical Materialism* 30, no. 3 (2022): 236–272; Klaud Meschkat, 'Helpful Intervention? The Impact of the Comintern on Early Colombian Communism', *Latin American*

Perspectives 35, no. 2 (2008): 39–56; Olga Ulianova, 'Desvelando un mito: Emisarios de Internacional Comunista en Chile', *Historia* 41, no. 1 (2008): 99–164.

7 Alan Beattie, 'Argentina: The superpower that never was', *Financial Times*, 23 May 2009. See also James Scobie, *Argentina: A City and a Nation* (New York: Oxford University Press, 1971) and David Rock, 'From the First World War to the 1930s', in *Argentina Since Independence*, ed. Leslie Bethell (Cambridge: Cambridge University Press, 1993), 139–72.

8 Nikita Sud and Diego Sánchez-Ancochea, 'Southern Discomfort: Interrogating the Category of the Global South', *Development and Change* 53, no. 6 (2022): 1123.

9 James Bryce, *South America: Observations and Impressions* (New York: Macmillan, 1913), 318.

10 Ibid.

11 José Vasconcelos, *Indología* (Paris: Agencia Mundial Librería, 1920), 135.

12 Julián Petrovick, 'Reseña de la pintura peruana', *Revista de Educación* (Santiago), October 1929, 774; Pablo Neruda to Héctor Eandi, letter dated 24 April 1929, accessible at https://neruda.uchile.cl/critica/eandi.html

13 Archivo General de la Nación Argentina, accessible at https://commons.wikimedia.org/wiki/File:Calle_Reconquista._Buenos_Aires_1929.jpg.

14 In Jason Wilson, *Buenos Aires: A Cultural and Literary History* (London: Signal Books, 2007), 3.

15 SSA, *El Movimiento Revolucionario,* 44.

16 Ibid., 148.

17 Ibid.

18 Ibid., 142.

19 Delegates used this Comintern wording throughout the conference. We could also describe Latin American states at this time – especially Argentina (and Brazil and Uruguay), which received large numbers of European migrants from the 1870s – as 'settler colonial' societies. On the benefits of doing so, see Michael Goebel, 'Settler Colonialism in Postcolonial Latin America', in Edward Cavanagh and Lorenzo Veracini (eds.), *The Routledge Handbook of the History of Settler Colonialism* (London: Routledge, 2017), 139–51. Several Latin American communists in Buenos Aires were of European descent themselves and likely for this reason dwelled less on recent European settlement in their countries than on the destructive impact of over-reliance on foreign, imperialist markets.

20 William Simons, 'The Sharpening Class Struggle in Latin America. A Tale of Two Conferences: Montevideo and Buenos Aires', *The Communist* 8, no. 8 (1929): 430.

21 SSA, *El Movimiento Revolucionario*, 238.

22 Ibid.

23 Simons, 'The Sharpening Class Struggle', 431.

24 Ibid., 430.

25 Michael Goebel, 'Forging a Proto-Third World? Latin America and the League against Imperialism', in Louro et al. (eds.), *The League Against Imperialism*, 71.

26 Ibid., 58.

27 Ibid., 69.

28 Ibid., 70.

29 In *Repertorio Americano* (San José), 4 July 1927.

30 On the 'successful' whitening of Argentina during the nineteenth century, see Erika Denise Edwards, *Hiding in Plain Sight: Black Women, the Law and the Making of a White Argentine Republic* (Tuscaloosa: University of Alabama Press, 2019).

31 SSA, *El Movimiento Revolucionario*, 237–9.

32 Ray Cline, *A Survey of Communism in Latin America* (Washington: Central Intelligence Agency, 1965).

33 Victor Figueroa Clark, 'Latin American Communism', in Naimark, Pons and Judge (eds.), *The Cambridge History of Communism*, 388–413. On similar splits afflicting the Communist Party of South Africa, see Robert Edgar, *The Making of an African Communist: Edwin Thabo Mofutsanyana and the Communist Party of South Africa 1927–1939* (Pretoria: Unisa Press, 2005).

34 The SSA was founded in 1925, to develop communist educational work in the region, support the formation of new national parties, and build links between them (Massó and Quiroga, 'Building a Continental Policy', 237).

35 On Irigoyen's government, see Joel Horowitz, *Argentina's Radical Party and Popular Mobilisation, 1916–1930* (University Park: Pennsylvania State University Press, 2008).

36 In Chile during Carlos Ibáñez del Campo's presidency, for example.

37 The offices of the Central Committee of the PCA and the SSA's *La Correspondencia Sudamericana* were located at 3054 Independencia.

38 Victor Jeifets and Lazar Jeifets, 'Introduction' to *The Latin American Revolutionary Movement: Proceedings of the First Latin American Communist Conference, June 1929* (Leiden: Brill, 2023), 22. They cite the memoirs of Luis Checcini, head of the PCA committee in Avellaneda.

39 Joel Horowitz, 'Football Clubs and Neighbourhoods in Buenos Aires before 1943: The Role of Political Linkages and Personal Influence', *Journal of Latin American Studies* 46, no. 3 (2014): 557–85.

40 Jeifets and Jeifets, *América Latina en la Internacional Comunista*.

41 Argentina had eight delegates: Victorio Codovilla, 'Contreras' (unknown identity), Paulino González Alberdi, Florindo Moretti, Francisco Muñoz, Leonardo Peluffo Cordoba, Pedro Romo and Jan Jolles. Speaking for Bolivia were José Antonio Arze and Alfredo Mendizábal, and for Brazil, Mario Grazini (under the pseudonym 'Gabrinetti') and Leoncio Bausbaum. Three delegates came from Colombia: Moises Prieto, Raul Mahecha and Heraclio Matallana. Two Cubans attended: Alejandro Barreiro ('Braceras') and Sandalio Junco ('Juarez'). Alberto Jaujo ('Arana') and 'Padilla' (unknown) came from Ecuador. Both representatives of El Salvador were unknown: 'Dieguez' and 'Márquez'. Representing Guatemala were Luis Villagran ('Villalba') and 'Taboada' (unknown). Renowned Mexican muralist David Alfaro Siquieros went by 'Suárez' and his compatriot Manuel Rodríguez appeared as 'Rosáenz'. 'Carignani' and 'Chavez' (both unknown) came from Panama. Also unknown was the Paraguayan emissary 'Dellepiane'. The Peruvian delegates were Hugo Pesce ('Saco') and Julio Portocarrero ('Zamora'). The Communist Party of Uruguay sent Felix Ramírez, Eugenio Gómez and Leopoldo Sala. There was just one Venezuelan delegate: Ricardo Martínez.

42 *La Correspondencia Sudamericana*, 15 August 1929, 24.

43 Ibid., 29.

44 SSA, *El Movimiento Revolucionario*, 105.

45 'Partidos representados en la Primera Conferencia Comunista Latino Americana', *La Correspondencia Sudamericana*, 15 August 1929, 24. Along with Humbert-Droz, these included Zacharij Rabinovich of the International Communist Youth, ICJ; Orestes Tomás Ghioldi and 'Schiappapietra' (unknown) of the South American Secretariat of the ICJ; and 'Meyer' (unknown) of the International Red Aid, founded by the Comintern in 1922.

46 Becker, 'Mariátegui, the Comintern, and the Indigenous Question', 450.
47 In SSA, *El Movimiento Revolucionario*, 89.
48 In Goebel, 'Forging a Proto-Third World?', 66.
49 SSA, *El Movimiento Revolucionario*, 89.
50 Figueroa Clark, 'Latin American Communism', 388.
51 In SSA, *El Movimiento Revolucionario*, 96.
52 Ibid., 128.
53 Meschkat, 'Helpful Intervention?', 45.
54 In SSA, *El Movimiento Revolucionario*, 110.
55 Mariátegui, 'Aniversario y Balance', *Amauta* 3 (1928): 3.
56 Mahler, 'The Red and the Black', 29. Mahler makes this assertion despite Soviets theorizing Marxism to include the peasantry by this point. Of course, the 'concrete realities of Peru' encompassed more than the peasantry, and within the peasantry there were specific conditions for Indigenous communities to take on board.
57 Hakim Adi, *Pan Africanism: A History* (London: Bloomsbury, 2018), 66.
58 Ibid., 65. Pan-Africanist George Padmore notes the input of Indian Communist Manabendra Nath Roy here too: 'From Mexico he turned up in Moscow in 1918, to be welcomed by Lenin, whom he assisted in drafting the Colonial Thesis for the Second Congress of the Third International'. See *Pan-Africanism or Communism: The Coming Struggle for Africa* [1956] (London: Denis Dobson, 1971), 278.
59 Ibid., 70.
60 See also Holger Weiss, *Framing a Radical African Atlantic: African American Agency, West African Intellectuals and the International Trade Union Committee of Negro Workers* (Leiden: BRILL, 2013).
61 Mark, 'Race', in Mark and Betts (eds.), *Socialism Goes Global*, 222.
62 *La Correspondencia Sudamericana*, 15 August 1929, 24.
63 Becker, 'Mariátegui, the Comintern and the Indigenous Question', 471.
64 Mark, 'Race', in Mark and Betts (eds.), *Socialism Goes Global*, 223.
65 In SSA, *El Movimiento Revolucionario*, 265–6.
66 Ibid., 288.
67 Mendizábal (Bolivia), for example, spoke of Communist ideas 'conquering' Latin America's 'Indians', and Márquez (El Salvador) asserted that the Indigenous 'stratum' needed to be 'dragged' along by the revolutionary movement. In ibid., 303 and 309.
68 Ricardo Melgar Bao, 'José Carlos Mariátegui y los indígenas: más allá de la mirada, diálogo y traducción intercultural', *Boletín de Antropología Americana* 31 (1995–7): 131–41.
69 *La Correspondencia Sudamericana*, 15 November 1926.
70 In SSA, *El Movimiento Revolucionario*, 282.
71 For example, *Amauta* 5, January 1927. See also letter from Chuqiwanka to Mariátegui, dated 6 February 1927, available at http://archivo.mariategui.org/index.php/carta-de-francisco-chuqiwanqa-ayulo-6-2-1927
72 Letter from Mariátegui to Arroyo Posadas, dated 5 June 1929, reproduced in José Carlos Mariátegui, *Mariátegui total: 100 años* (Lima: Biblioteca Amauta, 1994), 1997.
73 Tony Wood, 'Semicolonials and Soviets: Latin American Communists in the USSR, 1927–1936' in Becker et al. (eds.), *Transnational Communism*, 86.
74 Marc Becker, 'Indigenous Communists and Urban Intellectuals in Cayambe, Ecuador (1926–1944)' *IRSH* 49 (2004): 41–3.
75 Fellow leftist organizer, Rafael Núñez, remembered Mahecha as a 'man of the people'. Cited in 'Strikers or Revolutionaries? Strikers and Revolutionaries?', in

Ann Farnsworth-Alvear, Marco Palacios and Ana María Gómez López (eds.), *The Colombia Reader: History, Culture, Politics* (Durham and London: Duke University Press, 2017), 472–82.

76 In SSA, *El Movimiento Revolucionario*, 115–16.

77 Mahler, 'The Red and the Black', 18. Sandalio Junco, 'El proletariado negro de la América Latina y la Conferencia de Londres', *El Trabajador Latinoamericano* 32–33 (1930): 23–6.

78 'El problema de las razas en América Latina', in SSA, *El Movimiento Revolucionario*, 262–317.

79 In ibid., 266.

80 Ibid., 288.

81 Ibid., 274.

82 Ibid.

83 Ibid., 278.

84 Ibid., 289; and 'Problema de las razas', *La Correspondencia Sudamericana* 15 (August 1929): 25–30.

85 Ibid., 268–9. Siquieros (Mexico) made the same point (ibid., 304), and Mahecha indirectly referred to himself in these terms when talking about his mobilization of plantation workers in Colombia (ibid., 115).

86 Mariátegui in ibid., 282, and Siqueiros, 304.

87 Ibid., 282.

88 Ibid., 266.

89 Ibid., 270. Mariátegui seemed to ignore developments such as the Harlem Renaissance, and closer to home, the growing popularity of football club Alianza Lima, which was celebrated in the Peruvian press as the 'team of Blacks'. On debates about change and continuity in African American cultural traditions, see Sidney W. Mintz and Richard Price's ground-breaking text, *An Anthropological Approach to the Afro-American Past: A Caribbean Perspective* (Philadelphia: Institute for the Study of Human Issues, 1976).

90 Ibid., 284.

91 Ibid., 288.

92 'Resolución sobre la cuestión campesina en Latino-América', *Correspondencia Sudamericana* 15 (August 1929): 18–23.

93 Ibid., 21.

94 SSA, *El Movimiento Revolucionario*, 270.

95 Ibid., 287.

96 Ibid., 292.

97 See Mariátegui in ibid., 271, 284, 286–7; Bausbaum in ibid., 296–7; Barreiro Olivera in ibid., 302.

98 Ibid., 291–2.

99 Ibid., 293.

100 Ibid.

101 Junco went into more detail on this in Montevideo than in Buenos Aires. Bausbaum categorically denied that racism existed among the proletariat in Brazil. See ibid., 297.

102 Ibid., 294.

103 See Margaret Stevens, *Red International and Black Caribbean: Communists in New York, Mexico and the West Indies, 1919–1939* (London: Pluto Press, 2017).

104 At least four delegates – Siqueiros, Humbert-Droz, Chavez and Villagran – supported Junco on this. For more on the Cuban context, see Barry Carr, 'Identity, Class and Nation: Black Immigrant Workers, Cuban Communism, and the Sugar Insurgency, 1925–1934', *HAHR* 78, no. 1 (1998): 83–116.
105 Mark, 'Race', in Mark and Betts, *Socialism Goes Global*, 225.
106 Mahler, 'The Red and the Black', 28–30.
107 Ibid., 27.
108 In SSA, *El Movimiento Revolucionario*, 291.
109 Ibid., 301.
110 Ibid., 291.
111 The others were Jolles and Martínez. 'Resolución sobre el problema racial en la América Latina', Buenos Aires, 12 June 1929, RGASPI, F. 495, 3–5, accessible at https://www.yachana.org/earchivo/movrev/RGASPI_racial.php.
112 Mahler notes how Junco's Bolshevik-Leninist Party, a fringe group within the Communist Party of Cuba, opposed the struggle for Black self-determination in the country's eastern region because this made Black workers vulnerable to violent repression. Mahler, 'The Red and the Black', 21.
113 'Problema de las razas', 23–9.

3

Pan-Africa, African socialism and the 'federal moment' of decolonization

Marc Matera

Kwame Nkrumah wrote in his autobiography that the 1945 Pan-African Congress in Manchester stood for independence and 'the doctrine of African socialism'.[1] Narratives of decolonization and the triumph of nationalist independence movements across the African continent frequently begin with the event. Instead, this chapter uses it as a starting point for considering pan-African federalism and conceptions of African socialism among Black intellectuals in the former British Empire. The congress took place after the historic victory of the Labour Party in the first general elections in Britain after the Second World War. Labour's ascendence buoyed hopes for substantive colonial reforms and focused anti-colonial critique on the new government. African and Caribbean anti-colonialists' calls for internal self-government and dominion status evolved into demands for complete independence during the late 1940s and 1950s. However, many continued to view nationalism and the nation-state form as means to the ultimate goal of regional or continental federation.

Visions of pan-African federalism among anglophone Black intellectuals were in part a response to the revival of imperial federalism in the British Empire after the Second World War to contain and channel anti-colonialism.[2] In 1963, the Federation of Rhodesia and Nyasaland or Central African Federation, which was formed in 1953, dissolved under the weight of consistent but growing African opposition. The same year saw public debates across the African continent and the publication of Kwame Nkrumah's *Africa Must Unite* in the lead up to the Conference of Heads of Independent African States in Addis Ababa where the Organization of African Unity (OAU) was established in late May. On 5 June, the heads of the governments of Kenya, Tanganyika and Uganda declared their intention to form a post-colonial East African Federation by year's end, and on 20 July, eighteen African States and Madagascar signed a new convention of association with the European Economic Community in Yaoundé, Cameroon. For the main protagonists in these diplomatic forums, African journalists and writers and their readers, and Black radicals on both sides of the Atlantic, these developments were related.

Despite their full-throated opposition to the colonial federalist schemes, many African intellectuals viewed federation as the political framework best suited to securing economic and political liberation.[3] Advocates of federation on the regional or continental level cited long histories of interconnection, the unity and sense of Africanness developed in the ongoing struggle against colonialism, and the shared challenges and, if pooled, the substantial collective resources of post-colonial Africa. In their view, it could accommodate difference and some degree of local or regional autonomy while providing the scaffolding for unity of purpose and action, especially in economic development. The question of development fuelled federalist ambitions.[4]

Pan-African federalism was associated with what became known as African socialism during the late 1950s and 1960s.[5] Many African leaders held that the combination of the two, variously conceived, represented the best means of fostering rapid, equitable development across the continent. 'Indeed', the American sociologist Dorothy Nelkin observed in the mid-1960s, 'in all attempts to create supranational institutions on the African continent, African socialism has served as the unifying ideology. At the same time, the realization of the objectives of Pan-Africanism … is considered by Pan-Africanists to be a precondition for the success of African socialism in realizing the goal of continent-wide economic development.'[6] As Nkrumah wrote, 'At the core of the concept of African Unity lies socialism … Socialism and African Unity are organically complementary.'[7] By the end of 1962, when Léopold Sédar Senghor hosted a conference dedicated to the idea, African socialism appeared to be the most powerful ideological force on the continent. The British socialist and Labour MP Fenner Brockway wrote in 1963 that 'it is not too much to say that the most dynamic socialist movement in the world today is in Africa.'[8]

At base, as Emmanuel Akyeampong asserts, African socialism was 'a search for an indigenous model of economic development', and, as Priya Lal argues, it was the product of 'multiple imaginative genealogies.'[9] There were nearly as many different versions of African socialism as there were advocates of it, and the term was adopted as a rallying cry by leaders with contrasting, even opposed, positions, as the Dakar colloquium on African socialism demonstrated. Certain core elements linked most, if not all, iterations of African socialism. It entailed a commitment to self-determination and popular democracy, to equal opportunity for all and the abolition of material inequalities within society and at the level of the global economic order, and to mass mobilization and cooperation in pursuit of the collective interest. For Nyerere in the early 1960s, it was an ethos, 'an attitude of mind.'[10] For Nkrumah, 'socialism in Africa' represented 'a new social synthesis in which modern technology is reconciled with human values, in which the advanced technical society is realised without the staggering social malefactions and deep schisms of capitalist industrial society.'[11] Many justified socialism in an African context on the basis of African egalitarianism and humanism, evidenced by communal forms of social organization that were widespread prior to colonization and, to some extent, persisted down to the present. The trade unionist and Minister of Labor of Kenya, Tom Mboya, described African socialism as a combination of 'codes of conduct' and 'cosmological ideas which regard man, not as a social means, but as an end and entity in the society.'[12] By the late 1960s and early 1970s, critics, including Nkrumah, began distinguishing certain iterations of African socialism from what they termed 'scientific socialism.' Nevertheless, Nkrumah continued to maintain that 'the aim is to remold African society in the socialist direction; to reconsider

African society in such a manner that the humanism of traditional African life re-asserts itself in a modern technical community'.[13] The debate over the content, form and means of achieving African socialism played out among African leaders across the continent and, internally, within nearly every liberation movement.[14]

Like the arguments for pan-African federation, those made in support of African socialism referred to the cultural unity of African societies as well as parallel histories of colonialization and economic exploitation. Its proponents presented African socialism as the solution to the problem of post-colonial underdevelopment. After the Second World War, the Trinidadian radical George Padmore and Nkrumah viewed the distinction between industrialized and unindustrialized countries as the primary axis of exploitation and dependency in global economic relations. Development meant rapid industrialization, and state planning and a socialist economic model appeared to be the most equitable and efficient means of achieving it. The quest for socialist development and African economic liberation was related to – even, depended on – remaking north-south relations and dismantling global economic hierarchies. African socialists recognized that capitalist development in Europe and elsewhere was inseparable from imperialism, and at the core of African socialism lay an understanding of the anti-colonial struggle as class struggle. Padmore characterized the global anti-imperialist struggle as 'a manifestation of the class struggle in its acutest form, since the colonial masses are the "oppressed of the oppressed"'.[15] How could post-colonial African states develop economically without exploiting their neighbours or generating socio-economic inequality internally? Only the Soviet Union and emerging socialist states of Asia appeared to have done so, while, for Padmore and Nkrumah, the history of Latin America presented an ominous reminder of the possibility of continued underdevelopment in post-colonial Africa.[16] By contrast, Nyerere, whose vision of African socialism was rooted in his conception of *ujamaa* or 'familyhood', emphasized the distribution of wealth, both within African societies and globally, more than the mode of its production. In a world consisting of not only richer and poorer capitalist countries but of 'rich socialist countries and poor socialist countries', he believed that 'the class struggle will be transferred from a national to an international plane'.[17] Despite the difference in emphasis, Padmore, Nkrumah and Nyerere argued that socialism offered not only a set of economic principles likely to accelerate development and therefore raise African living standards, but also the best means of doing so while avoiding the social and economic cleavages and violent predations that accompanied the development of capitalism.

Why was there such a close link between various federalist alternatives and socialist dreams of development in decolonizing Africa? This chapter tracks the idea of pan-African regional or continental federation among radical Black intellectuals and African political leaders in the former British Empire from 1945 to the mid-1960s. The examples that follow demonstrate the broad purchase and staying power of the idea of federation as both a neocolonial and decolonial option, and compel us to consider pan-African federalism in relation to late imperial federal schemes, including the early history of European integration. British officials, white settlers and the African and Caribbean intellectuals who are the focus of this chapter all envisioned federalism as an engine of economic development. The latter recognized how the former parties employed federal schemes as part of a repertoire of strategies to control the course of development and to shape Africa's post-colonial future. While appropriating elements of the rationale used to justify imperial federations, such as economic complementarity and Africa's immense natural resources, they sutured federalism to the goals of Pan-Africanism, revising the content of the latter in the process. In their view, continental or regional federation and development along socialist lines in Africa would enable the continent to break out of the shackles of economic dependency and counter emerging modes of imperialist exploitation.

Towards pan-African socialism

Ninety delegates and roughly 200 people in total attended the Fifth Pan-African Congress in Manchester in 1945. A number of future post-colonial leaders in Africa, including Nkrumah, Jomo Kenyatta, Nnamdi Azikiwe, Obafemi Awolowo and Hastings Kamuzu Banda, were present. The participation of African intellectuals, trade unionists and political parties distinguished the Manchester conference from the earlier congresses, but the gathering was overwhelmingly one of people of African descent within the British Empire. Padmore and other members of the Pan-African Federation (PAF), including Kenyatta, the South African writer Peter Abrahams, and the Guyanese T. Ras Makonnen (born Thomas Griffiths), organized the event, seizing the opportunity provided by the conferences of the World Federation of Trade Unions in London and Paris in 1945. Nkrumah arrived in London in early 1945, after spending the previous decade in the United States, and soon joined the organizing effort. Abrahams recalled that Nkrumah 'had quickly become part of our African colony in London' and 'our protests against colonialism'.[18] He joined the West African Students' Union (WASU) and formed a West African secretariat to agitate for federation and independence in West Africa.

The congress unanimously adopted some twelve pages of statements and resolutions covering the United Nations Organization, the Caribbean and Africa. One declared:

> We demand for Black Africa autonomy and independence, so far and no further than it is possible in this 'ONE WORLD' for groups and peoples to rule themselves subject to inevitable world unity and federation … We condemn the monopoly of capital and the rule of private wealth and industry for private profit alone. We welcome economic democracy as the only real democracy.

Led by Nkrumah, the West African National Secretariat (WANS) drafted a separate set of resolutions on the region, declaring that 'the artificial divisions and territorial boundaries created by the imperialist powers are deliberate steps to obstruct the political unity of the West African people'.[19] Though the WANS was a direct outgrowth of the Pan-African Congress, it drew on regional political imaginaries and the legacy of the National Congress of British West Africa.[20] The WANS's main goals mirrored those of the WASU or represented an escalation of the latter's demands, and most of the WANS's members were active in both groups. At a meeting in December

1945, the founding members agreed that the WANS's purpose was to support and coordinate with 'progressive organizations in West Africa with a view to realising a West African Front for a United West African National Independence'.[21] Nkrumah formed a small vanguard group, dubbed The Circle, within the WANS to which 'only those who were ... genuinely working for West African unity and the destruction of colonialism' were admitted. The Circle aimed to serve 'as the Revolutionary Vanguard of the struggle for West African Unity and National Independence' and to 'create and maintain a Union of African Socialist Republics'.[22]

Both the PAF and WANS claimed the mantle of the 1945 Pan-African Congress and endeavoured to spread its message beyond the relatively small number who gathered in Manchester. The PAF's journal, *Pan-Africa*, published the conference resolutions. Abrahams situated the event within growing expressions of transcolonial or pan-'coloured' cooperation and linked it to a federalist political goal, concluding his contribution to Padmore's published volume of the proceedings with the call: 'FORWARD TO THE SOCIALIST UNITED STATES OF AFRICA! LONG LIVE PAN-AFRICANISM!'[23] The WANS and WASU organized a conference of West Africans, including representatives of two French colonies, in London in August 1946 with the intention of forming an All-West African Congress. The WANS published a journal, *The New African*, and several pamphlets, most notably Bankole Awoonor-Renner's *West African Soviet Union* (1946) and Nkrumah's *Towards Colonial Freedom* (1947). Awoonor-Renner wrote, 'It is only a united and independent West Africa, free from every vestige of foreign control, that could ensure security, happiness and prosperity'; 'help us ... to create a free, united, strong and independent West African Federated Nation.'[24] For Nkrumah and Awoonor-Renner, a united British West Africa would be a stepping-stone towards a larger federation encompassing all of West Africa.

Though Nkrumah remained a member of the PAF's executive committee, Abrahams remembered that he 'drifted away from us' and increasingly devoted his energies to 'his own West African group'.[25] Both the PAF and WANS made it clear that their ultimate goal was not merely independence along existing territorial lines but a union of socialist African states. Nkrumah returned to the Gold Coast in 1947 and led Ghana to independence a decade later. Awoonor-Renner embarked on a tour of West Africa in 1948 to generate support for a proposed West African National Congress. In Lagos, Nigeria, he urged his audience 'to intensify their present activities' in pursuit of the 'goal of West African, rather than Nigerian, nationalism'.[26]

Fabian imperialism and colonial regionalism

Far from entering the postwar period resigned to imperial disintegration and colonial independence, the political leaders and both the metropolitan and white-settler populations of European empires came out of the Second World War with outsized expectations for empire – to fuel reconstruction, to restore national grandeur or to ensure geo-political influence. At the same time, the atrocities of the Second World War, growing anti-colonial foment and the international climate of the early Cold War contributed to discrediting the old rationales for colonial rule and to the emergence of a new one – colonial development. Federalist schemes – at the imperial, regional and colony levels – became a popular neo-imperial tool in the French, Dutch, Portuguese and British empires. Though unsuccessful, these attempts to rebrand colonialism had significant implications not only for the course of decolonization, but also for the process of European integration and how decolonization was packaged and remembered in post-imperial societies across Western Europe.[27]

African and Caribbean anti-colonialists criticized colonial development policy, and the new constitutional arrangements justified in its name, as self-serving, ineffectual and an obstacle to political and economic liberation. The Conservatives' 'political blue-print of postwar Colonial Imperialism', Padmore and his partner and collaborator Dorothy Pizer wrote in *How Russia Transformed Her Colonial Empire* (1946), 'has been put forward' by Field Marshal Jan Smuts of South Africa, and 'bases itself upon a kind of condominium' grouping 'British Colonial regions into federal units according to their geographical position'.[28] As Mark Mazower notes, Smuts worked 'through the war on a plan for a new "Pan-African" superstate that would stretch right up to the equator'. In 1940, he reportedly told South African troops stationed in Kenya, 'the efforts you are making will, perhaps not in our time, bring about a United States of Africa'.[29] The proposals put forward by Smuts, imperial grandees such as Lord Frederick Lugard, and members of both the Labour and Conservative parties in Britain appropriated African anti-colonial demands and political imaginaries to buttress white hegemony in Africa. Padmore and Pizer contrasted the use of federalist schemes to perpetuate and deepen colonial exploitation and economic dependence with the Soviet model of an egalitarian federation of socialist republics. Padmore extended his critique of 'Fabian imperialism' and the Labour Party's approach to colonial development and again contrasted the British Empire with the Soviet Union in *Africa: Britain's Third Empire* (1949).

In *West African Soviet Union*, Awoonor-Renner, like Padmore, cited the Soviet example as a model for post-imperial federation, but like Nkrumah, he also turned repeatedly to the examples of India and the United States to support his arguments.[30] Awoonor-Renner held up Article 123 of the Soviet Constitution, which declared 'the equality of the citizens of the Union of Socialist Soviet Republics, irrespective of their nationality or race', as the solution to 'the whole question of this racial discrimination'. He also proposed a state-directed programme of industrialization and cooperative agricultural production for West Africa along with the model of the Soviet five-year plans.[31]

The Labour Party's leading voices on colonial issues, such as Secretary of State for the Colonies Arthur Creech Jones, were well known to African and Caribbean students and intellectuals in Britain. The West African Parliamentary Committee, formed in 1942, met weekly at Westminster Palace and consisted of Creech Jones and other Labour MPs, the South African economist Rita Hinden of the Fabian Colonial Bureau (FCB) and West Africans from the WASU and PAF, including R. W. Beoku-Betts, F. O. Blaize, Joseph Appiah and later Nkrumah.[32] WASU members labelled the FCB the 'unofficial mouthpiece' of the postwar Labour government.[33] Hinden cultivated relationships with African and Caribbean students and activists, and a number of them were members of the Fabian Society or had close contacts among the Fabians. While a student at Edinburgh University in 1949, Julius Nyerere joined the Fabian Society, and he remained a member for decades.[34]

The Labour government and FCB dismissed calls for independence as misguided before the achievement of dramatic improvements in social welfare and economic development.[35] African and Caribbean socialists countered that social democracy in Britain was built on colonial exploitation and seized on public statements by British socialists presenting the development of Africa as the solution to Britain's postwar problems. In prioritizing Britain's geopolitical interests and the needs of the metropolitan economy and domestic consumers, *Keep Left* (1947), written by the Labour MPs R. H. S. Crossman, Michael Foot and Ian Mikardo, reflected thinking on the Labour left.[36] The authors condemned the exploitative imperialism of the past but also presented the empire, particularly African human and natural resources, as the key to maintaining Britain's global standing. Economic development in Africa, they argued, 'should be our main colonial responsibility for the next twenty years'.[37] 'Public pronouncements by some of our leading "comrades" in the new Labour Government such as Creech-Jones, Bevin, and Morrison,' Appiah recalled, 'left us in no doubt what the difference between Labour-in-office and Labour-in-opposition was.' Socialist internationalism and social democracy in practice meant the continuation of imperialism under the guise of 'partnership' in development.[38]

During the late 1940s and early 1950s, two cases of colonial federalism – the imposition of a new constitution in Nigeria, which channelled African political participation into three regional units, and the formation of the settler-dominated Central African Federation – became focal points of anti-colonial protest. Preparations for the Pan-African Congress were carried out against the backdrop of a general strike of seventeen unions representing 150,000 workers in Nigeria. The repressive response to the strike, which included censorship to silence critics such as Nnamdi Azikiwe, helped turn a strike over wage demands and the rising cost of living into an anti-colonial cause, and Africans and Caribbeans in the WASU and PAF organized to raise money for the strikers and to attract publicity to conditions in Nigeria.[39] The Labour government's response to the calls for constitutional reform and greater African representation took the form of a new constitution that institutionalized regionalism by further dividing Nigeria into northern, western and eastern regions, and laid the groundwork for the post-colonial federalist system there. Azikiwe and the Lagosian intelligentsia as well as Black activists in the metropole denounced the so-called Richards Constitution. At a FCB conference on Britain's relationship to the colonies in April 1946, attended by Nkrumah, Padmore, Kenyatta, Abrahams and members of the WASU and West Indian Students Union, the Jamaican historian Elsa Goveia insisted, 'British rule in Africa has arrested the evolutionary growth of African territory.' The partition of Nigeria under the new constitution, she argued, 'has been unscientific and unreal. It was done by people who were scrambling for territory and had no thought about the good of the country.'[40] In a speech in July 1946, Azikiwe declared, 'The Richards Constitution divides the country into three zones which are bound to departmentalize the political thinking of this country ... it is obvious that regions will now tend more towards Pakistanization than ever before, and our future generations will inherit this legacy that is born out of official sophistry.'[41]

The Federation of Rhodesia and Nyasaland or Central African Federation (CAF) was the most ambitious example of postwar colonial federalism. The federation bound together the self-governing dominion of Southern Rhodesia (Zimbabwe) with its exclusively white legislature; the Northern Rhodesia protectorate (Zambia) which, due to the presence of the mining industry, bankrolled the CAF throughout its existence; and the Nyasaland protectorate (Malawi) which functioned largely as a large African labour reserve. Though Africans in the region and Britain mobilized against the CAF before and after its creation in 1953, the Conservative government that emerged from the 1951 general election, liberal white settlers and business leaders in Central Africa depicted it as a grand experiment in 'racial partnership' within a 'multiracial' African federation, contrasting it with apartheid in South Africa. The arguments in support of the CAF lauded the economic complementarity of the three territories and presented the federation as the best structure to attract investment, spur rapid development and facilitate 'African advancement'.[42]

This framing drew upon the rhetoric of the postwar Labour government, which led the way in redefining the terms of colonial relations around partnership in development. Though the FCB and some members of the Labour Party opposed federation in Central Africa because it would increase the power of white settlers in Southern Rhodesia vis-à-vis the British government, the party had originated the idea.[43] In fact, members of the Labour Party put forward the most ambitious proposals for territorial consolidation. In early 1948, the Labour MP Squadron Leader Ernest Kinghorn initiated a short debate on the topic of the 'United States of Africa' in the House of Commons. Kinghorn explained that he was not proposing consolidating political control of the continent under a single state, but rather calling attention to immense possibilities for development in Africa. Comparing Britain's colonies in Central and Eastern Africa to the United States, he declared that 'real salvation can be found, in my view, in the heart of our territories in Africa'.[44]

Opposition to the CAF and recognition of the growing threat of neocolonialism, particularly in light on European integration, informed debates over pan-African federalism as African and Caribbean territories moved closer to or attained independence during the 1950s and early 1960s. Nkrumah wrote, 'There is discernible a curious variance of purpose when one compares the British concurrence to the demand for regionalism in Nigeria and their refusal for so long to concede to African clamour for the dissolution of the Central African Federation.' Defenders of the CAF insisted 'that it made for economic cohesion and progress'. 'If a larger aggregate is good for one part of Africa, the settler-controlled part,' Nkrumah argued, 'then surely it must contain the same beneficent seed for the independent parts'.[45] For Nkrumah and other African anti-colonialists, Nigeria and the CAF revealed the hypocrisy of British developmentalist discourse. In their view, a concerted effort to delay political self-determination, preserve British and other foreign business interests, and guarantee access to mineral and other resources lay beneath the differences between the two cases.

African unity, balkanization and European integration

Nkrumah and Padmore remained close until the latter's death in 1959. Padmore spent his final years serving as Nkrumah's trusted adviser in Ghana. They organized two major conferences in 1957 and 1958 – the Conference of Independent African States and the All African Peoples Conference – held in Accra soon after Ghanaian independence. St Clair Drake, who arrived in Ghana in 1958, recalled that their aim 'was not fifty African states, it was continental government of the continent'.[46] The conferences stood for the 'ultimate goal[s] of a Commonwealth of African States or a United States of Africa' and 'Pan African socialism', the 'interim goal of regional federations' and the 'rejection of "tribalism"', and 'a new concept of "residential Pan Africanism"' encompassing everyone born or naturalized in African states.[47] At the end of his life, Padmore framed the anti-colonial fight for independence, socialist development and the transformation of economic relations, and the drive towards continental unity as a single revolution with three dimensions.[48] Nkrumah wrote in the 1962 foreword to *Towards Colonial Freedom*, a collection of his writings from the early 1940s: 'Twenty years ago my ideas of African unity ... were limited to West African unity. Today, ... I see the wider horizon of the immense possibilities open to Africans – the only guarantee, in fact, for our survival – in a total continental political union of Africa.'[49]

For Padmore and Nkrumah, Ghana was 'the standard-bearer of Pan-African Socialism', a stimulus and agent of unity and economic development guided by socialist principles and practices on a continental scale.[50] They insisted that only a United States of Africa would secure political independence and liberation from external economic domination. During the 1950s and 1960s, balkanization emerged as a common theme, part of a shared lexicon, among advocates of pan-African federation who warned of the limits of national independence and the threat of new forms of economic imperialism or neocolonialism.[51] 'Balkanisation is the major instrument of neo-colonialism and will be found wherever neo-colonialism is practised,' Nkrumah asserted. The 'only effective way to challenge this economic empire and to recover possession of our heritage, is for us to act on a Pan-African basis, through a Union government'.[52] Though balkanization became the most commonly used term, the region was not the only reference employed by advocates of African socialism and Pan-African federalism. While Azikiwe warned of the threat of 'Pakistanization', Nkrumah pointed to the unrealized dream of federation in nineteenth-century South America and cited the history of economic imperialism in post-colonial Latin America as a cautionary tale illustrating the twin dangers of neocolonialism and political fragmentation.[53] Without federation in the Caribbean and unity in Africa, Padmore told Drake, 'a lot of little Black banana republics would result' from decolonization.[54]

The five years between 1958 and 1963 witnessed growing coordination of anti-colonial struggles and ultimately political independence across much of the African continent. The conferences organized by Nkrumah and Padmore in Ghana quickened both.[55] Kamuzu Banda from Nyasaland, Harry Nkumbula and Kenneth Kaunda from Northern Rhodesia, Tom Mboya, Julius Kiano and Peter Mbiyu Koinange from Kenya and a number of other leaders of liberation movements attended the All African People's Conference in December 1958. Nyerere was also present at the conference of independent African states earlier that year as an observer.[56]

As states across the continent attained independence, the institutionalization of apartheid as 'separate development' and the Sharpeville Massacre in South Africa, the intensifying fight for independence in Portuguese colonies, French nuclear bomb tests in the Algerian Sahara and events in Congo, including the support that mining companies and settler politicians in the CAF provided to the breakaway Katanga Province and the covert machinations of Belgium, Portugal and the United States which culminated in kidnapping and murder of Lumumba, all augured a long struggle to come. The independent states of Africa were also divided by ideological differences, including the depth of their commitment to Pan-Africanism, and by their relations with the two sides in the Cold War and former European colonial powers. Two informal blocs – the so-called Monrovia group and the Casablanca group – emerged during the course of the debates that led up to the founding of the OAU in 1963. Led by Gamal Abdel-Nasser of Egypt, Sékou Touré of Guinea and Nkrumah, the latter advocated non-alignment in the Cold War, African socialism and federation in post-colonial Africa to facilitate coordinated development and African initiative at the geopolitical level. The Monrovia group, which included Nigeria, Liberia and former French colonies such as Senegal and Cameroon, stressed the importance of safeguarding the sovereignty and formal equality of newly independent states. When a majority of states at the 1963 Summit Conference of the Heads of State and Government in Addis Abba voted in favour of the Ethiopian plan over Ghana's proposal, internal stability and the hard-won sovereignty of new nation-states triumphed over political union.

Another fault line developed over the issue of association with the European common market after the signing of the Treaty of Rome which created the European Economic Community (EEC). At that time, the overseas colonies of France, Belgium, the Netherlands and Italy entered the framework as associated territories without the same rights as member states. The twelve former French colonies known as the Brazzaville group formed the *Union Africaine et Malgache* in 1961. Though the union floundered and was replaced by the even more limited *Union Africaine et Malgache de Coopération Économique* in 1964, these states represented the core of the Associated African and Malagasy states who signed an association convention with the six member-states of the EEC in July 1963. Peo Hansen and Stefan Jonsson suggest that the 'true historical purpose' of the 'EEC's "offer" of association to the Common Market' was 'to adjust Europe's foreign policy, modes of economic extraction and means of production to a nominally independent Africa, while ensuring that the continent's resources remained within Europe's reach'. For their part, 'leaders such as Nkrumah and Touré saw the EEC's Eurafrican design … as a deliberate attempt to frustrate the formation of any types of independently organized African integration and regionalization schemes'.[57] In Nkrumah's view, the Treaty of Rome could 'be compared to the treaty that emanated from the Congress of Berlin' in 1885. 'The latter treaty established the undisputed sway of colonialism in Africa, the former marks the advent of neo-colonialism in Africa.'[58]

Nkrumah's appeals for pan-African union, the effort to form a post-colonial federation in East Africa and the collapse of the CAF occurred against the backdrop of early European integration, and these issues were linked in public discourse. In early 1963, coverage of the dissolution of the 'bankrupt partnership' in Central Africa appeared alongside discussion of the upcoming conference of African heads of state in the *Evening News* in Ghana. An editorial lambasted Nigeria's leaders and those who believed that 'all that is needed is "closer association"' among independent African states, and asserted that the solution to Africa's problems lay in 'an organic unity on a continental scale directed against imperialism in all its forms and towards rebuilding a great Africa free from all subordinating ties to non-African states and power blocs'.[59]

As governor of Uganda after 1952, Andrew Cohen, who had served previously as Assistant Undersecretary for African Affairs under Creech Jones and was one of the architects of the CAF, proposed the creation of an East African Federation, presenting both as bulwarks against the spread of South African-style apartheid. Most Africans in London and East Africa opposed the idea for the same reasons that Africans rejected the CAF and earlier proposals for closer union in East Africa.[60] With independence on the horizon, however, leading anti-colonialists seized on the idea as a means towards Pan-African unity and economic cooperation in the region. Nyerere was a vocal opponent of the earlier proposals for federation in East Africa from his days as a student at Makerere College during the mid-1940s.[61] While a student at the University of Edinburgh between 1949 and 1952, Nyerere devoted some of his earliest published writings to the topic.[62] However, his friend and collaborator, John Keto, remembered that Nyerere's political vision already extended beyond independence for Tanganyika: 'Mwalimu', or teacher as Nyerere later became known, 'was talking about independence of Tanganyika, but this was within limits. He was talking more of an East African Federation – although this wasn't the term he was using.'[63]

At the second Conference of Independent African States in 1960, Nyerere called for east African federation. If the 'triumph' in the 'struggle against colonialism', which had forged 'the fundamental unity of the people of Africa', 'is to be followed by an equal triumph against the forces of neo-imperialism', Nyerere argued, 'the unity and freedom movements should be combined, and the East African territories achieve independence as one unit'. Like Nkrumah, he maintained that the 'balkanization of Africa is a source of weakness', and that the 'forces of imperialism and neo-imperialism will find their strength in this basic weakness'. Nyerere offered Canada, the United States, the United Arab Republic and the Republic of India (as opposed to the 'India/Pakistan situation') as examples of successful federations formed immediately at independence, contrasting them with the limited progress towards formalizing African unity. For Nyerere, this proved that, while 'it is difficult now to convince some of our friends that Federation is desirable, when it does not involve surrendering any sovereignty, it is going to be a million times more difficult to convince them later'.[64]

While denouncing the CAF as undemocratic and racist, the delegates at the first All Africa People's Conference in 1958 had outlined a roadmap towards continental unity built upon five regional units in Northern, Western, Eastern, Central and Southern Africa. By the time of the Summit Conference of Independent African States in 1963, Nkrumah and other radical pan-Africanists had come to reject regional federations, including in East Africa, as 'balkanization on a grand scale'.[65] Nyerere cast the disagreement as one over means, not ends. 'Our goal must be a United States of Africa,' he insisted, 'and it does not matter whether this is done by one step or by many, or through economic, political, or social development.'[66] Nkrumah argued that socialist economic development required political unification and that there was only a small window of opportunity to unify the continent. Nyerere's gradualism, in his view, was destined to play into the hands of neocolonial interests and to throw up new barriers to African union. During a fierce debate at the second meeting of the OAU in Cairo in 1964, Nyerere implied that Nkrumah's attitude was unrealistic, stating 'we do not believe there is a choice between achieving African unity step by step and achieving it in one act', but his defence of a gradual approach to African union contradicted his own reasoning regarding the need to take immediate action towards federation in east Africa at independence.[67]

In June 1963, Nyerere, Kenyatta and Milton Obote met and announced their intention to form a post-colonial federation by the year's end. The announcement helped to speed up the pace of Kenyan independence, but the East African Federation never materialized. In 1967, Kenya, Uganda and the United Republic of Tanzania established the East African Community, the successor to the colonial-era East African Common Services Organization, to foster economic integration and common provision of public health and other services. The East African Community existed, in its first iteration, for a little more than a decade but failed to rekindle enthusiasm for political federation as Nyerere hoped. As the prospect of East African Federation faded, public debate continued across the region, especially in Dar es Salaam and at the universities. Pan-Africanism and the idea of a socialist United States of Africa alternately complemented and competed with regional and national imaginaries.[68]

The emergence of the European Common Market, which many viewed as an instrument of neocolonial domination, provided a powerful rationale for regional and continental federalism. These issues dominated the contents of the short-lived pan-Africanist journal, *Spearhead*, edited by the South African of South Asian descent and African National Congress operative Frene Ginwala and published in Dar es Salaam.[69] In March 1962, *Spearhead* featured a forum of pieces on the economics of federation and regionalism in East Africa. The issue opened with coverage of Prime Minister Roy Welensky's desperate efforts to save the undemocratic CAF and included an opinion piece by the economist Vella Pillay on Africa and the EEC. The 'essence of the neo-colonialism of the Common Market,' Pillay maintained, was 'the perpetuation of colonial privileges through the creation of economic blocs in which the economies of the former colonies become integrated'. 'Above all,' he continued, 'the EEC has intensified economic and political divisions in Africa,' preventing industrialization and economic development beyond export-oriented, extractive industries.[70] Addressing an American audience in 1965, Nyerere argued that the common market being constructed in Europe demonstrated that meaningful economic cooperation required broader political and economic integration while warning that 'the special relationship which some countries of Africa have with the European Common Market' would 'adversely affect other parts of Africa, and complicate still further the final task of unification'.[71]

Across the continent in Ghana, the *Evening News* characterized association with the common market as a form of balkanization and neocolonialism creating 'a bloc [of African states] opposed to radical African nationalism and counselling "gradualism"'.[72] Following reports that Nigeria, Kenya, Tanzania and Uganda were considering joining the convention of association in September 1964, the Nigerian socialist and member of Nkrumah's Convention People's Party Samuel G. Ikoku, writing under the pseudonym Julius Sago, described the common market as 'a neo-colonialist web' in the Accra-based socialist journal *The Spark*.[73] An editorial on the same page claimed that the association convention harmed 'the economic interests of countries outside the customs boundaries of the Common Market' and contradicted 'the goal of economic co-operation between African countries as envisaged by the OAU Charter'. Association with the common market was 'old wine in [a] new cask'.[74]

In Nigeria, Remi Fani-Kayode continued to agitate for African continental federation 'on the same form as either the United States of America or the Union of Soviet Socialist Republics' until he was forced into exile in Britain. Fani-Kayode's philosophy of 'Blackism' resembled Nyerere's vision of building socialism in a United States of Africa. Like Nyerere, Fani-Kayode supported forming regional federations as building-blocks towards the final goal of continental unity, tracing support for federation in West Africa back to the National Congress of British West Africa and the activities of the WASU, which 'carried on … the political struggle of the National Congress' in London. Fani-Kayode chastised African leaders for ignoring the 'mass yearning for union' and described the EEC as 'the challenge of the era to a divided Africa'. 'If Britain joins the Common Market,' he wrote, 'a joint exploitation of Africa by Western Europe is assured, unless Africa stands firm.' After independence, he maintained, nationalism 'becomes, economically, a dead commodity, militarily, an outdated weapon' and 'politically, sheer suicide'. To facilitate 'peaceful progress and development', he recommended forming multilateral trade alliances with states outside Africa 'as a counter to the conspiracy of Western European union'. While collaborating in the realm of international economic relations in this manner, African states should 'coordinate their industrial and agricultural drive to eliminate unnecessary duplication and wastage'. Like many others of his generation, Fani-Kayode believed 'the creation of a political confederation of the independent African states' would provide the necessary political structure for such coordination. 'Africa can survive the present international struggle and thrive,' he asserted, echoing Nkrumah, 'but only as a united entity, a Union, a Federation or a Confederation, not as tiny little states'.[75]

* * *

The occasion of the sixth Pan-African Congress in Dar es Salaam in 1974 provided an opportunity for reflection for two of the twentieth-century's most influential Caribbean socialists, C. L. R. James and Walter Rodney. James admired Tanzania's Nyerere, describing him as 'a political figure today whose ideas, political prospects, and programs are not exceeded by any living politician'.[76] James initially planned to attend the Pan-African Congress, which, he said in an interview, stood for three things: 'self-reliance', 'the freedom of Southern Africa' and 'complete control over economic and financial life'. In the end, he disavowed the event because of the exclusion of nongovernmental delegations from the Caribbean and penned a stinging critique in which he outlined the history of the pan-Africanist movement and an expansive vision for its future. Transcending the nation-state through federation in the Caribbean and Africa was at the core of the latter. 'For us,' James declared, 'no longer is the national state an ideal.'[77] For the Guyanese historian and activist Walter Rodney, who taught at the University of Dar es Salaam during 1966 and 1967 and from 1969 to 1974, the actions taken on the part of Caribbean governments to exclude radical socialist and Black Power groups, such as the New Jewel Movement in Grenada and the National Joint Action Committee in Trinidad, and African governments' acquiescence to their demand spurred a 'necessary disillusionment' and an awakening to the realities of class struggle in post-colonial Africa and the Caribbean. He compared its impact to the coup that deposed Nkrumah in 1966.[78]

This was the context in which Rodney, having recently published his most influential book, *How Europe Underdeveloped Africa* (1972), wrote a piece on Pan-Africanism and the 'international class struggle in Africa, the Caribbean and America'.[79] Rodney viewed the failure to achieve the pan-Africanist dream of continental federation as the tragedy of decolonization.[80] He likened the 'African or Black petty bourgeois leadership' of the anti-colonial struggle to the 'Slav intelligentsia who advocated Pan-Slavism' in the late nineteenth century. Because the latter failed 'to unseat indigenous and external feudal oppressors', including imperial Russia, they 'were unable or unwilling to confront capitalist/imperialist partition; and the region gave rise to the term "Balkanization," as the supreme expression of failure to carry out the task of national liberation and unification'. Rodney charged that, in 'the very process of demanding constitutional independence', the leaders of African independence movements 'reneged on a cardinal principle of Pan-Africanism: namely, the unity and indivisibility of the African continent'. Economic imperialism and the African petite bourgeoisie's narrow class interests and swallow base of popular support, he contended, doomed the project of Pan-African federation, and instead, the first generation of post-colonial African leaders, who came from the former's ranks, 'accepted the balkanization' of the continent.[81]

During the period between the fifth and sixth Pan-African Congresses, especially the twenty years between 1945 and 1965, the focus of African intellectuals and leaders turned from how to secure democratic control of the state, or self-determination, to how best to achieve economic nondomination. Most maintained that the attainment of political and economic liberation required structures of unity and economic coordination which transcended the boundaries of colonial territories. A number of historians and political theorists have critiqued the methodological nationalism of histories of decolonization, but the debate typically ignores pan-African federalism and how it informed state-building practices, development schemes and conceptions of African socialism.[82] The question of political organization was premised on the need for rapid economic development and generating social returns from independence, and African intellectuals agreed that the content and future of political independence in Africa hinged on a radical transformation of Africa's place in the global economy, despite their differing views on how to do so. For African and Caribbean radicals, socialism and federation in Africa and the Caribbean were related components of the ongoing struggle against the evolving structures of economic imperialism.

Notes

1 Kwame Nkrumah, *Ghana: The Autobiography of Kwame Nkrumah* (1957; New York: International Publishers, 1971), 52.
2 Merve Fejzula, 'The Cosmopolitan Historiography of Twentieth-Century Federalism', *Historical Journal* 64, no. 2 (2021): 477–500 [487]. See also Ged Martin, 'The "Idea of Imperial Federation,"' in *Reappraisals in British Imperial History*, ed. Ronald Hyam and Ged Martin (London: Macmillan, 1975), 121–38; Martin Kolinsky, 'Federation and Partition in the Transformation of Empire', in *British Politics and the Spirit of the Age*, ed. Cornelia Navari (Keele: Keele University Press, 1996), 159–74; A. J. Stockwell, 'Malaysia: The Making of a Neo-Colony?' *Journal of Imperial and Commonwealth History* 26, no. 2 (1998): 138–56; John Darwin, 'What Was the Late Colonial State?' *Itinerario* 23, no. 3–4 (1999): 73–82; Daniel Gorman, *Imperial Citizenship: Empire and the Question of Political Belonging* (Manchester: Manchester University Press, 2006); Duncan Bell, *The Idea of Greater Britain: Empire and the Future of World Order, 1860–1900* (Princeton, NJ: Princeton University Press, 2017); Special Issue: 'From Aden to Abu Dhabi: Britain and State Formation in Arabia 1962–1971, a Retrospective', *Middle Eastern Studies* 53, no. 1 (2017).
3 Adom Getachew, *Worldmaking after Empire: The Rise and Fall of Self-Determination* (Princeton, NJ: Princeton University Press, 2019), 139.
4 Geoffrey Bing, *Reap the Whirlwind: An Account of Kwame Nkrumah's Ghana from 1950 to 1966* (London: McGibbon and Kee, 1968), 440.
5 For a succinct genealogy of African Socialism, see Emma Hunter, 'African socialism', in *Cambridge History of Socialism, Volume II*, ed. Marcel van der Linden (Cambridge: Cambridge University Press, 2023), 455–73.
6 Dorothy Nelkin, 'Socialist Sources of Pan-African Ideology', in *African Socialism*, ed. William H. Friedland and Carl G. Rosberg, Jr. (Stanford, CA: Stanford University Press for Hoover Institution, 1964), 63–79 [72].
7 Kwame Nkrumah, *Handbook of Revolutionary Warfare: A Guide to the Armed Phase of the African Revolution* (London: Panaf Books, 1968), 28; quoted in Opuku Agyeman, *Nkrumah's Ghana and East Africa: Pan-Africanism and African Interstate Relations* (Rutherford, NJ: Fairleigh Dickinson University Press, 1992), 88.
8 Fenner Brockway, *African Socialism* (London: Bodley Head, 1963), 17.
9 Emmanuel Akyeampong, 'African Socialism or the Search for an Indigenous Model of Economic Development', *Economic History of Developing Regions* 33, no. 1 (2018): 69–87 [70]; Priya Lal, *African Socialism in Postcolonial Tanzania: Between the Village and the World* (Cambridge: Cambridge University Press, 2015), 17.
10 Julius Nyerere, 'Ujamaa: The Basis of African Socialism' (1962), reprinted in *African Socialism*, 238–47.
11 Kwame Nkrumah, 'African Socialism Revisited', in *Africa: National and Social Revolution* (Prague: Peace and Socialism Publishers, 1967), available online in the Marxists Internet Archive: https://www.marxists.org/subject/africa/nkrumah/1967/african-socialism-revisited.htm (accessed 15 June 2023), 1–6 [1].
12 Tom Mboya, 'African Socialism' (1963) in *African Socialism*, 251.
13 Nkrumah, 'African Socialism Revisited', 1.
14 On versions of African socialism in the Portuguese colonies, see Natalie Telepneva, *Cold War Liberation: The Soviet Union and the Collapse of the Portuguese Empire in Africa* (Chapel Hill: University of North Carolina Press, 2022).
15 George Padmore, 'A Guide to Pan-African Socialism', in *African Socialism*, 224.

16 The Senegalese historian and politician Cheikh Anta Diop also warned of the 'South-Americanization of Africa' if a pan-African federal state was not established. See Cheikh Anta Diop, 'Alerte sous les Tropiques', *Présence Africaine*, no. 5 (1955–6): 8–33; Cheikh Anta Diop, *Black Africa: The Economic and Cultural Basis for a Federated State* (1974; Chicago: Lawrence Hill, 1987); Carlos Moore and Cheikh Anta Diop, 'Conversations with Cheikh Anta Diop', *Présence Africaine*, no. 149–50 (1989): 374–420 [385–6].
17 Julius Nyerere, 'Ujamaa: The Basis of African Socialism', in *African Socialism*, 162–3; Julius Nyerere, 'The Second Scramble', in *African Socialism*, 208.
18 Peter Abrahams, 'Nkrumah, Kenyatta and the Old Order', in *African Heritage*, ed. Jacob Draschler (New York: Crowell-Collier, 1963), 138. See also Marika Sherwood, 'Kwame Nkrumah: The London Years, 1945–1947', in *Africans in Britain*, ed. David Killingray (London: Frank Cass, 1994), 164–95.
19 Bankole Awoonor-Renner, *West African Soviet Union* (London: Wans Press, 1946), 14.
20 Hakim Adi, *West Africans in Britain: Nationalism, Pan-Africanism and Communism* (London: Lawrence and Wishart, 1998), 128–9.
21 Library of Congress, Washington, DC, National Association for the Advancement of Colored People Papers, Group 2, Box 44, 'Aims and Objectives', 8–9.
22 Nkrumah, *Ghana*, 60–1, 303.
23 Hakim Adi and Marika Sherwood, *The 1945 Manchester Pan-African Congress Revisited* (London: New Beacon Books, 1995), 60–1.
24 Awoonor-Renner, *West African Soviet Union*, 16.
25 Abrahams, 'Nkrumah, Kenyatta and the Old Order', 138.
26 Awoonor-Renner quoted in TNA, KV 1840, police commissioner of Lagos, Nigeria to police commissioner of Accra, Gold Coast (26 August 1948).
27 See Elizabeth Buettner, *Europe after Empire: Decolonization, Society, and Culture* (New York: Cambridge University Press, 2016); Peo Hansen and Stefan Jonsson, *Eurafrica: The Untold History of European Integration and Colonialism* (London: Bloomsbury, 2014); Giuliano Garavini, *After Empires: European Integration, Decolonization, and the Challenge from the Global South, 1957–1986* (Oxford: Oxford University Press, 2012).
28 George Padmore with Dorothy Pizer, *How Russia Transformed Her Colonial Empire* (London: Dennis Dobson, 1946), 160–1. See also Leslie James, *George Padmore and Decolonization from Below* (New York: Palgrave Macmillan, 2015); Theo Williams, *Making the Revolution Global: Black Radicalism and the British Socialist Movement before Decolonization* (London: Verso, 2022).
29 Mark Mazower, *No Enchanted Palace: The End of Empire and the Ideological Origins of the United Nations* (Princeton, NJ: Princeton University Press, 2009), 54.
30 Getachew, *Worldmaking after Empire*, 11; Kwame Nkrumah, *Africa Must Unite* (1963; New York: International Publishers, 1970), 205–15.
31 Awoonor-Renner, *West African Soviet Union*, 19.
32 On Hinden, see Charlotte Lydia Riley, 'Writing Like a Woman: Rita Hinden and Recovering the Imperial in International Thought', *International Politics Reviews* 9, no. 2 (2021): 264–71.
33 'Produce and Politics', *Wãsù* 12, no. 3 (Summer 1947): 5. On the FCB's relationship to the Labour Party, see R. M. Douglas, *The Labour Party, Nationalism and Internationalism, 1939–1951* (London: Routledge, 2004), 202–3; Kenneth O. Morgan, 'Imperialism at Bay: British Labour and Decolonization', *Journal of Imperial and*

Commonwealth History 27, no. 2 (1999): 233–54; Faridah Zaman, 'The Abstraction of Sovereignty: The Ottoman Empire in Early Twentieth-Century Socialist Thought', *Twentieth Century British History* 34, no. 1 (2023): 60–97.

34 Thomas Molony, *Nyerere: The Early Years* (Suffolk: James Currey, 2014), 144–6, 161–2. See also Saida Yahya-Othman, *The Making of a Philosopher Ruler*, Book One of Issa G. Shivji, Saida Yahya-Othman and Ng'wanza Kamata, *Development as Rebellion: A Biography of Julius Nyerere* (Dar es Salaam: Mkuki na Nyota, 2020), 67–90.

35 See e.g. Rita Hinden, 'Partnership and What It Means', *Wãsù* 12, no. 1 (March 1945): 9–10.

36 Williams, *Making the Revolution Global*, 231–2.

37 R. H. S. Crossman, Michael Foot, and Ian Mikardo, *Keep Left* (London: New Statesman and Nation, 1947), 44; quoted in Williams, *Making the Revolution Global*, 231.

38 Appiah, *Joe Appiah*, 162–3.

39 Williams, *Making the Revolution Global*, 224–5; Barbara Bush, *Imperialism, Race and Resistance: Africa and Britain, 1919–1945* (London: Routledge, 1999), 123.

40 FCB Papers Box 69, File 3 – Conference on the Relationship between the British and Colonial Peoples, Clacton-on-Sea (12–14 April 1946). On the links between the 1945 Pan-African Congress and the FCB conference, see Marc Matera, 'Partnership in/against Empire: Pan-African and Imperial Conferencing after World War II', in *Placing Internationalism: International Conferences and the Making of the Modern World*, ed. Stephen Legg, Mike Heffernan, Jake Hodder and Benjamin J. Thorpe (London: Bloomsbury, 2022), 216–33.

41 Nnamdi Azikiwe, 'Zik on Nigerian Constitutional Development', in *Zik: A Selection from the Speeches of Nnamdi Azikiwe* (Cambridge: Cambridge University Press, 1961), 100.

42 See Giovanni Arrighi, *The Political Economy of Rhodesia* (Mouton and The Hague: Institute of Social Studies, 1967); Ronald Hyam, 'Geopolitical origins of the Central African Federation: Britain, Rhodesia, and South Africa, 1948–1963', *Historical Journal* 30, no. 1 (1987): 145–72; Andrew Cohen, *The Politics and Economics of Decolonization in Africa: The Failed Experiment of the Central African Federation* (London: I. B. Tauris, 2017); Luise White, *Unpopular Sovereignty: Rhodesian Independence and the African Struggle for Decolonization* (Chicago: University of Chicago Press, 2015), 37–104; Clive Gabay, *Imagining Africa: Whiteness and the Western Gaze* (Cambridge: Cambridge University Press, 2018), ch. 5.

43 Michael Collins, 'Decolonisation and the "Federal Moment"', *Diplomacy and Statecraft* 24 (2013): 21–40 [22].

44 'African Territories (Development)', *Hansard* v. 447, cc. 2081–90 (25 February 1948). See also 'African Salvation? … "Colonial Cream"', *West Africa* 32, n. 1620 (6 March 1948): 215.

45 Nkrumah, *Africa Must Unite*, 176.

46 George Shepperson and St Clair Drake, 'The Fifth Pan-African Conference, 1945 and the All African Peoples Congress, 1958', *Contributions to Black Studies* 8 (September 2008): 35–66 [42, 50].

47 St Clair Drake, 'Pan Africanism: What Is It?' *Africa Today* 6, no. 1 (1959): 6–10 [9].

48 Padmore, 'A Guide to Pan-African Socialism', 228–9.

49 Kwame Nkrumah, *Towards Colonial Freedom* (London: Heinemann, 1962), x–xi.

50 Ibid., 237.

51 George Shepperson, 'Pan-Africanism and "pan-Africanism": Some Historical Notes', *Phylon* 23 (1962): 346–58 [357]; Basil Davidson, *Black Star: A View of the Life and Times of Kwame Nkrumah* (New York: Praeger, 1973), 121; Agyeman, *Nkrumah's Ghana and East Africa*, 47. On balkanization in decolonization in eastern Europe after the First World War, see James Mark and Quinn Slobodian, 'Eastern Europe in the Global History of Decolonization', in *Oxford Handbook of the Ends of Empire*, ed. Martin Thomas and Andrew S. Thompson (Oxford: Oxford University Press, 2018), 351–72.
52 Nkrumah, *Neocolonialism*, 14, 259.
53 Nkrumah, *Africa Must Unite*, 188; Getachew, *Worldmaking after Empire*, 149.
54 Padmore quoted in Kevin Gaines, 'Scholar-Activist St. Clair Drake and the Transatlantic World of Black Radicalism', in *The Other Special Relationship: Race, Rights, and Riots in Britain and the United States*, ed. Robin D. G. Kelley and Stephen Tuck (Basingstoke: Palgrave Macmillan, 2015), 80, 89.
55 See Matteo Grilli, *Nkrumaism and African Nationalism: Ghana's Pan-African Foreign Policy in the Age of Decolonization* (Basingstoke: Palgrave Macmillan, 2018).
56 Agyeman, *Nkrumah's Ghana and East Africa*, 60–1.
57 Hansen and Jonsson, *Eurafrica*, 269–70.
58 Kwame Nkrumah, 'Address to the Nationalists' Conference', 12; quoted in Hansen and Jonsson, *Eurafrica*, 270.
59 'The end of the Central African Federation is in sight' and 'Africa demands action now!' *Evening News* (18 February 1963): 5. See also Julius Sago, 'Anti-Imperialist United Africa Is the Goal', *The Spark* (17 May 1963): 1.
60 Robert Maxon, *Majimbo in Kenya's Past: Federalism in the 1940s and 1950s* (Amherst, NY: Cambria Press, 2017); Gabay, *Imagining Africa*; Ismay Milford, 'Federation, Partnership, and the Chronologies of Space in 1950s East and Central Africa', *Historical Journal* 63, no. 5 (2020): 1325–48.
61 Molony, *Nyerere*.
62 Molony, *Nyerere*, 141–2.
63 Keto quoted in Molony, *Nyerere*, 137.
64 Julius Nyerere, 'East African Federation', in *Freedom and Unity/Uhuru na Umoja: A Selection from Writings and Speeches, 1952–65* (London: Oxford University Press, 1967), 85–98 [85, 90–3, 97–8].
65 Robert S. Nye, Jr., *Pan-Africanism and East African Integration* (London: Oxford University Press, 1966), 16.
66 Julius Nyerere, 'A United States of Africa', in *Freedom and Unity/Uhuru na Umoja*, 189.
67 Julius Nyerere, 'African Unity – O.A.U. Cairo', in *Freedom and Unity/Uhuru na Umoja*, 300–2; Agyeman, *Nkruamah's Ghana and East Africa*, 73.
68 Chris Vaughan, Julie MacArthur, Emma Hunter and Gerard McCann, 'Thinking East African: Debating Federation and Regionalism, 1960–1977', in *Visions of African Unity: New Perspectives on the History of Pan-Africanism and African Unification Projects*, ed. Frank Gerits and Matteo Grilli (Basingstoke: Palgrave Macmillan, 2021), 49–75 [51]. See also Seth M. Markle, *A Motorcycle on Hell Run: Tanzania, Black Power, and the Uncertain Future of Pan-Africanism, 1964–1974* (East Lansing: Michigan State University Press, 2017); Christopher M. Vaughan, 'The Politics of Regionalism and Federation in East Africa, 1958–1964', *Historical Journal* 62, no. 2 (2019): 519–40; Ismay Milford, Gerard McCann, Emma Hunter and Daniel Branch, 'Another World? East Africa, Decolonisation, and the Global History of the Mid-Twentieth Century', *Journal of African History* 62, no. 3 (2021): 394–410.

69 George Roberts, *Revolutionary State-Making in Dar es Salaam: African Liberation and the Global Cold War, 1961–1974* (Cambridge: Cambridge University Press, 2022), 224–31.
70 Vella Pillay, 'Africa and the Common Market', *Spearhead* 1, no. 5 (1962): 24, 28.
71 Julius Nyerere, 'The Nature and Requirements of African Unity', in *Freedom and Unity*, 338–40, 346–8.
72 'Africa demands action now!' *Evening News* (18 February 1963): 5.
73 Julius Sago, 'The Common Market – a neo-colonialist web', *The Spark* (25 September 1964): 1.
74 'Old wine in new cask', ibid. See also Agyeman, *Nkrumah's Ghana and East Africa*, 68–70.
75 Remi Fani-Kayode, *Blackism* (Lagos, publisher not identified, 1965), 9, 12, 19, 25, 27, 56, 68.
76 'Dr. C. L. R. James talks to Geri Stark, Information Officer, Sixth Pan African Congress', Sixth Pan African Congress Temporary Secretariat, Dar es Salaam (n.d.), 5–6.
77 C. L. R. James, 'Towards the Seventh: The Pan-African Congress – Past, Present and Future', in *At the Rendezvous of Victory* (London: Allison and Busby, 1984), 236–50 [246].
78 'The *Black Scholar* Interviews: Walter Rodney', *Black Scholar* 6, no. 3 (November 1974): 38–47 [39–40].
79 Walter Rodney, 'Towards the Sixth Pan-African Congress: Aspects of the International Class Struggle in Africa', St Clair Drake Papers, Sc MG 309, Box 24, File 4; reprinted in Horace Campbell (ed.), *Pan-Africanism: The Struggle Against Imperialism and Neo-Colonialism* (Toronto: Afro-Carib Publications, 1975), 18–41.
80 See Rupert Charles Lewis, *Walter Rodney's Intellectual and Political Thought* (Detroit, MI: Wayne State University Press, 1988), 127–37; Milford et al., 'Another World?' 399.
81 Rodney, 'Towards the Sixth Pan-African Congress', 1–2.
82 Frederick Cooper, *Citizenship between Empire and Nation: Remaking France and French Africa, 1945–1960* (Princeton, NJ: Princeton University Press, 2014); Gary Wilder, *Freedom Time: Négritude, Decolonization, and the Future of the World* (Durham, NC: Duke University Press, 2015); Getachew, *Worldmaking after Empire*; Annette K. Joseph-Gabriel, *Reimagining Liberation: How Black Women Transformed Citizenship in the French Empire* (Urbana: University of Illinois Press, 2020); Collins, 'Decolonisation and the "Federal Moment"'; Fejzula, 'The Cosmopolitan Historiography of Twentieth-Century Federalism.' On pan-African federalism and development, see Agyeman, *Nkrumah's Ghana and East Africa*; W. R. Ochieng' and E. S. Atieno Odhiambo, 'On Decolonization', in *Decolonization and Independence in Kenya, 1940–1993*, ed. B. A. Ogot and W. R. Ochieng' (Athens: Ohio University Press, 1995), xi–xvii; Issa G. Shivji, *Pan-Africanism or Pragmatism? Lessons of the Tanganyika-Zanzibar Union* (Dar es Salaam: Mkuki na Nyota Publishers, 2008); Abena Dove Osseo-Asare, *Atomic Junction: Nuclear Power in Africa after Independence* (Cambridge: Cambridge University Press, 2019).

4

Socialism, internationalism and regime survival: The Guomindang, China and Taiwan in the 1940s and 1950s

Tehyun Ma

In 1943, not long after the publication of the 'Beveridge Report' in the UK, China – led by the Chinese Nationalist Party (GMD) – started to develop its own postwar social security plan. Less than a decade later, the Nationalists implemented an American-inflected redistributive programme of land reform on Taiwan, their last redoubt after Mao's victory in the Civil War (1946–9). Both projects suggest that GMD leaders were finally looking to fulfil their promise of ensuring the 'People's Livelihood': the avowedly socialist project of the party's founder, Sun Yat-sen. This paper asks what social security and land reform can reveal about socialism and development under a Nationalist regime that from the late 1920s onwards was trenchantly anti-Communist. In doing so, it situates China and Taiwan in global social democratic ideas and movements that encompassed Bismarckian Germany, the Soviet Union, Britain and the United States, and finally Japan under American occupation.

The Nationalists came of age in an era of anti-colonial mobilization, state planning and political experimentation. After the GMD brought most of China under its sway in the late 1920s, international recognition and the integration of its intellectual and administrative servants into transnational epistemic communities became imperative for a precariously unified nation-state. However, the GMD's dedication to internationalism was not purely instrumental; the impetus for building a Chinese developmental state shaped by models from overseas came too from experts whose professional aspirations overlapped with party leaders' ambitions to construct a warfare state capable of defeating internal and external threats to consolidation. The necessity of harnessing both people and resources for conflict – first for the battle to expel imperialists and unify China, then for the struggle against Japan, and finally (for the purposes of this chapter at least) in the early Cold War on Taiwan – not only thrust technocrats to the fore in national affairs, but also brought the GMD closer to its international allies in the realm of social policy. These considerations shaped the rationale, design and implementation of socialist ideas on Nationalist China and Taiwan.

Socialism in republican China, I argue here, had multiple meanings, the resonances of which depended on the domestic and international contexts in which they were invoked. Moreover the GMD was a broad coalition and the ideological, intellectual and factional divisions within its membership made socialism as an idea inherently unstable. It may be easiest to define it in Nationalist thought by what it was not. As Arif Dirlik suggests, for Sun, socialism meant 'non-capitalist development'[1] – or to reframe it negatively an alternative to the destructive tendencies of unrestrained enterprise – though even this is complicated by his heirs' tendency to equate socialism with a mixed economy or 'state capitalism'.[2] At points, especially in the 1920s and to a lesser degree between 1930 and 1949, socialism was used rhetorically to win foreign support; by the Cold War, on Taiwan, after 1949, the term itself was largely avoided in favour of a liberal discourse of legality and property ownership even as the GMD came closer than ever before to embracing the redistributive policies Sun had advocated. Socialism often served as short-hand for any state-led measure that sought to improve the welfare of the people. And as the first section of the chapter demonstrates, it also became a word that intellectuals and politicians both within and beyond the GMD tried to explain in terms that lessened its foreignness. Above all, though, socialism with Chinese republican characteristics was a means to an end: a weapon in the arsenal of nation-building rather than an end point of history or a template for a just society. The Nationalists – much like the socialists in Marc Matera and Nana Osei-Opare chapters in this volume and elsewhere – showed a pragmatic desire to pick, choose and indigenize items from the vast array of socialistic ideas that circulated in the first half of the twentieth century.[3]

Development and socialism in the politics of Sun Yat-sen

The GMD's entanglements with socialism sprang from the developmental vision of the party's founder, Sun Yat-sen. That vision is best articulated in his 1920 book *The International Development of China*. Sun's plan for the development of his country envisaged large-scale industrialization, the modernization of agriculture, the knitting together of the nation with rail and road, and the damming of the Three Gorges as a path to electrification and mass production. Historians have described the plan as ambitious, integrated and comprehensive, and have christened Sun as the 'father of the Chinese developmental state' for his modern economic vision.[4, 5]

Sun's programme of internationally financed development from above sought to yank into modernity a divided, poverty-stricken and semi-colonized nation in which wealth remained rooted in the land. Since the mid-nineteenth century, Western powers – the likes of Britain, France, Germany, Russia, the Austro-Hungarian Empire and more – had used gunboat diplomacy to continuously circumscribe the sovereignty of the Middle Kingdom and other landed empires like the Ottomans and Siam.[6] The resulting 'unequal treaties' led to a loss of tariff autonomy; the creation of mini-colonies in cities like Shanghai and Tianjin; the extension of extraterritorial rights to foreigners and their businesses; foreign control of major government revenue schemes; the exclusive rights for development in concessions and 'leased territories', which included mines and railroads; and, finally, the stationing of troops and warships on Chinese soil to ensure that 'free trade' arrangements were upheld by the late imperial court.[7] A major contributing factor in the demise of China's last dynasty in 1911 was popular dissatisfaction at the Qing court's inept handling of these foreign incursions and seemingly failed attempts at modernizing the empire out of its predicament. A new republic emerged in the Empire's wake, but within months, the post-revolutionary state had collapsed. After a brief attempt at imperial revival by the strongman Yuan Shi-kai, the authority of central government all but evaporated. For the next sixteen years, China was fragmented. Control devolved to local militarists, who acquired the pejorative term 'warlord'. These strongmen often worked with different empires to secure their fiefdoms, thus adding to the chaotic situation. What passed as a national government in Beijing did lead China into the First World War on the side of the Entente Powers, but at Versailles, negotiators received little for their citizens' sacrifices. News that German territory in China was to be handed over to Japan sparked a wave of nationalist protests that was dubbed the May Fourth Movement. But these protests did not hide the reality that China was a weak impoverished nation incapable of defending its interests. Thus for Sun and his successors, development was 'imperative to defend China's sovereignty and reassert China's importance in an unstable world'.[8]

That developmental programme, Sun hoped, would not only unify a fragmented polity, but would also give China the wealth and power to throw off the shackles of foreign domination.[9] A divided republic, this reasoning went, played into the hands of Western powers. In such a calculation the project can hardly be termed 'bourgeois' even if it found its strongest support among China's educated middle classes. Rather it made state and society cogs in a machine, the product of which would be a powerful and purposeful nation. As Richard Edmonds points out, 'the primary aim of Sun's plans was to transform China into a unified polity and economic development *per se* was of secondary importance'.[10] The path to power, though, required harnessing the energy of capitalism. Sun and his supporters saw that the wealth of the West and Japan had come from industrialization in which the interests of private property regimes overlapped to a greater or lesser degree with those of the state.[11] Indeed, the latter was able to throw off the shackles of semi-colonialism through state-led development. China needed to do the same.

But taking up capitalism as a tool to fight empire was fraught with danger. Reformers and revolutionaries of Sun's generation had lived and studied in Europe, the United States and Japan. While abroad in nations that seemed to be further ahead on the path to modern development, they witnessed the hardship, social dislocation, and class conflict intrinsic to industrialization.[12] The imperialist trajectory of industrialization had also led to rivalry across the globe that resulted not just in the destructive interventions in China, but also in major international wars.[13] This understanding was likely informed by Sun's engagement with J. A. Hobson and (whether directly or indirectly) Lenin's work on imperialism, which had taken East Asia as an example.[14] In part to guard against such risks, Sun proposed creating an international development agency to coordinate the financing of development in China without competition.[15] For Sun 'the appeal of a public international development institution was that it might be guided by better motives than the ones driving foreign private financiers and investors', which would create the foundation for a long-lasting peace in China and the world.[16] Sun's vision has thus led one scholar to dub him the 'pioneer of international development'.[17]

The social instability that came with capitalism led Sun and many other educated Chinese in the first decades of the twentieth century to gravitate towards socialist ideas. Socialism's appeal was reinforced by their disillusionment with Western liberalism after the disappointing returns at Versailles. But once again the ideas were a means to an end rather than the end in itself. The question for these GMD supporters lay less in how to achieve a socialist utopia marked by the abolition of private property and more in how to address the forthcoming social problems of capitalist development that would inevitably emerge as China followed a well-trodden path to modernization. This idea was perhaps best captured in Sun's own words in the *International Development of China*: '[I]t is my idea to make capitalism create socialism in China so that these two economic forces of human evolution will work side by side in the future civilization.'[18]

His socialist 'side' found ideological expression in the third of his Three Principles of the People. The Three Principles stood at the heart of Sun's revolutionary, anti-colonial political programme for a strong and prosperous China. First articulated in the late nineteenth century when Sun sought to overthrow China's last dynasty, they would become a mainstay of GMD developmental thought after Sun's death in 1925. The Three Principles encompassed the ideas of nationalism (*minzu*), democracy (*minquan*) and the People's Livelihood (*minsheng*). Nationalism was anti-colonial at its core, with the desire to seek independence from first the imperial dynasty – seen as a foreign occupier at this point – then the imperialist West.[19] 'Democracy' called for the political organization of China along constitutional lines, which would align the nation with stronger Western powers, and involved no concession on Sun's part to natural rights theory that sovereignty sprang innately from the masses.[20] The People's Livelihood, which for a time became synonymous with socialism in GMD ideology, sought to secure the nation's prosperity by freeing the people of 'the suffering caused by the unequal distribution of wealth'.[21]

By the 1920s, the People's Livelihood conveyed a communistic flavour. The radical implications of Sun's third principle are perhaps most evident in his land equalization policy, called Land to the Tiller, which envisaged the redistribution of rural property to downtrodden tenants. Such promises allowed Chinese Communists, who had formed an independent party in 1921, to claim they were the true heirs of Sun when they launched a violent programme of land reform in their base areas over the following three decades.

The place of Marxist-Leninism in Sun's thought, however, is questionable. Even before the Russian Revolution, Lenin saw Sun as a potential, albeit flawed, ally. Writing in 1912, the Bolshevik leader expressed his admiration for Sun's 'warm sympathy for the toiling and exploited people', and his 'faith in their strength and in the justice of their cause'. His followers were 'subjectively socialists because they are opposed to oppression and exploitation of the masses'. Sun's awareness that China's future lay in the cities rather than the countryside impressed the Russian revolutionary too. Sun had conceded, Lenin wrote, 'what reality forces him to admit', that 'in fifty years' China 'shall have many Shanghais'. Yet the Chinese nationalist erred, Lenin argued, in pushing a land reform programme that owed more to Henry George than to Marx.

His agrarian vision thus stood at odds with his prophecy of rapid urban and industrial development.

And despite Sun's own claim that the People's Livelihood was both 'communism' and 'socialism' in 1922, scholars have argued Marxist-Leninism as a social thought had a marginal place in Sun's thinking.[22] The Bolshevik emphasis on class conflict struck leaders preoccupied with national unification as dangerously disintegrative. China's poverty and social instability had already made it vulnerable to imperialist depredations, and embracing the destabilizing influence of communism would only invite more. Consequently, they saw socialism not so much an end point to which history tended, but as a tool to be used when necessary in the workshop of nation-building.[23] And if this sometimes implied a redistributive agenda – as it did in the countryside – that was offset by Sun's conviction that poverty, not inequality, was the bigger problem China confronted. Wealth had to be created before it could be shared around: indeed this recognition had impressed Lenin. Moreover, the socialist emphases in Sun's writing were partly a rhetorical strategy to show appreciation for Soviet assistance.[24] Despite the formation of a Chinese Communist Party, the Comintern aided Sun's campaign to refashion the Guomindang into a disciplined Leninist party that could oust warlords and imperialists from China, in the hope that social revolution would follow national liberation. Under the direction of the Soviet Union, the GMD entered a United Front with the Chinese Communist Party that lasted from 1923 to 1927.

But Sun's rhetoric also reflected the popularity of socialist ideas and the importance of the 'social question' among Chinese thinkers grappling with the Russian Revolution, domestic labour unrest, and their Indigenous cultural thought. In a period marked by eclectic political and aesthetic experimentation intellectuals translated and published extensively on the subject that bled into popular culture via science and utopian fiction. Yet Sun's insistence on couching his welfarist programmes under the label 'People's Livelihood' rather than using language from the Marxist canon is revealing. The term deliberately echoed the dynastic tradition of paternalism that would have been familiar to Chinese subjects reared on Confucian reverence for reciprocal obligations between the weak and the strong.[25] In choosing his words carefully, Sun not only distinguished his vision from communism, Margherita Zanasi has argued, but presented a socialism rooted in Chinese tradition.[26] In short, this was Sun's version of socialism with Chinese characteristics.

Sun's purposeful use of the People's Livelihood reflected his belief 'that communism was an important ideological adversary that needed to be nipped in the bud'.[27] Indeed, when we consider Sun's influences more closely, his aversion to anything that smacked of Bolshevism becomes apparent. Dirlik has pointed out that socialist works that were translated through his party magazine around the turn of the century were largely written by moderate Christian socialists who might best be described as coming from a social democratic tradition.[28] Meanwhile, Sun's ideas for tempering land inequality came mostly from the American reformer Henry George's design for land tax, which sought to curb rampant speculation, rather than from Marx's vision of a society in which property was held in common.[29] Sun would maintain this reformist outlook throughout his life.

And even Sun's land programme was more a means to a developmental end than an answer to inequity in itself. Zanasi has suggested that his design owed something to productivism, a school of thought that was taking hold across anti-communist European countries in the 1920s.[30] Productivists sought to expand national output as a means to improve social conditions and avoid class conflict. Sun, who was working on refining his programme in the early 1920s, would have been well acquainted with this development, while GMD leaders in the 1930s were drawn to related movements like Taylorism that sought to increase labour productivity.[31] Land to the Tiller in this vein was less about addressing inequality, and much more about augmenting national wealth by incentivizing newly independent farmers. That wealth could then grow faster through state-sponsored agricultural modernization, creating a virtuous cycle in which technology and the profit ethic worked together to strengthen China.[32] As Marie-Claire Bergère succinctly puts it, the People's Livelihood was both an 'idealistic goal and a strategy for development'.[33]

Yet it was hardly unique to the GMD. Sun's mingling of anti-colonialism and state-led development appeared across the political spectrum in the 1920s and 1930s and drew interest from China's utopian socialists, liberal democrats and fascist imitators. Their programmes for China bore striking similarities. They agreed on a need for rapid modernization and rejected the polarities of Bolshevik communism and laissez-faire capitalism. Both the left and the right, indeed, wanted to avoid the chaos of class conflict predicted by Marx through the embrace of unregulated capital.[34] Their focus, like Sun's, was less on addressing the question of uneven wealth distribution, and more on lifting China out of abject poverty. The desire for a 'third way' was reinforced by the fallout of the Great War and the global Depression that followed. Widespread disillusionment with Western civilization came not just from anger at China's Versailles settlement, but also from the savagery of the conflict it ended.[35] The scale and scope of the Great Depression's destructiveness further 'discredited the principle of the free market that underpinned liberal capitalism'.[36] At yet even as they sought to avoid the fate that had befallen much of the world they found precedents for successful state interventions in Meiji Japan, Bismarck's Germany and the New Deal United States. Their 'third way' took what they admired in such different settings and imagined pervasive state involvement in social and economic life, regulating conflict, developing resources, and lifting the nation out of the morass of poverty and imperialism.[37] In this respect they mirrored anti-colonial developmental politics elsewhere in the twentieth century from pre-Fascist Italy via Ataturk's Turkey to Nasser's Egypt.[38]

In China, moreover, such ideas chimed with the same traditional notions of good government as paternal that Sun had drawn on in formulating his third principle. State-led development, whether badged as socialist or not, offered a chance for China to achieve social harmony as envisaged in the classical concept of *datong*, which has been variously translated as the 'great commonwealth', 'great harmony', 'great unity' and even 'utopia'.[39] *Datong's* notion of harmony and universal welfare springing from the selfless and virtuous behaviour of the realm's subjects outlived the Qing. Indeed, writers in the first decades of the twentieth century utilized the concept to help indigenize socialism and communism by demonstrating their compatibility with Chinese tradition.[40] For some, even, socialism's appeal was rooted in the possibility of achieving utopia when

Confucianism as an everyday practice had failed.[41] Though the likes of Chinese liberals in the 1920s and 1930s, for instance, may not have articulated these ideas in the idiom of the 'great commonwealth', their desire for state intervention in development was rooted in the same desire to 'establish a perfect social order' for their country.[42] *Datong* was a key feature in Sun's Three Principles, and was further propagandised by the GMD in the 1930s, though by then the term had been imbued with Taylorist and militarized connotations, with social harmony coming through synchronized service to the state.[43]

Such ideas were pervasive enough to influence Mao to adopt a similar template in 1940 under the guise of 'New Democracy'. This manifesto challenged the Guomindang during the Sino-Japanese War (1937–45) by admitting that an immediate transition to socialism was not possible. Due to China's unique circumstances, the country, Mao argued, must undertake an intermediate stage of 'New Democracy', nestled between capitalism and socialism, before moving forward. His essay emphasized that China's path towards a socialistic future under the Communists would not be marked by violence or the abolition of private industry, but through prosperity built on a mixed economy and populated by a cross-class and anti-imperialist alliance of peasants, intellectuals, petite bourgeois and bourgeois led by the CCP. Mao's vision, Dirlik has pointed out, 'represented' not only 'a reappropriation or rephrasing' of Sun Yat-sen's vision, but also the insistence that the Communists were the 'more faithful' followers of Sun than their arch rival.[44] Though after the mid-1950s the People's Republic of China would move dramatically away from the premises Mao set down, it was his adaptation of Sun's vision that helped usher the CCP to power. In such respects Sun's Principle of the People's Livelihood, and the host of political projects with which it shared an affinity, marked an attempt to fuse socialist, social democratic and other developmental programmes to the specific needs and cultural traditions of China. For sure, the projects varied, with differences lying in the role of the masses, the place of Confucian values, and the precise understanding of democracy. But ultimately a broad consensus is evident as intellectuals and politicians envisaged development proceeding under the hands of a benevolent and powerful state.

Socialism and social security in wartime China

After Sun's death the GMD stood firmly in that current. 'Socialist, if illiberal and undemocratic, the GMD was, in its own way, a part of the social democratic mainstream in Chinese politics,' one historian has argued.[45] After it became the recognized government of China in 1927, with the success of Sun's son-in-law Chiang Kai-shek's Northern Expedition against warlords, its leaders publicly professed their mission to carry out their founder's programme. Over the following decade the party closely followed Sun's developmental blueprint. The GMD oversaw the creation of the National Reconstruction Commission in 1928 and the National Economic Council three years later, which coordinated all publicly financed projects for economic growth, and work on electrification and transportation infrastructure advanced in earnest, with a 50 per cent expansion in railway mileage.[46] The survey of the Yangzi Gorges – the first step towards making the Three Gorges Dam – took place in 1934.

Such activities have led scholars to label the GMD regime as a 'developmental state': one in which technocrats would have a key role in 'engineering' a new China, with government a visible hand directing economic life.[47] The outbreak of the Sino-Japanese War in 1937 would not only intensify this developmental imperative, but also direct it along more Soviet lines. Support for an industrial planned economy grew after the war for first the reconstruction of China and then the consolidation of Taiwan as an anti-Communist fortress. Such ambitions were shared by the CCP who would more or less follow the Soviet model of state planning between 1949 and 1958.[48]

In the 1930s, of course, such projects did not necessarily need the label 'socialist'. If the Soviet Union's communism offered a distinct path to rapid development that while premised on violent class conflict drew interest on account of its party organization, mobilized citizenry and commitment to centralized planning, other examples were available. In the likes of Italy and Germany, fascist and 'National Socialist' regimes tied infrastructural modernization to broader projects of national and racial rejuvenation. And the American New Deal saw the apogee of an interventionist new liberalism that looked vastly different to its nineteenth-century classical predecessor.[49]

These varied systems all had their adherents in the GMD. Fascism in particular drew interest – ironic though it may seem – as a means to anticolonial ends. Alex Lee, writing about East Asia in the 1930s, points to the appeal of what seemed 'to be an efficient technology for managing the economy to overcome the fallacies of liberal capitalism'.[50] The corporatism of fascist regimes, then, offered a similar path away from class conflict as Sun's reformist socialism.[51] But as David Motadel has argued, its draw lay too in its rejection both of a supposedly liberal Versailles system and of the Bolshevik alternative.[52] If GMD leaders were often impressed by disciplined, developed and highly militarized fascist societies, though, their own fascism – like their socialism – was for the most part instrumental rather than ideological. When it suited them they happily worked with the League of Nations and the International Labor Organization (ILO), and they shared an enthusiasm for state planning with regimes that had liberal, and communist tendencies too.

Though GMD made significant inroads in development during the Nanjing Decade (1927–37), a period of relative peacetime rule, the party struggled to live up to their founder's socialist promise of ensuring the People's Livelihood. In the countryside the party's insecure hold on power dissuaded leaders from launching a land reform programme. Chiang's Kai-shek's unification of China in 1927 had been achieved in part through military victory, but it hinged too on co-opting warlords and elites. The need for money to fend off recalcitrant strongmen also meant that the regime needed to maintain close ties to the moneyed classes in the cities. Thus to stay in power, the GMD had little incentive to challenge the status quo, and the threat of socialist-led rural and urban unrest troubled Chiang, who soon followed up his successful Northern Expedition with the massacre of Shanghai communists in 1927. For the following decade the party-state followed a corporatist line in managing industrial relations. The remnants of the Chinese Communist Party, meanwhile, were pursued into remote rural pockets of the republic, where the aggressive redistributive policies they pioneered would provide a template for their reemergence as a national force in the 1940s.

The government did, however, enact a handful of poorly enforced labour policies which addressed pay, working conditions and child labour. Such measures burnished China's credentials with the ILO and sought to tame worker militancy.[53] Even here, the limits of the legislation reflected structural problems as much as a failure of will, for both the party's left and right agreed in principle with the need to link social and economic development. Treaty obligations meant that foreign factories, which constituted most of the nation's manufacturing industry, were exempted from Chinese laws.[54] And some reformers evinced an impatience to move further and faster. The Nationalist authorities, working closely with the ILO, had translated a myriad of works on welfare after acceding to power.[55] And GMD policymakers also started preparations in 1934 for a compulsory social insurance bill, which was disrupted by the Japanese invasion of China in 1937.

The Nanjing Decade was therefore marked by a largely rhetorical commitment to Sun's Principle of the People's Livelihood, a concerted state-led push for planned economic development, and a ruthless anti-Communism that saw the persecution of radical socialists and a reluctance to embark on the kind of reforms the party's founder had once envisaged. However, war with Japan – which would become the first front in a conflict that eventually extended across the Pacific and Indian oceans – brought that decade to a close. In the face of immense nationalistic pressure, Chiang was forced into a reluctant alliance with his Communist opponents to fight Tokyo's forces, but after a series of reversals had to abandon his capital in Nanjing and retreat to China's mountainous west. The war exposed the frailties of the GMD government and left it ill-equipped to resist a resurgent Communist Party when that internecine conflict resumed centre stage in 1945.[56]

In older literature, the wartime era was cast as one of stagnancy and decline after the vibrant, energetic policies of the preceding period. Yet like the early 1900s, the sense of national crisis, and the connections the international situation created, opened space for experimentation, and created possibilities that would have been hard to imagine just a few years earlier.[57] Here, China's vital alliance with the Allied Powers, especially after the United States and Britain entered the Pacific War in 1941, would prove particularly important in enabling GMD policymakers to reconcile Sun's Third Principle with the social democratic ethos of the New Deal and the New Jerusalem.

Their plans, which the GMD cast as the realization of Sun's Principle of the People's Livelihood, owed much to the war. The Japanese invasion in 1937 sparked a refugee crisis which overwhelmed the capacity of traditional providers, such as lineage and charitable organizations, to meet relief demands. Here the state had stepped in instead. As Japanese forces swept down the East Coast, the government moved itself and important industries more than 1,500 kilometres inland to the western province of Sichuan. Officials put in place measures to provide work, housing, food, schooling and medical care for transplanted workers and their dependents. The state-enterprise system, as it was called, which would be taken up by the Chinese Communists after 1949, came out of this wartime contingency.[58] Wartime necessity therefore dramatically extended the scope of welfare provision even if it narrowed its geographic coverage: a process that would later be repeated on Taiwan.

The Nationalists established the state-enterprise system to better mobilize manpower in fighting a protracted war against a technologically superior enemy. However, this development took place amid a broader shift in expectations of how modern governments ought to act in times of war. If the Chinese people were expected to fight in the service of the nation, that nation had a responsibility to provide for their welfare. Such arguments rested on both biopower (healthy bodies were important in the fight) and republican ideology (citizens should be recognized for their patriotic sacrifice). Where the people's welfare was sacrificed for the greater good – most notoriously in Chiang's murderous decision to flood low-lying land around the Yellow River in order to halt Japan's advance – the Communists could reap the rewards.

Wartime policy therefore often was welfare policy. In 1940, the Nationalists created the Ministry of Social Affairs, which was partly modelled on US Social Security Administration.[59] The professed aim for the new government department was above all else to strengthen the state's capacity to mobilize and manage the population. According to the German-educated minister, Gu Zhenggang, 'the focus of social administration is to integrate in a scattered society … [i]n order to make our country a modern country and lead our people to become a modern citizen. In this war, to win a glorious victory depends on the manpower and material resources of our entire country. The basic requirement for wartime mobilization is to strengthen the organization of society.'[60] Yet, within this remit, the Ministry also created a Welfare Bureau designed especially to oversee relief and social policy projects as a corollary to its mobilization work.

This ambitious attempt to manage population pulled sociologists into the Ministry's employment. Indeed, the government required expertise on census and survey work to (among other things) organize conscription and food rationing, to manage labour in government industries, and to formulate plans for public health and relief. Many of the sociologists working with the government, such as the like of Yan Xinshe, Chen Da and Zhang Honjun, were either educated in the United States or trained by those who had been, and thus were well versed in the innovations of the New Deal.[61] Often networked into academies and associations across the globe, they were attuned to the latest trends in welfare provision and state planning, like the US Social Security Act of 1935 and the creation of the Tennessee Valley Authority as a way to bring jobs and power to poor rural communities. As early as 1941, not long after the creation of the Ministry, experts in the bureaucracy – with the help of the ILO – had started to collate material on social insurance policies across the world.[62] They would bring this know-how to put in place measures for the present and future China that aligned policy towards developments in the nation's allies. Soon their work translated into concrete proposals: a plan for social security in 1943. But it failed to get legislative approval.[63]

The tide, however, was turning. Over the course of 1943–4 government periodicals and academic sociologists began to sketch out increasingly ambitious plans for post-war reconstruction that borrowed from the tradition of social democratic politics Sun had followed closely. The social insurance policies adopted in Bismarckian Germany drew increased interest. So too did the prospect of a 'Chinese Beveridge

Plan,' which – taking its name from the wildly popular British blueprint – was generally taken to mean a 'social security (*shehui anquan*)' (another imported term) scheme for Chinese society.[64] These possibilities were given careful consideration. Could they, experts asked, be adapted to the primarily rural and clan-based nature of Chinese society?[65] Would the state have the finance and capacity to deliver such schemes?[66] At what point would industrialization render such a plan imperative, and was it better to wait until then or prepare now for that eventuality?[67] Such sceptical notes are not surprising: given the GMD's track record, the designs themselves are easy to dismiss as airy promises. Yet in May 1945, the GMD party congress affirmed its commitment to welfare provision, which it delegated to a new Central Insurance Bureau with a mandate to shepherd through the proposed schemes.[68] By 1947, provincial governments in southern China were trialling these new schemes for its civil servants.[69] The groundwork on welfare in these years would be continued after the GMD's retreat to Taiwan in 1949.

What explains this marked shift to 'social security' in the later war years? We should not discount the domestic anti-communism which had underpinned earlier welfare schemes during the Nanjing Decade; ad hoc social policy had proven a useful way of managing industrial relations and remained so in the 1940s. But that anti-communism also needs to be considered in international perspective. With the end of the war in sight, Chiang had aligned his nation with the United States, and saw the future global order as an American rather than Soviet one. As one of the 'Big Four', China could show it had moved with the times. Since 1941, the Allies had woven economic justice into human rights discourse, with the Atlantic Charter, Philadelphia Declaration, and new institutions like the United Nations Relief and Rehabilitation Association all committed to addressing material wants. Embracing social security enabled an authoritarian regime to position itself alongside liberal democracies: and in doing so augment its appeal to its sponsors in Washington, where support for Chiang had begun to waver in 1943 amid tension with US military leaders.[70] Chinese engagement of this sort had been part and parcel of its anti-colonial politics since the First World War, albeit with mixed success.[71] Now, once again, internationalism offered a way to strengthen the nation. Tellingly, the language of socialism affixed to such ideas in the 1920s appeared less often, with experts and policymakers more likely to root them in Roosevelt's 'Four Freedoms'.

Yet there is a risk of reducing social policy here to diplomatic calculation. To do so does a disservice to the Chinese experts who earnestly embraced the 'Rooseveltian moment' in welfare politics, and misses the GMD's long-standing commitment – which can be traced back to Sun – of state-led, socially cohesive development. Indeed social security was just one part of an integrated postwar vision the Ministry had for a reconstructed China: a comprehensive plan that promised to meet the agrarian, labour and health issues of what would become, under Nationalist direction, an industrialized nation.[72] War provided an impetus for improvisation, and alliances strengthened the epistemic networks and international incentives that brought welfare to the forefront of Nationalist politics, but China's Beveridge Plan was not hard to reconcile with earlier GMD developmental ambitions for China.

Land-to-the-Tiller on early Cold War Taiwan

The most concerted GMD effort to implement Sun's Third Principle occurred on Taiwan after the government's expulsion from China. By the early Cold War the socialistic elements of Sun's thought were muted in favour of an emphasis on legality and property ownership. These themes were stressed in the 1954 government publication *Agriculture and Land Programs in Free China*, which was intended for an international audience. The booklet laid out the programme of land redistribution that had taken place a year earlier, which enabled approximately 200,000 tenant-farmers[73] on Taiwan to '"climb the ladder" to farm ownership'.[74] Those without land, it continued, could now 'realise the aspirations they and their forefathers have always had'. The GMD propagandists at the Information Office indicated they were finally fulfilling the promise of the People's Livelihood, and doing so without the kind of bloodshed that typified Maoist land redistribution. The peaceful and lawful transfer of property on 'democratic' Taiwan, the document argued, not only ensured social stability, but also met the promise of social justice, and thus placed 'Free China' on a firmer footing in pursuit of industrial modernity.

Like social security, Land to the Tiller had long been delayed by the GMD, which had pandered to landlords in the 1930s. On Taiwan, though, the circumstances were more propitious for reformers. Taiwan had only recently re-entered the Chinese domain, though after 1949, it was just about all that remained of the GMD Republic of China. Japan ruled the island between 1895 and 1945. Over this period, imperial administrators turned it into a productive sugar colony, and imposed a rigorous regime of cultural assimilation. This 'Japanization' intensified during the war as the island served as the launchpad for the empire's southern advance in 1940.[75] At the end of the conflict, Taiwanese youths – though deemed 'ethnically' Chinese – spoke and dressed liked Japanese citizens.

Retrocession to China followed Japan's defeat. When Nationalist troops arrived on Taiwan, they were welcomed by the islanders, who expected to be treated as citizens rather than colonial subjects. However, the relationship quickly soured. Government corruption, a failing economy and rampant discrimination against the Taiwanese (who were often seen as traitors for working with the Japanese) led to an island-wide uprising in 1947 that was violently suppressed by the new government. The following years saw the imposition of martial law and the arrest and execution of dissidents. Amid the 'White Terror', islanders' perceptions of the GMD shifted, as the party came to be seen as illegitimate and incompetent occupiers.

In 1949, Mao defeated Chiang's Nationalist government, the remnants of which – amounting to approximately 1.5 million refugees – retreated across the Straits to Taiwan. The outbreak of the Korean War convinced a reluctant Truman administration to continue its sponsorship of the GMD, which warded off the immediate threat of invasion from the mainland. Despite this stay of execution, Chiang's regime was in disarray, and faced doubts over its legitimacy and longevity at home and abroad. Consolidating power and readying the population for conflict became, as in the Sino-Japanese War, imperative. The land reform first proposed by Sun Yat-sen provided one means to do so.

In the early 1950s, then, the GMD government finally embraced Sun's promise of 'land equalization'. Taiwan provided a more hospitable setting for such a reform. Unlike during the Nanjing Decade, the GMD had no entangling alliances with rural elites on the island, which gave party leaders greater freedom of movement. Moreover, just as in the 1940s, military crisis made action imperative. Indeed the redistribution of the property of Taiwanese landlords to their tenant farmers was intended to create a 'social base' required for mobilization. The term, which bore similarities to the Maoist 'mass line' (which GMD reformers also used), spoke to the need for a popular wellspring of support in warfare states: one, that as social security advocates had suggested a few years earlier, would come in part from a citizenry grateful for the government's protective embrace.[76] GMD reformers thus described the social base as an 'unmovable foundation' that would ensure their survival and even pave the path for their return to the mainland.

In a manner that mirrored wartime discussion of social security too, party leaders' ambitions converged with early Cold War American designs to reconstruct rural societies vulnerable to communism. Since the early 1940s, American planners searched for ways to secure both a long peace and US interests in the postwar world. Looking at Japan, planners came to the conclusion that the country's militarism was rooted in the unresolved problem of land inequality.[77] The redistribution of landed assets – which had been held by 'feudal landlords' with close ties to the military – would create a nation of owner-cultivators, who, much like the Jeffersonian yeomanry celebrated in American tradition, would defend democracy from its detractors. In occupied Japan, the principle was put into practice. A similar scheme of land redistribution was applied to South Korea.[78] Coupled to land reform were blueprints, often inspired by the New Deal, to bring development and stability to rural areas.[79] These designs became a lynchpin of Cold War policy.[80] The Economic Cooperative Administration (ECA), which oversaw Marshall Plan aid in Europe, would supply much of the financial and technical assistance that made land reform possible. Meanwhile, the American gospel of land reform would be propagated by itinerant experts, who carried ideas and experience across borders.

Taiwan provided the Americans a fitting testing ground to trial anti-Communist social policy. Land monopoly, according to US land reform advisers, was particularly acute, and the typical peasant's farmyard was 'among the worst' in the postwar world.[81] Moreover, as 'Free China' invited comparison to the Red China taking shape across the Straits, the GMD's redoubt presented an opportunity to demonstrate the viability of American-inspired liberal reform against a Maoist politics of confiscation and redistribution. Taiwan, then, served as a showcase for New Deal American liberalism as well as Chiang's developmental nationalism. Unsurprisingly in such a context, the 'socialism' of the GMD programme was downplayed, even as party leaders declared their desire to fulfil Sun's Third Principle.

As with the development of social security, work on the ground was enriched by a cadre of Chinese experts, who were connected to international networks, and able to act as intermediaries between the GMD and its American backers. Though the majority had stayed in China after 1949, a significant number had moved to Taiwan with the retreating government.[82] Among these technocrats were members of a Sino-American agency, the Joint Commission of Rural Reconstruction (JCRR). Created in 1948 as part of the continuing American economic assistance to China, the JCRR would help steer agriculture rehabilitation in Taiwan after 1949. Here the likes of Jiang Menglin (Chiang Molin) and Shen Zonghan, who sat at the head of the commission, had undertaken agricultural degrees in the New Deal-era United States.[83] Continuities with an earlier era are evident in the personnel: Sun had thanked Jiang in the preface of his *International Development of China* almost three decades earlier.[84]

Taiwan's land reform programme took the form of a series of measures that were enacted over three stages between 1949 and 1953. The first stage was the 375 Rent Reduction programme, which was launched in April 1949, which placed a ceiling on rent of 37.5 per cent of the value of the annual crop and was enshrined into law in 1951. The reduction was then followed by a wave of government land sales designed to transfer expropriated Japanese property to the landless. In 1953, the final stage – Land to the Tiller – mandated the purchase and transfer of excess lands from landlords to their tenants.

For both the GMD and the Americans, the 375 programme proved popular. Tenants prior to 1949 had typically handed over 55–60 per cent – and sometimes as much as 70 per cent – of their income to landlords.[85] The reduction was therefore significant. Investigations carried out by both the GMD and the Americans in 1951 suggested that the policy continued to elicit positive reactions from tenants and the public alike.[86] More households were able to purchase livestock, and more men could afford to marry. People were said to be dressing better and building better farmhouses.[87] The status of tenant farmers seemed to have improved.

But by the early spring of 1952, rural affairs seemed to have taken a turn for the worse. Party investigators began to pick up on a common complaint from villages that the 'good times do not last long' and that farmers' lives were 'hastening towards the hardship of the old days'.[88] The problem was rooted in the problem of taxation and credit. The state had now become a taxing master, replacing the old landlord class as an exploiter of rural labour. A large army, a swollen civil service and a hunger for foreign exchange led the government to place a heavy burden on peasants by, in effect, requisitioning rice and sugar.[89] With the absence of cheap credit in rural areas, those farmers became easy prey for usurious lenders.[90]

The party alleviated some of the fallout by helping peasants achieve their ambition of land ownership through the sale of government land, large tracts of which had come into GMD hands on Japan's defeat. But this programme yielded fewer benefits than expected after they got underway. Buyers tended to be owner-cultivators, rather than credit-hungry tenants. The party attempted to drum up public land sales through a publicity campaign which did little to stimulate demand.[91] In short, tenants had not escaped their condition.[92]

At first glance the story of early efforts at land reform might seem like a reversion to type for the GMD. The party's struggles to build a social base and impress American sponsors appeared to be dying a slow death. Indeed, the Nationalists' dire management of land sales moved land reform expert, Wolf Ladejinsky, to write directly to Chiang in August 1952, where he warned of the 'expression of universal ill-feeling' and 'disappointment' among farmers about the scheme.[93] But unlike in Ghana (addressed in another essay in this volume), popular frustrations here came less from opposition to the scheme itself, and more at the rapid erosion of benefits of an initially popular policy.

The GMD were well aware of the potential cost of failure. Internal reports warned that such a reversal would not only limit the party's ability to consolidate control over the island, but would weaken their appeal on the mainland, where Mao's bloody process of land reform was coming to a close.[94] Earlier that year the party commissioned a large survey designed to assess the impact of rent reduction on the peasants' livelihoods. More than a thousand GMD members working in the agricultural sector were mobilized to gather data on the likes of the pricing of commodities, the cost of production and the economics of rural households. The final report confirmed rural communities desperately needed credit. More disturbing, though, was the investigators assessment of the 'political outlook' of farmers, which indicated that the propaganda and land reform done thus far had not achieved their intended effect of creating a bulwark against communism.[95] Any 'social base' that had risen in the wake of rent reduction looked to be eroding fast.

On 24 July 1952, then, the GMD announced its intention to implement the final phase of their land programme in the new year. The Land to the Tiller scheme set out to transform vast numbers of tenant farmers to owner-cultivators, through the compulsory purchase and redistribution of private property from landlords. To signal the party's 'strong determination' to carry out this pledge, the GMD leadership made clear that this decision was taken in the presence of Chiang, who convened the meeting himself.[96] The highly publicized resolution stated that the measure would realize both Sun's teachings and the party's long-held position on land.

The announcement took the Americans by the surprise. In fact, the news horrified Washington policymakers, despite their support for land reform in the region. The GMD, they felt, was incapable of financing the scheme. If the Nationalists could not credibly pay off landowners or provide peasants with the means to finance the purchase themselves, the whole policy would become a 'fraud', and 'a lost opportunity' for both the Americans and the Chinese.[97] An American advisors pushed the Nationalists to postpone their plans until a more feasible option could be worked out.[98] '[F]ailure,' he warned, 'will entail substantial loss of popular support', and 'adversely affect the prestige of the government in Taiwan, on the mainland of China, and in other parts of Asia'.[99]

Despite the deep scepticism of US land reform experts, though, the GMD ploughed on to implement Land to the Tiller in 1953. The decision was driven by the imperative of mobilization. Promises had already been made to the Taiwanese that the party would finally deliver Sun's Third Principle. The desire to ready the population for war meant that this flagship reform could not be put off any longer. Here the Nationalist party-state mobilized the party-state in an unprecedented manner in order to deliver the peaceful transfer of property process on time and without American assistance. Given the intricacies of this land redistribution process, it was not easy. From training staff, mobilizing the legislature, circulating information, collecting data, surveying property, determining ownership, transferring deeds, predicting yields, issuing bonds, selling stock, arranging mortgages, compensating owners and punishing non-compliance, land reform presented a considerable challenge for a state with limited capacity. But both the process and outcomes offered opportunities to improve the party's standing among Taiwanese farmers whose counterparts on the mainland had flocked to the Communists; bolster the party's reputation to international observers; and establish a foothold in rural society. Following the campaign, the internal report to the GMD concluded land reform had become a powerful 'social campaign' that would act as a foundation for consolidation and mobilization of farmers.[100] 'The political effects' of Land to the Tiller, it continued, were 'to allow the revolutionary high-tide to reach deeply into the village', to 'advance and organise' farmers, and 'consolidate the party's mass foundation.'

* * *

The international climate of the 1950s differed markedly from the era in which Sun had engrafted the Three Principles of the People into Chinese Nationalist thought. In those earlier days the s-word – socialism – had been bandied around freely as China's intellectuals and aspiring leaders sought to chart a path that would navigate between the rocks of imperialism, laissez-faire capitalism, and the new Bolshevik order of the Soviet Union. By the early Cold War, the GMD's bitter conflict with Mao and the need to court an anti-Communist United States made reformers less likely to use the term. Even the term 'social security' largely disappeared from the party's idiom after the mid-1950s. Yet the actual policies the GMD implemented, though motivated by ambitions for national reunification by force, built on a longer engagement with socialist and social democratic ideas. Those ideas had been indigenized by Sun and his followers, explored by a generation of experts, and in projects like social insurance and land reform placed at the centre of republican governance.

It would be a stretch to call the GMD at any point a socialist party (even if some of its own leaders did so), but like so many anti-communist parties around the world over these decades, it continually engaged with socialist thought and practice. In this respect its anti-Maoist 'socialism' offered a model to likes of Diem's government in South Vietnam, which learned from Land to the Tiller,[101] while offering an alternative too to the non-aligned movement that came together at Bandung in 1956: American sponsorship, the GMD example revealed, could be used to pursue nationalist and developmental ends.[102]

Whether as a form of state legitimation, or as part of a concerted effort to reconcile Chinese circumstances with international developments, Nationalist leaders did so in ways that reveal their overlapping preoccupations with welfare (both of the people and of the nation as a whole) and warfare (both of the anticolonial and anticommunist variety). Generally hostile to Bolshevism, but cognizant of socialism's potential to serve as a counter to the disintegrative tendencies of laissez faire capitalism, these politicians and policymakers envisaged a road to modernization and mobilization made safe to travel through a modern paternal state.

Notes

1 Arlif Dirlik, 'Socialism and Capitalism in Chinese Socialist Thinking', *Studies in Comparative Communism* 11, no. 2 (1988): 149.
2 Michael Godley, 'Socialism with Chinese Characteristics: Sun Yatsen and the International Development of China', *The Australian Journal of Chinese Affairs*, no. 18 (1987): 109.
3 See also Nana Osei-Opare, 'Ghana and Nkrumah Revisited: Lenin, State Capitalism, and Black Marxist Orbits', *Comparative Studies in Society and History* 62, no. 2 (2023): 406; Emma Hunter, 'African Socialism', in *The Cambridge History of Socialism, vol. 2*, ed. Mercel Van de Linden (Cambridge: Cambridge University Press, 2022), 459; Alessandro Iandolo, *Arrested Development: The Soviet Union in Ghana, Guinea, and Mali, 1955–1968* (Ithaca: Cornell University Press, 2022), 2.
4 William Kirby, 'The Nationalist Regime and the Chinese Party-State, 1928–1958', in *Historical Perspectives in Contemporary East Asia*, ed. Merle Goldman and Andrew Gordon (Cambridge, MA: Harvard University Press, 2000), 217.
5 Eric Hellenier, 'Sun Yat-sen as a Pioneer of International Development', *History of Political Economy* 50, suppl. 1 (2018): 78.
6 Richard Horowitz, 'International Law and State Transformation in China, Siam, and the Ottoman Empire during the Nineteenth Century', *Journal of World History* 15, no. 4 (2004): 455–66.
7 Jürgen Osterhammel, 'Semi-Colonialism and Informal Empire in Twentieth-Century China: Towards a Framework of Analysis', in *Imperialism and After: Continuities and Discontinuities*, ed. Wolfgang Mommsen (London: Allen & Uwin, 1986), 290.
8 Kirby, 'The Nationalist Regime', 215.
9 Hellenier, 'Sun Yat-sen', 80.
10 Richard Louis Edmonds, 'The Legacy of Sun Yat-sen's Railway Plans', *The China Quarterly*, no. 111 (1987): 424.
11 Dirlik, 'Socialism and Capitalism', 135.
12 Ibid., 137.
13 Sun Yat-sen, *The International Development of China* (Shanghai: The Commercial Press, 1920), Preface, i; Helleiner, 'Sun Yat-sen', 88; Edmund S. K. Fung, 'State-Building, Capitalist Development, and Social Justice: Social Democracy in China's Modern Transformation, 1921–1949', *Modern China* 31, no. 3 (2005): 322–3.
14 A. James Gregor, *Marxism, China, and Development: Reflections on Theory and Reality* (Abingdon: Routledge, 1995), 187.
15 Sun, *International Development of China*, v.
16 Hellenier, 'Sun Yat-sen', 86. Sun, *International Development of China*, Preface i.
17 Ibid., 86.
18 Sun, *International Development of China*, 165.
19 Marie-Claire Bergère, *Sun Yat-sen* (Stanford: Stanford University Press, 1998), 362.
20 David J. Lorenzo, *Conception of Chinese Democracy: Reading Sun Yat-sen, Chiang Kai-shek and Chiang Ching-kuo* (Baltimore: John Hopkins University Press, 2013), 18.
21 Bergère, *Sun Yat-sen*, 368.
22 Ibid., 383.
23 Dirlik, 'Socialism and Capitalism', 137.

24 Margherita Zanasi, 'Fostering the People's Livelihood: Chinese Political Thought between Empire and Nation', *Twentieth-Century China* 30, no. 1 (2004): 23.
25 Ibid., 13.
26 Bergère, *Sun Yat-sen*, 383, 389; Fung, 'State-Building, Capitalist Development, and Social Justice', 331.
27 Zanasi, 'Fostering the People's Livelihood', 24.
28 Dirlik, 'Socialism and Capitalism', 142.
29 Bergère, *Sun Yat-sen*, 382–5 and Zanasi, 'Fostering the People's Livelihood', 20.
30 Zanasi, 'Fostering the People's Livelihood', 23; Bergère, *Sun Yat-sen*, 389.
31 Maggie Clinton, *Revolutionary Nativism: fascism and Culture in China, 1925–1937* (Durham: Duke University Press, 2017), 32–3.
32 Bergère, *Sun Yat-sen* 389; Fung, 'State-Building, Capitalist Development, and Social Justice', 331.
33 Bergère, *Sun Yat-sen*, 386.
34 Fung, 'State-Building, Capitalist Development, and Social Justice', 320; Nagatomi Hirayma, *The Making and the Unmaking of the Chinese Radical Right* (Cambridge: Cambridge University Press, 2022), 9; Brian Tsui, *China's Conservative Revolution: The Quest for a New Order, 1927–1949* (Cambridge: Cambridge University Press, 2018), Introduction.
35 Edmund S. K. Fung, 'Nationalism and Modernity: The Politics of Cultural Conservatism in Republican China', *Modern Asian Studies* 43, no. 3 (2009): 781.
36 Fung, 'State-Building, Capitalist Development, and Social Justice', 320–1.
37 Ibid., 320.
38 A. James Gregor and Maria Hsia Chang, 'Nazionalfacismo and the Revolutionary Nationalism of Sun Yat-sen', *Journal of Asian Studies*, 39, no. 1 (1979): 37.
39 Bergère, *Sun Yat-sen*, 386.
40 Nicola Spakowski, 'Dreaming a Future for China: Visions of Socialism among Chinese Intellectuals in the Early 1930s', *Modern China* 45, no. 1 (2019): 103.
41 Wen-Hsin Yeh, 'Middle County Radicalism: The May Fourth Movement in Hangzhou', *The China Quarterly*, no. 140 (1994): 906, 919.
42 Fung, 'State-Building, Capitalist Development, and Social Justice', 320, 324.
43 Bergère, *Sun Yat-sen*, 412; Spakowski, 'Dreaming a Future for China', 103. Tsui, *China's Conservative Revolution*, 55–6 and Clinton, *Revolutionary Nativism*, 32–3.
44 Arif Dirlik, 'Socialism in China: A Historical Overview', in *The Cambridge Companion to Modern Chinese Culture*, ed. Kam Louie (Cambridge: Cambridge University Press, 2008), 165.
45 Fung, 'State-Building, Capitalist Development, and Social Justice', 331.
46 William Kirby, 'Engineering China: The Origins of the Chinese Developmental State', in *Becoming Chinese: Passages to Modernity*, ed. Wen-hsin Yeh (Berkeley: University of California Press, 2000), 141.
47 Kirby, 'The Nationalist Regime', 212.
48 William Kirby, 'Continuity and Change in Modern China: Economic Planning on the Mainland and on Taiwan, 1943–1958', *The Australian Journal of Chinese Affairs*, no. 24 (1990): 127–33.
49 Jeremy Rayner, Susan Falls, George Souvlis and Taylor C. Nelms, 'Introduction: Back to the 30s?', in *Back to the '30s? Recurring Crises of Capitalism, Liberalism, and Democracy*, ed. J. Rayner, S. Falls and G. Souvlis, T. Nelms (New York: Palgrave Macmillan, 2020), 4.

50 Alex Taek-Gwang Lee, 'The Spectre of the 1930s in Asian Nation-Building: Global Fascism, Colonial Biopolitics and the Origins of Modern Asia', in *Back to the 30s: Recurring Crises of Capitalism, Liberalism and Democracy*, ed. J. Rayner, S. Falls, G. Souvlis, and T. C. Nelms (London: Palgrave Macmillian, 2020), 336.
51 Tsui, *China's Conservative Revolution*, introduction. See also William Kirby, *Germany and Republican China* (Palo Alto: Stanford University Press, 1985) and Clinton, *Revolutionary Nativism.*
52 David Motadel, 'The Global Authoritarian Moment and the Revolt Against Empire', *American Historical Review* 124, no. 3 (2019): 846–7.
53 Aiqun Hu, 'Social Insurance in Twentieth-Century China: A Global Historical Perspective', PhD diss. (Northeastern University, 2007), 143, 171–2, 175.
54 Hu, 'Social Insurance in Twentieth-Century China', 142.
55 Nara Dillon, *Radical Inequalities: China's Revolutionary Welfare State in Comparative Perspective* (Cambridge, MA: Harvard University Press, 2015), 48.
56 Dillon, *Radical Inequalities,* 55.
57 On this topic, see articles in the special issue of *European Journal of East Asian Studies* 11, no. 2 (2012).
58 Morris Bian, *The Making of the State Enterprise System in Modern China* (Cambridge, MA: Harvard University Press, 2005), 131.
59 Yan Ming, *Zhongguo shehuixue shi: yi men xueke yu yige shidai (A history of Chinese sociology: a discipline and an era)* (Beijing: Qinghua University Press, 2010), 261.
60 Gu Zhenggang, 'Di yi ci quanguo shehui xingzheng huiyi (weiyuanzhang xunci) (The director's speech at the first National Social Administration Conference), *Shehui gongzuo tongxun* 1, no. 1 (1944): 2.
61 Tehyun Ma, 'The Common Aim of the Allied Powers': Social Policy and International Legitimacy in Wartime China, 1940–1947', *Journal of Global History* 9, no. 2 (2014): 261.
62 Hu, 'Social Insurance in Twentieth-Century China', 183.
63 Ibid., 184.
64 Ma, 'The Common Aim of Allied Powers', 257.
65 Shi Kejing and Zhen Junying, 'Lun shehui baoxian yu woguo shishi de wenti (A discussion of social insurance and the problems of implementation in our country)', *Zhongyang ribao*, 23 July 1947; Ta Chen, 'The Foundations of a Sound Social Policy for China', *Social Forces* 26, no. 2 (1947): 140.
66 Lin Liangtong, 'Shehui xingzheng yu shuihui baoxian (Social administration and social insurance)', *Zhongyang ribao*, 8 October 1942; Wu Jian, 'Woguo zhanhou shehui Anquan chubu sheshi shishi jiahua juyao (A summary of our country's social security implementation plan)', *Shehui jianshe* 1, no. 4 (1944): 4.
67 Chen, 'The Foundations of a Sound Social Policy for China', 140.
68 Chinese Ministry of Information, *China Handbook, 1938–1945: A Comprehensive Survey of Major Developments in China in Eight Years of War* (New York: Macmillan, 1947), 52.
69 Guangdong sheng chouban she fu baoxian, 17 July 1947, 026.00000.3636A, Neizhengbu, Academia Historica, Taiwan.
70 Ma, 'The Common Aim of Allied Powers'.
71 Guoqi Xu, *China and the Great War: China's Pursuit of a New National Identity and Internationalization* (Cambridge: Cambridge University Press, 2005), chapter 1.
72 Shehui bu, *Si da shuhui zhengce ganglin ji shishi banfa* (The big four social policies and their implementation methods) (Nanjing: [publisher unknown], 1946).

73 T.H.Shen, *Agriculture and Land Programs in Free China* (Taipei: Government Information Bureau), 1.
74 Shen, *Agriculture and Land Programs in Free China*, 5.
75 Seiji Shirane, *Imperial Gateway: Colonial Taiwan and Japan's Expansion in Southeast Asia, 1895–1945* (Ithaca: Cornell University Press, 2022).
76 'Zhongyang weiyuanhui di 339 ci huiyi jilu', 9 May 1952, RG 6.42/35.9, Guomindang Party Archives, Taipei, Taiwan.
77 Dayna L. Barnes, *Architects of Occupation: American Experts and the Planning for Postwar Japan* (Ithaca, NY: Cornell University Press, 2017).
78 Michael Albertus, *Property without Rights: Origins and Consequences of the Property Right Gap* (Cambridge: Cambridge University Press, 2021), 282.
79 Ethan Kapstein, *Seeds of Stability: Land Reform and US Foreign Policy* (Cambridge: Cambridge University Press), chapter 4.
80 David Ekbladh, *The Great American Mission: Modernization and the Construction of an American World Order* (Princeton: Princeton University Press, 2011), 117.
81 Wolf Ladejinsky, *Agrarian Reform as Unfinished Business: The Selected Papers of Wolf Ladejinsky*, ed. Louis Isaac Walkinsky, (Oxford: Oxford University Press, 1977), 168.
82 Kirby, 'Continuity and Change in Modern China', 136.
83 James Lin, 'Sowing Seeds and Knowledge: Agricultural Development in Taiwan and the World, 1925–1975', *East Asian Science, Technology and Society: An International Journal* 9, no. 2 (2015): 136–7.
84 Sun, *International Development of China*, Preface ii.
85 Ladejinsky, *Agrarian Reform*, 96. Only 5–8 per cent of tenants paid rents less than 40 per cent. See also 'Conference on Land Tenure Reform Program of Taiwan', 27 August 1949, Box 38, UD410, RG469, National Archives at College Park, College Park, MD [hereafter NARA].
86 ' "San qi wu" jianzu jixiao diaocha zonghe baogao (shang)', *Taiwan dangwu* 16 (1951): 21–9; Chinese Institute of Land Economics, 'Research Report on Rent Reduction in Taiwan', enclosed in letter from JCRR Commissioner J Baker to J. Nason (ECA, Washington), June 1950, Box 38, UD410, RG469, NARA.
87 Yan Ming, 'Nongmin shenghuo diachao zhi yiyi yu jiazhi', *Gaizao* 38 (1952): 30.
88 Ibid.
89 Taipei to ECA Washington, 'United State Economic Mission to China', 6 December 1950, Box 73, UD 409, RG469, NARA.
90 Ladejinsky, *Agrarian Reform*, 146.
91 Zhongyang weiyuanhui mishuchu, Zhongguo Guomindang zhongyang gaizao weiyuanhui huiyi yijue'an huibian ([unknown]: Zhongyang weihuiyuan mishuchu, 1952), 447, 449.
92 Ibid., 163.
93 Schenck to MSA Washington, 'Land Reform Progress', 21 August 1952, Box38, UD410, RG469, NARA; Howard P. Jones (Charge d'Affaires), American Embassy, Taipei to State Department, 'Conversation between Premier Ch'en and Mr. Ladejinsky on Formosan Conditions', 8 August 1952, Box70, UD409, RG469, NARA.
94 Zhongyang weiyuanhui mishuchu, Zhongguo Guomindang zhongyang gaizao weiyuanhui huiyi yijue'an huibian, 163.
95 Di liu zu, 'Shehui diaocha tongxun', *Zhongyang* 7 (March 1953): 11.
96 JCRR Land Division, 'Text of the Kuomintang Resolution to Introduce the Private Land Purchase Program in Taiwan in 1953', 28 July 1952, Box38, UD410, RG469, NARA.

97 EA to DCM, 'Sponslor's Comment on Land Reform Program', 31 July 1952, Box 38, UD410, RG469, NARA.

98 Ibid.

99 MSA Taipei to MSA Washington, 'Chinese Government Long-Range Plans for Economic Improvement', 12 August 1952, Box 72, UD409, RG469, NARA; MSA Taipei to MSA Washington, 'Agricultural Field Trip in Taiwan, by Wolf Ladejinsky', 16 September 1952, Box 2, UD409, RG 469, NARA.

100 Zhongyang weiyuanhui mishuchu, Sishiyi sishier niandu fan'gong kang'e zongdongyuan yundong huibao juilu huibian ([unknown]: Zhongyang weiyuanhui mishuchu, 1954), 373.

101 See James Lin, 'Martyrs of Development: Taiwanese Agrarian Development and the Republic of Vietnam, 1949–1975', *Cross-Currents: East Asian History and Culture Review* 33 (2019): 53–83 and Simon Toner, 'Imagining Taiwan: The Nixon Administration, the Developmental States, and South Vietnam's Search for Economic Viability, 1969–1975', *Diplomatic History* 41, no. 4 (2017): 782. For Taiwan and exchanges with the Global South, see also Philip Liu Shiao-pong, 'Planting Rice on the Roof of the UN Building: Analysing Taiwan's "Chinese" Techniques in Africa, 1961-present', *China Quarterly* 198 (2009): 381–400.

102 Hao Chen, 'Resisting Bandung? Taiwan's Struggle for "Representational Legitimacy" in the Rise of the Asian People's Anti-Communist Leagues, 1954–57', *The International History Review* 43, no. 2 (2021): 244–63.

5

Three logics of Indian socialism: Historicizing development under capital

Matthew Shutzer

Introduction

> *The objective of the Party will be to achieve a classless and casteless socialist society by peaceful means.* (The wordings in this clause are subject to final approval.)[1]
>
> Manifesto of the Socialist Party and Kisan Mazdoor Praja Party, 1952

In an article published in 2009, 'Thinking between the Posts', Sharad Chari and Katherine Verdery staged a possible dialogue between postcolonial studies and post-socialism, a turn in historical anthropology focused on the aftermath of 'actually existing' socialist countries within the former Eastern bloc. Their suggestion was that scholars in these fields had much to learn from one another, and that they were perhaps best poised, when read together, for apprehending the complex legacies of the Cold War in our present. While Chari and Verdery's proposal was enthusiastically received by scholars working on post-socialism within the former Soviet Union, for those writing in the tradition of postcolonial studies, their article arrived more like a dead letter.[2] Perhaps one of the reasons for this uneven reception lay in what Chari and Verdery had already anticipated as postcolonial studies' strategic 'retreat' from the lineages of Marxist thought undergirding the state socialisms of the erstwhile Third World. Emerging as an intellectual formation amidst attacks on state socialism by neoliberal restructuring during the 1980s, the postcolonial turn echoed a similar disenchantment with the post-colonial itself. A generation of younger scholars instead embraced culturalist 'critiques of Orientalism and Enlightenment rationality' to explain modes of power and knowledge that marked continuities across colonial and post-colonial regimes.[3] There was little here to identify post-colonial socialisms, or their discredited aftermath, as an historical experience deserving separate study.

Nowhere was this generalized disenchantment with post-colonial socialism more clearly expressed than in the histories of Indian 'development' that first emerged in the mid-1990s. As the founding site of the postcolonial collective of Subaltern Studies – itself originating as an intellectual formation reacting to the Indian 'Emergency' of the 1970s and the complicity of many of the country's left-wing parties in that authoritarian project – it is not surprising that such tendencies were so pronounced for scholarship on modern India.[4] Defined by the work of Partha Chatterjee and Gyan Prakash, early postcolonial writing on this topic was characterized by the marginalization of socialism as a meaningful category, and an emphasis instead placed on Foucauldian-inspired readings of 'development' as a discourse of elite legitimation and bureaucratic expertise. Post-colonial development was here conceived as an extension of the symbolic and governmental forms of colonial power, expressed most prominently in the post-colonial state's commitments to 'scientific modernity'.[5] These de-historicized renderings of development were further supported by the influential work of the political scientist James Scott, an admirer of the early Subaltern Studies' emphasis on 'histories from below'. South Asianist readers of Scott's book, *Seeing Like a State*, came to understand Indian development as part of a transhistorical conceptual vocabulary of what Scott called 'high modernism', or the violent abstractions used by states to control people and territory.[6]

Taken together, these approaches instilled a methodological anti-statism in the writing of India's history of development, defined by a suspicion that what passed as the nationalist promise of post-colonial prosperity and freedom was, at its core, an inescapable 'grammar of modern power' and repressive 'unitary reason'.[7] In more recent years, however, this gloomy consensus has become somewhat displaced. A new body of scholarship since the 2010s has painted a different picture of Indian development as a social phenomenon more decentralized than previously thought, emerging not only as a technical project of post-colonial nationalism and state-building, but as an evolving set of transnational ideas and exchanges framed by the Cold War.[8] Rather than a top-down imposition, several new works seem to converge on the argument that development was the medium by which the interests of common people were brought into relation with the state.[9] While this process may have been messy and incomplete, development appears in these new works as a *dialogic* strategy of statecraft, oftentimes exposing the very limits of any singular developmentalist vision when counterposed against India's heterogeneous social realities.[10]

Yet for all the talk of a 'new history of development', there are common threads connecting old to new. Development remains coded primarily as a discourse or category of knowledge, subject to the modes of interpretation that historians of development now seem to prefer: symptomatic political and cultural readings that render development as a symbol or an imaginary, as a technocratic practice concretizing pre-existing ideological commitments, as a legitimating discourse for the self-promoting strategies of 'experts', or as a type of statist (and now, transnational) form of knowledge for mediating state-society relations and inculcating an appropriate post-colonial citizen-subject. If one of the main problems of postcolonial scholarship was the paucity of empirical materials it used to explain development – it relied, fundamentally, on an *a priori* programme of post-structural analysis – the remaking of 'development' as an object of deep empirical enquiry by contemporary scholars has not quite escaped the post-colonial provocation of locating its subject primarily in the realm of the discursive.[11]

There remain strikingly few historical studies, for instance, that centre development as a question of political economy, or as a response to actual forms of social conflict, historical tendencies of capital accumulation, or asymmetries of global economic power within the postwar world system.[12] This absence is all the more peculiar given that India's developmentalist turn in the 1950s was explicitly socialist, and that many of its practitioners understood the socialist model of development as a direct response to historical structures of inequity within the global system. The relativization of the 'economy' as a mere discursive artefact of expert knowledge has had the perverse effect of drawing scholarly attention away from historically produced political economic structures that called into being the ideas and practices that came to be called 'development'. This inattention to historical structure has become so ingrained that the history of Indian socialism is now framed as simply one example of a technocratic repertoire of developmental ideas, with practically no attention to why or how so many in India's post-colonial milieu recognized *socialist* development as an appropriate diagnostic for Indian society.[13]

In this chapter, I would like to offer a few methodological reflections on how one might pair a history of Indian socialism with a history of political economic structure. My intention is not to recuperate a rosier vision of Indian socialist political economy, nor to overstate the influence of socialist politics within India's post-colonial economic life or democracy. As the historians David Engerman and Taylor Sherman have demonstrated, socialism, as it came to be consolidated under India's first prime minister, Jawaharlal Nehru, after 1956, not only lacked ideological coherence as a governing principle, but was a faction-ridden political project unable to assert sustained degrees of influence on the Indian state.[14] Socialism in India was neither an anomalous state-form in comparison to the other 'mixed economy' planning states of much of the Cold War world, nor the majority of its policy prescriptions outliers to the liberal market discipline championed at the time by the Bretton Woods institutions of the International Monetary Fund and the World Bank.[15] The import-substitution-industrialization socialism that became associated with the Nehruvian regime (1950–64) was defined by a strong dose of liberal moderation in its respect for prevailing distributions of property and power.[16]

Nevertheless, Indian socialism functioned as both an explicit project of developmental governance, as well as a powerful mode of political economic critique spanning both the late-colonial and post-colonial periods. Because socialism in post-colonial India was not reducible to a singular political project, I want to suggest that the concept is best understood as a broad set of left tendencies which sought to counterpose the *juridical* independence of decolonization against the revolutionary *socio-economic* transformations that many believed independence was supposed to bring. This conceptual framing is not meant to minimize the meaningful ideological differences or direct party conflicts that defined the history of Indian leftism throughout the Cold War. Nor is it to provide an exhaustive cognitive map of Indian socialist ideas. It is rather to call attention to how various types of political and developmentalist positions that adopted the mantle of 'socialism' were activated in relation to claims about embedded socio-economic structures preventing fuller forms of freedom. This position is intended to take seriously the socialist worldview of historical development – not as an expression of empirical truth, but also not as some purely ideological position produced in contexts unmoored from social life. The interpretive issue at stake is rather to ask why, within a given historical moment, socialist economic development could appear as a plausible idea at all.

In what follows, I will pursue this alternative understanding through what I call 'three logics of Indian socialism'. The framework of 'logics' situates socialist ideas in relation to the historical conditions of their emergence, while also connecting three different visions of socialist development separated by distinctive historical conjunctures.[17] The idea of development shared across these three case studies is significantly different from the way that term is used by historians today. If development is now conceived as an historical subject merely *constructed* by the knowledge forms and technical interventions of post-colonial states and transnational agencies and experts, development was, for the socialist thinkers discussed below, both a framework for technical intervention into political economy, and an *historical condition* produced by extant forms of social power and the patterns of capital accumulation operating at global and national scales. This idea of development as a form of historically produced social structure is one of the positions that separated socialist thought from its liberal developmentalist variants, which attributed India's economic 'underdevelopment' to the primacy of other factors: cultural values, weak institutions and indeed the insufficiency of India's exposure to capitalist markets or principles of competition.[18]

The three exemplary logics of socialism I present here track this idea of development from its emergence in the interwar period to its fundamental reformation and crisis under the political economy of Indira Gandhi's Emergency regime of the 1970s. Section one briefly examines the formation of Indian socialist politics amidst the global crises of interwar capitalism. Indian socialist economic ideas ascended as alternatives to a capitalist system held responsible for global economic immiseration and warfare, but they were also assembled to legitimate the Indian nationalist movement's wider turn towards '*purna swaraj*', or complete freedom. Indian anti-imperialists who became socialists believed that socialist political economy could serve as both a mechanism for controlling capital, as well as a set of normative political commitments for transforming the nationalist movement into a mass politics for social democracy. It was this complex duality – socialism as a governing principle of development, and socialism as a political project beyond statist institutions – that would challenge every advance of Indian socialism into the post-colonial era. In section two, I highlight some of the limits of these developmentalist politics by focusing on an archetypal case study of post-colonial state socialism: an oil pipeline project undertaken by the socialist politician, K. D. Malaviya. This section resituates the Indian state's socialist turn through the oil discoveries and energy infrastructures that made that political imaginary possible. And finally, in section three, 'Socialism without Socialists', I consider the transformations of the Indian economy during the crisis-ridden decade of the 1970s and the country's authoritarian 'socialist' turn that reorganized national capital accumulation for a post-Bretton Woods global order.

Socialism as freedom

The history of leftism in the years immediately following the partition of the subcontinent was defined by state suppression. In many states across India, such as Bengal from 1948 to 1951, the Communist Party of India was officially banned, with party cadre languishing in prison under preventative detention. As the Indian National Congress (INC) began the process of consolidating its power over the institutions of the former colonial state, in Calcutta Communist cells and trade unionists took to the streets, engaging in violent urban warfare against the city's European-owned businesses, the police and the homes of Congress party officials. Police surveillance reports documented bomb-throwing, arson, looting and efforts to organize *hartals* or general strikes in and around the docks of Calcutta's port. Strike-breaking labour gangs, led by the Congress party, fought with striking mariners and dockworkers at the water's edge. Breakaway communist underground groups like the Indian Bolshevik Party and the Revolutionary Communist Party recruited members from these actions with the hope of seeding future struggles in both the port and the holds of European-owned steamers.[19]

This period marked an early challenge to the legitimacy of the INC as the institutional successor to the mass politics of the anti-colonial movement. Not only was the interim government confronted with managing the unprecedented violence and dislocation caused by the partition of the subcontinent, but across the country workers and farmers began to seize opportunities to realize the gains of *political* freedom in the economic sphere.[20] In the provinces, reports began to filter through that peasants had come to believe the abolition of empire meant the abolition of land rents. For the large agrarian estates in Bihar and Bengal, no-rent campaigns appeared continuously between 1948 and 1954, and only a few of these were connected to any identifiable political party.[21] In the main coal-mining regions of central and eastern India – territories long dominated by foreign-owned firms – mineworkers rose up against Indian foremen and European mining managers in strike waves that had to be suppressed by military police.[22]

In the background of these events, the INC began to institutionalize an ideology of governance that emphasized the simultaneous moderation of post-independent social change and the grounding of a developmental politics within the apparatus of the state itself.[23] The INC sought to reconcile the divergent identitarian and class interests of the Indian polity through a Janus-faced appeal to national identity: looking backward, the party called upon its historic connection to Gandhi and the anticolonial movement, and looking forward it presented itself as the sole arbiter of a future of socio-economic upliftment for the many.[24] This is what Partha Chatterjee described as the process through which nationalism became a 'state ideology' which appropriated 'the life of the nation into the life of the state'.[25] Yet there were also significant exclusions in terms of the types of ideas and political affiliations the INC tolerated within its own ranks. Despite influential members within the Congress Party, including Jawaharlal Nehru, whose ideological investments in economic planning stemmed from an earlier engagement with Fabian socialism, the INC as a whole during the immediate post-independence period worked to exorcise the influence of socialist and communist factions in the name of party unity.[26]

Socialism as a political and ideological project had emerged in colonial India amidst the broader remaking of anticolonial nationalism in the 1920s and 1930s. The premier nationalist party, the INC, founded in 1885, had been the primary institution for expressing the then-prevailing bourgeois ideology of a parliamentary road towards federated reconciliation with the British Crown. As younger political actors joined and inspired new mass social movements, Indian nationalism began to represent its demands in terms of the abstract entity of the Indian 'people', and through the idiom of *purna swaraj*, complete freedom.[27] The notion of *purna swaraj* was open to a range of interpretations. For radicals like M. N. Roy, one of the founders of the Communist Party of India in 1925, *purna swaraj* meant an open-ended struggle against both imperial capitalism *and* bourgeois nationalism leading to worldwide revolution.[28] Others, such as the socialist insurrectionist Bhagat Singh, understood *purna swaraj* as a break from both the Brahminical elitism of Gandhi's leadership and the vanguardist internationalism of the Comintern. Singh instead sought a strategic positioning of what he called 'Left Communism' oriented towards the amorphous figures of the peasant and the labourer.[29]

Neither the mainstreams of the Congress nor the party's tactics of Gandhian *satyagraha* (non-violent truth force) were immune from left-wing challenges. Congress socialism developed in the 1930s on the fringes of the party, responding both to the perceived tactical failures of the Congress leadership, and to the growing wave of mass labour and peasant unrest that began in the 1920s and accelerated in the wake of the global great depression. Early socialist figures like Jayaprakash Narayan were especially influenced by the rise of the *Kisan Sabha* or peasant union movement in the state of Bihar after 1929, along with the radical agrarian platform put forward by the Communist Party of India at the same moment.[30] Between 1932 and 1933, Narayan helped to form a socialist group amongst jailed nationalists held under colonial detention in the Nasik Road Central Prison. At the All-India Congress Committee in Bihar in 1934, Narayan and others formed the Congress Socialist Party, or CSP, a caucus within the INC to push the party in a left-leaning direction.[31]

Much of the early political-institutional hope of the Congress Socialists was placed in Jawaharlal Nehru, the scion of a wealthy barrister's family from northern India, whose father, Motilal, had previously served as president of the Congress. Nehru never joined the CSP, but his own election to the Congress presidency in 1936 was widely viewed as a recognition of the growing influence of socialist ideas within the nationalist movement. In his speech accepting the office, Nehru announced, 'Socialism is for me not merely an economic doctrine which I favor; it is a vital creed which I hold with all my head and heart.'[32] This description of socialism as an overarching belief system, a 'vital creed' rather than a definitive politics, reflected the contradictory assimilation of socialist ideas by the nationalist movement. On the one hand, Congress Socialists close to Nehru called for the organization of future state institutions for challenging the prevailing distributions of wealth and power within Indian capitalism. Under Nehru after 1936, the Congress embarked on drafting the first technocratic documents for building India's post-colonial developmental state. Nehru even appointed socialists like Narayan, and the national education movement figure, Acharya Narendra Dev, to the Labour Research Department of the Congress, a working committee where they honed ideas concerning the global economic conjuncture of the interwar period and the unlikely future of capitalism as a hegemonic system.

On the other hand, however, even the Indian socialists who supported Nehru expressed a deep ambivalence towards state power. Their distrust of state institutions reflected the factional splitting between Indian communists and socialists, in which the heterodox orientations of the CSP's founders led them towards a view of state developmentalism as a potential vehicle for anti-democratic tendencies. The technical and institutional concentration of economic forces within the state was understood as emblematic of prevailing monopolistic tendencies within global capitalism, embodied in the mirror-image forms of the Fordist corporation and the Stalinist 'command economy' state.[33] Many of the CSP's members believed economic redistribution needed to be determined by mass political awakening, not merely the technical leadership that was often presented by Nehru as the pragmatic alternative to socialist revolution. Figures like Narayan and Narendra Dev looked to traditions and practices of agrarian self-help and trade union organizing as alternatives to planning committees and advisory boards.[34] These were the broad fault-lines over which Indian socialism would come to form and reform itself over the next several decades: socialism as a governing ideology of statist political economy, and socialism as a politics of social democracy.[35]

The anti-statist tendencies of those to the left of Nehru in the socialist milieu have often been taken as evidence of the relatively weak commitments of Indian socialists to a radical redistributionist politics at the scale of the nation. There is good cause for such an assessment, especially as one considers the subsequent splintering of the different socialist factions in the 1950s and 1960s on precisely these questions.[36] A parallel line of critique, however, might suggest that what socialism gave to the nationalist movement was an articulation, born of the interwar moment of defining the meanings of freedom under *purna swaraj*, that anti-colonial nationalism was not rendered legitimate by its incorporation into the state alone. It required instead, a deeper commitment to both economic equality and mass democratic participation. Indeed, Acharya Narendra Dev's own writings on the growth of global fascism in the 1930s diagnosed the capacity of state institutions to be overcome by authoritarian movements putatively acting in the name of national unity and economic progress. State power was a necessity, but not the *telos*, of popular political struggle.[37]

It is not surprising that this emphasis on the popular as the locus of socialist struggle was one of the main ideological divisions that kept the members of the CSP from entering the upper ranks of the Congress Party after 1947. The Congress viewed itself like a railway switchman in a great marshalling yard of unruly political tracks. To a lesser extent than the communists (who were basically banished from the memory of the nationalist movement), the main socialists too were culled in the 1950s as the INC sought to assume full control over the trade union movement. In 1952, former members of the CSP created the Socialist Party, contesting national elections on their own and winning a vote share three times as much as the next leading opposition party, the Communist Party of India. After the election, the leaders of the Socialist Party and another faction, the Kisan Mazdoor Praja Party, joined to form the Praja Socialist Party. Despite a great deal of disunity, the political factions of the socialist movement were guided by the sense that the electoral dominance of the Congress made sustained opposition from within the INC no longer possible.[38] What this overlooked, however, was the very institutionalization of a new type of state socialist developmentalism that would emerge from within the Congress itself by the late 1950s. This articulation of state socialism was not to be born out of social upheaval. Rather, what would become India's official 'socialist turn' after 1956 was materialized in part through the new political possibilities opened up by the postwar economy of oil.

Petro-socialism at the limits of the political

> *Socialism is neither Marxian nor Gandhian. It is the necessity of the present times and belongs to me as much as it belongs to Gandhi or Marx.*[39]

The Ministry of Natural Resources and Scientific Research (NRSR), founded in 1952, became one of the most important bureaucratic bodies for advancing the socialist political economy championed by India's post-colonial government. The portfolio and membership of the NRSR would shift over time, but its main functions were related to mineral, resource and energy research and development. As the environmental historian Megan Black has observed, Cold War-era governmental agencies with these types of portfolios were at the centre of an emergent geopolitics concerning the ownership of the earth's subterranean resources.[40] Institutions like the NRSR played a fundamental role in determining the trajectory of post-colonial mineral economies by grounding wider ideological debates about capitalist and socialist development, resource nationalization and foreign investment, post-colonial sovereignty and neo-imperial imposition, and autarkic national economy and liberal economic interdependence.

The most significant political figure to come out of the NRSR was undoubtedly Keshav Dev or K. D. Malaviya. Malaviya had long been associated with the socialist factions of the Congress and was an ally of Nehru as the latter rose to party dominance during the 1930s. Although never part of the socialist parties that broke away from the Congress after independence, Malaviya distinguished himself from other senior Congress members in ministerial posts as a vociferous advocate for integrating socialist planning principles into India's developmental policies. Malaviya was specifically interested in the question of energy, and he viewed India's reserves of coal and petroleum as the bedrock of the country's future industrialization. Calling attention to the material significance of these resources was one thing, but Malaviya would also come to understand fossil fuels as a political stage for contesting existing claims of British capital in India's mining industries, as well as the advancing geopolitical power of US oil companies. For Malaviya, energy was the economic basis to assert both India's political claims to national self-determination and for establishing materially derived socialist solidarities to aid other Third World nations. By the late 1950s, Malaviya led the Indian state towards building one of the post-colonial world's first integrated public sector oil companies organized explicitly to curtail the power of foreign oil firms.[41]

In his letters, speeches and writings from the late 1950s and early 1960s – the height of India's experimentation in a type of petro-socialist politics – Malaviya frequently imagined India's energy infrastructures as a centralizing grid for promoting both social democracy and economic advancement. He continuously contrasted Indian socialism with that of Maoist China, insisting that although a process-oriented democracy might stymie India's rate of developmental transformation in comparison to more authoritarian socialisms, it remained the primary legitimating tool for determining the aims and desires of Indian society.[42] 'The world,' Malaviya wrote in 1961, 'has entered into a stage where individual interests have to be completely submerged into that of the society.'[43] But the key to that process was, at least in his rendering, for the state to guarantee 'fundamental rights to every member of the society to overthrow a regime which is not justly and fairly serving the over-all cause of the society'.[44] He reserved his most brutal invective for the invidious 'feudal' and 'capitalist' interests that stood in the way of such a compromise, seeking to arrogate to themselves the common wealth of the nation as a private source of profit. Malaviya viewed these reactionary domestic interests as the natural allies of postwar neo-imperial formations embodied most of all by the United States.

The cornerstone of what would become Malaviya's oil programme in the late 1950s was a pipeline project to bring oil from India's northeast to a network of new refineries. Malaviya had initially based his oil programme on a discovery in the Naharkatiya area of upper Assam in 1953, an undeveloped reserve that had been awarded to the Assam Oil Company in the 1930s, a subsidiary of British-owned firms that would subsequently become British Petroleum. Malaviya expropriated the colonial-era geophysical license claimed by the Assam Oil Company, insisting that Naharkatiya's oil had become the sovereign wealth of the Indian people. The oil discovery in Naharkatiya ultimately enabled the formation of a public-sector oil company for producing, refining, and distributing state-owned petroleum.

In practice, however, the technical and capital requirements for constructing a state-owned oil company necessitated extensive public-private partnerships with both existing oil firms and foreign governments, including the United States and Britain. The British oil companies leveraged their political influence to remain involved in the Indian oil sector by offering infrastructural and financing support once they were otherwise shut out of any future prospecting or concessions claims. Malaviya in these cases preferred to turn to the assistance of the Soviet Union and the eastern bloc, but this was not always possible. Malaviya's ambitions of energy self-sufficiency ultimately produced new contradictory forms of interdependence.

The Assam pipeline project exemplified these tendencies. Pipelines, as scholars like Tim Mitchell and Laleh Khalili have shown, are infrastructures of mediation intended to reorganize existing distributions of labour, capital and territorial claims over space.[45] The initial idea behind the Assam pipeline was to decentre the existing concentration of oil storage infrastructures first constructed during the colonial period and centred around the Port of Calcutta. While Assam boasted the oldest refinery in India going back to 1901, the flows of India's oil wealth moved towards Calcutta's manufacturing areas, and were mediated by British-owned river transport companies that moved kerosene, batching oil, and other petroleum products up and down the great river systems of India's eastern states. These companies, owned under a consortium of firms affiliated to the Peninsular and Oriental shipping company, maintained an entrenched financial interest in Indian shipping routes well after decolonization. The inland water transport firms, or IWT's as they were known, were the primary conduits for taking the oil, tea, and jute produced in both Assam and what became East Pakistan into global markets.

The partition of the Indian subcontinent fundamentally challenged the existing business model of the IWTs. The river routes that had once served as highways from productive hinterlands into the markets and ports of Bihar, Calcutta and Dacca were now sub-divided by the new geopolitical demarcations of India and Pakistan. Not only were their South Asian investments suddenly internationalized, but so was their labour force. The IWT's depended on contracts with the communist-affiliated Bengal Mariners Union or BMU, one of the first trade unions that became affiliated with the Communist Party of India founder Muzaffar Ahmed in the 1920s. The BMU had stood in an oppositional relationship with the Congress Party since independence, viewing their leadership in West Bengal as too conciliatory with the British firms that dominated Calcutta's port. On 8 October 1952, 35,000 employees of the BMU struck for higher wages and for the appointment of their General Secretary, Mansour Gilani, who had just defeated a Congress-backed candidate in union elections.[46] Although the strike was concentrated in eastern India, BMU workers were able to disrupt the entire system of inland water transport. Mansour Gilani meanwhile travelled directly into Assam and East Pakistan intending to stop cargo flows. Alarmed by the disruption of river traffic, the Indian Tea Association in London and the IWT consortium in Calcutta demanded the government dispatch security forces to detain Gilani and to provision their auxiliary steam ships with emergency supplies of coal and food grains.[47]

Deliberations on the proposed Naharkatiya pipeline unfolded amidst this wave of strike activity, which lasted intermittently into 1955 when a labour tribunal finally forced a renegotiation between the BMU and the IWTs. B. C. Roy, the Congress Chief Minister for West Bengal, used the tribunal to cull both Pakistani citizens and members of the CPI from the BMU's ranks, declaring both to be 'non-Indian nationals' and thus excluded from representation under Indian labour law.[48] The central government meanwhile had moved ahead on plans to obviate the IWT's oil routes by calling for engineering proposals for a pipeline spanning the Brahmaputra River and connecting Naharkatiya with a prospective refinery project in Bihar. The government cited security concerns relating to the proximity of Naharkatiya to the East Pakistan border and the volatility of the labour situation as justification for pipeline investment. The IWTs argued the opposite position. In correspondence with Malaviya and other members of Nehru's cabinet, the IWT consortium called attention to the recent attack on the British-owned Iraqi oil pipeline in 1956 after the signing of the Baghdad Pact. Unlike pipelines, whose routes were fixed and exposed, IWT tankers, the consortium insisted, could shift courses in times of conflict, and store oil all along a decentralized route.[49]

The ultimate decision came down to a complex triangulation of interests. Malaviya and the socialist members of his ministry were able to get approval for Romanian and Soviet assistance in the construction of new refineries at Nunmati (Guwahati) in Assam and Barauni in Bihar. Political leaders in Assam who had demanded a greater share of the rents and royalties extracted from their state were moderately appeased, even though they had at one point privately consulted with naval architects in Britain for a private fleet of IWT oil tankers to retain the river routes. The consortium of British oil companies, shut out from the refinery deals, reinserted themselves into the state-run oil programme by brokering a three-million-pound loan from the Bank of England to the Indian government in 1959. The British state had initially balked at approaches from Malaviya for financing for the pipeline project, but with the eastern bloc proposal for the refineries approved, there was greater geopolitical interest in retaining such an investment.[50] According to the British oil managers involved, Western support for a state-owned pipeline would demonstrate a good faith commitment to India's ideas of oil sovereignty.

In his pioneering monograph, *The Magical State*, the anthropologist Fernando Coronil argued that modern petrostates are not uniform creatures, but rather composed of all sorts of contradictory ideological claims, competing institutional priorities, conjunctural performances of legitimacy, and sedimented histories of political and social power. One of his most important insights was that, before the discovery of oil in the early twentieth century in his case country of Venezuela, the state was neither a strong nor socially cohesive administrative unit. But in the aftermath of oil, the state was able to *appear* as 'an independent agent imposing its dominion over society' because it became capable of mediating between foreign oil companies and the fragmented interests that comprised the Venezuelan nation.[51] Coronil's analysis has a great deal of explanatory power for understanding both Malaviya's project and the Indian turn to 'socialist' development in the late 1950s. The 1,157-kilometre pipeline that would come to distribute Assamese oil across the Gangetic basin of northern India indeed produced a new regime of bureaucratic centralization, but this infrastructure was simultaneously embedded within a deeply fractious political and social field. The logic of the pipeline was not 'production first and production last', the phrase that Malaviya used to disdain socialist ideologues motivated by a narrow economism. It was rather a logic of conjuncture, shaped by notions of socialist autarky and Third World internationalism, as much as by layered histories of labour militancy, colonial capital, Indian federalism and Cold War rivalry.

Socialism without socialists

The late 1960s witnessed a fundamental reorientation of Indian political life and the idea of socialism within it. With Nehru's death in 1964 following the disaster of the Indo-China War, the Congress Party faced an unprecedented succession crisis. Casting about for the future leadership of the party that had led India continuously since independence, the INC elected Nehru's daughter, Indira Gandhi, to both the head of the party and the Prime Minister's Office in 1966. That summer, Gandhi's election coincided with the outbreak of massive drought and crop failure in Bihar and eastern Uttar Pradesh.[52] Rising prices in the cities for basic foodstuffs and petrol were seized upon by a new generation of communists and trade unionists seeking to topple regional governments that remained loyal to both the post-Nehru Congress and the Stalinist parliamentarians of the mainline Communist Party of India.

By the late 1960s, extra-parliamentary fronts of left-wing inspired political violence opened up across India's eastern states and northern Andhra Pradesh. This was exemplified most of all in the formation of the Maoist 'Naxal' movement and its proliferating networks of underground affiliated cells, real and imagined, during this period. In the iron-ore mines of Singhbhum near the Tata-owned 'steel city' of Jamshedpur, company officials began calling for special police action against refractory workers and unruly trade unionists by sensationalizing their affiliation with 'secret' Naxal units. Tribal or *adivasi* activists associated with the secessionist party, the Birsa Seva Dal, were held under police protection for raising anti-landlord slogans and for allegedly seeking Naxalite affiliation. The Naxal movement was blamed by Indian police for radicalizing Bihar's Communist Party to begin a 'land grab' programme in tribal villages. State-led paramilitary units, such as the Central Industrial Security Force, were brought into being in 1969, justified on the grounds that special security was required to halt a rising tide of left-wing violence against industrial property. By 1970, government officials estimated that Naxals had killed more than thirty people – violence concentrated especially in 'landlord extermination' campaigns in northern Bihari districts of Darbhanga and Muzaffarpur – while 850 suspected Naxals were being held in Bihari jails.[53]

These events bracketed Prime Minister Indira Gandhi's experience of heightened political turbulence, as well as her sense that the era's politics were to be defined by a rhetoric of socialist revolution. In 1969 she was expelled from the Congress Party by its most senior and conservative members for losing elections to an alliance of socialist parties known as the SVD, even as she retained majority support from the party overall. Recognizing that her popularity as a national political figure was no longer dependent on the blessings of the old men that populated the party's senior leadership, Gandhi formed a new organization, Congress (R) to contest new elections in 1971. Her election campaign mobilized a more radical political language to appeal to the simmering discontent and stagnating economic possibilities felt by many millions. The campaign's theme, *garibi hatao desh bachao*, 'abolish poverty save the country', promised to go beyond the more conciliatory socialist politics that had marked the Congress' agrarian and domestic economic policies in the past, and to finally bring to conclusion long-vaunted reforms like land reform, bonded labour abolition and land ceiling enactments. The campaign was a stunning success. Gandhi not only effectively erased the socialist inroads made by the non-Congress SVD, but utterly demolished all rival parties, emerging as a singular national figure ideologically connected to the agrarian poor.

Socialism legitimized Gandhi's political ascendancy. But structurally the Indian economy was already in the throes of a gradual liberalization of the socialist economic model that was shakily put in place under Nehru.[54] Already in 1964, the World Bank had begun to push more directly for the Indian government to loosen its economic controls regime and to devalue its currency.[55] The drought and monsoon failures of 1966–7 gave Indira Gandhi cause to follow this course, leading her to agree to a devaluation and moderate price reform, and to deepen India's connection to US food aid and the Bank-backed Aid India Consortium. USAID head John Lewis, along with Bernard Bell at the World Bank, also used this reformist moment to push the advancement of the capital and petro-chemical intensive agriculture that would become the hallmark of the Green Revolution.[56] This turn towards food aid and new, petrol-intensive agricultural technologies was to have determinative implications for the reorganization of the Indian economy under Gandhi's regime.

When Gandhi returned as prime minister in 1971, her commitments to a renewed socialist political economy covered over the new nexus of food-energy interdependence by claiming that India's newest Five-Year Plan would bring the country 'towards self-reliance'. This claim was, however, unceremoniously met by the realities of the inflationary dollar crisis that followed the 'Nixon shock' of 1971 and the subsequent OPEC oil price hike in 1973. Between 1972 and 1975, rising oil and dollar costs pushed India's petroleum imports from $264 million to $1.4. billion. Global agronomists understood that with the need to constrain petrochemical imports under austerity, India would stand to lose nearly 7 per cent of its total cereal coverage in 1974.[57]

The tools and ideologies that Gandhi's administration had on hand to combat this macroeconomic volatility were the blunt instruments of a crisis-ridden nationalization. In 1969 Gandhi had already taken a first step in this direction by nationalizing major commercial banks. After 1971, Gandhi and one of her closest allies, the Communist Party of India member Mohan Kumaramangalam, began to fully nationalize the coal sector. In 1973 Gandhi enacted a short-lived nationalization of wheat distribution networks – building off of the preexisting authority of the government-controlled Food Corporation of India – as a way of eliminating black market trading and controlling nominal prices. And in 1974 the government began nationalizing all of the remaining foreign oil companies and their refineries. Overall, the unprecedented extension of the Indian state in this conjuncture, and its reformation into a new rentier apparatus, appeared to represent the socialist advancement promised by the *garibi hatao* campaign. Such an appraisal was underscored by Gandhi's own claim that her administration represented a 'socialist' revolution, a term that she then inserted into a 1976 amendment to the constitution that declared India a '*socialist* secular democratic republic'.

But Gandhi's regime, if socialist in any sense, was a socialism lacking meaningful commitments to redistribution, economic equality, or the mobilization of a mass socialist politics.[58] Nor was her socialist turn somehow conducted in opposition to global or national capital, or the logic of market performance. As Christophe Jaffrelot and Pratinav Anil have recently argued, Gandhi's political economy was characterized as a corporate dirigiste regime, centred on close alliance with the large capitalist interests of India's advanced industries and a commitment to an anti-inflationary provisioning of key consumer items like energy and food.[59] Workers suffered immensely under Gandhi's regime, experiencing direct government pressure driving wage stagnation, bonus and dearness sequestration, rental increases and labour disciplinary measures barring strikes.[60] Paired with these tactics, nationalization was in some cases able to deliver unprecedented production increases.[61] But this was a commitment to a socialism of bland productivism.

In 1975, Gandhi declared a political 'emergency' to resist a judicial ruling that would have nullified her electoral victory in the previous election. For nearly two years Gandhi presided over an authoritarian regime with the full suspension of civil liberties and democratic procedures. In the name of national unity and socialist self-reliance, Gandhi used the executive powers under the emergency clause to deepen the state's absolute control over trade unions and to allocate unprecedented investments in new police paramilitary units for the protection of industrial property. As Gandhi jailed thousands of political prisoners, and hundreds of thousands more organized in the streets for her overthrow, even the World Bank praised the type of 'socialism' Indira had at last brought to India, which for them meant authoritarian labour controls, governing efficiency and counter-inflationary policymaking.[62]

Gandhi's authoritarianism was well-suited to the Bank's paradigm of growth for the late 1970s. Her reliance on India's unelected bureaucracy and their creditors in Washington D.C. was a predictable power pairing to those socialists who had long separated themselves from the immobilizing tendencies of the Congress' left-wing rhetoric. Writing in 1971, the Odia social activist for the Praja Socialist Party, Kishen Pattnaik, already observed that Gandhi's electoral rebranding as the socialist candidate demonstrated that 'slogans against poverty, unemployment, economic disparity, and rising prices' continued to animate the popular consciousness of political legitimacy. Gandhi was, at least for this moment, more skilled at channeling the collective aspirations associated with those forms of political speech, but her commitments to their actual realization were much more shallow. Gandhi had no organized social base or grassroots party infrastructure for actually implementing her redistributionist vision. Instead, her power depended on a collection of party bosses – who were themselves largely taken from the elite strata of upper-caste agrarian landowners and the urban bourgeoisie – and the institutional authority of the permanent bureaucracy. Neither of these groups could ever 'tolerate any kind of agitation or struggle for equality'. The fundamental question of the moment, according to Pattnaik's diagnosis several years before the declaration of Emergency, was to understand how Gandhi will 'manage to hold power even without implementing her socialist promises, for socialism for her is a necessity for the sake of remaining in power'.[63]

Conclusion

In a speech from Japan in May of 1985, the famed US economist Walt Rostow cast a synthetic eye over the relationship between development economics and the place of underdeveloped countries in the world economy. He argued that one of the casualties of the Cold War competition between capitalism and socialism was that it had produced an incorrect and ideologically driven presumption that optimal economic solutions were a zero-sum game. From Rostow's vantage, the proliferation of developmental states in the 1950s did not reflect the success of any one economic ideology, but was rather the result of underdeveloped nations needing to manage both domestic distributional conflicts and macroeconomic volatility. The result was the creation of a new 'state bourgeoise' that had progressively come to monopolize ever greater areas of economic life. The cause of the hour, according to Rostow, was to shift power from this state bourgeoise to the entrepreneurial competition of the private sector. This was not a call for anything approaching a 'Friedmanesque' devotionalism to the market, Rostow cautioned. State management was still needed in some areas, but the dictates of national growth within a changing world economy required a measured shift in the balance from state institutions to markets.[64]

There were once many names for diagnosing what Rostow called the 'state bourgeoise'. Michal Kalecki, the Polish Marxist economist who had consulted on development strategy in India in the 1950s, originally called this formation an 'intermediate regime.'[65] The Pakistani Marxist sociologist Hamza Alavi understood this peculiar state form as a lingering social-institutional consequence of what he called the 'colonial mode of production'.[66] Kishen Pattnaik, the socialist apparatchik mentioned above, diagnosed things with greater rhetorical effect: 'India's new feudal class,' he called the experts and bureaucrats who filled out the organs of the state. Despite the divergent implications of these analyses, what Rostow, Kalecki, Alavi and Pattnaik shared was a way of understanding midcentury development as a process that produced particular state forms out of the complex and historically contingent interweaving of social structure and ideology. Theirs was an appeal to state form embedded in political economy – not the other way around – and conceived as the expression of national class and political configurations standing in relation to the competitive pressures of global capital.

In this chapter I have tried to take these much older concerns with development as an historical structure and to pair them with a conjunctural account of the conditions of possibility for Indian socialism. Socialist development has here been presented as a project that sought to remake elite nationalism into a popular politics of social democracy, as a conflict between state bureaucracy and labour militancy, and as the ironic vehicle for the 'de-socialization' of developmental tactics and policies that would carry India into the 1980s. These moments contextualize the wider political and economic fields that rendered Indian socialism both a plausible and implausible Cold War project. The prospect of a more efficacious or transformational socialism was never solely contingent on ideological commitments, nor on the technocratic savvy of developmental bureaucrats. These of course mattered deeply. But socialist developmentalism was always dependent on its political capacity to transform the historical structures underlying India's economic integration into the postwar world.

In moving away from histories of Indian socialism, I wonder if historians have been too dismissive of socialist thought as either representing only a minor tendency within a broad set of Indian 'developmental ideas;' or as functioning as merely an elite discourse with little connection to the social realities and political expectations of a heterogeneous post-colonial polity. There is certainly ample evidence to suggest otherwise. To reflexively situate these histories in the present would require a more deeply empirical engagement with both ideology and political economy as mutually constituting vectors of socialism in the postwar world. But it would also require moving away from the condescending vantage of posterity that has come to see the socialist worldview as just some confused 'grand narrative' so far removed from the putatively post-ideological and disenchanted commitments of academic critique. Such a turn might help to uncover why the socialist imaginary of development remained such a durable form of national political life in India throughout the late twentieth century, and the narrowing horizons of political and economic potentiality that have now come to replace it.

This as I take it would be part of restaging the conversation between post-socialism and post-colonialism originally suggested by Chari and Verdery. If post-colonialism represented an *internal* critique of anticolonialism and its statist aftermath, might it be possible to articulate a postsocialist critique that is not strictly a form of disavowal? It might then allow us to read the epigraph that began this paper with less cynical eyes. The parenthetical notation that the Socialist Party's commitment to a classless and casteless society would be 'subject to final approval' is a tragic articulation of the self-defeating dilemmas that characterized Indian socialist strategy at the time. But read slightly differently, this halting deferral is also exemplary of a political language in-the-making, whose iterative articulations of the problematic of an emancipatory equality after capitalism remain glaringly unfinished to this day.

Notes

1 Statement of Acharya Narendra Deva and Acharya Kripalani, Manifesto of the Lucknow Agreement between the Socialist Party and the KMPP, 1952.
2 Douglas Rogers, 'Postsocialisms Unbound: Connections, Critiques, Comparisons', *Slavic Review* 69, no. 1 (2010): 1–15.
3 Sharad Chari and Katherine Verdery, 'Thinking between the Posts: Postcolonialism, Postsocialism, and Ethnography after the Cold War', *Comparative Studies in Society and History* 51, no. 1 (2009): 11.
4 For an early statement on the impact of Emergency for the thinking of one of the collective's founders, Ranajit Guha, see: Ranajit Guha, 'Indian Democracy: Long Dead, Now Buried', *Journal of Contemporary Asia* 6, no. 1 (1976): 39–53.
5 Partha Chatterjee, 'Development Planning and the Indian State', in *State and Politics in India*, ed. Partha Chatterjee (New Delhi: Oxford University Press, 1994), Gyan Prakash, *Another Reason: Science and the Imaginary of Modern India* (Princeton: Princeton University Press, 1999), Akhil Gupta, *Postcolonial Developments: Agriculture in the Making of Modern India* (Durham: Duke University Press, 1998), Srirupa Roy, *Beyond Belief: India and the Politics of Postcolonial Nationalism* (Durham: Duke University Press, 2007). India's colonial history itself became the implicit template for crafting Foucauldian accounts of a durable 'colonial power' writ large. See for instance: David Scott, 'Colonial Governmentality', *Social Text*, no. 43 (Autumn, 1995): 191–220; Ahmad Shokr, *Remaking the Plantation: Cotton and the End of Empire in Egypt* (Palo Alto: Stanford University Press, forthcoming).
6 James Scott, *Seeing Like a State: How Certain Schemes to Improve the Human Condition Have Failed* (New Haven: Yale University Press, 1998).
7 Prakash, *Another Reason*; Ronald Inden, 'Embodying God: From Imperial Progress to National Progress in India', *Economy and Society* 24, no. 2 (1995): 261.
8 For works that have displaced state-centric approaches and focused instead on development as a logic of dispersal, decentralization, and transnational exchange, see: Subir Sinha, 'Lineages of the Developmentalist State: Transnationality and Village India, 1900–1965', *Comparative Studies of Society and History* 50, no. 1 (2008): 57–90; Nicole Sackley, 'The Village as Cold War Site: Experts, Development, and the History of Rural Reconstruction', *Journal of Global History* 63, no. 3 (2011): 481–504; Daniel Immerwahr, *Thinking Small: The United States and the Lure of Community Development* (Cambridge: Harvard University Press, 2015); Benjamin Siegel, 'The Kibbutz and the Ashram: Sarvodaya Agriculture, Israeli Aid, and the Global Imaginaries of Indian Development', *The American Historical Review* 125, no. 4 (2020): 1175–204.

9 Benjamin Siegel, *A Hungry Nation: Food, Famine, and the Making of Modern India* (Cambridge: Cambridge University Press, 2018); Nikhil Menon, *Planning Democracy: Modern India's Quest for Development* (Cambridge: Cambridge University Press, 2022).

10 Taylor Sherman, 'From "Grow More Food" to "Miss a Meal:" Hunger, Development, and the Limits of Post-colonial Nationalism in India, 1947–1957', *South Asia: Journal of South Asian Studies* 36, no. 4 (2013): 571–88.

11 Stephen J. Macekura and Erez Manela (eds.), *The Development Century: A Global History* (Cambridge: Cambridge University Press, 2018). On the pervasiveness of linguistic models of historical analysis inherited from the historical turn to poststructuralism, see: Anna Yu Krylova, 'The Agency Dilemma', *American Historical Review* 128, no. 2 (2023): 883–937.

12 For a recent challenge to this absence, see: Aditya Balasubramanian, *Toward a Free Economy: Swatantra and Opposition Politics in Democratic India* (Princeton: Princeton University Press, 2023); Medha Kudaisya, '"A Mighty Adventure": Institutionalising the Idea of Planning in Post-Colonial India, 1947–1960', *Modern Asian Studies* 43, no. 4 (2009): 939–78.

13 More recently, socialist development has been replaced by the terminology of 'economic planning', whose rise as a governing project appears as a result of Indian elites jockeying for power and influence within the post-colonial state. Menon, *Planning Democracy*.

14 David C. Engerman, *The Price of Aid: The Economic Cold War in India* (Cambridge: HUP, 2018); Taylor Sherman, '"A New Type of Revolution:" Socialist Thought in India 1940s–1960s', *Postcolonial Studies* 21, no. 4 (2018); Daniel Kent-Carrasco, 'A Battle Over Meanings: Jayaprakash Narayan, Rammonhar Lohia, and the Trajectories of Socialism in Early Independent India', *Global Intellectual History* 2, no. 3 (2017): 370–88.

15 Charles Bettelheim, *India Independent* (New York: Monthly Review Press, 1969), Amy Offner, *Sorting out the Mixed Economy: The Rise and Fall of Welfare and Developmental States in the Americas* (Princeton: PUP, 2018), Johanna Bockman, *Markets in the Name of Socialism: The Left-Wing Origins of Neoliberalism*; Matthew Shutzer, 'Oil, Money, and Decolonization in South Asia', *Past and Present* 258, no. 1 (2023): 212–45.

16 Nasir Tyabji, *Forging Capitalism in Nehru's India: Neocolonialism and the Indian State, 1940–1970* (New Delhi: Oxford University Press, 2015).

17 On these methods of ideas in history, see for instance: Angela Zimmerman, 'Three Logics of Race: Theory and Exception in the Transnational History of Empire', *New Global Studies* 4, no. 1 (2010): 1–11; Andrew Sartori, 'Hegel, Marx, and World History', in *A Companion to Global Historical Thought*, ed. Prasenjit Duara, Viren Murthy, and Andrew Sartori (New York: Wiley, 2014); Rebecca Karl, *The Magic of Concepts: History and the Economic in Twentieth Century China* (Durham: Duke University Press, 2017).

18 For a classic statement of this type of position in the world of mid-century development economics, see: Gunnar Myrdal, *Asian Drama: An Inquiry into the Poverty of Nations* (New York: Allen Lane, 1968) 3 vols.; Morris David Morris, 'Values as an Obstacle to Economic Growth in South Asia: An Historical Survey', *The Journal of Economic History* 27, no. 4 (1967): 588–607.

19 See for instance: Office of the High Commission for the United Kingdom, Foreign Office, Political Registry, Communism in the Far East, DO 133/113, 1948–1952.

'Note on developments in connection with communism in India subsequent to despatch no. 7, 24th February, 1949'.

20 On the violence of this federal moment, see: Sunil Purushotham, *From Raj to Republic: Sovereignty, Violence, and Democracy in India* (Palo Alto: Stanford University Press, 2021).

21 Jawaharlal Nehru Memorial Museum and Library (JNMML), Individual Collections, Syama Prasad Mookerjee Collection, Subject File: No. 59, 'Zamindari System: 1948–1951'.

22 National Archives of India (NAI), Ministry of States, P Branch, 1950, File No. 17 (85) – P/50, 'Murder of Mr. J.V. Bell, late manager, Umaria Colliery, Vindhya Pradesh'; JNMML, Institutional Collections, Bengal Coal Company Papers 17th Installment, No. 22, R-12414.

23 For a retrospective accounting of the party's structure under Nehru that worked in favour of such ideological moderation, see: Christophe Jaffrelot and Pratinav Anil, *India's First Dictatorship* (London: Oxford University Press, 2021), Ch. 5.

24 Francine Frankel, India's Political Economy: The Gradual Revolution, Ch. 2; Vinita Damodaran, *Broken Promises: Popular Protest, Indian Nationalism, and the Congress Party in Bihar, 1935–1946* (Delhi: Oxford University Press, 1992).

25 Partha Chatterjee, *Nationalist Thought and the Colonial World: A Derivative Discourse?* (Minneapolis: University of Minnesota Press, 1986), 166. See also Upendra Baxi, 'Accumulation and Legitimacy: The Indian Constitution and State Formation', *Delhi Law Review* 15 (1991).

26 Shalini Sharma, '"Yeh azaadi jhooti hai!": The shaping of the opposition in the first year of the Congress raj', *Modern Asian Studies* 48, no. 5 (2014): 1358–88.

27 Mrinalini Sinha, 'The Political in Question: Anatomy of a People's Politics', in *Political Imaginaries in Twentieth Century India,* ed. Mrinalini Sinha and Manu Goswami (London: Bloomsbury, 2022); Manu Goswami, 'A Communism of Intelligence: Early Communism in Late Imperial India', *Diacritics* 48, no. 2 (2020): 90–109.

28 M. N. Roy, *India in Transition* (Geneva: J. B. Target, 1922).

29 This was also the position taken by the Communist leader Muzaffar Alam and his cadre in Calcutta. See, Suchetana Chattopadhyay, *An Early Communist: Muzaffar Ahmed in Calcutta* (New York: Columbia University Press, 2012).

30 Walter Hauser, *The Bihar Provincial Kisan Sabha, 1929–1942: A Study of an Indian Peasant Movement* (Delhi: Manohar, 2019); S. K. Mittal and Irfan Habib, 'The Congress and the Revolutionaries in the 1920s', *Social Scientist* 10, no. 6 (1982): 20–37; Uma Shankar Singh, 'The Politics of Mass Mobilization in Eastern Uttar Pradesh, 1920–1940', *Social Scientist* 3, no. 5/6 (2015): 93–114. On the interwar rise of communist organizing, see: Ali Raza, *Revolutionary Pasts: Communist Internationalism in Colonial India* (Cambridge: Cambridge University Press, 2020).

31 John Patrick Haithcox, *Communism and Nationalism in India: M.N. Roy and Comintern Policy, 1920–1939* (Princeton: Princeton University Press, 1971), Ch. 9.

32 Quoted in A. V. Bhuleshkar (ed.), *Indian Economic Thought and Development* (Bombay: Popular Prakashan, 1969), xiii. See Nehru's full account of socialism's necessity in, Jawaharlal Nehru, *Whither India?* (Allahabad: Kitabistan, 1933).

33 Susan Buck-Morss, *Dreamworld and Catastrophe: The Passing of Mass Utopia in East and West* (Cambridge: MIT Press, 2002); Greg Grandin, *Fordlandia: The Rise and Fall of Henry Ford's Forgotten Jungle City* (New York: Picador, 2010).

34 On Narendra Dev's socialist thought, see: Rakesh Ankit, 'Marxist *Guru*, Socialist *Neta*, Buddhist *Acharya*, Gandhi's *Shishya*: The Many Narendra Devas (1889–1956)', *Global Intellectual History* 2, no. 3 (2017): 350–69.

35 This socialist critique of the state, built through creative appropriations of Marx, Laski, and Gandhi, appeared across the nationalist political spectrum. See: Karuna Mantena, 'On Gandhi's Critique of the State: Sources, Contexts, Conjunctures', *Modern Intellectual History* 9, no. 3 (2021): 535–63.

36 Sherman, 'A new type of revolution'.

37 Narendra Deva, 'Socialism and the Nationalist Movement', (1934), in *Socialism and the National Revolution*, ed. Yusuf Meherally (Bombay: Padma Publication, 1946).

38 Acharya Narendra Dev, 'The Indian National Congress and Socialism', *Janata*, 27 February 1955, in *Selected Works of Acharya Narendra Deva, Volume Four, 1952–1956*, ed. Hari Dev Sharma (New Delhi: Radian Publishers and the Nehru Memorial Museum and Library, 1999).

39 JNMML, Individual Collection, K.D. Malaviya Private Papers, Subject File 30, 'Notes on socialism', 4 March 1961.

40 Megan Black, *The Global Interior: Mineral Frontiers and American Power* (Cambridge: HUP, 2018).

41 Shutzer, 'Oil, Money, and Decolonization in South Asia'.

42 On alternative comparisons between India and China at this same time, cast through imagined projections of self-sufficient village communities, see: Yasser Nasser, 'Asia as a Third Way? J.C. Kumarappa and the Problem of Development in Asia', in *The Lives of Cold War Afro-Asianism*, ed. Su Lin Lewis and Carolien Stolte (Amsterdam: University of Amsterdam Press, 2022).

43 JNMML, Individual Collections, K.D. Malaviya Private Papers, Subject File 30., Malaviya to Jawaharlal Nehru, 6 October 1962.

44 Ibid.

45 Tim Mitchell, *Carbon Democracy: Political Power in the Age of Oil* (New York: Verso, 2011), Laleh Khalili, *Sinews of War and Trade: Shipping and Capitalism in the Arabian Peninsula* (New York: Verso, 2020).

46 London Metropolitan Archive (LMA), Rivers Steam Navigation Company, Ltd., Inchcape Group, Private Papers, 'Jagannathganj Strike – Bengal Mariners Union', Ms 28 063/1.

47 LMA, Rivers Steam Navigation Company, Ltd., Inchcape Group, Private Papers Telegram, Indian Tea Association, 10 October 1952, MS 28 063/1.

48 LMA, Rivers Steam Navigation Company, Ltd., Inchcape Group, Private Papers Circular, Labour Commissioner, Government of East Pakistan, 10 October 1952, MS 28 063/1.

49 LMA, Rivers Steam Navigation Company, Ltd., Inchcape Group, Private Papers Letter to Sri R.K. Ramdhyani, Secretary, Ministry of Scientific Research and Natural Resources, 4 January 1957, Bulk Oil Carriage.

50 British Petroleum Archives (BP), Ref 131546, G Richmond to R.P. Smith, Private and Confidential, 6 April 1959, Minutes and Correspondence – India Oil Policy, Burmah Oil Company Limited, 1954–1959.

51 Coronil, *The Magical State: Oil, Money, and Modernity in Venezuela* (Chicago: University of Chicago Press, 1997), 4.

52 Paul Brass, 'The Political Uses of Crisis: The Bihar Famine of 1966–67', *Journal of Asian Studies* 45, no. 2 (1986): 245–67.

53 National Archives of the United Kingdom, Foreign Office Bihar – Political Situation Internal, 133/191. 'Restricted – 10 June 1970'.

54 On the oscillating patterns of Indian liberalization prior to the vaunted 1990s reforms, see: Vijay Joshi and I. M. D. Little, *India: Macroeconomics and Political Economy, 1964–1991* (Washington D.C.: The World Bank, 1994).

55 World Bank Economic Mission, *Report to the President of the International Bank for Reconstruction and Development and the International Development Association on India's Economic Development Effort,* Volume One, Main Report, 1 October 1965.
56 Engerman, *The Price of Aid*, 248–52; David B. H. Denoon, 'Cycles in Indian Economic Liberalization, 1966–1996', *Comparative Politics* 31, no. 1 (1998): 43–60; C. Subramaniam, *The New Strategy in Indian Agriculture* (New Delhi: Vikas Press, 1979).
57 Lyle P. Schertz, 'World Food Prices and the Poor', *Foreign Affairs* 52, no. 3 (1974): 522.
58 Lucas Chancel and Thomas Piketty, 'Indian Income Inequality, 1922–2015: From British Raj to Billionaire Raj?', *The Review of Income and Wealth* 65, no. 1 (2019): 33–62.
59 Jaffrelot and Anil, *India's First Dictatorship.*
60 Ibid., 103–7.
61 'Coal Sector Summary', World Bank Report, Number 3601-IN, *India: Coal Sector Report*, South Asia Programs Department, 14 September 1982.
62 World Bank Archives, Travel Briefs, India, 1976. Records of the President Robert S. McNamara, WB/IBRD/IDA 03 EXC-10-4540S, 'The Political Situation'.
63 Kishen Pattnaik, "Death of Non-Congressism," *Mankind* (April–May 1971), 28–32.
64 NMML, Individual Collections, B.K. Nehru Private Papers, B. K. Nehru correspondence with W. W. Rostow, Subj. File 10, 1984–1985.
65 Kalecki, 'The Intermediate Regimes' (1966); K. N. Raj, 'The Politics and Economics of Intermediate Regimes', *Economic and Political Weekly*; Malgorzata Mazurek, 'Polish Economists in Nehru's India: Making Science for the Third World in an Era of De-Stalinzation and Decolonization', *Slavic Review* 77, no. 3 (2018): 588–610.
66 Hamza Alavi, 'India and the Colonial Mode of Production', *Economic and Political Weekly.*

6

Socialism and the question of Third World development in the ideas of the Indonesian Socialist Party (PSI)

Pradipto Niwandhono

Socialism was a central component of almost all Indonesian political currents in the post-colonial era, although with various interpretations.[1] The Indonesian people generally claimed to be a communal society, reject individualism as an alien principle, and identify capitalism with colonialism. However, the evolution of socialist ideas in Indonesia or the Third World differed from their development in Europe, which was based on industrial capitalism. With society and the economy largely in the pre-capitalist stage, socialism had an important impact in two forms: *first*, as an idea that inspired liberation from colonial exploitation, and *second*, as a stimulus for modernization, economic planning or development in general. In this respect, the Indonesian Socialist Party (PSI) and its intellectuals saw modernization as a continuation of national liberation, namely as a social transformation of Indonesian society towards a democratic and egalitarian order. The history of the PSI, Sutan Sjahrir (1909–66), and his networks of followers is well known in Indonesian political discourse, and a subject that is poorly understood at the same time, especially as part of the intellectual history of socialism. It still occupies a marginal position amidst the proliferation of Western scholarship on Asian Marxism and communism.[2]

Generally speaking, the PSI's ideological development was influenced by three streams of democratic socialist-related thought, namely continental European social democracy, British Fabian socialism and Asian socialist internationalism in the 1950s. European social democracy was an ideological stream with a strong influence on working-class movements and Dutch East Indies colonial reform, particularly during the Ethical Policy era. Meanwhile, Fabian socialism in England represented a kind of socialism emphasized by the role of intellectuals-technocrats and planned economic policies as a form of 'socialism from above'. It was implemented by a gradual reform to improve social welfare by avoiding class conflicts.[3] While Sjahrir was mostly influenced by mainland European socialism, then the influences of Fabianism were represented by two other PSI intellectuals, Soedjatmoko (1922–89) and economist

Sumitro Djojohadikusumo (1917–2001). In principle, Indonesian socialism was far from a single and unified ideology, but rather a sum of multiple influences and interpretations by its figures in post-colonial Indonesia.

Sjahrir, European socialism and national liberation

Sjahrir, along with Mohammad Hatta, belonged to the earliest generation of Indonesian socialist intellectuals forged by a transnational anti-colonial struggle. The greatest influence on the ideas of early Indonesian democratic socialism came from Dutch and Western European socialism, as well as from the League Against Imperialism movement between 1925 and 1933 which was supported by, and later dominated by the Third International, or the Comintern.[4] The rejection of both Stalinist communism and conservative Dutch social democrats eventually defined the ideological orientation of Indonesian democratic socialism espoused by Hatta, Sjahrir and their followers in the study club of Indonesian National Education, also called PNI-Pendidikan (PNI-Education), or PNI-Baru (New-PNI) and the Indonesian Socialist Party.

In the Netherlands, the Social Democratic Labor Party (SDAP), formed in 1894, played a central role in Dutch colonial reform, particularly its ethical and social welfare policies. The SDAP's official views on colonial affairs were represented by the arguments of Henri van Kol at the Second International Congress in 1907. Van Kol argued that the mission of socialists in colonial states, which according to Marx represented societies with 'Asiatic modes of production',[5] was to pave the way to full capitalism before a socialist order could be established. This was done by supporting progressive politics and reducing the excessive exploitation of colonial rule.[6] On the other hand, for the German socialist Karl Kautsky, considering that the new European imperialism was synonymous with the growth of industrial capitalism, it needed the 'backward' non-European peripheries as fields for investment, which could mean nothing but conquest and exploitation.[7] Support for socialist colonial politics – or 'social imperialism' – was common among both revisionists and Fabians, while orthodox Marxists firmly repudiate it.

Criticism on SDAP continued in the late 1920s, for instance in polemics between Hatta and J. A. Stokvis. Following the policy of the Second International, Stokvis defended the continuity of colonial relation, its role in ripening the stage towards socialism and preparing for independent, or autonomous status only when the colony has attained maturity in the international relations.[8] Differences on similar colonial issues led to the separation of the Dutch Social Democratic Student Club – which Sjahrir joined in the early 1930s – from the mainstream Dutch socialist movement. Some of its figures, such as Salomon Tas and Jacques de Kadt later formed the Independent Socialist Party (*Onafhankelijke Socialistische Partij*, OSP) from 1932 to 1934, while Sjahrir who returned to the Indies in December 1931, joined the Indonesian National Education club or the New-PNI. The principal objective of the New-PNI which became the central character of the study club formed by Sjahrir was to cultivate a 'rational-hygiene', a clear reasoning of the national liberation movement, especially those with a socialist-Marxist orientation, and to draw a clear distinction from the political irrationality of the more traditional-oriented nationalists.[9] The roots of the problem came from two sources: *first*, political conservatism among colonial scholars, and *second*, Eastern cultural revivalism and/or nationalism and its various derivations. These two factors were intertwined. In colonial policy, there were some trends derived from orientalist perspective: the preservation of Eastern 'otherness', with the basic assumption that most native peoples cannot be governed based on Western democratic principles instead of the deeply rooted collectivist traditions, and only its middle-class segment could be modernized. A similar view was reflected in Boeke's 'dual economy' theory which was a problem in the development of former colonial states in general.[10]

A different stance between the Hatta-Sjahrir camp and the Sukarno camp was reflected in the difference of their attitudes towards nationalism and Marxist socialism. Both Sjahrir and Sukarno used the class theory of Marxism in a looser and more instrumental manner; for Sukarno, Marhaenism as 'Marxism applied in Indonesia' was aimed for national unity and liberation of the colonized people as a representative of the oppressed class. While for Sjahrir, Marxism provided a theoretical foundation for the struggle for liberation from exploitations towards an equal, democratic society. National unity is only a means for the emancipation of humankind, which cannot be carried out by merely revolutionary actions, but through political education that will keep all forms of obscurantism away. For Sjahrir, Javanese aristocratic culture or the so-called Eastern philosophical wisdom, celebrated by cultural nationalists and many European orientalists was a sort of worldview akin to medieval feudalism. Adopting the Nietzschean perspective, Sjahrir viewed the principle of self-annihilation embodied in Hindu-Javanese mystical terms as a kind of 'slave morality' that transformed the state of powerlessness into the highest virtue.[11] In his pamphlet '*Perdjoeangan Kita*' (Our Struggle) in November 1945, Sjahrir exclaimed that the aim of the revolution was not limited to achieving national independence, but also to establish democracy by eliminating the feudal mentality especially the habit of being submissive to superiors, or leaders. Even while he was thinking in a Marxist way by advocating the establishment of a vanguard party, Sjahrir's critique was somewhat different from that of the leftists in general. If the orthodox Marxist-Leninist put forward a political economy framework in colonial or feudal exploitation, then for Sjahrir and his followers this exploitation was preserved through mental-cultural constructions.

As a political manifesto, '*Perdjoeangan Kita*' has an important meaning as a call for the formation of the Socialist Party, which was supported by some activists of the anti-fascist movement. In February 1948, the party was split into Amir Sjarifuddin's communist and Sjahrir's socialist factions, in which the latter named their party as the Indonesian Socialist Party (PSI). The '*Perjuangan Kita*' also contained an international political view that provided as a basis for diplomatic efforts to win an official recognition of the sovereignty of Indonesian nation-state from both Western and Asian countries. We could see, then, the internationalist roots of Sjahrir's democratic socialism, that was moving between the activism of the 'Third World,' or Afro-Asian post-colonial nations and the international anti-communism sponsored by the United States.

Arguably the most significant manifestation of PSI's international political stance was its participation in the forum of Asian Socialist Conference (ASC) between

1952 and 1960. The first ASC meeting in January 1953 discussed several core issues of the democratic socialist movement in Asia: Afro-Asian decolonization, inequality between industrial countries and underdeveloped post-colonial states, as well as global political bipolarity due to the Cold War.[12] However, affirming neutrality and distance towards the West while most of Asian former colonial countries were in need of support for economic growth and nation-state development was one of the most complex issues.[13] The relation with the European-based Socialist International (SI) was hindered by SI's conservatism in addressing decolonization and fears that a Third World solidarity would more easily influenced by communism.[14] Sjahrir argued that one of the main problems of Third World socialism was its emergence as an integral part of anti-colonial nationalism, which in its extreme manifestation could lead to 'totalitarianism and disaster'. Nevertheless, even Marxism-Leninism, which according to him, contained more political rationality, under Stalin's regime had degenerated into a kind of quasi-socialism which subordinated worker's internationalism as a servant to Soviet Russian imperialistic nationalism.[15]

During his chairmanship of the PSI, Sjahrir wrote treatises to emphasize the stance of Indonesian democratic socialists towards various aspects of Marxism-Leninism, and polemics against the Indonesian Communist Party (PKI) in particular.[16] This was a consequence of the resolution of the first PSI congress in February 1952 which abolished Marxism as the official party ideology and reduced it to a mere framework of social analysis. By taking references from Bernstein's revisionism, as well as from Marxist theorists of imperialism such as Rudolf Hilferding or Rosa Luxemburg, Sjahrir identified a number of errors in Marx's predictions. These concerned, first, the impoverishment (*verelendung*) of the workers that exacerbated class conflict, and second, the final crisis situation that will cause the collapse of capitalism.

In fact, the economic conditions of the working-class tended to improve due to the surplus capital obtained from the colonial territories, so that the workers succeeded to rise themselves as skilled workers, or managers. In other words, there had been a sort of 'embourgeoisiement' of the working-class movement which Lenin called as 'labour aristocracy'.[17] This process led to changes in the functioning of the state in Europe during the early twentieth century, particularly during the Great Depression, when the welfare state model was widely adopted in Western Europe and Scandinavia. As a result, the labour movement had inclined to become more pro-capitalist since the European welfare states had been able to work towards improving labour conditions, even though society as a whole had not moved away from the capitalist mode of production. Sjahrir argued that the changing nature of global capitalism since the Great Depression had changed the socialist movement as a whole. Henceforth, the majority of the Third World people tended to support welfare systems and economic planning by the state rather than market-based free competition. If the state was unable to do so, they will soon be taken over by the communists as happened in post-Second World War China.[18]

The ideas of Sjahrir were consistently characterized by anti-totalitarianism which was not only targeted at international communism under Stalin or Mao Zedong of China, but also towards the potential for military domination in developing countries, which was used as a tool in anti-communist campaigns. The PKI versus PSI antagonism culminated in the PRRI/Permesta revolts and thereafter which resulted in the dissolution of the party by Sukarno's Guided Democracy regime and the arrest of its figures, including Sjahrir.[19] In addition, Sjahrir's ideological emphasis on socialism as a humanitarian struggle, more or less affecting intellectual-cultural activism in a number of study groups or cultural movement such as *Poedjangga Baroe* (New Poet) and *Kritiek en Opbouw* (Criticism and Construction).[20] This groups evolved into a kind of cultural wing of Indonesian democratic socialism. They espoused an artistic cosmopolitanism, an anti-ideologization of arts, and at one point became part of a global anti-communism campaign. These phenomena, which later led to depoliticization of Indonesian cultural activism after the events of 1965, have implications that go in line with the creation of a politically stable developmental state governed by Western scientific principles.[21]

Fabian socialism and Asian development

In his classic study, Herbert Feith that the ideology of PSI contained 'more elements of Fabianism than Marxism'.[22] The Fabians' main objective was to strengthen the role of intellectuals in directing a country's political economy towards socialism. The Fabian Society, established in January 1884 was a think-tank organization that promoted evolutionary and gradual social(ist) reform based on scientific inquiries, with deep roots in the professional middle-class. Its influence could be traced back into the 1930s, mostly for Indonesian socialists who were associated with the bureaucratic or technocratic spheres, including individuals such as Amir Sjarifuddin, particularly during his short-term career in the Indies Department of Economic Affairs,[23] Sumitro Djojohadikusumo and to a lesser extent Mohammad Hatta. To some extent, Hatta's concept of economic democracy was inspired by the guild socialism of George Douglas Howard Cole, as well as the Owenite cooperative movement. To some extent, Hatta got the inspiration for his concept of economic democracy from the guild socialism of George Douglas Howard Cole, as well as Owenite cooperative movement. He wrote an article on guild socialist movement in the New-PNI's newspaper *Daulat Ra'jat*.[24] Unlike in the most of former British colonies, the influence of Fabian socialism in Indonesia was indirect and was interpreted through the ideas of Indonesian socialist intellectuals.

Guild socialism was a communitarian movement inspired by the model of medieval guilds to modern working-class communities.[25] Cole argued that a sort of industrial democracy, and the transfer of economic control from capitalists to workers and craftsmen, should come about through the medium of national guilds. The restoration of the guild system implied some basic features of the movement including the emphasis of creative labour as the primary objective of social transformation, the rejection of state collectivism – as upheld by the Fabians – and the decentralization of economic power with the key role given to trade unions.[26] Nevertheless, the main connecting link between Fabianism and Asian post-colonial development lies in the presence of the London School of Economics (LSE), which produced some of the most important economic thinkers in the field of development theory.

As their social democratic counterparts in continental Europe, the Fabians' impact on imperial policy and colonies' development cannot be overlooked. Since the turn of the century the socialist think-tank has become closely associated with debates around social imperialism, a term referring to social reforms relying on imperial development abroad.[27] The relatively decentralized political institutions and socio-economic maturity of England prevented the country from taking the Marxian revolutionary path to socialism, instead of carrying out gradual reforms. In respect to colonial questions during the Boer War era (1899–1902), the Fabians, divided between a minority faction led by Ramsay MacDonald, which argued that Britain must educate [colonized] people towards self-rule, while the majority represented by Sidney Webb or George Bernard Shaw advocated for the more centralized, technocratic-based control of the British Empire.[28] The strong desire towards social reform and planning rather than reinforcement of class consciousness among European democratic socialist currents goes hand in hand with the need to win the support of the working-class for the national and imperial interests of the European countries. It exerted strong influences among British former colonial states and commonwealth as in British India and Malaya. In India, the impact of Fabian principles was more visible in a pragmatic sense, as the private sector also contributed in industrialization while the economy was being transformed into one dominated by public sector, along with Soviet-type five-year economic plan.[29]

Two of the Fabian and LSE-connection figures made most impact in the developmental thought among Indonesian socialists were Harold Joseph Laski (1893–1950) and the African-descent William Arthur Lewis (1915–91), who both an influence on Sumitro. Living in North America during the First World War, Harold Laski was initially interested in US progressive politics – he was an admirer of Roosevelt's New Deal – and arguably influenced by pragmatist thinker John Dewey. In 1920, Laski returned to England after having accepted a position at the London School of Economics. Since 1926 onwards, he was increasingly attracted to more leftist, Marxian thoughts in response to critical situation induced by the economic crises, fascism and war, in which he blamed capitalism as the main cause. An international peace, therefore, was likely to be established under socialism, and Laski once predicted that Soviet Russia's transformation under Stalinist dictatorship was only a temporary stage that led to liberation.[30] As a Labour Party supporter and intellectual-activist, Laski remained critical during Clement Attlee's reign (1945–51) and argued that the government should prioritize socialist reform over its international manoeuvres.[31]

The other influential figure was the African-Caribbean economist Arthur Lewis based at the LSE since 1940. Lewis researched and advised various government ministries on colonial economics and development from 1942 to 1951.[32] In London, Lewis came into contact with left-wing socialist and pan-Africanist activism that made him critical to the Fabians' top-down technocratic orientation. In 1939 the Fabian Society published a pamphlet by Lewis on labour protests that spread across the West Indies, in which he proposed a strategy to alleviate poverty and reduce unemployment by social welfare measures and intensified industrialization. He was also critical to racial prejudices among colonial scholars and policymakers which had been a barrier to development 'from below'.[33]

While he mostly worked for the needs of colonial reform during and after the wartime, Lewis' developmental economics was influential among the Third World intellectuals. Mohammad Hatta in his pamphlet, '*Ekonomi Terpimpin*' (Guided Economy) in 1960 cited Lewis's views on underdeveloped regions whose people possessed almost no capital savings, justifying an increased role by government. 'Planning in backward countries imposes much bigger tasks on government than does planning in advanced countries [which is left to the entrepreneurs]. It has to create industrial centres to put through an agricultural revolution, to control the foreign exchange more strictly, and to make up a great leeway of public services and of ordinary economic legislation.'[34] Lewis's ideas on industrialization and the role of the state in post-colonial economic planning, specifically impacted Sumitro's ideas and policies within his developmental plan in the 1950s and beyond.

Sumitro's technocracy and economic planning

The term 'technocracy' was coined after the First World War to describe the rule over society by the people with technical competence or expertise.[35] Its origin was inseparable from the Industrial Revolution and was specifically linked to the utopian socialist thought of Claude Henri de Saint-Simon. He argued that an egalitarian society could only be materialized through industrialization and state governance based on the principles of modern science.[36] A similar vision was shared by Fabian socialists such as Sidney Webb, who stated that governance should be a matter for the experts and 'the key word of political science is efficiency.'[37]

Theories concerning the role of technocratic intellectuals in a socialist state generally originated from Trotskyist circles as a criticism of Stalin's regime. The most important treatise was arguably the new class theory of the Yugoslav Marxist intellectual, Milovan Djilas. According to him, the bureaucratic class in communist states such as the Soviet Union had origins that 'were not subject to the communist party or the state apparatus but came from the revolutionary intellectuals as the core of the party itself before they came to power'. It was Lenin himself who gave birth to a new class as the basis for state capitalism or 'bureaucratic collectivism' during Stalin's time.[38] Meanwhile, James Burnham described the rise of a new bureaucratic-managerial class to replace the capitalists as a result of the economic crises and revolutions between two world wars. Ultimately, the Great Depression resulted in a sort of 'statist turn' in global scene. Likewise, the US Marshall Plan project to fund the postwar economic development had a more significant impact on the application of planned economy, including in former colonial countries.

In Indonesia, the key figure for economic planning based on this scheme was Sumitro Djojohadikusumo, who as a member of Sjahrir's group together with Soedjatmoko played an important role in diplomatic lobbies in the United States and Europe during the revolution. He was a theorist of Keynesian-oriented developmental economics, which had almost no connection to democratic socialism outside of his career as a PSI politician. As the son of a Javanese aristocrat, R. M. Margono Djojohadikusumo, who was also an activist of the cooperative movement of the Great Indonesia Party

(Partai Indonesia Raya, Parindra), Sumitro was initially more interested in efforts to improve the social welfare of the native people during the 1930's Great Depression. It became the theme of his dissertation at the University of Rotterdam, the Netherlands, entitled '*Het Volkscredietwezen in de Depressie*' (People's credit in the Depression era) which he completed in 1943.[39] At the time, Parindra was a Javanese aristocratic-based party which had considerable attention to improve welfare, and by using the Japanese as main reference, it sought to develop the society by integrating Eastern tradition and Western modernity.[40] Sumitro criticized the colonial credit economic system, also recommended by Boeke, as a scheme to maintain the 'dual economy' and the economic position of rural communities at the subsistence level. Furthermore, he supported the cooperative system as a potential solution to elevate local farming and trading communities into self-employed entrepreneurs.[41]

In planning future economic development programmes, Sumitro was mainly concerned with overcoming the dualism of the colonial economy that became an inhibiting factor in the process of modernization. At the time, the Dutch academia were divided into the 'Leiden school' and the 'Rotterdam school'. The first one consisted of orientalists who supported a sort of cultural determinism, while the second group prioritizes purely economic factors in development planning. According to Leiden Indologists, traditional societies lacked the innate potential for socio-economic progress. This opinion was contested by Sumitro as having no empirical basis from an economic point of view.[42] Furthermore, the polemic between Sumitro and the supporters of the dualism theory led to his increasing distrust on colonial scholarship, which in turn brought him closer to the views of American development experts as well as Fabian socialists in England, such as Harold Laski of the London School of Economics (LSE), which he once attended lectures as student.[43] This was reinforced during his diplomatic mission in the United States between 1947 and 1949. His criticism towards the conservatism of the Dutch was also seen at the Round Table Conference (Konferensi Meja Bundar, KMB). Sumitro refused to impose foreign debt of the Republic of the United States of Indonesia (Republik Indonesia Serikat, RIS), the successor state of the Netherlands Indies, as a condition for transferring sovereignty.[44]

Sumitro's technocratic project and his collaboration with the American technical assistance mission took place during his tenures as Minister of Finance and Minister of Trade during the Natsir (1950–1), Wilopo (1952–3) and Burhanuddin Harahap (1955–6) cabinets. At the time, he was profoundly influenced by the development and modernization theories by William Arthur Lewis and Walt Whitman Rostow, and persistently supported the industrialization programme as a stimulus for social transformation and the most likely solution to moving away from the situation of dualism. If Rostow's modernization theory tended to be linear, overlooking the dual nature of the society, then Lewis' theory of industrialization was particularly consistent to Sumitro's views. According to Sumitro, the low productivity of the subsistence economy and the overpopulation of underdeveloped regions created an almost limitless supply of labour, a condition that appeared to be underemployment, which can only be overcome by channelling this employment potential into modern industrial sector.[45]

The Economic Urgency Plan or Sumitro Plan formulated in April 1951 focused on industry as a basis for strengthening Indigenous entrepreneurial sector and stimulating the growth of domestic capital. In addition, an Industrialisation Committee was established, which set three main goals for industrial development: a balanced economic structure, the absorption of a growing population into productive sectors, and an increase in national income.[46] One of the implications of the industrialization programme and Sumitro's efforts to develop the national entrepreneur-capitalist class was by launching the 'Benteng (fortress) Program', supported by nationalist parties and reached its peak during the first Ali Sastroamidjojo cabinet (1953–5). However, the programme ended up failing since the protection policy addressed to the interest of domestic middle-class entrepreneurial class, in fact was used by Chinese traders, big Indonesian businessmen or their political patrons.[47]

Sumitro's industrialization plan and the inefficiency of the Benteng Program which had several weaknesses were sharply criticized by a politician and economist from the modernist Islamic party of Masjumi, Sjafruddin Prawiranegara (1911–89). Unlike Sumitro, who was more oriented towards the United States or Britain, Sjafruddin was closer to Dutch economists and administrators.[48] He criticized Sumitro's industrialization for ignoring the fact that most Indonesian people have so far lived based on agriculture and subsistence sectors. Aside of considering the agricultural sector that should be put into priority, Sjafruddin advocated a gradual development model that emphasized the human factors (including religious-based moral values, and an enhanced technical expertise) rather than material factors before an accelerated industrialization programme could be implemented. The failure of the Benteng Program was largely due to a lack of technical-managerial expertise to support the rise of an Indigenous entrepreneurial class. In order to improve the Indonesian people's technical skills, the transfer of technology and economic growth, the government needed to license foreign private companies since state's control was limited to vital economic sectors.[49] In contrast, Sumitro considered that Sjafruddin's economic views were too conservative, because after all industrialization cannot completely replace the agrarian basis of Indonesian economy except as a balancing factor and a stimuli for growth.[50] Nevertheless, on some other issues both figures agreed, particularly dealing with the need to increase the level of expertise by involving technical and financial aids from Western countries.

After the the Second World War, the US technical and economic assistance programme targeting Third World countries directly spread the discourse of developmentalism and American scientific management. It was inseparable from the context of Cold War, in which the US campaign was characterized by two main points: first, an emphasis on the freedom as the principle of universal humanity, along with economic improvement and the creation of social welfare to prevent the spread of communism's influence.[51] In Indonesia, the provision of aid was carried out by focusing on economic development and the formation of a managerial class by involving a number of higher education institutions such as Massachusetts Institute of Technology (MIT), Cornell University and Yale University. One of the most important scientific research projects in supporting development in Indonesia was the Ford Foundation-MIT Project, chaired by Canadian economist Benjamin Higgins, and Rufus Hendon as field team leader. Between 1952 and 1958 the project produced several research in the fields of economics, sociology and anthropology, including some of Clifford Geertz's studies on the division of religious-cultural streams and the problem of involution in the rural economy of Java.[52] While MIT's focus was on economics and had closer connection to Sumitro and some development planning institutions, Cornell's Indonesian study project was more engaged in the socio-political and humanities field.

Eventually, the greatest legacy of Sumitro Djojohadikusumo lies not in his economic policy experiments in the 1950s – soon swept away by the wave of nationalization of foreign private assets – but in his technocratic projects involving two major powers: the United States and Indonesian Army's leadership. In 1956, as an economist and the founder of the Faculty of Economics at the University of Indonesia (UI), Sumitro sent his best students such as Widjojo Nitisastro, Mohammad Sadli and Emil Salim to the University of California, Berkeley.[53] He also brought in many experts from the United States to replace the Dutch colonial administrators. These UI-Berkeley graduated economists formed the core group of development thinkers at the National Development Planning Board (Bappenas) and President Suharto's team of economic advisers at the beginning of the New Order era. While living a period as one of the leading rebels and political exiles between 1957 and 1967, Sumitro established a network of technocrats who closely collaborated with the Army and the United States to plan a post-Sukarno development scheme.[54]

Even under Sukarno's Guided Democracy system, the state adopted a system of economic nationalism that drew on Sumitro's ideas. However, it was soon clear that this kind of nationalism became a battleground between the military's business interests and the communists. At the time, the PKI was the only political party in Indonesia that consistently opposed Western intervention, alongside the pro-Western technocrats or bureaucratic capitalism in general.[55] With the collapse of communism in Indonesia, the political development under the new regime was dominated by various groups that supported Western-style economic policies, namely the technocrats who supported a top-down approach and intellectual-activists who emphasized bottom-up initiatives and economic democracy as a pillar of development and social transformation. The last group, dominated by former PSI and Masjumi members, formed moderate opposition to the New Order government. The crackdown following the catastrophic 1974 student protests [*Malari*] ended the political activism of Indonesian democratic socialists, but not their intellectual tradition.

Indonesian human development according to Soedjatmoko

Soedjatmoko's contribution to the history of intellectuals in Indonesia, among other things, lies in the fact that he was one of the earliest figures who think about the role of public intellectuals in Third World countries as an independent class. Like Sumitro, he expressed few ideas within the framework of Marxian socialism. Nevertheless, in contrast to Sumitro, who was more state-centric, Soedjatmoko was someone who lived up to Sjahrir's ideals of socialism as human liberation, by focusing on individual intellectual freedom. Thus, while Soedjatmoko's role as a development thinker transcended all ideological affiliation, he was considered the ultimate role model for the PSI intellectual.

Soedjatmoko Mangundiningrat was born into a Javanese noble-bureaucratic family. Since he was a teenager, he had been interested in politics thanks to various readings of political thoughts and philosophy, especially after a traumatic experience during the Japanese occupation era that made him drop out of school. He often gathered with his colleagues from the medical school (*Ika Daigaku*), including Soebadio Sastrosatomo and Subandrio, also members of a study group formed by Sutan Sjahrir. Soedjatmoko's involvement in Sjahrir's group led him to be a diplomat, as well as a journalist and a critical thinker. Together with Rosihan Anwar, Soedjatmoko founded the official newspaper and magazine of the Indonesian Socialist Party, namely *Pedoman* (guidelines) and *Siasat* (strategy).[56]

In the period between 1947 and 1951, Soedjatmoko was assigned to the United States to raise support for Indonesia's decolonization both politically and economically. In December 1947 as a member of the Indonesian diplomatic team of experts, Soedjatmoko had warned his colleagues of the possibility of weakening Indonesia's bargaining position before the United Nations, which was dominated by the United States, given the strong anti-communist paranoia in that country. It especially targeted the Indonesian leftists. Too obvious a strengthening of socialist politics would provoke the United States to defend Dutch interests and seriously undermine the legitimacy of the Indonesians' right of self-determination on the international stage.[57] It was likely that Soedjatmoko's 'warning' accelerated the schism of Sjahrir's democratic socialist faction from their communist counterparts who later formed the People's Democratic Front (FDR) by the initiative of Amir Sjarifuddin. From America, Soedjatmoko travelled through Europe for nine months visiting several socialist-communist countries – including Yugoslavia – to see how far the impact of socialist ideology had on the process of socio-economic transformation of a country.[58] His observations during the trip seem to have given rise to distrust, and at the same time a distance towards various political ideologies.

Upon his return to Indonesia, Soedjatmoko started his career as socio-cultural thinker, and was loosely associated with the Gelanggang group, formed in 1946. Following international recognition of Indonesia's independence and sovereignty, artists affiliated with the PSI weekly journal, *Siasat*, declared themselves 'heirs to world culture' to affirm Indonesia's position among other nations and perceive Indonesian culture in continuous interaction with the outer world.[59] The cosmopolitan spirit of the Gelanggang group was revived by the journal *Konfrontasi* between 1954 and 1960. One of the initiators of this journal's publication was Soedjatmoko, an ardent supporter of modernization. Like his mentor and brother-in-law Sutan Sjahrir, he expressed sharp criticism of feudalism and nationalism which relied on traditional conservatism. In an article entitled, '*Mengapa Konfrontasi*' (Why, confrontation) in the inaugural edition of *Konfrontasi*, July–August 1954, Soedjatmoko revealed the potential for a crisis due to limitations in the nationalist perspective at that time in facing the challenges of post-colonial modernity. He advocated for 'creative adaptation' by exploring and renewing cultural sources or potentials that are uniquely Indonesian to respond to the changing era.[60]

In the second edition of *Konfrontasi*, Soedjatmoko wrote an article entitled 'Economic Development as a Cultural Problem'. In the article, he showed how development was a matter of transforming society, which was more determined by non-economic factors. Soedjatmoko mentioned two important issues as inhibiting factors. First, the lack of attention of politicians to development issues, except as a mere political commodity. Second, too much emphasis on collectivism as a force of development, as in the cooperative movement. Overall, he saw the potential problems in Asian nationalism, namely anti-industrialism, and the implications of anti-capitalism in the anti-colonial struggle, as ideological obstacles to development. For instance, Gandhi's promotion of a conservative form of economic independence (*swadeshi*) and its rejection of Western industry would create unlimited demand and dependence on machines. However, many of these doctrines had been abandoned by the Indian government under the leadership of Jawaharlal Nehru, a modernist nationalist and adherent of Fabian-style democratic socialism.[61]

However, the experience of being involved in politics had changed Soedjatmoko's views on the relation between tradition and modernization. Following the general election of 1955, Soedjatmoko joined the PSI to be nominated as the party's representative in the Constituent Assembly.[62] At the time, the PSI was a minor political party, and its electoral failure at least prompted Soedjatmoko to rethink the nature of Indonesian politics and its relation to post-independence sociocultural transformation. Soedjatmoko admitted that anti-colonial roots of Indonesia's party tradition made them nearly identical – they use a similar 'socialist' or 'nationalist' rhetoric. In fact, at that time, very few Indonesian people were aware of politics. The success of political parties in mobilizing mass support was almost entirely determined by traditional authorities and local charismatic figures. Given that Indonesian agrarian society was undergoing a revolutionary transition towards an independent state, this resulted in the disintegration of the feudal order and the mobilization of the peasant class against the old elites. While the nationalist and Islamic parties were able to use traditional elites to their interests, and the PKI to use new revolutionary forces, the PSI seemed unlikely to take advantage of this opportunity.[63] Furthermore, Soedjatmoko argued that political parties in Indonesia only have limited effective power due to following situations: *First*, Indonesian politics in the 1950s was relatively decentralized. *Second*, the lack of efficiency in the party organization. *Third*, cultural factors in which most decision-making is based on deliberation and consensus; hence it will take a longer time. Under these conditions, Soedjatmoko calculated the possibility of having extra parliamentary power – the president or the army – that would take more political initiatives.[64]

Experiences in the 1955 elections as well as a constituent assembly member and representative of the PSI between 1956 and 1959 had changed Soedjatmoko's ideological orientation from a radical modernizer to closer to a nationalist position. Even though the PSI and democratic socialists were major exponents of a multi-party system, they increasingly expressed criticism against the party system of parliamentary democracy. In a condition that the party was marginalized due to the involvement of some of its cadres in regional insurrections, Soedjatmoko was one of the few PSI figures who were able to escape persecution, partly because of his close relations to Sukarno and his foreign minister, Subandrio.

The political constellation of Guided Democracy in the form of the 'power triangle' of Sukarno – PKI – The Army did not escape the attention of Sjahrir and Soedjatmoko.[65] For Sjahrir, a nationalist government under Sukarno's rule was still better than a regime controlled by the military or communists. In addition, the implementation of the Guided Democracy system was actually the biggest obstacle for the PKI to come to power – as they would almost the first communist party to succeed in seizing power in a democratic and non-revolutionary way.[66] Even under house arrest, Sjahrir advised Soedjatmoko that he and other PSI figures would continue to contribute and assist Sukarno's government when needed. Soedjatmoko's long-standing connection to Subandrio made this possible, and in March 1963 Soedjatmoko was involved in drafting an economic recovery plan in response to an IMF economic aid offering, which became known as the Economic Declaration (Deklarasi Ekonomi, or Dekon). This new policy sought to find a middle ground between economic nationalism and integration with global market to stimulate growth.[67] Although this policy later fell apart due to the politics of confrontation against Malaysia, at least it managed to establish a technocratic role of PSI intellectuals within the government, which would continue during the New Order era.

Another major impact on Soedjatmoko's thoughts was his participation in the development of social sciences and humanities, particularly in his association with Cornell Modern Indonesian Project under George Kahin.[68] It started with the first seminar of history in December 1957 and continued when he became a guest lecturer at Cornell University between 1961 and 1962. In the seminar that was organized to formulate a concept of national history apart from colonial scholarship tradition, a fierce debate ensued between Mohammad Yamin and Soedjatmoko. While Yamin supported the formulation of a nationalistic philosophy of history which situated Indonesian nation-state as a continuation of the ancient civilization of the archipelago, Soedjatmoko defended the independence of historiography, as well as history as a scientific discipline, to be free from any ideological content. His intellectual commitment was later manifested in a collaborative project with Cornell published as '*An Introduction to Indonesian Historiography*' (1965), in which he wrote an article entitled 'The Indonesian Historian and His Time'. Soedjatmoko insisted that the main obstacle to the construction of national history or the decolonization of Indonesian history was its 'ahistorical' elements. While nationalism, on one side, has been a driving force for modernization, it did not break off from its agrarian cultural roots. In fact, it often revitalizes elements of tradition in the name of anticolonialism and/or anti-Westernism. Then Marxism itself, as the most rational aspect of anti-colonialism, still adhered to a philosophy of deterministic historical progress. According to Soedjatmoko, the solution lies in studying history using a critical method, which emphasizing the mentality and cultural-political aspects of Indonesian societal development.[69]

One of the writings that represented Soedjatmoko's views more comprehensively on culture and religion in Indonesia was '*Indonesia: Problems and Opportunities*' (1967). It was a reflection on the failure of Sukarno's Guided Democracy as well as a reassessment of how Indonesian political elites used traditional institutions and symbolism for modern purposes. Inspired by studies by Clifford Geertz and Herbert Feith, Soedjatmoko categorized Indonesia's political tradition in two variants: Javanese – *priyayi* and *abangan,* and Islamic. While some aspects of this Javanese tradition could be transformed into modernity by incorporating Marxist elements of the anticolonial struggle, then Islam had more troubles in relation to secular modernism due to its exclusive character as a legalist religion. These characters often evoke a 'fundamentalist' reaction when confronting external pressures.

Soedjatmoko's writing on intellectuals was one of his great contributions. Intellectuals refer to the educated class or intelligentsia with a vanguard role; they are mostly distinguished from ordinary disciplinary academics by their broad range of thinking and active involvement in moral and political matters. The role of 'Third World' intellectuals as modernizers has been discussed by sociologist Edward Shils,[70] which commented by an article of Soedjatmoko titled '*Peranan Intelektual di Negara Sedang Berkembang*' (the role of the intellectulas in developing countries, 1970). Soedjatmoko insisted how the role of intellectual-modernizers contained a dillematic position between being more politically involved but at the expense of their original idealism, or surviving and being alienated among conflicting values in the society. On the other hand, many of the people from former colonized countries were only ready to accept a unifying leadership and were not accustomed to the more critical political tradition. Hence, intellectuals in developing countries must excercise restraint in pursuing their ideals, and every stage of modernization should take into account and utilize the inherent irrational elements in the processes of forming and liberating of a nation.[71]

Concluding remarks

Indonesian democratic socialism was intertwined and profoundly influenced by various Asian internationalist movements, both in terms of Third World solidarity and socialist internationalism. As a fighter for Indonesian national liberation, Sjahrir had strong ties to the independent wing of Dutch social democratic movement. However, the experience of political repression and anti-fascism struggle altered Sjahrir's orientation towards a more pragmatic one. His diplomatic career during the revolutionary years, and his conviction that Western hegemony would still determine the fate of post-colonial states, led him to advocate a sort of socialist planning system within a capitalist economic framework.

This new orientation brought socialist party's leading intellectuals as Soedjatmoko, and particularly Sumitro, towards political economic thinking influenced by British Fabians. This would also allow them to mediate between Western interests in the Cold War, while also seeking to maintain independence among developing Third World nations. Issues regarding the position of intellectuals in response to sociocultural transformation in developing nations seemed to be of more concern to Soedjatmoko than to the technocratic Sumitro. Unfortunately, the independent role of socialist intellectuals faded along with the rise of New Order developmental state which depoliticized most aspirations of civil society in Indonesia.

Notes

1 Jeanne Mintz mentioned three ideological sources of socialism in Indonesia, namely the Indigenous spirit of communalism, the Islamic concept of social justice, and Western class struggle-based socialism, mostly Marxism. See Jeanne S. Mintz, *Mohammed, Marx, Marhaen: The Roots of Socialism in Indonesia* (London/Dunmow: Pall Mall Press, 1965).

2 Exceptions include Robert J. Myers, *The Development of Indonesian Socialist Party* (PhD Thesis, Chicago, Illinois, USA: University of Chicago, 1959); Mintz, *Mohammed, Marx, Marhaen*; J. D. Legge, *Intellectuals and Nationalism in Indonesia: A Study of the Following Recruited by Sutan Sjahrir in Occupation Jakarta* (New York: Cornell Modern Indonesia Project, 1988), and Rudolf Mrazek, *Sjahrir: Politics and Exile in Indonesia* (Ithaca/New York: Cornell Modern Indonesia Project, 1994).

3 On Fabianism and Fabian Society and aspects of the political economy of democratic socialism in Britain in general, see Noel Thompson, *Political Economy and the Labour Party: The Economics of Democratic Socialism 1884–2005* (London/New York: Routledge, 2005). For the more general historical account, see Margaret Cole, *The Story of Fabian Socialism* (Stanford: Stanford University Press, 1961).

4 For the recent study of the anticolonial league see Fredrik Petersson, 'We Neither Visionaries nor Utopian Dreamer: Willi Munzerberg, the League Against Imperialism, and the Comintern, 1925–1933 (Doctoral thesis, Turko, Finland: Abo Akademi University, 2013).

5 The socio-economic condition of precapitalist society is characterized by the absence of personal ownership of land, autonomous rural communities, and the emergence of a despotic state with centralized power. The term 'Asiatic modes of production' was never clearly defined by Marx himself, except in a few segments from the *Grundrisse* (1857–8), and the third volume of *Das Capital.*

6 On the debate at the Stuttgart Congress see Ruth T. McVey, *The Rise of Indonesian Communism* (Singapore: Equinox Publishing, 2008), 4–5.

7 Richard B. Day and Daniel Gaido (eds.), *Discovering Imperialism: Social Democracy to World War I* (Leiden/Boston: Brill, 2012), 26–7.

8 On argumentations between Hatta and Stokvis after the former's arrest as a member of the League Against Imperialism see Harry A. Poeze, *Di Negeri Penjajah: Orang Indonesia di Negeri Belanda 1600–1950* (Jakarta: KITLV/Kepustakaan Populer Gramedia, 2008), 215–17.

9 The term 'rational hygiene' or clarity of reason is taken from the writing of Sal Tas, 'Souvenirs of Sjahrir', *Indonesia*, no. 8 (1969): 153.

10 Regarding J. H. Boeke and his dissertation in 1910 (updated in 1953), 'Economics and Economic Policy of Dual Societies as Exemplified in Indonesia', see Hanneman Samuel, *Genealogi Kekuasaan Ilmu Sosial Indonesia* (Depok: Kepik Ungu, 2010).

11 Sutan Sjahrir, *Renungan Indonesia* (Yogyakarta: Bakung Putih, 2019), 173–4.

12 There were several recent studies on Asian Socialist Conference, including Titia van de Zande, *A Third World Concept: The Asian Socialist Conference, Ideologies of Neutrality and Anti-Imperialism in the laboratory of the 1950s* (Leiden: Master Thesis University of Leiden, 2017); Su Lin Lewis, 'Asian Socialism and the Forgotten Architects of Post-Colonial Freedom', *Journal of World History* 30, no. 1–2 (June 2019): 55–88.

13 Van der Zande, *A Third World Concept*, 41–2.

14 For further discussion on the relation between Asian and European socialist internationalism, see Talbot C. Imlay, *The Practice of Socialist Internationalism: European Socialists and International Politics 1914–1960* (Oxford: Oxford University Press, 2018), 422–9.
15 Sutan Sjahrir, 'Nationalism and Internationalism', speech delivered at the first Asian Socialist Conference, January 1953, in *Indonesian Political Thinking, 1945–1965*, ed. Herbert Feith and Lance Castles (Ithaca: Cornell University Press, 1970), 235–6.
16 See Sutan Sjahrir, *Sosialisme Indonesia, Pembangunan* (Jakarta: Lembaga Penunjang Pembangunan Nasional, 1982).
17 Regarding the concept and debate about the labour aristocracy, see Anthony Brewer, *Marxist Theories of Imperialism* (London/New York: Routledge, 1990).
18 For a complete discussion of the 'missed' predictions of the Marxists according to the democratic socialists' point of view, see Sutan Sjahrir, *Sosialisme dan Marxisme: Suatu Kritik terhadap Marxisme* (Jakarta: Penerbit Djambatan, 1967).
19 About PRRI/Permesta and various intrigues surrounding US efforts to make the insurrection part of anti-communist campaign in Southeast Asia, see George McTurnan Kahin dan Audrey R Kahin, *Subversi Sebagai Politik Luar Negeri: Menyingkap Keterlibatan CIA di Indonesia* (Jakarta: Pustaka Utama Grafiti, 1997).
20 Regarding intellectual-cultural activism around Sjahrir, which also involved several socialist figures including Amir Sjarifuddin, Marcel Koch, and J. de Kadt, see Mrazek, *Sjahrir: Politics and Exile in Indonesia*, 160–3.
21 This anti-communist intellectual activism was mostly associated with the existence of Congress for Cultural Freedom (CCF) forum funded by the US intelligence agency, the CIA. Further study of the institution, see Gilles Scott-Smith, *The Politics of Apolitical Culture: The Congress of Cultural Freedom, the CIA, and the Post-War American Hegemony* (London/New York: Routledge, 2002).
22 Herbert Feith, *The Decline of Constitutional Democracy in Indonesia* (Jakarta: Equinox Publishing, 2007), 130.
23 Amir Sjarifuddin, the second prime minister of the Republic of Indonesia (1947–8) was a leading left-wing nationalist figure before the war. In 1940, shortly after the Nazi occupation of the Netherlands, he was arrested on charges of being a member of an underground communist plot. See Gerry van Klinken, *Lima Penggerak Bangsa Yang Terlupa: Nasionalisme Minoritas Kristen* (Yogyakarta: LKiS, 2010), 200–1.
24 Mohammad Hatta, 'Gilden Socialisme', *Daulat Ra'jat* 4, no. 87 (10 February 1934), quoted in Mrazek, *Sjahrir: Politics and Exile in Indonesia*, 74.
25 Matt Beech and Kevin Hickson, *Labour's Thinkers: The Intellectual Roots of Labour from Tawney to Gordon Brown* (London/New York: Tauris Academic Studies, 2007), 31–40.
26 Thompson, *Political Economy and the Labour Party*, 33.
27 For discussion on social imperialism, see Geoff Elley, 'Social Imperialism: Use and Abuse of an Idea', *Social History* 1, no. 3 (October 1976): 265–90.
28 See also an article on Max Beer, 'Social Imperialism' (September 1901) in *Discovering Imperialism: Social Democracy to World War I*, ed. Richard B. Day and Daniel Gaido (Leiden/Boston: Brill, 2012), 249–53.
29 Padma Desai, 'Socialism and Indian Economic Policy', *World Development* 3, no. 4 (April 1975): 223. See also Taylor C. Sherman, *Nehru's India: A History in Seven Myths* (Princeton/Oxford: Princeton University Press, 2022), 85–117.
30 Peter Lamb, 'Harold Laski (1893–1950): Political Theorist of a World in Crisis', *Review of International Studies* 25 (1999): 329–32.

31 Ibid., 334.
32 Barbara Ingham and Paul Mosley, 'Marvellous Intellectual Feasts: Arthur Lewis at the London School of Economics, 1933–1948', *History of Political Economy* 45, no. 2 (2013): 195–203.
33 Ibid., 208–10. See also Marc Matera, *Black London: The Imperial Metropolis and Decolonization in the Twentieth Century* (Oakland: University of California Press, 2015), 90–1.
34 Mohammad Hatta, *Ekonomi Terpimpin* (Jakarta: Penerbit Djakarta, 1960), 32.
35 Jens Steffek, *International Organization as Technocratic Utopia* (Oxford: Oxford University Press, 2021), 16.
36 See the review on the origin of technocracy by Dawam Rahardjo, 'Teknokrasi: Dari Gerakan Sosial ke Dominasi Tekno-Ekonomi', *Prisma* XIII, no. 3 (Maret 1984): 14–26.
37 The statement of Sidney Webb quoted in the intellectual biography of Isaiah Berlin, a liberal thinker who was critical to the idea of managerialism, see Joshua L Cherniss, *A Mind, and Its Time: The Development of Isaiah Berlin's Political Thought* (Oxford: Oxford University Press, 2013), 89–90.
38 Milovan Djilas, *The New Class: An Analysis of the Communist System* (London: Thames & Hudson, 1957).
39 His dissertation was later translated into Indonesian and published under the title, Sumitro Djojohadikusumo, *Kredit Rakyat pada Masa Depresi* (Jakarta: LP3ES, 1989).
40 Parindra is commonly associated with the 'organicist' or quasi-fascist ideas of Indonesian politics. Parindra's connection with the Japanese was represented by one of its main figures, Mohammad Husni Thamrin (1894–1941), see Sony Karsono, 'Indonesisa's New Order 1966–1998: Its Social and Intellectual Origins' (PhD thesis, Athens, Ohio: College of Arts and Sciences of Ohio University, 2013), 234.
41 Djojohadikusumo, *Kredit Rakyat*, xviii.
42 For his refutation of the theory of dual economy, see Sumitro Djojohadikusumo, *Perkembangan Pemikiran Ekonomi: Dasar Teori Ekonomi Pertumbuhan dan Ekonomi Pembangunan* (Jakarta: LP3ES, 1994), 72–3.
43 See the introduction by Tarli Nugroho in M. Dawam Rahardjo, *Nasionalisme, Sosialisme dan Pragmatisme: Pemikiran Ekonomi Politik Sumitro Djojohadikusumo* (Jakarta: LP3ES, 2017).
44 Aristides Katoppo et al., *Sumitro Djojohadikusumo: Jejak Perlawanan Begawan Pejuang* (Jakarta: Sinar Harapan, 2000), 95–8.
45 About the economic theories of Arthur Lewis, a British-Caribbean economist who studied at the LSE, see Djojohadikusumo, *Perkembangan Pemikiran Ekonomi*, 92–6.
46 Howard Dick, 'Formation of the Nation-State', in *The Emergence of a National Economy: An Economic History of Indonesia 1800–2000*, ed. Howard Dick et al. (Honolulu: University of Hawaii Press/Asian Studies Association of Australia, 2002), 176–7.
47 Regarding the Benteng Program as a manifestation of economic nationalism and the formation of state capitalism in the 1950s, see Richard Robison, *Indonesia: The Rise of Capital* (Jakarta/Singapore: Equinox Publishing, 2009), 44–5.
48 For intellectual biography of Sjafruddin Prawiranegara, see M. Dawam Rahardjo, *Ekonomi Neoklasik dan Sosialisme Religius: Pragmatisme Pemikiran Ekonomi Politik Sjafruddin Prawiranegara* (Bandung: Mizan, 2011).
49 About the argumentations of Sjafruddin against those of Sumitro, see Sjafruddin Prawiranegara, 'Recollection of My Career', in *Recollections: The Indonesian Economy 1950s–1990s*, ed. Thee Kian Wie (Singapore: Institute of Southeast Asian Studies, 2003), 78–84.

50 Sumitro Djojohadikusumo, *Persoalan Ekonomi di Indonesia* (Djakarta: Indira, 1953).
51 Scott-Smith, *The Politics of Apolitical Culture*, 34.
52 Samuel, *Genealogi Kekuasaan Ilmu Sosial Indonesia*, 81–2.
53 Katoppo, *Sumitro Djojohadikusumo*, 191–2.
54 Regarding the US-Indonesian connection in the technical aid project and the eradication of communism, as well as the origin of the term 'Berkeley Mafia', see David Ransom, 'The Berkeley Mafia and the Indonesian Massacre', *Ramparts* 9, no. 4 (October 1970): 26–8 and 40–9. See also Bradley R. Simpson, *Economist with Guns: Authoritarian Development and U.S-Indonesian Relations* (Stanford: Stanford University Press, 2008).
55 In 1950's the PKI divided the Indonesian middle class into a national bourgeoisie sought to build domestic capital independently from elements of Western (imperialist) capitalism, feudalists and comprador bourgeoisie which functioned as an extension of the interests of foreign capital. Bureaucratic capitalism refers to the consequence of economic nationalism when efforts to reinforce the bourgeoisie and national capital, in fact gave rise to a new class – the military entrepreneurs – that were predatory and, like the compradors, more supportive to the interests of Western imperialism. See Olle Tornquist, *Dilemmas of Third World Communism: The Destruction of the PKI in Indonesia* (London: Zed Books, 1984).
56 There are several biographical sources or studies on Soedjatmoko's intellectual aspects, see, for example, M. Nursam, *Pergumulan Seorang Intelektual: Biografi Soedjatmoko* (Jakarta: Gramedia Pustaka Utama, 2002).
57 See Soedjatmoko's letter to Soebadio Sastrosatomo dated 16 December 1947, as quoted in Frances Gouda and Thijs Brocades Zaalberg, *American Vision of the Netherlands East-Indies/Indonesia: US foreign Policy and Indonesian Nationalism 1920–1949* (Amsterdam: Amsterdam University Press, 2002), 209–10.
58 Interview with Soedjatmoko, as quoted in Legge, *Intellectuals and Nationalism*, 130.
59 About the Gelanggang group and its cultural activism, see Jennifer Lindsay, 'Heirs to World Culture 1950–1965: An Introduction', in *Heirs to World Culture 1950–1965: Being Indonesia*, ed. Jennifer Lindsay and Maya H. T. Liem (Leiden: KITLV Press, 2012), 10.
60 See Soedjatmoko, 'Mengapa Konfrontasi', and the translation of excerpts from Soedjatmoko's article, 'The Need for Creative Adaptation', in Feith and Castles, *Indonesian Political Thinking, 1945–1965*, 238–40.
61 Soedjatmoko, 'Pembangunan Ekonomi sebagai Masalah Kebudayaan', in *Dimensi Manusia dalam Pembangunan: Pilihan Karangan*, ed. Soedjatmoko (Jakarta: LP3ES, 1983), 11–15.
62 Nursam, *Pergumulan Seorang Intelektual*, 106.
63 Soedjatmoko, 'The Role of Political Parties in Indonesia', in *Nationalism and Progtess in Free Asia*, ed. Philip W. Thayer dan William T. Phillips (Baltimore / Cambridge: The John Hopkins Press / Oxford University Press, 1956), 129–34.
64 Ibid., 135–40.
65 Regarding the activism of the PSI figure in response to the political climate of the Guided Democracy era, see Rosihan Anwar, *Sebelum Prahara: Pergolakan Politik Indonesia 1961–1965* (Jakarta: Pustaka Sinar Harapan, 1981).
66 Quoted from Guy Pauker in Olle Tornquist, *Dilemmas of Third World Communism: The Destruction of the PKI in Indonesia* (London: Zed Books, 1984), 116–18.
67 On the link between the Economic Declaration and IMF aid, see Simpson, *Economist with Guns*, 109–12.

68 For Kahin's testimony from his experience working with Indonesian scholars and intellectuals including Soedjatmoko, see George McT. Kahin, *Southeast Asia: A Testament* (London/New York: Routledge, 2003).
69 Soedjatmoko, 'The Indonesian Historian and His Time', in *An Introduction to Indonesian Historiography*, ed. Soedjatmoko (Jakarta/Kuala Lumpur: Equinox Publishing, 2007), 404–15.
70 Edward Shills, 'Intellectuals in the Political Development of the New States', in *Political Change in Underdeveloped World*, ed. John H. Kautsky (New York/London: John Wiley and Sons, 1967).
71 Soedjatmoko, 'Peranan Intelektual di Negara Sedang Berkembang', in *Cendekiawan dan Politik*, ed. Aswab Mahasin and Ismed Natsir (Jakarta: LP3ES, 1983), 32–8.

7

Cuban *Internacionalismo*: A Cuban contribution to the history of internationalisms

Berthold Unfried and Claudia Martínez Hernández

Internacionalismo was the name of Cuba's civilian and military assistance to countries in Africa, Asia and Latin America in its heyday in the period of Cuban membership in the Council for Mutual Economic Assistance (CMEA). This official denomination had a strong normative connotation of solidarity and economically disinterested assistance with nations on a 'socialist path of development'. It included civilian personnel: advisors, experts, specialized workers, teachers and doctors, as well as military personnel dispatched in a mission of 'International Solidarity' to countries of the 'Three Continents'. This chapter focuses on the civilian 'internationalist' personnel: Cuban experts, advisors and teachers in Africa and their encounters with their African counterparts. It looks at 'Internationalism' in practice 'on the ground' as a development project dealing with inequality, living with and bridging diversity in international and inter-cultural personal encounters.[1]

Here, we present Cuban *Internacionalismo* as a genuinely Cuban contribution to the history of internationalisms in practice. Thus, we systematically distinguish this Cuban *Internacionalismo* specifically used to denominate Cuba's civilian and military assistance to countries in Africa, Asia and Latin America from the general notion of 'Internationalism'. We will specifically address the Cuban *Internacionalismo* during the Cuban membership in the CMEA, that is, from 1972 to 1991. Cuban *Internacionalismo* was part of socialist development efforts in order to systematically tackle inequality in the world in the perspective to achieve convergence, that is, more similarity out of inequality in situations of profound inequalities. We point to the forms of education and of self-education in mission as part of a process of socialist education. 'Internationalists' are studied as 'people on the move', as a form of international mobility.

The literature on the subject is still quite sparse. The historical periodization of revolutionary Cuba's history introduced by Carmelo Mesa-Lago in the 1970s continues to provide a valuable framework. Mesa-Lago has distinguished periods of politically driven 'voluntarism' from periods of 'realism', both notions calculated on the relation between the island's capacities and its political ambitions in the world. He interpreted the second half of the 1960s as such a period of economic 'voluntarism' when Cuba tried to build its own independent path to socialism, followed by a period of 'realist' alignment to the CMEA, a larger economic unit capable and willing to provide economic assistance.[2] Even without access to Cuban archive material, some international scholars have produced well-informed works on Cuban 'Internationalism' in general and in the field of education and health services.[3] In Cuba itself, *Internacionalismo* is seen as a guiding principle of Cuban foreign policy and as a permanent high-principle mission to follow by Cuban citizens. This hampers an approach as a subject of history. Berthold Unfried has tried to bring together the fields of Cuban, CMEA and migration studies in a recent article interpreting Cuban-East German cooperation in the CMEA and triangular cooperation in Angola as situations of *entanglement* engendered by dense and systematic interactions.[4] The 'mobility' aspect of the socialist world has been treated in several large Leipzig project volumes and especially by Christina Schwenkel for Vietnamese contract workers and students.[5]

Regarding Cubans in Angola, we can build on the valuable book by Christine Hatzky on Cuban civilian *Internacionalismo* in Angola.[6] The principal value of this book, based on new Angolan yet hardly any Cuban archival sources, lies in the extensive use of memories of Cuban Internationalists captured by interviews.[7] A recent volume builds on a facet of the legitimizing Cuban narrative of the intervention in Angola: that the two countries were linked by the past of slavery and that descendants of slaves would return to the country of origin of their ancestors to definitely liberate it from colonialism.[8]

Most works on Cuban *Internacionalism*o have been written, already in the 1970s and 1980s, by scholars from outside Cuba and without access to Cuban archives.[9] Among recent contributions are the pioneering works of Piero Gleijeses.[10] He mobilized new Cuban archives that offer insight into the organization of what the Cubans called *Internacionalismo* and he focuses on its military side. While the Cuban Party archives that Gleijeses consulted are not open to the public, we had access to archival sources of the Party's youth organization: the Young Communists League, *Unión de Jóvenes Comunistas* (UJC) in Havana. As many 'Internationalists' were young people, the Party delegated part of the framework of organization and supervision to the youth organization. This material illustrates the institutional framework to the activity and the everyday life of the Cuban 'Internationalists'. These copious documents imply that the Cuban side is much better documented than the Angolan one which in most cases only appears indirectly.[11] That imbalance in sources constitutes a certain asymmetry in this contribution like in all others before.

Cuban *Internacionalismo* has not yet been ranged into a broader perspective on Internationalisms. Recent works which try to give a synthesis of Internationalisms do not mention it.[12] It is equally absent in recent conceptualizations on the 'globalization' of the socialist world.[13] This is all the more striking as Cuban *Internacionalismo* has already in the 1980s been addressed as 'Globalism', understood as global activism.[14] Recently, the Cuban efforts to establish an own International have caught attention in historiography.[15] The 'Tricontinental' Cuban Internationalism of the 1960s was driven by logics distinct from that of the CMEA-period on which we put our focus. The non-white racial rhetoric in the 'Tricontinental' which was in part a reaction to Chinese efforts to define the 'Third World' in racial terms was not assimilated in Cuban's CMEA-period 'Internationalism'.[16] There might be a line, however, to the official discourse about a 'Latin American-African nation' as an ideological underpinning of the Cuban intervention in Angola.[17] More important than the rhetoric: both fought under the banner of 'anti-imperialism',[18] but their means differed largely: guerrilla groups and a dominance of non-state actors – liberation movements – in the period of the 'Tricontinental' in contrast with large-scale military and civilian assistance in cooperation with the CMEA states in the CMEA period.

In this chapter, first we focus on civilian assistance and insert Cuban *Internacionalismo* into a broader CMEA perspective. The CMEA was the economic organization of the Socialist World System and Cuba was one of its three non-European and – following the Cuban self-denomination – 'underdeveloped' members. We present Cuban intercontinental personal mobilities as a bridge among European members of the organization and countries at the fringes of the CMEA in Asia, Africa and Latin America. Second, we show how these personal mobilities were the occasion for education and self-education. Not only the Angolans were to be educated but also the Cubans were to undergo a process of education and self-education in mission.

Phases and forms of Cuban *Internacionalismo*

The Cuban revolution triggered a major global revolutionary wave. It sent shock waves of revolutionary activism first to Latin America, then to other parts of the world. A Cuban cycle of *International Solidarity* with revolutionary movements in Asia, Africa and Latin America in the 1960s found its organizational expression in the establishment of an own International of revolutionary liberation movements, the *Tricontinental*, as an alternative to the Soviet and Chinese orbits. The *Tricontinental* – this organization's official name was: 'Solidarity Organisation of the peoples of Africa, Asia and Latin America' – can be seen as an effort to organize revolutionary liberation movements and countries steering between the orbits of Soviet and Chinese socialist internationalism.[19] Even though we perceive the *Tricontinental* as an important Cuban chapter in a Global History of internationalisms, it is not part of the Cuban denomination of *Internacionalismo Cubano*. This International, a comparatively loose organization of heterogeneous movements, lost its raison d'être with Cuba's integration into the CMEA – this short life being no exception from precedent international political associations like the three Labour Internationals. Our focus is on the ensuing period of Cuban international activities.

This *guerrillero* and *Tricontinental* period was followed by a cycle in the framework of Cuban membership in the CMEA which is the timeframe of our analysis and where Cuban *Internacionalismo* played the highly important role of an intermediary between the European socialist countries and its allies in the 'Three Continents' in the 1970s and 1980s. Cuban *Internacionalismo* changed its methods from the guerrilla of Che Guevara in the Congo and in Bolivia to large-scale interventions with a military side complemented by civilian assistance, thereby morphing into a new form of Internationalism.[20]

The 1970s were the period of a massive Cuban outreach to Africa, most importantly to Angola after 1975 and to Ethiopia after 1977. Cuban military assistance proved decisive in the civil war which the leftist MPLA (*Movimento Popular de Libertação de Angola*) fought against rival national liberation movements supported by the United States, China and South Africa. Cuban military alongside Soviet advisors and weapons saved the revolutionary military government of Ethiopia from the Somalian invasion in 1977–8.[21] At this time, Cuba also became a provider of not only military but also civilian assistance to countries of the 'Three Continents'. In sub-Saharan Africa alone, in the peak year of 1979, 8,250 civilian 'Internationalists' were on mission, nearly 6,700 of them in Angola. This number levelled off at 5,000–6,000 at the beginning in 1978, to drop to a level of 3,000 in 1988.[22] In contrast to this trend in Africa, in Nicaragua there was a peak in the number of 'Internationalists' at the beginning of the 1980s until this number dropped for political and security reasons from the mid-1980s.[23] Cuban 'Internationalists' were withdrawn from places with a high probability of being attacked by the 'Contras' in the escalating civil war in Nicaragua. All women were sent back from this country to Cuba. At the beginning of the 1980s around 25,000 Cuban 'Internationalists' were believed to have been on mission in the 'Three Continents'.[24] Following Noemí Benítez de Mendoza, in the 1980s head of the section *Exportación de Asistencia Técnica y Desarrollo Industrial/Export of Technical Assistance and Industrial Development* of the *Centro de Asistencia Técnica*/Center of Technical Assistance of the *Comité Estatal de Colaboración Económica*/State Committee (Ministry) for Economic Cooperation (CECE), the number of Cuban 'Internationalists' sent on mission between 1963 and 2001 totalled 120,000.[25] These are considerable numbers.

The Cubans sent in particular doctors and nurses, and above all, teachers, the two latter categories mostly female. Five thousand Cubans were on civilian mission in Angola at the beginning of the 1980s, of which 1,500 of them in primary and secondary education, 120 in higher education, 400 doctors, 180 health workers and 200 agricultural specialists.[26] At the beginning of the 1980s, the director of the sending agency *Cubatécnica* spoke of '25,000 compañeros', comrades overseas as overall figure of Cubans abroad, including the young Cubans sent to socialist Europe to be trained as skilled workers.[27] Other figures refer to 25,000 'Internationalists' – that denomination did not include these workers – and of these around 3,000 in the educational sector.[28] Thus, these would be considerably higher figures. For the purpose of comparison, in the case of the Soviet figures, at the end of 1970s more than 40,000 Soviet specialists (engineers, experts and trained workers) were working in 'developing countries'.[29] These figures were 30–40 times more than such from the GDR but not much more than Cubans.[30]

Who were the Cuban 'Internationalists'? At large, four groups of Cuban personnel were operating globally. Two of them were Cuban students and workers sent to European CMEA countries under bilateral agreements. The other two groups were denominated as 'Internationalists'. That was the military and civilian personnel which the Cuban State sent as assistance to politically friendly states in the 'Three Continents' from Angola to Nicaragua: some tens of thousands of military personnel, some thousands of agrarian specialists, engineers, doctors and nurses, and a lot of teachers and educational advisors.

A specific group of civilian 'Internationalists' were the *Destacamentos Pedagógicos Internacionalistas*, 'internationalist pedagogic departments' of students who had not yet finished their university education and who were sent to teach in Angola.

This model of sending brigades of pre-graduate students as teachers had already been implemented in Cuba in secondary-level boarding schools in the countryside (*Escuelas Secundarias Básicas en el Campo*).[31] Starting in 1978, prospective teachers of the *Destacamentos Pedagógicos Internacionalistas* were sent to Angola. They comprised more than 2,000 altogether. More than half of them were women. This was a considerable part of a total of around 11,500 'Internationalists' in Angola's education sector, of which just under 500 were in higher education.[32] This experiment was repeated in Nicaragua a few years later. In sending pre-graduate students or trainees out into the international arena, Cuba was closer to the *US Peace Corps* model than to the *Friendship* or *Komsomol* Brigades, as the *Peace Corps* promoted a model based on sending non-fully trained youngsters. The *Friendship* or *Komsomol* Brigades which represented the overall political model were constituted of fully trained young people.[33]

In the Cuban official discourse, accomplishing an 'internationalist mission' was presented as a duty and an historical debt to settle (*deuda para saldar*).[34] That did not mean that civilian 'Internationalism' was obligatory.[35] It was a privilege and a recognition to be sent on such an internationalist mission. There were several modes of recruitment. Many offered themselves as voluntary candidates. Twenty-four thousand Cubans responded to a national campaign of recruitment for *internationalist* missions to Nicaragua and 4,000 out of them were chosen, in their majority *maestras*, mainly female secondary and primary school teachers.[36] Others were asked to go on mission. Interviewees remember that they were approached by the personnel of their work unit, in the case of teachers the Ministry of Education.[37] Executive personnel like the Cuban civil administration in Angola were often recruited in an informal way by colleagues and comrades with whom they had shared the professional or political career.[38] Committees for the selection were constituted under the leadership of the Party, by representatives of the youth organization UJC, the 'mass organizations' *Comités de Defensa de la Revolución* (CDR, the political neighbourhood organizations), *Federación de Mujeres Cubanas* (FMC, or Federation of Cuban Women), the unions *Central de Trabajadores Cubanos* (CTC, or Workers Central Union), the local governmental structures and the peasants' organization; these organizations, in the military sector alongside military representatives, selected the candidates.[39] Some people however refused to go to Angola when approached for the civilian or military mission.[40] This could be seen as a serious political 'error'.[41]

As Cuban institutions adapted to the model of the European socialist states in the second half of the 1970s, the Ministry for Economic Cooperation was founded. This ministry and its implementation agency *Cubatécnica* were charged with the administrative and procedural work of sending personnel abroad.[42]

In the framework of its 'internationalist' programme, Cuba was not only sending personnel abroad. It received, given its specialization in educational services, approximately 40,000 young people, mostly secondary-level students from Africa, Asia and Latin America, especially in its 'Internationalist Schools' on Cuba's largest sub-island, the *Isla de la Juventud* (Youth Island). It was possible to be an 'Internationalist' without leaving Cuba. In 1979, the category of *Internacionalista* was extended to all those teachers who, fulfilling certain requirements, worked in 'internationalist schools' which were concentrated on the *Isla de la Juventud*.[43] Cuba became the CMEA's study centre for students from the 'Three Continents', second in the socialist world only to the USSR and with greater numbers than the GDR. Up to 22,000 students – this term included the secondary school – populated the *Isla de la Juventud* and got their education there.[44]

The thousands of Cuban unqualified young worker-trainees sent to Czechoslovakia, East Germany, Hungary and Bulgaria under bilateral agreements between 1978 and 1990 were not included in the category of *Internacionalistas*. They were called 'socialist collaborators' instead. Their task was different from the 'Internationalists'. They were to be trained as qualified workers in the work process, thus in the same time contributing to compensate for the labour shortage in the European socialist countries. However, the Cuban authorities explicitly associated the 'revolutionary task' of working and acquiring a qualification with high patriotic and internationalist sentiments.[45] But this level of interaction was part of the sphere of 'scientific-technical cooperation', which was more operating with the logics of the mutual economic interest, and not of the sphere of 'International Solidarity'. While Cuba had an abundance of unqualified young people, this was not the case with the qualified 'Internationalists' sent on mission in the 'solidarity' line of Cuban international activities. Cuba had an economic interest in the European labour programme whereas such an economic interest never came to dominate the Angolan endeavour despite the fact that part of the services was financially compensated by the Angolan government for a few years (cf. infra).

Modes of implementation: Internationalism on the ground

Angola was the setting for one of those 'hot wars amid the Cold War', which, in the final phase of the competition between the two systems, seemed to shift the balance of power in favour of the socialist world system.[46] Following independence in 1975 in the wake of the revolution in Portugal in 1974, a civil war broke out between competing liberation movements. As a consequence of this devastating war and the exodus of the Portuguese, the colonial economy broke down. The colonial administration collapsed and a new state apparatus had not yet been built. Cuba, as a new CMEA member state, brought the CMEA into play as a development organization thanks to its massive military and civilian aid. Angola was supposed to become a showpiece for the development policies of the CMEA countries. It seemed an appropriate country for demonstrating how decolonization could be accomplished successfully on the basis of rich natural resources 'along the path of socialist development'.

Three years after joining the CMEA, at the request of the MPLA government of Angola, Cuba started a massive military and civilian intervention in Angola, upon its own decision and not executing a Soviet masterplan, to save that socialist – according to its self-definition – regime as a candidate for CMEA activity in the 'Three Continents'. The massive deployment of Cuban troops decided the military situation in favour of the MPLA.[47] Cuban specialists followed in the wake of the military: coffee and sugar experts, teaching personnel, chicken production and citrus fruit experts, and transportation and civil engineers and staff. A civil emergency programme was planned to get the Angolan economy going in replacement of the Portuguese colonial administration and its experts. The decisive contribution of Cuba consisted in supporting the Angolan State by massive military and civilian assistance, the latter above all in the education and health sectors. Several thousands of Cuban teachers, doctors and specialists of all sorts were deployed to Angola to work and live there for several years.[48]

How did the Cubans deal with the inequality with the local population they encountered in Angola? And what were the regulations and practices for dealing with situations of inequality in habits and standards? A look at practices of coexistence on the ground shows that the political claim of 'international solidarity' or 'Internationalism' went hand-in-hand with a separation from the local population in living environments. In Angola, the Cubans lived in separate communal lodgings (*predios*). They were organized in collectives, as was typical of the then current social and political life in Cuba.[49] In Party and youth organization meetings, the participants gave accountability reports on their professional and personal development; they were evaluated, and cases of irregular and deviant behaviour were discussed further and punished. In Angola, the food supply often even came from Cuba because there was nothing to buy in the country itself. All of this gave rise to a specifically Cuban life-world in Angola: Cuban enclaves where the 'Internationalists', many of whom had left the island for the first time in their life, found a Cuban ambiente. This aspect of reproducing the same surroundings around the globe can be seen as a sort of international projection of a national culture.

These Cuban communities had limited exchanges with the surrounding population. External contacts were restricted by the Cuban authorities as a potential security risk in a country ravaged by war. In a civil guerrilla war, the enemy cannot be distinguished and may be your neighbour or the father of your school-children. External contacts were also undesirable in a realistic assessment of potential perils due to uncontrolled interactions between and the mixing among such unequal groups of people. Everyday life had shown the merging of bodies (sexuality, prostitution) and objects (illicit barter) to lead to undesirable phenomena, such as conflicts on the basis of different ways of life and customs, resulting in black market activities, prostitution or conflicts based on different ways of living.[50]

A paramount instruction by the Cuban authorities was to respect local customs and not behave in an attitude of superiority towards them. Yet, interviews show the difficulties they had accepting all of them. Memories of Cuban 'Internationalists' contain expressions such as 'beasts of burden' to describe the traditional role of women in Angolan society or 'backward tribal' habits to refer to the importance of traditional medicine in Angola.[51] In the archives, one finds repeated entreaties to 'respect the laws and customs of the country' (of mission), giving the impression that this had to be repeatedly emphasized. The Cuban 'Internationalists' thus found themselves faced with the challenge of all those living and working in situations of gross inequality. Inequality in material living conditions – with so many starving people around – reminded Cuban 'Internationalists'[52] of 'backward' habits that Cuba's society had overcome, such as poor hygiene, appalling relations between men and women, and seemingly apathetic attitudes towards death that bewildered them. All this gave the impression of people living in very different realities.[53]

Such inequalities represented elements of real-life separation from the local population, which were grounded in distinct cultures and ways of living. The prescription of solidarity had to coexist with this feeling of profound material and cultural differences. In an address to the Cuban Party Organization in Angola, the head of the Cuban civil administration in Angola, Jorge Risquet, described the 'cultural backwardness, technical ignorance, illiteracy' as the 'main problems of the Angolan people'.[54] The prescriptions for respecting differences had to coexist with the essentially socialist drive for 'progress' expressed by this highest civilian representative in Angola. That was the essence of socialist developmentalism. After all, the Cubans had come to Angola, along with other citizens of socialist countries, to assist that country as agents of change on its 'socialist path of development' as shared objective – which was a path of profound change on all levels and on that path Cuba was definitely considered as more advanced and 'progressive'. Additionally, the fight against 'regionalism, tribalism and racism' as 'reflections of pre-capitalist production relationships and colonial domination' which together with lack of discipline in production and distribution hampered progress towards socialism was shared by the Angolan leading Party MPLA.[55]

Education and self-education in mission

The 'internationalist' mission of Cuban personnel also was a mission of education and self-education within the Party collective. The mission should contribute to the Internationalists' self-education, to their progress towards an integrally developed socialist personality (*allseitig entwickelte sozialistische Persönlichkeit*). Some advanced in this process, others failed and were sent back to Cuba. Just as they did in European socialist countries such as the GDR or Czechoslovakia,[56] the Cubans built in accordance with the MPLA government self-governance structures in Angola, thereby re-creating, to a certain extent, life in Cuba. In Angola, these structures of civilian self-government were the corollary of the independent military mission. They consisted of an Economic Office, Party and Youth Organisation structures, the heads of mission of the different sectors of collaboration, a security apparatus and logistical structures. This self-government replaced non-existing or deficient Angolan structures for each sphere of everyday life. The head was the Cuban ambassador to the country. In Angola, in the first years, this position was filled by Jorge Risquet, who managed the huge Cuban infrastructure in Angola. He was the Africa specialist of the Party leadership, a veteran of the 1965 Cuban 'internationalist' military mission in Congo-Brazzaville, and later on Cuban minister of labour.[57] This was Cuban Internationalism in practice, the organizational expression of a special way of dealing with what were later called 'intercultural' encounters.

Part of this Cuban self-administration was a complementary Party structure. The disciplinary apparatus of the Party and its youth organization provided education and discipline. Just like the East Germans who were sent abroad and who built their own Party life in the countries of mission,[58] the Cubans had their own Party life like in Cuba. The UJC archives reveal the reality of this internal life 'through the Party's eye'. The Party and its youth organization acted as educational organizations for their members: 'The UJC worked to raise the labour demeanour of internationalist youth, improving their discipline, strengthening the social prestige of their professions and for raising their efficiency as workers.' Discipline, formal education and social behaviour were the tasks and functions undertaken by the UJC members sent abroad.[59]

In the Party and Youth organizations, Cubans abroad underwent constant evaluation. The archival materials show a framework of individual plans and reports, self-evaluations, autobiographical sketches recording personal development, and trimestral and annual evaluations of the work and personal performance.[60] Time and again, self-criticism was emphasized for the process of educating oneself.[61] These young Internationalists were 'worked over' more or less mildly in Angola in the meetings of the UJC collective by means of 'criticism and self-criticism'. The same applied to Cuban organizations in the socialist countries in Europe. These self-statements were complemented by personal evaluations conducted by the Party or UJC organization. This was part of the plan that the mission contributes to a process of '*crecimiento*', the growth of the socialist personality. The positive aspect of this personal evaluation was demonstrating the progress made while in the country of mission. The mission was thus seen as part of the personal development of the *internationalist* developers. The *internationalist* mission was to upgrade the person of the *Internacionalista*. According to the official newspaper of the Communist Party of Cuba, the *internationalist* mission was seen as a process of learning to improve oneself: 'El internacionalismo cubano como aprendizaje para ser mejores' – 'Internationalism as learning to be better'.[62] This idea is reappropriated by interviewees who refer to Cuban Internationalism as the 'highest stage of human development'.[63] 'La causa más bonita', the most beautiful cause, called it Risquet, the head of the Cuban civilian administration in Angola.[64]

Negative evaluations could lead to the conclusion that the person in question had lost 'all authority' and thus revealed himself as a non-advanced personality. Infractions could reveal such a deficient personality. There were a number of infractions that were considered punishable. These included: infractions against the strict contact and leave regulations, like leaving the Cuban compound during curfew; and black market activities. Sexual 'irregularities', such as homosexuality in combination with other 'deficiencies', were analysed as a symptom of a corrupted personality. Homosexuality was in this time considered as incompatible with the norms and values of the Party, thus also a personal deficiency in the 'internationalist' mission. In the Angolan cases, it was not sanctioned *eo ipso*, but as a symptom, when problematic consequences were associated with it. It is, however, difficult to distinguish from the rather laconic qualification that acts of homosexuality had led, as is often stated, to a 'complete loss of respect' for the incriminated person before the collective, that such a loss of prestige made the position of the person untenable; or if such a statement came more or less automatically together with the allegation of homosexuality.[65]

Lack of cooperation with local counterparts and conflicts were also punished. In the case of such conflicts with locals, the Cuban authorities showed a tendency to punish their co-nationals quite severely rather than to pass over such an affair, as the following case demonstrates. A Cuban collaborator of the Angolan Young Pioneers Organization, driving at night accompanied by an Angolan nurse, got into an accident with an Angolan bus driver. They got into an argument during which the Cuban fired several shots at both the bus and driver, ultimately wounding the driver. The secretary of the Cuban youth organization on the ground decided to remain silent about this incident, but it became a public matter through a strike of the Angolan bus drivers. As it had become a public and political issue, the case was given to Cuban security authorities, which decided to hand over the Cuban transgressor to be tried in the Angolan justice system. The civilian Cuban authority proposed to expel the transgressor as well as his accomplices from the ranks of the youth organization while also expelling them from the Cuban 'internationalist' mission.[66] This was the 'civilian' side of the treatment of that infraction. Such cases also occurred with Cuban worker trainees in the GDR.[67] Their handling – the transgressors were sent back to Cuba to be tried there – was an expression of the Cuban self-governance.

'Cuban Internationalism' and 'international solidarity' in the socialist world

'Internationalism' is used in this contribution in the sense that groups of activists wanted to spread their practices, concerns and ideas beyond their own nation to other parts of the world because they thought those practices, concerns and ideas were universally applicable. In this sense, all great revolutions had their 'internationalist' phases. In the understanding applied in this text, a universalistic grounding, the claim of speaking to the entire humanity, is a *conditio sine qua non* of 'Internationalism'.

When revolutions established socialist developmental states in the world outside Europe, beginning with China 1949, followed by Korea, Cuba, Mongolia and Vietnam, 'international solidarity' took the form of the exchange of qualified personnel (experts) and personnel to be qualified (workers, students) between socialist Europe and these states. Cuba provided a large part of the personal glue for that entanglement. Together with the Soviet Union, Cuba became the largest provider of personnel to the CMEA. In the 1980s, Cuba is said to have been the country with the highest percentage of citizens sent on civil foreign missions in the world.[68] Around 30 per cent of the delegates of the Party congresses in 1980 and 1986 had undertaken 'Internationalist' missions.[69] Cubans went to a much higher number to the 'Three Continents' than citizens of European socialist countries. This was an expression of 'Internationalism' as projecting Cuban personnel, and with it, Cuban influence into the world.

The Cuban 'Internationalists', in comparison with their European colleagues in Angola, had a reputation of simplicity and modesty. They lived without great material needs and demands. They were known for their adaptability to work in conditions without expensive technical devices. They agreed to work in much more frugal conditions as their East German colleagues.[70] The 'Internationalists' lived in more modest settlements and their cost was thus considerably lower than that of specialists from European CMEA countries. Cubans got a monthly allowance of 425 Birr (the local currency of Ethiopia), while the Soviets got in contrast 1,000–1,250 Birr, local expenditures (housing, medical services) and half of the transport paid by the Ethiopian side.[71] Cuban human qualities were generally appreciated. Cuban 'Internationalists' were coveted partners in many respects. In Tanzania for instance, female West German project personnel gladly fraternized with Cuban doctors.[72] Despite all measures of separation, their way of living was considered as closer to the African population. A contribution to this feeling of closeness was that the Cuban government sent black Cubans by preference in the military sector with the ideological credentials of a community of descent and a 'historical debt' contracted by Cuba by slave trafficking: it was supposed that the descendants of African slaves came back from Cuba to assist in the liberation of Africa and the building of independent States.[73] This also had a root in contemporary realities: the highly mestiço dominated MPLA faced ressentiments by the pronouncedly black UNITA – a sentiment which led Soviet representatives in Angola to speak of 'black racism'.[74] This opinion was expressed by Neto towards the Cuban representative in Angola, Jorge Risquet, as early as 1976.[75] The basis of the Nito Alves uprising was massive resentment among black MPLA supporters against the MPLA leadership around Neto, in which a disproportionately high number of mestizos was represented.[76] This resulted in conflicts that were carried out in an armed manner. In May 1977, a wing of the MPLA under Interior Minister Nito Alves staged a coup against party and government leader Agostinho Neto and was subsequently liquidated. The Cubans actively supported Neto in this armed conflict.[77] There were rumors that Nito, despite the mentioned pejorative remarks by Soviet representatives, had been on the other hand supported by the Soviet Union.[78]

Cuba tried to bring the CMEA closer to the 'Three Continents'. It provided its 'internationalist' personnel services for politically friendly countries as a part of 'International Solidarity' free of charge, making exceptions for those countries endowed with foreign currency. Angola, with its oil and coffee production, was for some years (1978–83) part of that category, before once again receiving assistance at no cost.[79] After unsuccessful efforts to get European CMEA countries on this line of 'internationalist' personnel sending free of charge – the Cuban proposition in 1977, that the CMEA member states should consider to render assistance free of charge as a rule[80] was not supported by other CMEA delegations – Cuba followed the logics of remunerated personnel dispatches for a while. From the end of the 1970s, it operated a distinction between countries endowed with convertible valuta – including Angola with its income in petrol-dollars – and countries without such resources – Moçambique, Nicaragua, but also Ethiopia despite its coffee-dollars. With its increasing personnel dispatches which could also be seen as *exportaciones de servicios técnicos*, the export of technical services, Cuba followed the CMEA policy to 'immaterial exports' promoting the export of experts and advisory services.[81] A treaty of November 1977 stipulated rates of remuneration for Cuban civilian 'Internationalists' in Angola.[82] Thereafter the number of them was reduced from 7,000 to 4,000. The introduction of remunerations thus also served to curb the ever-increasing demand for Cuban 'Internationalists' free of charge.

Similar to the GDR and other European socialist states, the Cuban state distinguished between 'internationalist' assistance, free of charge, 'scientific-technical cooperation' under advantageous conditions for the recipient country, and economic relations in the 'mutual interest' (*Colaboración Económica*), thus with economic returns. But the weighting was different than in the socialist European countries. There were barter trade protocols between Cuba and Ethiopia as well as Angola to be sure.[83] Thus a small layer of economic relations between Cuba and African countries came into being in the sector of expertise in health, education, building, sugar production and agricultural infrastructure.[84] But this commercial sector remained very small in comparison with the much more important 'internationalist' assistance sector where no economic returns were expected. For the Cuban economy, this personnel dispatch was a loss in any case. On the active side certainly was the training in action, especially for the students of the *Destacamentos Pedagógicos*. As opposed to the Cuban dispatch of unskilled labour to Europe, this dispatch was not underlain by a labour surplus in Cuba.[85] The sending of Cuban 'Internationalists' was no export of superfluous work-force. It had essentially political reasons.

Linking the continents

Cuba's role in linking the continents is retrospectively called 'South-South cooperation'.[86] This notion was not used at that time. The distinction was made between non-European CMEA member countries, countries on a 'socialist path of development' while not CMEA members, and 'developing countries' oriented towards a capitalist model of development. What today is called the 'Global South' thus was distinguished into three different spheres treated differently in terms of preferential relations. Cuba acted as an advocate for non-CMEA countries from the 'Three Continents' on a 'socialist path of development' in the CMEA. These included countries such as Ethiopia, Angola, Mozambique and Nicaragua, which a revolution or a war of independence had orientated towards the 'Socialist World System' without being members of the CMEA. Through its *Internacionalismo* Cuba became a major actor of 'International Solidarity' in the 'Socialist World System' on an inter-continental scale.

Cuba was not alone in the role of sending professionals to the 'Three Continents'. Another extra-European CMEA member, war-torn Vietnam, sent not only students and workers to Europe for training, but also thousands of professionals to Africa to train African personnel.[87] Vietnamese military advisors tried to convey to Nicaraguan colleagues their experiences of guerrilla warfare against (US-trained) troops.[88] In 1983, the special trade representative of the GDR attempted to arrange a triangular trade deal, whereby Angola would supply the GDR with additional coffee for rice from Vietnam.[89] But Cuba's personnel dispatches were the most impressive in numbers. Some tens of thousands of civilian 'Internationalists', from teachers, doctors and civil engineers to coffee and citrus fruit specialists, chicken breeders and construction workers were sent to that country joining Soviets, East Germans, Czechoslovaks, Yugoslavs and even Vietnamese experts there. This was the CMEA in action, though not as a multilateral organization but via its member states. While the experts from the European CMEA countries mostly worked as consultants or trainers, the Cubans also worked operationally, that is to say their teachers taught Angolan children in place of the Angolan teaching staff, who were unavailable or missing. In the first half of the 1980s, they represented more than three-quarters of the teachers in the secondary sector.[90] This provision of personnel kept the Angolan state alive or, put better, it helped to develop it in the first place. The Cubans tried to make Angola a showpiece for a CMEA-driven development of an 'underdeveloped' country on a 'socialist path of development', linking the continents.

We could establish a system of personal inter-continental mobility in the Socialist World: interwoven flows of educational, labour and professional migration between Cuba, the European center of the Socialist World and the Three Continents. This shows the inequality between these regions as a trigger factor of personal mobilities destined to achieve *convergence* between unequal societies and people. Mobility and inequality, or mobility to bridge inequality are the lead terms of such an approach. This study shows the socialist nation-states disposed of mobile professionals as liaison to parts of other continents embarking on a path of development to a similar socialist society. Thus, they became the personal glue of the inter-continental extension of the 'Socialist World System' if we may speak of such a system.[91] They were, besides the international revolutionaries and politicians and the traders the mobile elites of that system.

What Internationalism?

Which type of Internationalism was put into practice by the Cuban 'Internationalists'? Certainly, this 'Internationalism' was distinct from *cosmopolitanism*, understood as the capacity – usually of educated elites – to move in different cultural contexts and to adapt to various lifestyles, adopting hybrid ways of life, and from having an itinerant life, moving between different cultural contexts as a recurrent pattern. In contrast to such a vision, 'Internationalist' was no permanent profession and identity. The Cuban 'Internationalists' were to return to Cuba and re-integrate themselves after one or two or three missions. They were not supposed to distinguish themselves from 'ordinary' Cubans lacking that 'Internationalist' experience. The primary distinction was not the capacity to move between different cultures. They were supposed to acquire a strengthened Cuban national conscience as a consequence of their mission.[92] They were regarded as representatives of the Cuban socialist national state, not as a cosmopolitan global elite in Cuba. The interviews with 'Internationalists' do not show them having adopted a special 'internationalist' way of thinking and of living. They declared to feel primarily Cuban and secondarily 'Internationalist'.[93] Contrary to a *cosmopolitan* identity, many of them actually claim a Cuban national identity enforced by the mission. It is thus a quite special 'Internationalism' which we encounter on the personal level of these men and women sent on 'Internationalist' missions. This was *patriotic* Internationalism.

On the institutional level, Cuban *Internacionalismo* was conceived as 'Internationalist Solidarity', as an economically disinterested assistance for countries on a 'socialist path of development'. In this sense, Cuban *Internacionalismo* can be inserted into the history of 'development' projects of the kind which was ex posteriori called 'South-South cooperation'. Cuba forwarded part of the assistance received from the European centre of the CMEA to extra-European countries and to movements at the fringes of the CMEA. One of the main tasks was to assist the building of nation-states out of former colonies – nation-states with citizens educated and endowed with a national identity and a state apparatus capable to 'plan' and direct the nation-states' economy. Making Angolans out of Ovimbundos and Bakongos, Mestiços and 'Whites'. In this sense, Cuban 'internationalist' assistance to Angola was essentially assistance in nation-building. Angola ceased to follow 'socialist' developmental models in the economy already in the mid-1980s, years before the fall of the planned economy systems in Europe. What remained of the massive Cuban 'Internationalist' military and civilian assistance was an Angolan State strong enough to survive the civil war yet with no more 'socialist' aspirations.

Where then, and into which larger histories, can we purposefully insert Cuban 'Internationalism'? First, Cuba, member of the CMEA from 1972, made such 'internationalist' personnel deployment its specialty. Through its agency, Cuba became the CMEA's personnel pool for the extra-European sphere, linking the European centre of the CMEA to the extra-European world, to the 'Three Continents'. Cuban 'Internationalism' thus was part of the 'globalization' of the 'Socialist World System' if we understand by that notion its extra-European extension. Cuban *Internacionalismo* was certainly one of the most vigorous efforts in the history of the post-colonial period to bring societies on a similar path of development, thus to make *converge* very diverse parts of the world. It was an 'Internationalism' in the sense that groups of activists, in our case organized by the State and the Party, tried to spread their concerns and ideas beyond their own nation to other parts of the world because this programme was thought to be potentially applicable to the whole world. The idea was to set 'underdeveloped' states 'on the socialist path of development' in order to achieve convergence in the 'Socialist World'. In this perspective, we also see *Internacionalismo cubano* as part of development efforts, of efforts to systematically tackle inequality in the world in the perspective to achieve *convergence*. Main examples were the educational and expertise transfers from Cuba to Angola.

This opens quite a few occasions for comparison. Civilian 'Internationalists' can be compared with developmental efforts of all political orientations on the level of personnel dispatches. *Destacamentos Internacionalistas* can be compared with Youth sending organizations from *Peace Corps* and West German *Entwicklungshelfer* or French *Volontaires du progrès* to Soviet *Komsomol* and GDR *Friendship Brigades.* Cuban International Schools can be compared with those in Moscow and Leipzig, in a wider perspective with US, British or French educational programmes towards what was called in their terminology, the 'Third World'.

A Global History perspective studying inter-continental and inter-cultural connections, transfers, but also disruptions as a consequence of interactions, seems to us a fresh and rewarding approach to Cuban *Internacionalismo*, making that experience part of the global history of education. Mobility was seen as a mover towards education in a broad sense – that is to say education of the populations of the newly independent countries in the 'Three Continents' setting out on the 'socialist path of development' as well as the education of their educators, the 'Internationalists', by continuous self-evaluation and evaluation by the Cuban collective.

Finally, Cuban *Internacionalismo* can be integrated as a part of migration history in the large understanding of that field in Global History which includes temporary forms of mobility. We see these 'people on the move' as a form of inter-national mobility, thus a contribution to the history of global mobilities. It is further part of the history of global development efforts, understood as policies aiming at achieving more convergence between hitherto divergent parts of the world. We analyse Cuban *Internacionalismo* as a form of international political action, as a form of living with strong educational features, and as an effort of education in action. The effort had a clear aim: elaborate models of socialist development for the 'Three Continents'. And the history of Cuban *Internacionalismo* is, after all, part of the history of Internationalisms, understood as efforts at unifying the world, to bring more convergence, more sameness to the world, and as efforts to make the globe the theatre of action.

Notes

1 This contribution is based on material from archives and interviews in Cuba and Germany and presents results of the research project 'Entanglements Cuba-GDR: mobilities, exchanges, circulations within the CMEA' sponsored by the FWF/Austrian Science Fund from 2019 to 2023 (project leader/principal investigator Berthold Unfried). Available online: https://socialist-entanglements.univie.ac.at/en/. This article profited from various comments by the editors, Su Lin Lewis and Nana Osei-Opare.

2 C. Mesa-Lago, *The Economy of Socialist Cuba. A Two-Decade Appraisal* (Albuquerque: University of New Mexico Press, 1981); C. Mesa-Lago, *Breve historia económica de la Cuba socialista. Política, resultados y perspectivas* (Madrid: Allianza Editorial, 1994).

3 J. Domínguez, *To Make a World Safe for Revolution. Cuba's Foreign Policy* (Cambridge, MA, and London: Harvard University Press, 1989); M. Erisman and J. Kirk, *Cuban Foreign Policy Confronts a New International Order* (Boulder, CO and London: Lynne Rienner, 1991); J. Kirk and M. Erisman, *Cuban Medical Internationalism. Origins, Evolution, and Goals* (New York: Springer, 2009); A. Hickling-Hudson, J. Corona González, and R. Preston (eds.), *The Capacity to Share. A Study of Cuba's International Cooperation in Educational Development, New York-Houndmills* (Basingstoke, 2012); J. M. Feinsilver, 'Fifty Years of Cuba's Medical Diplomacy: From Idealism to Pragmatism', *Cuban Studies* 41 (2010): 85–104.

4 B. Unfried, 'A Cuban cycle of development socialism? Cubans and East Germans in the Socialist World System', *Journal für Entwicklungspolitik* 33, no. 3 (2017): 69–90.

5 A. Calori, et al. (eds.), *Between East and South. Spaces of interaction in the globalizing economy of the Cold War* (Berlin and Boston, MA: De Gruyter, 2019); J. Mark, A. M. Kalinovsky, and S. Marung (eds.), *Alternative Globalizations. Eastern Europe and the Postcolonial World* (Bloomington: Indiana University Press, 2020); C. Schwenkel, 'Rethinking Asian Mobilities: Socialist Migration and Postsocialist Repatriation of Vietnamese Contract Workers in East Germany', *Critical Asian Studies* 46, no. 2 (2014): 235–58.

6 C. Hatzky, *Kubaner in Angola. Süd-Süd-Kooperation und Bildungstransfer 1976–1991* (München, 2012; English translation C. Hatzky, *Cubans in Angola. South-South Cooperation and Transfer of Knowledge, 1976–1991* (Madison, WI: University of Wisconsin Press, 2012).

7 Most of the contributions to Hickling-Hudson, *The Capacity to Share*, are also based on interviews.
8 K. Argyriadis, G. Bonacci, and A. Delmas, 'Reconfiguring the Cuba-Africa Encounter', in *Cuba and Africa, 1959–1994. Writing an Alternative Atlantic*, ed. K. Argyriadis, G. Bonacci, and A. Delmas (Johannesburg: Wits University Press, 2020), 1–26. This ideological justification of 'Internationalism' is also discussed in Hatzky, *Kubaner in Angola*, 92–104.
9 S. Díaz-Briquets (ed.), *Cuban Internationalism in Sub-Saharan Africa* (Pittsburgh PA, 1989); Domínguez, *To Make a World Safe for Revolution*.
10 P. Gleijeses, *Visions of Freedom. Havana, Washington, Pretoria, and the Struggle for Southern Africa, 1976–1991* (Chapel Hill: University of North Carolina Press, 2013).
11 In Cuban and East German reports. These are complemented by the Angolan archive material and the interviews with Angolans realized by Hatzky in her book, *Kubaner in Angola*.
12 G. Sluga and P. Clavin (eds.), *Internationalisms. A twentieth-century history* (Cambridge, 2017); D. Brydan, and J. Reinisch (eds.), *Internationalists in European history. Rethinking the twentieth century* (London: Bloomsbury, 2021).
13 Mark, Kalinovsky and Marung eds., *Alternative globalizations*.
14 M. Erisman, *Cuba's International Relations. The Anatomy of a Nationalistic Foreign Policy* (Boulder, CO and London: Westview, 1985).
15 Recently, the proceedings of an international conference on the occasion of the 50 year anniversary of the 'Tricontinental' have been published: J. R. Parrott, and M. A. Lawrence (eds.), *The Tricontinental Revolution. Third World Radicalism and the Cold War* (Cambridge: Cambridge University Press, 2022), containing a contribution by Anne Garland Mahler. author of an earlier, race-centered book: A. Garland Mahler, *From the Tricontinental to the Global South. Race, Radicalism, and Transnational Solidarity* (Durham: Duke University Press, 2018).
16 J. R. Parrott, 'Introduction: Tricontinentalism and the Anti-Imperial Project', in Parrott and Lawrence (eds.), *The Tricontinental Revolution*, 19–20, and contributions by Jeffrey James Byrne, 'The Romance of Revolutionary Transatlanticism: Cuban-Algerian Relations and the Diverging Trends within Third World Internationalism', in Parrott and Lawrence (eds.) *The Tricontinental Revolution*, 163–90; Jeremy Friedman, Reddest Place North of Havana. The Tricontinental and the Struggle to Lead the 'Third World', in: *From the Tricontinental to the Global South*, (2020), 193–215; Eric Covey, From Playa Girón to Luanda. Mercenaries and Internationalist Fighters, in: ibid., 304–31.
17 More on that discourse in Hatzky, *Kubaner in Angola*, 92–104.
18 J. Friedman, *Shadow Cold War. The Sino-Soviet Competition for the Third World* (Chapel Hill: The University of North Carolina Press, 2015), 212–13; Unfried, 'A Cuban cycle of development socialism?', 85; S. Mohandesi, (2023), *Red Internationalism. Anti-Imperialism and Human Rights in the Global Sixties and Seventies* (Cambridge: Cambridge University Press, 2023), identifies an era of 'anti-imperialism' to be replaced in the 1970s by 'human rights' as the 'dominant idiom of internationalism', a shift already analyzed by E. Traverso, Le passé, modes d'emploi (Paris, 2005), ibid., European Memories. Entangled Perspectives, in: Jürgen Mittag/Berthold Unfried/Eva Himmelstoss (eds.), *The Memory of Labour and Social Movements. A Global Perspective* (Leipzig: Akademische Verlagsanstalt, 2011), 33–51, but not referred to by Mohandesi who neither refers to Cuban 'Internationalism' of this period.
19 This interpretation as an effort to create a new ('Fifth') International is highlighted by J. Gerassi, 'Havana: A New International is Born', in *Latin American Radicalism.*

A Documentary Report on Left and Nationalist Movements, ed. I. L. Horowitz, J. de Castro, and J. Gerassi (New York: Jonathan Cape, 1969), 532–42.

20 U. Berthold, and C. Martínez Hernández, 'El Internacionalismo, la Solidaridad y el interés mutuo. Encuentros entre cubanos, africanos y alemanes de la RDA', *Estudos Históricos* 61 (2017): 425–47.

21 Gleijeses, *Visions of Freedom*; R. Yordanov, *The Soviet Union and the Horn of Africa during the Cold War* (Lanham: Lexington Books, 2016); B. Unfried, 'Friendship and Education, Coffee and Weapons. Exchanges between Socialist Ethiopia and the German Democratic Republic', *Northeast African Studies* 1 (2016): 15–38.

22 E. Bestard Pavón, *La colaboración de Cuba con los países de Africa Subsahariana (1959–1988)*, tesis MA, La Habana ISRI, Anexo VII (1989); Gleijeses, *Visions of Freedom*, 84, indicates 7,000 civilian 'Internationalists' in Angola in 1978.

23 Gleijeses, *Visions of Freedom*, 321.

24 J. A. Díaz Vázquez, 'Cuba: colaboración económica y científico-técnica con países en vías de desarrollo de África, Asia y América Latina', *Economía y Desarrollo* 68 (mayo-junio 1982): 28–9.

25 Noemí Benítez de Mendoza, Modalidades de la Colaboración, manuscript kindly provided by the author.

26 Vermerk über die Tagung der Handelsräte der ML RGW in der VRA am 22.4.1982, BA Berlin DL2/10624.

27 *Colaboración internacional* 1982: 14–16.

28 Díaz Vázquez, 'Cuba: colaboración económica y científico-técnica con países en vías de desarrollo de Africa, Asia y América Latina', 28–9.

29 Bericht über die Ergebnisse der Expertentagung der interessierten ML/RGW über die Bedingungen der Entsendung von Spezialisten in EL, Warna 25.-28.9.1979, BA Berlin DL 2/20039.

30 See Berthold Unfried's forthcoming (de Gruyter 2024) book: *'Entwicklungshilfe' und 'Internationale Solidarität': Globalisierungsunternehmen in Zeiten der Systemkonkurrenz.*

31 Archivo Central de la UJC, Secretariado Nacional 1972, 4.0.2: Actas de reuniones: 4-2-110/2.

32 Bestard Pavón, *La colaboración de Cuba con los países de Africa Subsahariana (1959–1988)*, 54; N. Jiménez, *Mujeres sin fronteras*, La Habana: Editora Política, 2009), 96–7; Hatzky, *Kubaner in Angola*, 109.

33 The "international solidarity" activities of the Komsomol serving as an example for the Cuban youth organization are described by Robert Hornsby, The post-Stalin Komsomol and the Soviet Fight for Third World Youth, in: Cold War History 1/2015, 89–94.

34 Hatzky, *Kubaner in Angola*, 92–104.

35 Carta de Secundino Guerra Hidalgo a Luis Orlando Domínguez, La Habana 4.2.1976, Archivo Central de la UJC, Sección 5 Primer Secretario 1976, 7-4-220/1: 5.0.8 Documentos recibidos del Partido. Interview of Berthold Unfried with Emiliano Manresa, former head of the Economic Office of the Cuban civil administration in Angola, La Habana 26.10.2015. Interview of Berthold Unfried with Santiago Castro, La Habana, 28.10.2015.

36 Gleijeses, *Visions of Freedom*, 321; Fidel Castro, in a speech published in the Cuban 'Revista Bohemia' (7.12.1979): 57, gives the number of 29,500 volunteers; S. Roca, 'Economic Aspects of Cuban Involvement in Africa', in *Cuba in Africa*, ed. C. Mesa-Lago and J. S. Belkin, (Pittsburgh, 1982), 172.

37 Interview of Berthold Unfried with Ester Moncada, former teacher in Nicaragua, La Habana 19.10.2015.
38 Interview of Berthold Unfried with Emiliano Manresa, former head of the Economic Office of the Cuban civil administration in Angola, La Habana 26.10.2015.
39 Carta de Secundino Guerra Hidalgo a Luis Orlando Domínguez, La Habana 18.3.1976, Archivo Central de la UJC, Sección 5 Primer Secretario 1976, 7-4-220/1: 5.0.8 Documentos recibidos del Partido.
40 Carta de Secundino Guerra Hidalgo a Luis Orlando Domínguez, La Habana 4.2.1976, Archivo Central de la UJC, Sección 5 Primer Secretario 1976, 7-4-220/1: 5.0.8 Documentos recibidos del Partido.
41 Acta 3 Reunión del Grupo de Colaboradores de la JMPLA, 1.10.1976, Archivo Central de la UJC, Seccion de Cuadros, Documentos sobre Grupo de Colaboracion en la Rep. Popular de Angola, 8-3-245/1.
42 Interview of Berthold Unfried with Noemí Benítez de Mendoza, sub-director of the CECE, La Habana 13.3.2015.
43 Carta de Luis Orlando Domínguez a Asela de los Santos, La Habana 5.12.1979, Archivo Central de la UJC, Sección 4 Primer Secretario 1979, 9-3-281/1: 4.0.23 Sobre selección trabajadores internacionalistas.
44 The Cuban number is mentioned in documents of the Departamento de becas del MINREX, Archives of the Min. of Foreign Affairs (MINREX), Havana. For the Soviet Union: Katsakioris, C. (2007), Transferts Est-Sud. Echanges éducatifs et formation de cadres africains en Union soviétique pendant les années soixante, *Outre-Mers*: 354–5, 90–1, tables of the figures of African students until 1980.
45 Informe del trabajo de la UJC en el exterior. La Habana 8.1982, Archivo Central de la UJC, Sección 7 Organización 1982, 11-2-340/1: 7.0.18 Sección atención a organizaciones de base en el exterior.
46 P. Gleijeses, 'Kuba in Afrika 1975–1991', in *Heiße Kriege im Kalten Krieg*, ed. B. Greiner, C. Müller and D. Walter (Hamburg, 2006), 469–510.
47 For the history of the Cuban military engagement in Angola see P. Gleijeses, *Conflicting Missions. Havana, Washington, and Africa, 1959–1976* (Chapel Hill et al, 2002).
48 Gleijeses, *Visions of Freedom*; Hatzky, *Kubaner in Angola*; Unfried and Martínez, 'El Internacionalismo, la Solidaridad y el interés mutuo. Encuentros entre cubanos, africanos y alemanes de la RDA', 425–47.
49 The organization of everyday life is vividly described by Hatzky, *Kubaner in Angola*, 249–92.
50 This issue is discussed at some length in a chapter on the sanctioning of 'indisicplines' in Berthold Unfried's forthcoming book: *'Entwicklungshilfe' und 'Internationale Solidarität': Globalisierungsunternehmen in Zeiten der Systemkonkurrenz.*
51 Personal memories in: Hatzky, *Kubaner in Angola,* 319–21.
52 A recurrent topic in interviews, eg. Interviews of Berthold Unfried with Nancy Jiménez, La Habana 18.3.2015 and 24.10.2015.
53 Memories of Cuban 'Internationalists' in: Jiménez, *Mujeres sin fronteras*; Hatzky, *Kubaner in Angola*, 302–5, 318–20. We do not dispose of correspondent Angolan memories to reproduce their view of the Cubans.
54 Zusammenfassung einer Rede von Jorge Risquet, Mitglied des Sekretariats des ZK der KP Kubas, gehalten zum Abschluss der II. Konferenz der Parteiorganisation der Zivilen Kubanischen Mission in der VR Angola, 10.10.1976, BA Berlin DY 30/27031.

55 First Party Congress MPLA Dec. 1980, cit. in P. F. M. Bondo, *The History of Angolan Education 1930–1980. The Convergence of Colonialism, Religion, and Decree* (Manhattan/Kansas, 2015), 241–2.
56 B. Unfried, 'Sozialistisches Weltsystem? Wie tauglich ist diese Selbstbezeichnung für die historische Forschung? Eine Erörterung anhand der Praxis außereuropäischer internationaler Zusammenarbeit der DDR', *Zeitschrift für Weltgeschichte* 1–2 (2022): 144–5; Alena K. Alamgir, '"Inappropriate Behavior': Labor Control and the Polish, Cuban, and Vietnamese Workers in Czechoslovakia" in *Labor in State-Socialist Europe, 1945–1989: Contributions to a Global History of Work* Ed. Marsha Siefert (Budapest-New York: Central European University, 2020), 111.
57 Gleijeses, *Visions of Freedom,* 82–3; Hatzky, *Kubaner in Angola,* 204.
58 Berthold Unfried, 'Scènes de la vie quotidienne des coopérants de la RDA en Afrique: normes de comportement et transgressions', in 'Coopérants et coopération en Afrique: circulations d'acteurs et recompositions culturelles', dossier thématique, Outre-mers 101:384–385 (2014), 247–66.
59 Informe del Comité de la UJC en la RPA a la V asamblea de balance, renovación y ratificación de mandatos de la UJC en la RPA e Informe del segundo chequeo de emulación especial del II.Contingente del DPI 'Che Guevara', Archivo Central de la UJC, Sección 18: Relaciones exteriores, Subsección 18.2 África y Medio Oriente, 18.2.1 Documentos relacionados con el país: Angola: 9-5-295/6.
60 Primera asamblea de balance de la UJC en la RDV, 9.2.1975, Archivo Central de la UJC, Sección 31: Relaciones internacionales 1975, 31.0.10.
61 Informe sobre el viaje a la Unión Soviética en ocasión del 50 aniversario de Komsomolskaia Pravda, 26.5.-4.6.1975, p. 11, Archivo Central de la UJC, Sección 31: Relaciones internacionales 1975, 31.0.10.
62 Granma 19.1.2016, http://www.granma.cu/cuba/2016-01-19/el-internacionalismo-cubano-como-aprendizaje-para-ser-mejores-19-01-2016-15-01-33 (23.2.2016).
63 Interview of Berthold Unfried with Isabel Martín González, 'Internationalist' in Angola, La Habana 26.10.2015; Interviews of Berthold Unfried with Nancy Jiménez, La Habana 18.3.2015 and 24.10.2015.
64 P. Gleijeses, '"La causa más bonita": Cuba y Africa 1975–1988', in *Cuba – Africa. Historia común de lucha y sangre*, ed. P. Gleijeses, J. Risquet and F. Ramírez (La Habana, 2008), 1–79.
65 Archivo Central de la UJC, Primer Secretario 1979, 4.0.9 Resoluciones 9-3-280/2.
66 'Boris' to Francisco García, member of the UJC Bureau (1977), Archivo Central de la UJC, Primer, Sección 9 Sección de Cuadros, 9.0.1 Documentos sobre Grupo de Colaboración en la República Popular de Angola, 8-3-245/1.
67 Unfried, 'Sozialistisches Weltsystem? 149–51; H. Bortlová-Vondráková, and M. Szente-Varga, 'Labor Migration Programs Within the Socialist Bloc'. Cuban Guestworkers in Late Socialist Czechoslovakia and Hungary, *Labor History* 62, no. 3 (2021): 297–315.
68 M. Erisman, M. and J. Kirk, J., (1991), *Cuban Foreign Policy Confronts a New International Order* (Boulder, CO and London: Lynne Rienner, 1991): 87–8.
69 Domínguez, *To Make a World Safe for Revolution,* 281.
70 MfAA/Generalsekretär Alfred Neumann, Information über die Reise einer Delegation des MfAA in die Volksrepublik Angola, Berlin 1.9.1977, BA Berlin, SAPMO DY 3023/1463, fol. 37; Unfried and Martínez Hernández, 'El Internacionalismo, la Solidaridad y el interés mutuo. Encuentros entre cubanos, africanos y alemanes de la RDA'.

71 Embassy of the GDR in Socialist Ethiopia, Commercial Section/Handelspolitische Abt. Addis Abeba Handelsrat und Attaché für WTZ Haenel an MAH/Leiter Abt. WTZ mit EL/Genn. Dr. Streber, Jahresanalyse über die fondsfinanzierte WTZ Äthiopien, 20.11.1989, BA Berlin, DL 3/74.

72 Interview of Berthold Unfried with Heinz Esche, West German project leader in Tanzania, Berlin 8.11.2014.

73 F. Castro, 'Ser internacionalista es saldar nuestra deuda con la humanidad', in *Colaboración Internacional* (La Habana, 1990), 38; see Hatzky, *Kubaner in Angola*, 92–104.

74 R. Soares de Oliveira, *Magnificent and beggar land. Angola since the civil war* (London, 2015), 7–10; J. Friedman, *Ripe for Revolution. Building Socialism in the Third World* (Cambridge, MA: Harvard University Press, 2011), 196, 205–6, 200.

75 Jorge Risquet to Fidel Castro, Luanda 13.7.1976, Wilson Digital Archive, https://digitalarchive.wilsoncenter.org/document/jorge-risquet-fidel-castro (7.5.2024).

76 This emerges strikingly from conversations that journalist Lara Pawson conducted with Nito Alves supporters 40 years after the events: Lara Pawson, *In the name of the people. Angola's forgotten massacre,* London et al. 2016.

77 Ottaway/Ottaway, Afrocommunism, 115.

78 Nicola Miller, Soviet relations with Latin America 1959–1987, Cambridge u.a. 1989, 116; Duncan, Cuba's Impact on Soviet Behavior in Sub-Saharan Africa, 188–89; Jorge Domínguez, To Make a World Safe for Revolution. Cuba's Foreign Policy, Cambridge/Mass. 1989, 158–159; William LeoGrande, Cuban-Soviet Relations and Cuban Policy in Africa, in: Carmelo Mesa-Lago, June S. Belkin, eds., *Cuba in Africa* (Pittsburgh: University of Pittsburgh Press, 1982), 29–30; Christine Hatzky, Hierarchien? Die Sowjetunion, Kuba und Angola. Ein Fallbeispiel, in: Jost Dülffer/Wilfried Loth (Hg.), Dimensionen internationaler Geschichte, München 2012, 398–399.

79 Gleijeses, *Visions of Freedom,* 327; Acuerdo Especial, 5.11.1977, Wilson Digital Archive, digital scan, https://digitalarchive.wilsoncenter.org/document/117931 (accessed 13.10.2021). Before: S. Díaz-Briquets, and J. Pérez-López, 'Internationalist Civilian assistance: The Cuban Presence in Sub-Saharan Africa', in *Cuban Internationalism in Sub-Saharan Africa*, ed. S. Díaz-Briquets (Pittsburgh PA, 1989), 52–4; Domínguez, *To Make a World Safe for Revolution,* 154–6.

80 Bericht über die Tagung der Stv. der Minister der ML/RGW, die für die Fragen der Außenwirtschaftsbeziehungen zuständig sind im Rahmen der SKTU, Plovdiv 21.-23.9.1977, BA Berlin DL 2/20077.

81 This momentum is the subject of my forthcoming book: *'Entwicklungshilfe' und 'Internationale Solidarität': Globalisierungsunternehmen in Zeiten der Systemkonkurrenz.*

82 Acuerdo Especial, 5.11.1977, Wilson Digital Archive, http://digitalarchive.wilsoncenter.org/document/117931 (19.2.2015); Gleijeses, *Visions of Freedom,* 327.

83 Memorandum a Viceministro Gerardo Mazola: Informe del cumplimiento del plan de trabajo de preparación del cro. Fernando Prats Mari, consejero en Etiopía, 10.6.1986, MINREX, Dirección de África Subsahariana, Archivos MINREX La Habana, Caja Etiopía; Agreements signed between Cuba and Angola in 1976 (extracts), in Nazario, O. and Benemelis, J., *Cuba's Relations with Africa*, in Díaz-Briquets, *Cuban Internationalism in Sub-Saharan Africa*, 27–8.

84 *Colaboración Internacional*, 1985: 22.

85 Contrary to suppositions by M. Falcoff, 'Cuba: First among Equals', in *The Red Orchestra. Instruments of Soviet Policy in Latin America and the Caribbean*, ed. D. L. Bark (Stanford: Hoover Institute Press, 1986), 77.
86 Already termed like this by A. Hickling-Hudson, 'South–South collaboration: Cuban teachers in Jamaica and Namibia', *Comparative Education* 40, no. 2 (2004): 1–29; Hatzky, *Kubaner in Angola*, and D. Benzi, and X. Zapata, 'Good-Bye Che? Scope, Identity, and Change in Cuba's South-South Cooperation', in *South-South Cooperation Beyond the Myths*, ed. I. Bergamaschi, P. Moore, and A. Tickner (London: Springer, 2017), 79–106.
87 A. Alamgir, and C. Schwenkel, 'From Socialist Assistance to National Self-Interest: Vietnamese Labor Migration into CMEA Countries', in *Alternative Globalizations*, ed. J. Mark, A. Kalinovsky, and S. Marung (Bloomington: Indiana University Press, 2020), 105; S. Bayly, 'Vietnamese Intellectuals in Revolutionary and Postcolonial Times', *Critique of Anthropology* 3 (2004): 334–9.
88 L. H. Nguyen, 'The Vietnam Decade: The Global Shock of War', in *The Shock of the Global. The 1970s in Perspective*, ed. N. Ferguson et al. (Cambridge, MA-London: Belknap Press, 2010), 168.
89 Information über den Aufenthalt des Sonderbeauftragten, Genossen Klaus Häntzschel, vom 5.-14.10.1983 in der VR Angola, BA Berlin SAPMO, DY 3023/1464, 189.
90 Following Angolan sources, in: Hatzky, *Kubaner in Angola*, 232.
91 Not every scholar is willing to see the socialist countries as forming a socialist world system. See for the discussion of this issue: C. Chase-Dunn (ed.), *Socialist States in the World-System* (Beverly Hills-London-New Delhi: Sage, 1982); Z. Gorin, 'Socialist Societies and World System Theory: A Critical Survey', *Science & Society* 49, no. 3 (1985): 332–66; Unfried, 'Sozialistisches Weltsystem? 183–207.
92 Unfried and Martínez Hernández, 'El Internacionalismo, la Solidaridad y el interés mutuo. Encuentros entre cubanos, africanos y alemanes de la RDA'.
93 Around thirty interviews conducted between 2015 and 2020 with ex-*Internacionalistas* in La Habana, following a snowball system.

8

The politics of development at Afro-Asian women's conferences

Su Lin Lewis and Wildan Sena Utama

In February 1958, a group of Asian and African women convened in Colombo to attend a conference that styled itself as a 'women's Bandung'; the organizing committee hailed from the five nations that had, in that same city, dreamed up the Afro-Asian Conference in Bandung three years earlier: Burma, Ceylon, India, Indonesia and Pakistan.[1] Yet it was partly overshadowed by the Afro-Asian People's Solidarity Conference held in Cairo over a month earlier. In contrast to Bandung, this conference had billed itself as an Afro-Asian conference for the 'people', led and organized by non-state movements, rather than statesmen, primarily from World Peace Council and the broader international left. It was followed by its own 'First' Afro-Asian Women's Conference in 1961. While the Colombo conference aimed – unsuccessfully – to be 'apolitical', the Cairo's women's conference, like AAPSO, put anti-imperial politics at the heart of the agenda.[2]

Recent years have seen a plethora of scholarship on the Bandung era, from the politics and performance of Bandung, often seen as an origin point for Third World internationalism, to other events involving activists, writers, film-makers and political leaders throughout the 1950s that signalled the breadth of Afro-Asian solidarity.[3] Yet three crucial dimensions remain relatively unexamined: women, development and the politics of the left. While the mere mention of Bandung invokes sentiments of Afro-Asian solidarity that have lasted well into the twenty-first century, Afro-Asian women's conferences have received comparatively little coverage.[4] This erasure mirrors, too, that of women in the early history of development – for these were very much conferences about development, and the centrality of internationalist socialist women to discourses of development in the Afro-Asian world. Both conferences focused on women's education and political participation, while the Colombo conference also included discussions on public health, slavery and trafficking, and labour. All these issues continue to be central concerns of development practitioners today.

Scholarship on women and development traces their inclusion in development discourse to the 1970s, specifically the United Nations 'Decade of Women' from 1975 to 1985, marked by a series of conferences in Mexico City, Copenhagen and Nairobi that put women at the centre of economic development.[5] But as scholars and activists from the Global South have argued, what Jocelyn Olcott terms 'consciousness-raising' began not with the UN but with networks of Third World women working via local organizations to campaign for a visible platform for women's concerns at the United Nations.[6] The UN Charter on Human Rights was revised by figures like Minerva Bernardino, chair of the Inter-American Commission on Women and Hansa Mehta, who organized the 1933 All-Asian Women's Conference in Lahore, a precursor to the Afro-Asian Conference of Women. Moreover, various scholars have argued that it was the Women's International Democratic Federation, a transnational alliance of women of the Communist and anti-Fascist Left who pushed for the 1975 International Women's Year which inaugurated the UN Decade.[7] It was a landscape of transnational networking across the South that nurtured developmental thinking in internationalist forums.

Transnational networking across the South fed into development thinking in international forums at the same that national development priorities put women at the heart of the agenda. This was a symbiotic relationship: as Amina Jamal has argued with reference to Pakistan, 'women leaders … during the 1950s and 1960s positioned themselves within the modernist project of the developmental nation-state to demand their rights, [while] the feminist women's movements of the 1980s and early 1990s constructed itself through elite women's disillusionment with the nation-state'.[8] In creating educational, professional, and political opportunities for women, designing social welfare priorities, and revising legislation to protect women's rights, women who participated in these networks worked closely with national governments. They faced challenges particular to postcolonial states, primarily around mass education, literacy and the minority of women in the workforce.[9]

While the Colombo conference was clearly nestled within the rise of a development discourse shaped by both national development priorities and international institutions like the United Nations, at the Cairo conference, 'development' took on a much more insidious flavour, with foreign aid seen as a cover for business and military interests of Western powers. The 'nominal' independence given to some Asian and African countries was hamstrung by the provision of conditional economic aid, which could only continue colonial domination, political oppression and economic exploitation.[10] The Cairo conference placed the discourse of development within a global framework of independence and liberation. Delegates believed that the development of colonized peoples was hampered by colonialism, and new manoeuvres in the form of neocolonialism sought to steer development in the postcolonial world to benefit former imperial powers. On the other hand, pillars of development did exist, particularly in terms of improving the condition of women. The Soviet Union was seen as a model of 'the gigantic development which a people can realise after achieving their national independence'.[11]

Despite these differences, we must be careful not to view these two conferences within the binary constrictions of conventional Cold War historiography, labelling one side liberal and another socialist. Elisabeth Armstrong's insistence that the Colombo conference hailed from the social reformist strand of Asian (or perhaps more accurately, Indian) feminism has merit, but her distinction of the conference from the 'leftist' strand of feminism present at earlier conferences like the 1949 Women's

International Democratic Federation conference in Beijing is in danger of falling into this trap. Many postcolonial Asian governments could be placed in a broad spectrum of the left in the 1950s and 1960s. They appealed to the public through the rhetoric of eradicating inequality, alleviating poverty and expelling foreign capitalists. By 1958, four of the states which organized Colombo's Afro-Asian Conference of Women were led by nominally socialist parties or leaned socialist. Ceylon's Sri Lanka Freedom Party had come to power in 1956 on 'socialist democratic' principles mixed with resurgent Sinhalese nationalism, propelled by workers, peasants and young urban voters.[12] U Nu and the Burma Socialist Party jointly governed Burma since its founding in 1947, bolstered by Burma's growing labour movement. Both Nehru's India and Sukarno's Indonesia were founded on socialist principles, despite challenges by nominally 'socialist' and 'communist' political parties.[13]

On the surface, attending countries at the Colombo conference represented multiple 'camps' of the global Cold War: Thailand, the Philippines and Pakistan in the US orbit; resolutely non-aligned Burma, Indonesia, India, Egypt and Ceylon; and communist China and North Vietnam. Yet as this chapter will show, Cold War alignments did not always point to stark differences in development aims, particularly around the social welfare provision that underlay the conference's key themes. With the participation of Vietnam and the People's Republic of China, the conference highlighted the way in which liberals, socialists and communists engaged in dialogue with each other about women's development and the direction of the postcolonial state. This was despite the Chinese delegation's walk-out at the speeches of observers from UN agencies, due to the UN's refusal to officially recognize the PRC. While the delegation had arrived one week early to unsuccessfully pressure Ceylonese authorities to prevent UN participation, PRC delegates continued to attend, considering the conference too important a forum to engage with Asian and African delegates.[14]

At the same time, the aims of the Colombo conference to be 'apolitical' – which proved unsuccessful – were at odds with the heightened context of decolonization and the Cold War. If the Colombo conference signalled the cooperation between women affiliated with multiple camps of the Cold War, Cairo's 'First Afro-Asian Women's Conference' in 1961 signalled the militancy of the left to campaign against the persistence of imperialism in the Afro-Asian world; decolonization was necessary for development, and true solidarity relied on the elimination of colonialism in all forms. Afro-Asianism, like women's internationalism, was thus not a linear development but led by multiple campaigns, activists and regions that prioritized different aims. Both connections and cleavages between leftist, women's and Afro-Asian movements would go on to shape the discourse, and the practice, of development in the Global South.

Internationalizing women: Colombo's Afro-Asian Conference of Women

Since the interwar era, Asian women had been campaigning for suffrage, access to education, an end to polygamy and access to rights to divorce and to hold and inherit property. In the 1950s, they had the legislative space to realize these changes.

Postcolonial governments needed women. Women were simultaneously symbols of the nation, of virtue and tradition, but also of cosmopolitan modernity.[15] Their entry into the workforce was also seen as a key to economic progress. Moreover, with the granting of universal suffrage, women voters could secure a political party's electoral chances. Women's organizations and their leaders were thus key interlocutors for postcolonial governments as well as the international organizations seeking to gather information about women in the developing world.[16] They were organizations led by educated, often middle-class women who claimed to represent women throughout the nation and the issues directly affecting women's lives.[17]

Through conference sessions, national women's organizations highlighted their close cooperation with their governments to enact legislation related to social welfare and women's issues. As Ghana's representative Mercy Ffulkes Crabbe noted, the Federation of Ghana Women, founded in 1953, was ready to support 'whichever political party in power' to improve the status of women.[18] Along with national women's organizations from the host countries, other organizations also included the Afghan National Association of Women, the Tunisian Women's Association, as well as the National Women's Federation of the PRC and Vietnam Women's Union. National organizations also indicated their integration with local organizations; Kowani, the Indonesia's Women's Congress, served as an umbrella organization for Muslim, Protestant and Catholic women's organizations, women's branches of political parties as well as independent and non-political women's organizations.[19] While it worked closely with government, it also cooperated with local organizations to encourage women to vote, promoted adult education for women labourers, established nurseries and health centres, provided scholarships and created a national cooperative women's bank.[20]

Delegates were drawn largely from the elite and burgeoning middle class, representing a range of professions: authors, educators, administrators, lecturers, MPs, journalists, social workers, nurses, lawyers and municipal councillors, as well as one aviator/pioneering broadcast journalist from Japan (Fuji Egami). While most women worked as educational and medical professionals, a few were first women ministers, including China's Shi Liang (Minister of Justice); India's Lakshmi Menon (Minister of State); Indonesia's Maria Ulfah Santoso (Minister of Social Welfare) and S. K. Trimurti (Minister of Labour); Burma's Khin Kyi (Minister of Social Welfare); the DRV's Le Minh Hien (Vice-Minister of Social Assistance); and first ambassadors, including the Philippines Trinidad Legardad (a former teacher and beauty queen). Some had participated in international forums including the League of Nations, the UN and the World Inter-Parliamentary Union, as well as inter-Asian conferences in the years prior to Bandung, including the 1947 Asian Relations Conference and the 1953 Asian Socialist Conference. Notably, no women from the working or agricultural classes were represented in such forums. The conference operated largely in English, given that many of the delegates came from states that were former British colonies; members of the Indonesia's political elite, meanwhile, increasingly used English as the language of internationalism. While this posed problems of representation and discursive imbalances in terms of linguistic fluency of the delegates, it was the most practical solution for transnational communication at the time, particularly for a conference run on a shoestring budget. The conference was unable to pay for delegates' travel and accommodation, though many of the delegations were sponsored by their own governments.

As in Bandung, the African continent was under-represented (only Egypt, Tunisia, Uganda and Ghana sent delegates); the conference only invited countries that had secured their independence. While the Cairo conference was dominated by over sixty participants from the United Arab Republic (UAR), Egypt's participation in Colombo was limited to three women. The Ghanaian delegation 'charmed all the delegates' in informal sessions but contributed little in formal sessions, apart from an opening statement that internalized the European missionary impulse, describing tangible achievements to improve the social and legal status of women, while also referring to 'purely illiterates living the primitive way, found mostly on farms, who must be brought to the light of the New Day'.[21] As an indicator of the cleavages that were to come, the Tunisian delegation – composed of three young women – was preoccupied with the recent French bombing of their borders during the Algerian War, and went against the conference's apolitical protocol by asking delegates to commemorate those killed in the raid; all delegates eventually obliged, and a number of delegates promised to support them.[22]

The conference's 'apolitical' stance was designed to ensure that delegates of all political backgrounds could come to the table and discuss key issues involving women's development. This was in line with the Bandung powers' foreign policy of positive neutralism, a point which the Burmese delegation stressed.[23] Yet already in the opening speeches of the conference, some delegates pushed back on this: Singapore's Shiridin Fozdar, a participant of the All-Asian Women's Conference and a 1934 League of Nations Conference on equality, expressed her disappointment that the conference had not brought together women from Egypt and Israel, North Korea and South Korea, Formosa and China: 'We must not continue to be our men's voice, but must courageously express our own feelings which could be heard in the world's parliaments and compel men to eliminate war.'[24] The delegate from the DRV saw the conference as an opportunity to bring North and South Vietnam together – though South Vietnam was not represented. The trope of women as peacemakers ran through all three major international conferences that sought to define the shape of Asian feminism in the postwar era, from the 1949 Women's International Democratic Federation conference in Beijing to Colombo to the 1961 Cairo conference.[25]

In contrast to the emotional flair of the conference's opening speeches, the main plenary sessions were far more technocratic, relying on an emerging lexicon of development, some drawn from international organizations as well as American aid bodies and civic organizations – some, like the YWCA, operated in Asia since the interwar era. The Ugandan delegation – notably represented by the Ugandan Indian Women's Association – attributed the 'dawning of the conception of woman as an individual' to the YWCA, which had taken on a multi-racial identity in East Africa.[26] A ILO report on Asian women's labour was circulated before the conference and was referenced by Burmese, Ceylonese and Tunisian delegates (this was the product of a mission undertaken to seven Asian countries in 1955–6, written in dialogue with various Asian women's organizations; Frieda Miller, who undertook the mission, found 'the organised women of Asia' preferable to parts of the women's movement of the West).[27] The ILO delegate, Emma Broisman, also used the opportunity to network and collect data from Asian and African women's organizations on all aspects of women's and children's welfare including health, education and labour conditions; particularly from China and Mongolia, previously inaccessible to the organization.[28]

The representatives of international organizations were keen to stress both their internationalism and their link to Asian women's movements. UNICEF's French representative began her report on its work in Asia and Africa with an account of supplies of material aid from various wealthy nations in the Global North, recounting a story of a Burmese midwife relying on a Japanese bicycle, Australian soap, Swedish basin and medical equipment from the United States, Canada, France and the UK, before using a German scale to weigh a 'healthy baby that has come into the world with the help of many nations – all pooling their resources and good will through the United Nations Children's Fund'.[29] The account served to reinforce a point about the organization's internationalism and work through national governments, but also resulted in highlighting inequalities in resources between the Global North and Global South.[30] By contrast, the UNESCO representative, Malcolm Adiseshiah, was an Indian developmental economist and educator whose mother was involved in the Indian women's movement, a connection which he stressed in his opening remarks; Adiseshiah could thus create an affective link between Afro-Asian women's organizations and UNESCO, urging them to recognize and join the work of the organization to improve educational opportunities for girls at a more egalitarian and emotional level.[31] The WHO was represented by its Indian representative, R. L. Tuli, a specialist on maternal and child health. The work of Asian (and particularly, Indian) delegates within international organizations – as Taylor Sherman also notes in this volume – was crucial in adding both expertise and legitimacy to their work in the Global South.

All the plenary sessions were led by an appointed discussion leader who circulated a background paper on key topics. Many showed an impressive comparative understanding of development challenges throughout African and Asian countries, including China and Vietnam, with background papers referencing both UN reports and reports commissioned by postcolonial governments. The session on education, led by Begum Aziz Ahmed of the All-Pakistan Women's Association, referred to the personal challenges faced by women on both continents in choosing between motherhood and further education, as well as the societal and governmental challenges of both valuing and funding girls' education. Indonesia's Hurustiati Subandrio led the discussion on health problems affecting women and children in Asia and Africa, including malnutrition, sanitation, and infant mortality and the heavy burdens borne by women as labourers and mothers; she pointed to the need for preventative work, health centres and voluntary organizations dedicated to promoting public health, as well as interventions provided by international organizations. Similarly, Anahita Kiramuddin described the training of health personnel in Afghanistan, underlining the role of the WHO and UNICEF, who since 1948 worked with Afghan governments to institute preventative measures, sanitation and health education, including midwifery education and establishing rural health development units.

Many of the papers, particularly in the realm of public health, thus served to validate the role of international organizations. They provided not only sources of data, but also frameworks for comparison and grounds for expertise. Family planning was an international arena where experts from the Global South – particularly women – played a major role. The organizer of the conference was Avadai B. Wadia, a pioneer of the London-based International Planned Parenthood Movement and long-standing member of the All-India Women's Conference. Despite her concerns about the eugenics aspect of the movement, Wadia believed in the independence and health benefits that family planning provided to women.[32] Avoiding any suggestion of controversial, top-down imposition of family planning measures, Wadia was careful to mention that any adoption of family planning had to be a matter of voluntary choice of an individual married couple. She spoke broadly about the links between family welfare services and social welfare, focusing holistically on the family unit rather than individual. Indonesia's Hurustiati Subandrio also joined the movement while living in London from 1949 to 1954 with her husband, Indonesia's first ambassador to the UK (where she may have met Wadia). After returning from the Soviet Union, where her husband had served as ambassador from 1956, she opened a family planning clinic in Jakarta and founded Indonesia's first Family Planning Association. She argued at the conference that the establishment of a 'welfare state' in Asian and African countries was directly correlated with the need for population control; birth rates in both Asia and Africa were exploding, while governments sought to elevate the standard of living.[33] She noted that both China and India were organizing family planning programmes on a large scale, while Egypt, Ceylon and Japan had established family planning programmes to different degrees.[34]

State feminism was in full force in the plenary session on women and citizenship, where women from Egypt, Turkey, the PRC and Iran detailed the achievements of their governments and national women's movements in educating women, securing women's legal rights and granting women the vote. Delegates provided accounts of the overall picture of conditions for women in their own countries, coalescing around the issue of equal rights and the representation of women in government. Many linked their women's movements with struggles for equal and political rights in the colonial era. Others – such as the Ceylonese and Pakistani delegations – stressed non-governmental efforts of women to instil civic consciousness. The Mongolian delegate noted presciently that despite the recognition of equal rights, 'there is a great distance between the proclamation of equality and the complete fulfilment of it'.[35] The Ghanaian delegate deplored the lack of representation of women in the Legislature, while the Burmese delegate pointed to reasons why women did not take up public office, including the lack of economic freedom and experience as well as interference with social welfare activities.[36] Discussion centred around encouraging women's participation in politics via civic education and party registration, as well as the need to educate men to change their attitudes towards women candidates.[37]

What Armstrong calls the 'social reformist' school of feminism was particularly prevalent in the session on trafficking, where delegates lamented the prevalence of prostitution, while others denied its existence.[38] Interwar and colonial era efforts – in conjunction with the League of Nations – had abolished brothels.[39] Delegates diagnosed multiple causes, including exploitation, war, the dowry system, as well as 'broken homes, poverty, unemployment, and feeble-mindedness' and the 'sexual appetite' of men in 'creating a demand and the need for money on the part of women'.[40] Shirin Fozdar shocked the delegates – and drew the wrath of her government – for declaring Singapore to be 'one big brothel'.[41] The PRC discussed its efforts to tackle prostitution through rehabilitation centres and the provision of social relief; in contrast to other country reports, some of which vilified or debased the prostitute, it stressed compassionate social attitudes towards prostitutes, who were not discriminated against but 'received sympathy and concern' and recognition of social and economic factors that led women to turn to prostitution.[42] Women, the PRC delegate argued, could be productive members of society, citing an example of a former prostitute elected as an 'outstanding worker' in her factory.[43] The Indonesian delegation similarly detailed government efforts to assist destitute and unmarried mothers, and provide accommodation to homeless persons and hostels for women workers.[44]

The session on labour indicated the most similarities across countries of various camps of the Cold War as multiple countries discussed the shape of social security schemes. The concept of 'equal pay for equal work' – a concept often associated with the United States and Europe – had been written into Indonesian and Chinese laws.[45] China had also set up restrooms and canteens for pregnant women working in factories, as well as crèches and nurseries in factories and mines all over Asia. Vietnam had in its opening remarks highlighted generous maternity leave policies, nursery groups and mutual help groups to look after the children of peasant women.[46] Asian socialist governments grasped early on that ensuring women's productivity was essential to the economic growth of the Third World.

The final session was on the promotion of closer links between Asian and African women. Some delegates advocated for more school exchanges, girl guide jamborees and international leadership courses as venues for interaction. The Philippines delegation pressed for the study of Asian and African languages, while the Singapore delegate suggested the promotion of import, export and barter goods from Asian and African countries. Notably, most suggestions came from Asian delegations – there were few contributions from African delegates, apart from the Ghanaian delegates' suggestions of a permanent bureau where publications might be exchanged. The session was an indicator of one of the core problems of the conference, and one that also plagued Bandung: despite acting as a forum for Afro-Asian solidarity, the lack of comparative representation by Africans meant that most of the sessions were shaped by Asian voices.[47]

Apart from its regional biases, the conference demonstrated that ideological differences could be put aside in the interests of women's development. The Chinese delegation's decision to stay despite its grievances about UN organizations, alongside the presence of Vietnamese and Mongolian delegations, made the conference more representative of a broad spectrum of Asian social policies – even more so than Bandung – particularly where it came to childcare and women's labour. The Vietnamese Women's Union had enthusiastically accepted the invitation to the conference, which provided an opportunity to build networks among Asian and African women beyond the Women's International Democratic Federation.[48] The conference also provided an opportunity for women of different political backgrounds to join together in a national context; the Indonesian delegation brought together S. K. Trimurti from Gerwani (the Indonesian Women's Movement), a radical women's organization affiliated with the PKI (Indonesian Communist Party), and Maria Ulfah, from the anti-communist PSI (Indonesian Socialist Party); such women cooperated in the women's movement up until the late 1950s, while their parties were often at loggerheads in Indonesian national politics.[49]

On the other hand, as Trimurti observed, ideological differences were more difficult to reconcile when it came to colonialism.[50] While the organizers of the conference attempted to steer the conference away from politics, the Indonesian and Tunisian delegations nonetheless addressed the issues of colonialism in Algeria and West Irian in their speeches. Here, unlike other conference delegates, the Indonesian delegation was united, as they were in 1931 at the All-Asian Women's Conference, when they refused to take part if the conference was led by a European rather than an Asian. Maria Ulfah, head of the Indonesian delegation, referred to the execution of four young women freedom fighters in Algeria and the issue of the Dutch occupation of West Irian as proof that the existence of colonialism that threatened world peace. As Ulfah argued, 'How can we, women and mothers, carry out welfare programme, if there is no world peace.'[51] Meanwhile, the Tunisian delegation gave an emotional address about the effects of the French military bombing of an Algerian village where dozens of women and children were killed and trucks distributing aid from international agencies were destroyed, resulting in Tunisians fleeing to Algeria. Nazli Tlabar of Turkey then complained that the chairman 'should have stopped such a speech right away'.[52] At the end of the conference, there was no AACW resolution – a rarity compared to previous Afro-Asian conferences – to avoid the arguments that had ensued around passing a resolution on colonialism.

Despite the lack of a resolution, women returned to their states with new policy ideas around women's development, viewing their own government's and organization's achievements or failures within a comparative global framework. Personal networks between women had also been formed, some crossing ideological lines, and efforts were made to sustain the conference's spirit of solidarity. Chinese delegate Tsao Meng-Chun invited Shirin Fozdar to visit the PRC in 1959. The Iranian government invited Wadia, Lakshmi Menon and Kamaladevi to discuss the idea of having an Asian Women's Congress. Wadia argued that national women's organizations should create international sections to build outward links and inform their correspondence and international activities. Yet any attempt to formalize an organization of Afro-Asian women was unsuccessful. At the conference, delegates from China and Indonesia tried to institute a Federation of Afro-Asian Women as proposed at the Colombo conference – but the suggestion was shut down by the executive committee.[53] Wadia travelled to East Africa in 1961 after a UNESCO Seminar in Addis Ababa to search for a suitable place for a second conference, proposing Accra, Dar es Salaam, Lagos and Addis Ababa.[54] She noted that despite the receptiveness of a few African and Asian women in Kampala, communal tensions between Asians and Africans would pose problems.[55] African cities with large Indian communities, such as Dar es Salaam, were the most receptive, and Wadia noted that a speech given about the cross-cultural, apolitical platform provided by the AACW was well received from both African and Asian women as well as Julius Nyerere, who Wadia met at his home.[56] Wadia hoped to set up second conference immediately after Conference on Women's Education in Ethiopia, planning for February 1961; an African conference, she hoped, 'would provide our Asian delegates with a new world to explore, and open up wide vistas of future cooperation'.[57] This plan never materialized, however, as it was overshadowed by a Cairo conference that placed African women firmly at the centre of Afro-Asian solidarity.

Mobilizing women: The 'First' Afro-Asian Women's Conference, Cairo

The 'First Conference of Asian-African Women' was held from 16 to 20 January in 1961, 'first' presumably to disregard the Colombo conference and situate Cairo, rather than South Asia, as the new hub of the Afro-Asian solidarity movement.[58] The conference was a legacy of the 1957 Afro-Asian People's Solidarity Conference in Cairo, which positioned itself within the lineage of Bandung, but involved far more countries, particularly from the African continent, and a far broader spectrum of activists, trade unionists, writers and artists. After the nationalization of the Suez Canal, Nasser's Egypt became the beacon of a decolonizing world; it was also the new centre of the Afro-Asian world thanks to the efforts of both state and non-state actors in building what Reem Abou El-Fadl has called 'infrastructures of solidarity': associations, media and political capital.[59] Unlike Bandung, which sought to remain non-aligned by not inviting the Soviet Union, the Cairo conference received hefty financial support from the Soviet Union and was organized largely by activists working with the World Peace Council – leading Western powers to blanketly regard it as a propaganda exercise for Moscow.[60] Unlike Bandung, too, women were highly prominent at the initial 1957 Cairo conference, with veteran peace activist and Indian poet Rameshwari Nehru opening the conference, and Egypt's Dr Ayesha Abdel Rahman speaking on the conditions of women and children.[61] The Cairo conference established the Afro-Asian Peoples' Solidarity Organization (AAPSO) and a women's section headed by Egyptian activist Bahia Karam to study the position and condition of women in Asia and Africa.[62] The rationale behind the 1961 Afro-Asian women's conference was that colonialism had usurped social rights and exploited women. Women activists throughout Asia and Africa needed to mobilize for full independence to allow women to effectively assume their rightful roles and attain equitable positions within society.

More than 200 delegates representing thirty-six Asian and African countries arrived at the AAWC, including nineteen countries from the African continent and large contingents from the UAR and Lebanon. Among the participants – most of whom were full-time activists – were Karima El Said (UAR), Rameshwari Nehru and Hajrah Begum (India), Iwanah Prijono and Francisca Fanggidaej (Indonesia), Mamia Chentouf (Algeria) and Adelaide Tambo (Union of South Africa), while the African American activist Shirley Graham Du Bois and Nigerian activist Funmilayo Ransome-Kuti came as observers. In contrast to the 1958 AACW, the number of African countries at the AAWC outnumbered the participation of Asian countries. The 1961 AAWC did not limit invitations to independent countries and followed the model of the 1957 Cairo conference in encouraging the widest possible participation.[63] The AAWC's call for solidarity with national independence led women activists to undertake long journeys to come to Cairo. While many made use of the expanded opportunities of air travel,[64] others, like the Kenyan delegate Peres Wera Ambitho, travelled by foot to avoid colonial authorities. Ambitho was arrested en route in Uganda, though was eventually able to come to Cairo with the help of the Sudanese government.[65]

In Cairo's former Senate Hall, decorated with national flags and a striking emblem of a loosely veiled woman – which graces this book's cover – the atmosphere buzzed with the energy of an activists' conference, bolstered by the support of Afro-Asian leaders. Kwame Nkrumah praised the arrival of 'Afro-Asian womanhood' on the international scene, while Sukarno's message to the conference focused explicitly on the role of women in development: 'It is very important also to mobilise all the energies of the Asian-African women for Development, because it is only with the help of the women that Development can be carried out in full, and only through Development can we achieve prosperity and a decent living for the peoples of Asia and Africa.'[66] Nikita Khrushchev's rousing message referred to the efforts of colonizers in Algeria, the Congo, Laos and the Caribbean to inhibit development, 'alleging as before that the colonial peoples have not matured to govern their countries. The experience of many newly independent states of Asia and Africa shows that this is a lie.' He accused colonial powers of failing to train their own specialists in education and administration, of suppressing a wellspring of local talent, and referred, by contrast, to the commanding presence of leaders from Asia, Africa and Latin America in the UN General Assembly.[67] After the first session, the delegation held a march signalling their solidarity with liberation struggles in colonized countries, paying a surprise call on President Nasser, who was said to have 'overwhelmed them with joy' and shook hands with every delegate.[68]

It was the height of the political crisis in the Republic of Congo following its nominal independence from Belgium, during which the Belgian government had re-deployed forces in Katanga to protect its mining interests there.[69] The conference's timing accentuated its focus on national liberation and world peace, seen as inseparable from the context of continued imperialism in the Congo, as well as in Algeria, Laos, Vietnam and Palestine. The Egyptian press reported that the UN peacekeeping operation 'seemed close to collapse', as one country after another served notice of withdrawal of its military contingent from UN Command.[70] In the eyes of the African continent and the wider Afro-Asian world, the UN had lost its credibility.[71] Rameshwari Nehru, president of the Indian Association for Afro-Asian Solidarity, in her opening address at the AAWC emphasized that the participants were 'meeting at a time when the colonial powers are making the most desperate efforts to retain their strangle-hold over our two continents'.[72] Like the 1958 Colombo conference, the 1961 Cairo conference still referenced the authority of the UN, but only insofar as it worked to assure independence from colonialism: 'At present time it is our main aim to ensure that the will of the peoples expressed in the Declaration to make [sure] an end of colonialism is carried out.'[73] Whereas the Colombo conference had taken pains to sweep politics under the proverbial carpet in the interests of development, the Cairo conference put the politics of a decolonizing world front and centre of the agenda – pledging solidarity with anti-colonial movements while railing against the persistence of Western political, military and economic hegemony in the Afro-Asian world. Nehru's speech asserted that the AAWC would 'be a landmark in the struggle of the Afro-Asian peoples against the forces of imperialism and war'. She added that the Indian people would give full support to the problems in Congo, Algeria, Laos, South Africa, the Portuguese colonies and elsewhere where 'imperialism threatens the freedom and peace of mankind'.[74]

Whereas the Colombo conference's final report captured a range of views but indicated its failure to come to an agreement, the Cairo conference provided not only a set of resolutions but a general report, composed collectively before the conference's official opening to be read out during the event. It commented on women's role in independence struggles and maintenance of peace, the political rights of women, economic equality between men and women, social and cultural rights. Yvonne Quiles, a reporter for the WIDF journal *Woman of the World,* said that the section on the role of women in the struggle for independence and peace was 'the most vehement, the liveliest, and the longest in coming to an agreement'.[75] Was this because the list of colonial grievances was too long and complex or was there disagreement among participants on these issues? Conference dynamics were difficult to discern as reports by the international media and observers of the conference were limited, focusing on the political and anti-imperialist nature of the conference. However, the *New York Times* reported that although the AAWC adopted 'a slate of resolutions approving a neutralist-communist line', there was 'one major dissenter'.[76] In a reversal of the Turkish delegates' complaint in Colombo about the apolitical nature of the AACW, Iranian delegate Safia Shinazi called on the Cairo conference to leave political issues alone, but her opinion was soundly defeated by the majority. UAR delegates complained to British diplomats in Cairo that 'the impression given by the press of an almost entirely political and anti-colonial conference, was misleading'.[77] The report noted that other topics of women's political, legal, social and cultural rights and the issue of women's equality in the economic field were equally important but the media was more interested in reporting on the political resolution (of the anti-colonial struggles) 'as being more newsworthy'.[78]

A key section of the report was, indeed, concerned with the continued political, economic, and military influence of Western powers in Africa, the Middle East and Asia. Accusations of 'neo-colonialism' had been prominent at previous pan-African conferences, presided over by Kwame Nkrumah.[79] Imperialist powers, the conference report asserted, were driven by their pursuit of economic gains and political dominance to strategically control natural resource in the Third World countries, even after their attainment of formal independence.[80] The AAWC revealed that an estimated 200 American firms were at work exploiting Africa's abundant mineral resources, thereby reaping considerable profits from the extraction of uranium, diamond and cobalt from the Congo; copper, chromium and manganese from the Federation of Central Africa; bauxites from Ghana; rubber from Liberia; and lead from Morocco.[81] Moreover, the profits generated by American oil interest in the Middle East experienced a twofold increase from 1952 to 1957, while American, British, French and West German monopolies dominated the economies of Angola, Mozambique, Guinea and other African countries.[82] The report noted the disquieting transaction totalling 500 million dollars of American military aircraft sold to France for the Algerian War.[83]

The participants of the AAWC were relentless in their condemnation of foreign imperialists for granting nominal independence to certain Asian and African countries, while providing conditional economic aid that made them dependent on former colonial powers. The report lambasted the French government's plan for a 'Franco-African Community' in twelve African countries, maintained by military forces and retaining strategic positions for French officials, as ostensibly presenting equality between African nations and France.[84] Meanwhile, the 'most subtle and dangerous' form of imperialism came from the United States, which devised mutual aid pacts as cover for military bases and troop deployments. This included the creation of US-backed military blocs in Europe, the Middle East and Southeast Asia including NATO, CENTO and SEATO;[85] this, the report asserted, was neocolonialism: 'colonialism departs from the main exit to return from the back door'.[86] As colonialism and neocolonialism prevented the consolidation of independence, hindering the emancipation of women, the conference advocated that the 'historic mission' of women in Asia and Africa was primarily the complete elimination of colonialism and imperialism.

In the economic field, the conference recommended the development of a national economy founded on industry.[87] Newly independent countries, such as India, China, Burma, the UAR, Indonesia and Guinea, were commended for their successful establishment of self-reliant and nationally driven industrial economies with the assistance of friendly nations (possibly the Soviet Union). In this regard, the conference embraced state-led economic planning and state-led industrialization. But to do so required not only expertise but foreign aid; most non-aligned states including India, Indonesia and Burma – played both sides of the Cold War in the early 1950s, accepting aid from both the United States and the Soviet Union.[88] By the end of the 1950s, Indonesia, Burma and newly independent Ghana turned increasingly towards the Soviet Union and Eastern Europe as a model and source of development aid given their overtures to the Third World and the imposition of 'conditional' American aid.[89]

Political and economic independence were certainly not the only concerns of the conference; delegates also addressed gender equality and social issues raised at the 1958 conference, including women's political rights, gender equality in the economic field, social, educational and cultural rights. Still, these issues had a political flavour: speeches accused colonial regimes of inhibiting development, while elevating successful development efforts of the Soviet Union and Asian and African countries. Far from veering towards totalitarianism, a charge often levied against the Soviet-aligned left, the conference encouraged Asian and African countries to build free and democratic societies, 'in which the creative abilities of the people can be fully expanded without any discrimination on the base of sex, race, etc.'[90] A similar resolution that had been posed at the anti-Soviet Asian Socialist Conference almost a decade earlier.[91] Without full political independence and freedom within a country, women's political rights would not be fully achieved. Despite this, the report noted that in sovereign Middle Eastern countries such as Afghanistan, Iran, Saudi Arabia, Yemen and Jordan, there were no broad women's movements against foreign oppression or for peace and democracy, and no suffrage.[92] Meanwhile, the Soviet Union, China and Mongolia were praised for enshrining women's rights within the constitution and implementing laws against the discrimination of women and replacing unequal marriage laws; in the economic sphere, women's work and wage rights were granted on an equal basis with men, and in recognition of invisible labour of housewives in the home.[93] Such claims echoed those made by the Chinese and Vietnamese delegations at the 1958 Colombo conference.

Participants also shared their views on the challenges faced by women in achieving equality in the economic field. The United States and other monopolies that dominated Afro-Asian economies continued to profit from the exploitation of labour, particularly women's labour.[94] Income inequality cut across continents: the wages of women working in Indonesia's rice-fields were half that of men's; in India, the average daily wage of women was 82–89 per cent of men's wages; and in Japan the average wage of women workers in all industries was 41.1 per cent of that of men.[95] In the Southern UAR region, the law stipulated a minimum wage of 19 piastres for men and 12 piastres for women in agriculture. Women workers in agriculture, cottage industries or contract labour were often not given maternity benefits, despite laws against this in many Asian and African countries. The conference then issued comprehensive and specific recommendations on economic equality for all working women, industrial women workers, agricultural women workers, women officials, women workers in unorganized trade and housewives.

On social rights, the report advocated for women's education and laws to 'free women from the shackles of tradition and superstition'.[96] In so doing, delegates styled themselves as 'modern', educated and progressive women, like women at the Colombo conference. But, like Colombo, women operated within a state feminist framework, and the focus on the achievements of postcolonial governments held delegates back from directly criticizing their lack of progress on women's rights;[97] nonetheless, in Cairo, they agreed collectively to urge their respective governments to eliminate enforced marriages, set an appropriate minimum age for marriage, and enact laws that limited the number of wives to one and prevent men from abusing their right to divorce. Against the continued legalization of polygamy was in Indonesia, Malaya, Burma, Pakistan, Sudan, UAR and some Arab countries, delegates cited the examples of Tunisia and Turkey, which had adopted personal laws limiting wives to one. The development of the social situation in Tunisia became 'the subject of controversial discussion in an impromptu conversation during the conference', and the Tunisian delegates shared their views with other delegates from Arab countries who were curious about the application of personal status laws.[98] Delegates argued that the number of maternity homes, childcare centres and nurseries should be increased and provided free of charge.[99] Just like the 1958 AACW, the conference underscored the importance of family planning.

Meanwhile, in the discussion around women's cultural rights, the main concern of the participants was education. Emphasizing the importance of independence, participants compared the progress in education since the era of colonial domination.

After independence, the number of schools and people attending them had increased, while illiteracy rates had considerably decreased thanks to the role of women's organizations, as happened in Sudan, Iraq, Vietnam, Korea and Indonesia. Decolonization in education was demonstrated in the conference recommendations that education was a natural right to every individual regardless of gender, colour and class; education should be free and compulsory for both men and women and women were encouraged to pursue education to the highest level; and education should prioritize local languages and cultures over foreign languages and cultures. The report cautioned vigilance against 'the plots of imperialism' and 'rotten American culture', particularly through the organization of popular campaigns and the exchange of publications and information among Asian and African countries.[100]

After the Cairo conference, delegates returned to home countries to share examples of women's progress elsewhere. At the Indonesian Organization for Afro-Asian Peoples' Solidarity (OISRAA) two months after the Cairo gathering, Iwanah Prijono, head of the Indonesian delegation to the AAWC, gave examples of educational conditions in the Democratic Republic of Vietnam and the large number of women holding government positions in independent and socialist countries, although she noted that polygamy still prevailed in some countries which were in various ways protected by law.[101] But as Anna Baldinetti and Martina Biondi argue, while anti-colonialism was the bond of solidarity between Asian and African women activists in Cairo, the Afro-Asian women's solidarity movement lost its unifying factor after independence was achieved.[102] Moreover, the improvement of the status of women politically, socially and economically were dependent on the interests of the state. In Indonesia, for instance, after 1961, Kongres Wanita's activism on women's issues were subsumed within a discourse of anti-imperialism as Sukarno attempted to incorporate parties and organizations into a united front supporting the state's commitment to ending imperialism and neocolonialism.[103]

In the wake of the Cairo gathering in 1961, the AAWC established an Afro-Asian Women's Section in the Permanent Secretariat of AAPSO. The Section published the *Bulletin of the Afro-Asian Woman*, of which Bahia Karam was the editor-in-chief, as the main outlet for the exchange of information and knowledge on the condition of women and women's struggles across Asia and Africa. Although the bulletin was expected to be the main medium of interaction of the Afro-Asian women's solidarity network, Karam expressed with regret that it was not possible to publish the bulletin on a regular basis. She said that 'the main reason is that, in spite of repeated efforts, our Afro-Asian sisters have not been very responsive and few of them only took the trouble to furnish the "Woman's Section" at the Permanent Secretariat'.[104] Although the next conference was scheduled to take place in Tanganyika, this plan never materialized. The second AAWC conference was only held in 1972, eleven years after the first conference. As with many of the conferences of the era, Afro-Asian solidarity, despite its symbolic appeal, was difficult to consolidate in practice amidst the persecution of the left, the rise of authoritarianism and geopolitical conflict amid a global Cold War.

Conclusion

While the 1958 Colombo conference aimed to be apolitical, providing space for a range of views on issues of women's development, the 1961 Cairo conference put anti-colonial politics centre stage, creating a shared framework for the discussion of such issues. Even so, the Colombo conference showed that anti-colonialism and decolonization were difficult to disentangle amidst the activism of Asian and African women's movements; delegates from several countries recognized the profound impact of colonialism on women's development, pointing to anti-colonial struggles in West Irian and Algeria. Although the two Afro-Asian women's conferences differed in vision and strategy, they each provided a platform for women activists to exchange views at a time when women were seen as central to the future of the postcolonial state. At both conferences, the state was omnipresent precisely because both political leaders and activists could not separate the construction of the nation with the building of a post-colonial world.[105] Yet they also reflected two sides of the same coin: on the one hand, a willingness to participate in international development forums in the interests of transnational exchange, expertise and the possibility of multilateral development aid; and on the other, a de-legitimization of an economic, political and military order that prioritized Western interests over the real needs of the Global South.

Even if Afro-Asianism proved difficult to consolidate in practice, both conferences served as a starting point for cooperation between women activists across Asia and Africa. The issues they discussed – education, women's rights and political participation, along with labour and trafficking – have formed the bedrock of women's development concerns for the past seventy years, at both UN conferences and conferences of activists meeting in South-South forums. Such conferences serve as sites of interaction between women from various political backgrounds and ideological camps seeking to better the advancement of women. But the core argument of the Cairo conference, pointing to the use of foreign aid as a political weapon, spoke to the continued desire for postcolonial nations to build a world free of imperial ties. The persistence of the non-aligned movement as a mode of countering the hegemony of the West, the attempts of Third World women's movements to centre their own claims and concerns, and the frustration with the hypocrisy of the West's human rights discourses as a condition of aid are indications that these continue to be fundamental concerns of the Global South.

Notes

1 Cindy Ewing, 'The Colombo Powers: Crafting Diplomacy in the Third World and Launching Afro-Asia at Bandung', *Cold War History* 19, no. 1 (2019): 1–19.

2 Elisabeth Armstrong, 'Before Bandung: The Anti-Imperialist Women's Movement in Asia and the Women's International Democratic Federation', *Signs* 41, no. 2 (2016): 305–31.

3 Christopher J. Lee (ed.), *Making a World after Empire: The Bandung Moment and Its Political Aftermath* (Athens: Ohio University Press, 2010); Vijay Prashad, *The Darker*

Nations: A People's History of the Third World (New York: The New Press, 2007); Carolien Stolte and Su Lin Lewis (eds.), *The Lives of Cold War Afro-Asianism* (Leiden: Leiden University Press, 2022).

4 Some scholars have covered the 1961 Afro-Asian Women's Conference, see Laura Bier, 'Feminism, Solidarity, and Identity in the Age of Bandung', in *Making a World After Empire: The Bandung Moment and Its Political Afterlives*, ed. Christopher J. Lee (Athens: Ohio University Press, 2010), 143–72; Prashad, *The Darker Nations*.

5 See Judith Zinsser, 'From Mexico to Copenhagen to Nairobi: The United Nations Decade for Women, 1975–1985,' *Journal of World History* no. 13, vol. 1 (2002): 139–168.

6 Joceyln Olcott, *International Women's Year: The Greatest Consciousness-Raising Event in History* (New York: Oxford, 2017); Amrita Basu (ed.), *The Challenge of Local Feminisms: Women's Movements in Global Perspective* (Boulder: Westview, 1995); Chandra Mohanty, Ann Russo, and Lourdes Torres (eds.), *Third World Women and the Politics of Feminism* (Bloomington: Indiana University Press, 1991); Devaki Jain, *Women, Development, and the UN: A Sixty-Year Quest for Equality and Justice* (Bloomington: Indiana University Press, 2005).

7 Francisca de Haan, 'Continuing Cold War paradigms in western historiography of transnational women's organizations: The Case of the Women's International Democratic Federation (WIDF),' Women's History Review Vol. 19, no. 4 (2010): 547–573.

8 Amina Jamal, 'Transnational Feminism as Critical Practice: A Reading of Feminist Discourses in Pakistan', *Meridians* 5, no. 2 (2005): 57–82.

9 Kumari Jayawardena, *Feminism and Nationalism in the Third World* (London: Zed, 1986); Mina Roces and Louise Edwards (eds.), *Women's Movements in Asia: Feminism and Transnational Activism* (Abingdon: Routledge, 2010).

10 Bahia Karam, *The First Afro-Asian Women's Conference* (Cairo: Amalgamated Press of Egypt, 1958), 33.

11 Karam, *First Afro-Asian Women's Conference*, 65.

12 Manifesto and Constitution of S.L.F.P. (1951), as quoted in D. K. Rangnekar, 'The Nationalist Revolution in Ceylon', *Pacific Affairs* 33, no. 4 (1960): 361–74.

13 See Taylor Sherman, Matthew Schutzer, and Pradipto Niwandhono elsewhere in this volume.

14 Emma Broisman, 'Report on Mission to the Asian-African Conference of Women, Colombo', WN 5027-1, International Labour Organization Archives (ILOA), Geneva.

15 Beth Baron, *Egypt as a Woman: Nationalism, Gender, and Politics* (Berkeley: University of California, 2005).

16 Laura Bier, *Revolutionary Womanhood: Feminisms, Modernity, and the State in Nasser's Egypt* (Stanford: Stanford University Press, 2011); Elizabeth Martyn, *The Women's Movement in Post-colonial Indonesia: Gender and Nation in a New Democracy* (New York: RoutledgeCurzon, 2005); Tharapi Than, *Women in Modern Burma* (London and New York: Routledge, 2014).

17 Joanna Crow's chapter elsewhere in this volume also speaks to the claims of middle class and elites at international conferences to represent broader publics.

18 *First Asian-African Conference of Women: Report of the Proceedings, 15–24 February 1958* (Colombo: Asian-African Conference of Women, 1958), 29 [henceforth FAACW].

19 Kongres Wanita Indonesia, *Sejarah Setengah Abad Kesatuan Pergerakan Wanita Indonesia* (Jakarta: Balai Pustaka, 1986).

20 *FAACW*, 36. See also Kongres Wanita Indonesia, *Sejarah Setengah Abad*.

21 *FAACW*, 29. Rose Parsons, 'Confidential Report to the International Council of Women of Asian-African Conference February 15–24, 1958', Committee of Correspondence Records (CoCR), SSC-MS-00340, Smith College Special Collections, Northampton, Massachusetts.
22 *FAACW*, 56; Parsons report.
23 *FAACW*, 15.
24 *FAACW*, 52.
25 Armstrong, 'Before Bandung', 305–31; Suzy Kim, *Among Women across Worlds: North Korea in the Global Cold War* (Ithaca: Cornell University Press, 2023).
26 Eleanor Tiplady Higgs, 'Becoming "Multi-Racial": The Young Women's Christian Association in Kenya, 1955–1965', in *Gender and Diversity Issues in Religious-based Institutions and Organizations*, ed. Blanche Jackson Glimps and Theron Ford (Hershey: IGI Global, 2016), 24–50.
27 Eileen Boris, *Making the Woman Worker: Precarious Labor and the Fight for Global Standards, 1919–2019* (New York: Oxford University Press, 2019), 89–104.
28 Broisman, 'Report on Mission'.
29 *FAACW*, 123–34.
30 Ibid., 114.
31 Ibid., 80–95.
32 Avabai Bomanji Wadia, *The Light Is Ours: Memoirs & Movements* (London: IPPF, 2001). Wadia memoir (page unknown – to get again).
33 Hurustiati's contemporary, the Southeast Asianist R. Chatterji, analysed the attraction of the concept in 'The Welfare State Concept in Indonesia and Cambodia', *India Quarterly* 18, no. 2 (1962): 154–66.
34 *FAACW*, 154.
35 Ibid., 169.
36 Ibid., 167–8.
37 Ibid., 170.
38 Armstrong, 'Before Bandung'.
39 Stephen Legg, 'Of Scales, Networks and Assemblages: The League of Nations Apparatus and the Scalar Sovereignty of the Government of India', *Transactions of the Institute of British Geographers* 342 (2009): 234–53.
40 *FAACW*, 196.
41 'S'pre Woman Explains Remark on Brothels', *South China Morning Post*, 11 March 1958, 12.
42 *FAACW*, 199.
43 Ibid., 201.
44 Ibid., 206.
45 Ibid., 259.
46 Ibid., 63.
47 Gerard McCann, 'Where Was the Afro in Afro-Asian Solidarity: Africa's "Bandung Moment" in 1950s Asia', *Journal of World History* 30, no. 1–2 (2019): 89–123.
48 *Women of Vietnam* 1 (1958). This bulletin was circulated among participants of the Colombo conference, and highlighted both the domestic and international activities of the Vietnamese women's movement. See 'Asian African Conference on Women, February 1958' File no. 5027-1. ILO archives.
49 Pradipto Niwandhono, 'The Making of Modern Indonesian Intellectuals: The Indonesian Socialist Party (PSI) and Democratic Socialist Ideas, 1930s to mid-1970s' (PhD diss., The University of Sydney, 2021).

50 S.K. Trimurti, 'Oleh-Oleh dari Konferensi Wanita Asia-Afrika (bagian IV)', *Harian Rakjat*, 6 March 1958, 3.
51 *FAACW*, 35.
52 *FAACW*, 57.
53 Parsons, 'Confidential Report', (CoCR), SSC-MS-00340, Smith College Special Collections.
54 Avabai Wadia, Letter to Steering Committee, 20 January 1961, Ibid., 10.
55 Ibid., 5.
56 Ibid., 8.
57 Ibid., 9.
58 This was not lost on the FCO. See Savingram to the Secretary of State for the Colonies, 'Afro-Asian Women's Conference, Cairo, April, 1960', 13 January 1960, FCO 141/7209, The National Archives (TNA), London.
59 See Reem Abou-El-Fadl, 'Building Egypt's Afro-Asian Hub: Infrastructures of Solidarity and the 1957 Cairo Conference', *Journal of World History* 30, no. 1–2 (2019): 157–92.
60 Homer Jack, 'The Cairo Conference', *Africa Today* 5, no. 2 (1958): 3–9. On the WPC see Carolien Stolte, 'The People's Bandung: Local Anti-imperialists on an Afro-Asian Stage', *Journal of World History* 30, no. 1/2 (2019): 125–56.
61 See *Afro-Asian Peoples' Solidarity Conference, Cairo, 26 December 1957–1 January 1958* (Moscow: Foreign Language Publishing House, 1958).
62 Speech of Miss Karam, *The First Afro-Asian Women's Conference*, 15 [henceforth *FAAWC*].
63 Wildan Sena Utama, *'Engineering Solidarity: Indonesia, Afro-Asian Networks, and Third World Anti-imperialism 1950s–1960s'* (PhD diss. forthcoming, The University of Bristol, 2023).
64 Su Lin Lewis, 'Skies That Bind: Air Travel in the Bandung Era', in *Placing Internationalism: International Conferences and the Making of the Modern World*, ed. Stephen Legg, Mike Heffernan, Jake Hodder, and Benjamin Thorpe (London: Bloomsbury, 2021), 234–51.
65 *FAAWC*, 1; Yvonne Quiles, 'Hand in Hand: Cairo Plays Host to The First Afro-Asian Women's Conference', *Women of the Whole World*, no. 4 (1961): 10.
66 *FAAWC*, 4–6.
67 *FAAWC*, 7.
68 Confidential Report from British Diplomatic Mission in Cairo to Information Research Department, Foreign Office, 21 January 1961, FO 1110/1480, TNA.
69 Georges Nzongola-Ntalaja, *The Congo from Leopold to Kabil: A People's History* (London: Bloomsbury, 2002).
70 *Egyptian Gazette*, 18 January 1961, 2.
71 See Margot Tudor, *Blue Helmet Bureaucrats: United Nations Peacekeeping and the Reinvention of Colonialism, 1945–1971* (Cambridge: Cambridge University Press, 2023), 114–61.
72 *FAAWC*, 14.
73 *FAAWC*, 19.
74 *FAAWC*, 14.
75 Quiles, 'Hand in Hand', 7.
76 *New York Times*, 21 January 1961, 21.
77 Confidential Report from British Diplomatic Mission in Cairo to Information Research Department, Foreign Office, 24 January 1961, FO 1110/1480, TNA.

78 Ibid.
79 See Frank Gerits, *The Ideological Scramble for Africa: How the Pursuit of Anticolonial Modernity Shaped a Postcolonial Order, 1945–1966* (Ithaca: Cornell University Press, 2023), 66–70.
80 *FAAWC*, 35.
81 Ventures of a powerful conglomeration of US and European oil companies were well-known at the time; see, for instance, the work of American anthropologist Alvin Wolfe in an anti-colonial newsletter of the period, 'The "Team" Rules Mining in Southern Africa', *Towards Freedom* 11 (1).
82 See Giulio Garavini, *The Rise and Fall of OPEC in the Twentieth Century* (Oxford: Oxford University Press, 2019), 107; G. and H. S. 'The First Arab Petroleum Congress', *The World Today* 15, no. 6 (1959): 246–53.
83 While France had asked the United States for this amount, it is unclear whether the United States agreed. See Matthew Connolly, *A Diplomatic Revolution: Algeria's Fight for Independence* (Oxford: Oxford University Press, 2003), 123.
84 *FAAWC*, 37.
85 W. M. Roger Louis and Ronald Robinson, 'The Imperialism of Decolonization', *The Journal of Imperial and Commonwealth History* 22, no. 3 (2008): 462–511.
86 *FAAWC*, 38.
87 *FAAWC*, 32.
88 See David Engerman, *The Price of Aid: The Economic Cold War in India* (Cambridge: Harvard University Press, 2018).
89 See Bradley Simpson, *Economists with Guns: Authoritarian Development and US-Indonesian Relations, 1960–1968* (Palo Alto: Stanford University Press, 2008); See also James Mark and Paul Betts, 'Introduction: When Socialism Went Global', in *Socialism Goes Global: The Soviet Union and Eastern Europe in the Age of Decolonisation* (Oxford: Oxford University Press, 2022); Kristin Roth-Ey (ed.), *Socialist Internationalism and the Gritty Politics of the Particular: Second-Third World Spaces in the Cold War* (London: Bloomsbury, 2023).
90 *FAAWC, 20.*
91 See *Report of the Asian Socialist Conference* (Rangoon: Asian Socialist Conference, 1953), 92.
92 *FAAWC*, 49.
93 *FAAWC*, 51.
94 *FAAWC*, 54. The source of these statistics is curious but one – Japan's – roughly maps onto that of the 1958 ILO report on conditions labour for Asian governments. A summarized report is here: 'Report to the Governments of Ceylon, India, Indonesia, Japan, Pakistan, the Philippines, and Thailand on Conditions of Women's Work in Seven Asian Countries' (Geneva, ILO, 1958).
95 *FAAWC*, 54.
96 FAAWC, 58.
97 Geraldine Forbes argues that despite sporadic criticism – particularly from women in the Indian Communist Party – the Indian government's record on women's equality was not seriously challenged until 1974. See *Women in Modern India* (Cambridge: Cambridge University Press, 2008), 226.
98 Quiles, 'Hand in Hand', 9; Amy Aisen Kallander, *Tunisia's Modern Woman: Nation-building and State Feminism in the Global 1960s* (Cambridge: Cambridge University Press, 2021), 75.
99 *FAAWC*, 30.

100 *FAAWC*, 68.
101 *Harian Rakjat*, 1 April 1961, 1.
102 Anna Baldinetti and Martina Biondi, 'Unfolding Transnational Female Networks: Algeria, Libya, Morocco, and Tunisia's Delegates at the First Afro-Asian Women's Conference (1961)', *Journal of Asian and African Studies*, OnlineFirst, June 9, 2023, 11.
103 Jayawardena, *Feminism and Nationalism in the Third World.*
104 Bahia Karam, 'Editorial', *Bulletin of Afro-Asian Woman*, January 1963, 1.
105 Cindy Ewing, 'Troubling the Global South in Global History', in Paul Thomas Chamberlin and others, 'On Transnational and International History', *The American Historical Review* 128, no. 1 (2023): 270–4.

9

Ahmad Ali Kohzad's visit to China (1958): A Voice from the Past

William Figueroa

In studies of the history of development and of postcolonial societies, voices from Central Asia, especially Muslim voices, are often at the periphery rather than at the centre. Kelvin Ng's chapter makes an important contribution in this regard by examining the thought of Mirsaid Sultan-Galiev (1892–1940), a Tatar Bolshevik revolutionary and Muslim socialist thinker, in an international context. This short piece is an attempt to make a further contribution by introducing another voice from the region into the conversation, one which highlights the ways in which intellectuals and politicians across Asia were actively working to build a common sense of national identity and international solidarity. These various projects, which emerged from a variety of different colonial, political and ideological contexts, found common ground by promoting a shared historical identity and by drawing on the anti-colonial and developmental discourses that were circulating globally, especially in the Non-Aligned, Afro-Asian and international socialist movements.

The following is an essay originally published in Dari, the style of Persian spoken throughout Afghanistan, in the magazine *Āryānā*, on 22 December 1958.[1] Its author, Ahmad Ali Kohzad (1907–82), had just returned from China and was eager to extol the virtues of that country and its political and economic development over the last decade. Kohzad was a renowned historian whose work shaped modern national narratives of m Afghanistan based on Afghan (Pashtun) identity.[2] A graduate of Lycée Esteqlal, a Francophone school and one of countries oldest and most prestigious institutions, his knowledge of French and participation in French archaeological research in Afghanistan in the 1920s and 1930s led him to a career in publishing, scholarship and public service. Throughout the 1930s he worked for the publication department of the royal government, as a secretary to the embassy of Afghanistan in Italy and as head of the Kabul Museum. In 1942, he was appointed the founding director of the *Anjoman-e Tarikh-e Afghanistan* (Historical Society of Afghanistan), where he became the leading spokesperson for a particular narrative of the national history of Afghanistan that was rooted in its pre-Islamic past.

Kohzad's personal history and association with European governments reflect the colonial history of Afghanistan, which was often at the centre of rivalries between the Great Powers. The most famous is the proverbial 'Great Game' between Britain and Russia, in which the two imperial nations vied with one another to wield political and economic influence in Central Asia through diplomacy and military intervention. Britain intended to establish Afghanistan as a friendly buffer state between Russia and the British Raj, and invaded the kingdom twice in the First (1839–42) and Second (1878–80) Anglo-Afghan Wars to enforce their will. Ultimately, Afghanistan was defined as a part of the British sphere of influence in the Anglo-Russian Agreement of 1917, and its history has traditionally been told through this colonial lens, with the aspirations and agency of Afghans themselves left to the side.[3] But more recent works have begun to excavate the local and global activities of Afghan elites and everyday people, and portray the nation as more than just a pawn in a Eurocentric competition. Scholars like Robert D. Crews, Marjan Wardaki and Elisabeth Leake, just to name a few, have emphasized the global dimensions of the Afghan national project, and the deep roots that contemporary developments have in the longer history of the country.[4] This includes connections to other nations like Germany and France, and efforts on the part of Afghan elites to modernize their country through the use of European knowledge. The school in which Kohzad studied, the Lycée Esteqlal, was founded by King Amanullah Khan in 1922, as part of a wider series of reforms to the social, political and education system. Kohzad's efforts can be read as part of these efforts on the part of Afghan elites to define their own history, culture and relationship with the world.

In attempting to provide the state with a national history, Kohzad was simultaneously asserting Afghanistan's right to exist as an independent nation-state. Reacting to the prevailing norms of nationalist, 'civilizationalist' historiographies in European academia and political discourse, Kohzad attempted to provide Afghanistan with a primordial national history of its own. Along with a generation of government-sponsored historians at the Historical Society, he was heavily influenced by nationalists such as Mahmud Tarzi, who had developed his ideas while living in exile in the Ottoman Empire. Tarzi was himself influenced by the Young Turks and the Committee of Union and Progress, which promoted a centralizing approach to building Turkish national identity and a state-centric process of national development. Although the legacy of similar top-down projects initiated in Afghanistan are hotly contested to this day, where many view them as an imposition on the part of the ruling Pashtun elites, Kohzad had a major impact on a generation of intellectuals in Afghanistan. Nile Green considers Kohzad 'the most influential historian of pre-Islamic Afghanistan whose writings during his twenty-year directorship of the Afghan Historical Society formulated a new historical identity for his fellow citizens'.[5]

The magazine in which Kohzad wrote, *Āryānā*, was the official publication of the Historical Society and was one of the most influential journals among educated elites.[6] Sayyid Ali Al-Dawood, writing in the *Great Islamic Encyclopaedia*, considers it 'the most important magazine that has been published in Afghanistan'.[7] Printed in Kabul from 1942 to 1978, it covered a variety of subjects including language, geography, archaeology, folklore and above all else, history. Kohzad was the founder and first director of the magazine, and continued to be an active contributor until the forced dissolution of the Historical Society of Afghanistan after the coup of 1978, which brought the Soviet-aligned People's Democratic Party of Afghanistan (PDPA) to power and set the stage for the Soviet invasion of Afghanistan. Its longevity is a testament to its influence and enduring popularity, and was partly due to the fact that it hosted articles from a range of prominent scholars from Iran and Afghanistan, making it widely read by academics and educated elites in both countries. Given its audience, we can see this letter as an attempt to inform its relatively educated and influential readers about the historical and contemporary ties between China and Afghanistan, as well as to persuade them to support the government's ongoing efforts to forge economic and political connections with China.

In 1958, Kohzad visited China as part of a cultural delegation sent by the government of Afghanistan to cement their growing relationship with China. These ties came about in the context of Kabul's flexible approach to Cold War politics. In the words of Indian historian Ved Pratap Vaidik, 'The Afghan rulers, right from Mohammad Daud Khan to Babrak Karmal, have emphatically claimed that Afghanistan is "one of the oldest non-aligned countries"'. Vaidik also cites the great historian of Afghanistan Rawan A. G. Farhâdi, who described Kabul's approach as 'a foreign policy which, contemplated as a whole, would one day become that of the non-aligned countries.'[8] At the First Non-Aligned Conference in Belgrade in 1961, then-Prime Minister Daud Khan said, 'Although the term "non-alignment" has been used to describe the policy of each member of this conference, it must be noted that Afghanistan's policy of neutrality far antedates the events which have given rise to the term "non-alignment"'.[9] In practice, non-alignment often meant playing to both sides in order to advance the government's agenda. While still maintaining links to the United States, Afghanistan developed especially close relations with the Soviet Union after Pakistan gained independence in 1947.[10] Nationalist Pashtun elites made irredentist claims to the whole of what they considered the historical region of Pashtunistan, which included parts of newly independent Pakistan.[11] Both the Soviet Union and the United States provided support to Afghanistan throughout the Cold War, with the United States stepping up its support to compete with the Soviets after 1947.[12]

Drawing closer to the Soviets opened up the possibility of improving relations with China as well. From the Chinese perspective, relations with Afghanistan were part of a larger push for closer relations with the Third World post-Bandung. Although Afghanistan recognized China almost immediately after the revolution in early 1950, the PRC was initially hesitant to establish relations due to the presence of 'large-scale United States construction of military projects'.[13] But as Mohammad Zahir Shah began to pursue closer relations with the Soviets, PRC leaders were more willing to engage and established a formal relationship in January 1955.[14] At first, things proceeded slowly, but they quickly gained speed with the conclusion of the Bandung Conference in April 1955, after which China redoubled its attempts to build ties to the newly decolonized nations of the world.[15] This is highlighted by the fact that despite being officially appointed in March 1955, a Chinese ambassador did not actually arrive in Kabul until three months after the two sides made direct personal contact at the Bandung.[16] Relations slowly developed over the next few years, culminating in a high-profile visit by Premier Zhou Enlai in 1957. Shen-Yu Dai, a Chinese political scientist who taught at universities across the United States, Pakistan and Liberia from the 1950s to the 1970s and wrote extensively about Beijing's foreign policy at that time, described the exchange between Zhou and the leaders of Afghanistan based on Chinese media sources:

> To his hosts, the Chinese Premier stressed that … 'The victory attained by the Afghan people in their struggle for national independence … inspired the Chinese people in fighting for their own national independence.' … His hosts, in turn, deprecated criticism against the neutralism advocated by Afghanistan. 'Those who criticise neutrality are, in fact, trying to find an excuse for their own blocs,' observed Premier Sardar Mohammed Daud Khan. 'It is evident that the present system of blocs has been the cause of discord and has especially created differences among the peoples of Asia and Africa.' Kabul's Mayor echoed agreement on 'historical ties,' and expressed hope that 'more efforts would be exerted to extend the exchange in economic, cultural and technical fields as well as in personal contacts.' … the Afghan press declared the old Silk Road reopened.[17]

A joint communique released following the visit spoke of the need to develop 'favourable economic relations' and to 'support the efforts of the Asian and African peoples to safeguard their freedom and independence'.[18] It also emphasized support for 'the principles of the Bandung Conference' and their belief that 'participation in the Asian-African [Bandung] Conference does not preclude cooperation with the rest of the world'.

Kohzad interpreted his visit to China through a similar lens, one which highlights three important themes of this volume: anti-colonial internationalism, South-South solidarity and state-led economic development. He draws these together by describing how he personally experienced the shared history of the two states by retracing the steps of the Timurid ambassadors who travelled to Ming China 500 years before. Kohzad weaves a narrative that juxtaposes the much older idea of China as an exotic, far-off locale behind a veil of mystery and the modern notion of China as a successful, rapidly developing modern Asian nation, one which can serve as a model for other states with similar economic and historical paths of development. For him, relations with China were a natural historical dynamic that had been severed by the influence of colonial oppression and internal disorder, leaving the people of Afghanistan ignorant of their Far Eastern cousins.

The relationship that Kohzad envisioned with China was similar to the type of Unfried and Hernández chapter in this volume on Cuban *internationalismo,* the policy of providing civilian and military assistance to countries in Africa, Asia, and Latin America. But while Kohzad's vision is almost utopian, Unfried and Hernández demonstrate that the reality was often far more fraught with cultural misunderstanding and clashing priorities. Where the two pieces converge is on the way international solidarity is deployed to reinforce a sense of national consciousness and benefit nation-building projects at home; or, as Unfried and Hernández put it, to create a 'patriotic internationalism' through appeals to a shared historical experience. Furthermore, whatever this shared past may have been, whether ancient ties across Asia, the international socialist movement or the common experience of colonial domination as part of the Third World (or Global South), its current goal should be the political and economic revitalization of the nation through 'development'. Thus, the past is put in the service of the development and construction of a shared present, in the sense of a common set of economic and political standards, what Unfriend and Hernández call 'convergence' on a single developmental path.

Through a shared historical experience linked by the spread of Buddhism, the exchange of diplomatic missions and economic exchange along the Silk Road, Kohzad is able to imagine Afghanistan as part of a broad community of Asian states, despite the difference in their recent history, political systems and ideological convictions. By juxtaposing this shared history with the impact of colonialism and issues of economic development, his essay brings into focus the links between the various socialist, nationalist and development discourses that animated the Non-Aligned and Afro-Asian movements. These linkages were a key factor in the appeal of these movements and the development of ties between nations with significant practical differences in their approach to politics and economic development. Personal essays like this one can do much to give us a glimpse into the mindset of Asian elites as they grapple with the changes sweeping across Asia and the world and try to place them in the service of their own goals, aspirations and nationalist projects.

'China'

Monday, 22 December 1958
Ahmad Ali Kohzad

Not one week has passed since I returned from China, and I still must say a few words about this country to everyone that I meet, whether I want to or not. Fifteen days in China may not seem like a long time, but because the journey is by plane – in fact by a jet plane – whatever one might claim about having only seen very little, there is time to see quite a lot. The era of the journeys of Marco Polo or the ambassadors of Herat,[19] who dedicated three years to travelling back and forth from *Khanbaliq* (Beijing), has now passed, and so these short trips are very valuable to promoting mutual understanding between different people and nations.

Today our thoughts focus on the West to such an extent that the land of the East has fallen behind a curtain of darkness and obfuscation, and the distance between us, which was already very great, becomes even greater; in such a way, even for those of us who are from the East and who reside on the threshold of Central Asia, the majority of the East seems to be either completely unknown, or else very far from our minds, as if it is located beyond the limits of dreams and imagination.

With the exception of Japan, which was jolted awake sixty years ago[20] and began to follow the caravan of civilization, and which has now participated in great international wars and gained worldwide fame for its industrial products, the rest of the Eastern lands of Asia have either been hidden behind the veil of colonialism, or held captive by internal disputes, so much that they have fallen into obscurity. They have neither their own voice to introduce themselves nor anybody who takes note of their existence.

China is one of the countries located to the east of Afghanistan, specifically in the northeast corner, through the Wakhan Corridor on the eastern outskirts of the Pamirs. It has several kilometres of common borders with us and is 1,715,510 square miles in size. Its population is 650 million and increases every week by as much as the population of the city of Kabul, and every year by as much as the entire population of Afghanistan.

The land is composed of mountain chains, high plateaus, and flat and expansive plains, as well as the basins of the two large rivers (the Yellow River and Yangtze River) that form the most fertile and populated areas, which have created a great Mesopotamia in the centre of China.

China is a fertile land and is counted as one of the early centres of human civilization. Signs of human life from 500,000 years ago have been excavated near the outskirts of Beijing. The history of China is well-recorded, from the cave-dwelling period to the era of half-history and half-legend to the heroic historical eras of the Han, Tang, Song, Ming, and Manchu dynasties, among others, each of which lasted from 200 to 300 or 400 years. In the last nine years, a new chapter in the life of this old country has been opened, and while it is possible to review all these developments, it is obvious that we cannot go into it here. One could attempt a comparison of some of China's cultural and artistic products and historical issues with their corresponding eras in Afghanistan, but there is no room to explore these issues in this essay of just a few brief lines …

During their fifteen-day stay in China, the cultural group of Afghanistan[21] dedicated one week to seeing Beijing and the nearby environment within a 120-kilometre radius. During the second week, on the way from Beijing to Canton, we passed through several provinces while travelling 3000 kilometres in southern China and stopped at some cities along the road, such as Xi'an, Luoyang, Longmen, and Canton.

Beijing is located on plains that are no more than 165 feet above sea level. The closest mountain ranges are west of the city, and the Great Wall of China is located behind that same mountain range. Due to the fact that it is located 90 km from the city, it can be seen from some high points in Beijing.

During their one-week stay in Beijing, the cultural delegation of Afghanistan visited the royal palaces of the Ming Dynasty, which were contemporary with the Timurids of Herat. Today the National Museum of China occupies most of this space. The cultural delegation visited Peking University, the Academy of Fine Arts, the Foreign Language Press, a series of spring and summer gardens, a number of palaces and promenades, the Great Wall of China, and the shrines of the emperors of the Ming Dynasty, most notably the tomb of Yongle, the great emperor of the Ming that established friendly relations with Shahrukh Mirza,[22] the Timurid Shah of Herat. The Ming Dynasty ruled from between 1368 and 1644, about 276 years, during the fourteenth, fifteenth, and sixteenth centuries, and at one time they were contemporaries with our Timurids of Herat. Friendly relations were established in the middle of the ninth century of the Hijri calendar (in the middle of the sixteenth century in the Christian calendar), especially between Shahrukh and his sons, Ulugh Beg Mirza[23] and Mirza Baysunghur,[24] and the Great Ming Emperor, Yongle.[25] Envoys of goodwill and ambassadors were repeatedly exchanged between Herat and Khan Baliq (Beijing). In volume two of the book *Maṭla ʿ-e sa ʿdayn va majma ʿ-e baḥrayn*,[26] using the words of Ghiyāth al-dīn Naqqāsh of Herat,[27] who himself was counted among one of the goodwill delegations and was ordered by Baysunghur to write a travelogue from Herat to Beijing. Using the words of others, Molānā Kamāl-al-Dīn ʿAbd-al-Razzāq Samarqandī delivers the reflection of the memories of these goodwill delegations of the Timurids of Herat to our ears.

Explaining the relations between the court of the Timurids and the court of Tang and *Dai Ming*, which means the Great Ming [in Chinese], would require many articles and treatises, but there is not enough space or time in this essay for that. Before I left Afghanistan, I took with me some notes on the *Maṭlaʿ-e saʿdayn*, especially that which was reported by Ghiyāth al-dīn Naqāsh of Herat after his five months stay in Peking. I had read everything and brought the notes with me.

The writings of Naqāsh of Herat that were related to the palace of the Great Ming Emperor had a great deal of importance to us, as they described the courtroom of Yongle and listed what hospitality was provided to envoys, among other things. We saw many of those things that were mentioned in his writings, and inside the paved plazas and old buildings and gardens of the Ming courts, the same tables and chairs and Chinese ceramics and large bronze incense burners mostly still existed exactly as he described them. The reader can imagine how happy the Afghan cultural group felt, reading these notes taken by one of their countrymen 500 years ago while seeing the palace of the Ming Emperors.

Luckily, prior to the arrival of the Afghan delegation to Peking at the area of the grave of Yongle, a crypt was discovered, and in the crypt, an enormous number of gold utensils and jars and ceramic pots and vases from that era were discovered, along with hundreds of very exquisite pieces and tools. All of them were put on display in the Drum Tower of the Northern Gate of the Royal Palace, and on the last day of our stay in Peking, we also went to see them. Anyway, to describe every place and location that we saw in one week in Peking would be too much. During the second week of our journey, we travelled 3000 kilometres through the southern parts of China, and we passed by and stopped in the different cities that I have named.

Among these cities, Xi'an attracted more of our attention than the others. Compared to everywhere else we had been, we had a more enjoyable time in this historic city. Xian is one of the historic cities of China and was the capital during the era of the Tang dynasty in the first two or three centuries of the Hijri calendar, which was contemporary with the emergence of the auspicious religion of Islam in Afghanistan. Buddhism had spread widely in China due to the activities of missionaries and monks of Gandahara and Kapisa during the previous few centuries. The leading Chinese scholar of Buddhism, Xuanzang, who has gained great fame in the historical memory of Afghanistan and who was himself from Xi'an, had entered Afghanistan in 631 of the Christian calendar, and as everyone knows, passed through Qanduz (Kohan Dej), Balkh, Bamyan, Kapisa (Bagram), Hadda (Habilu), etc. After his trip to India, he would again pass through the valleys and mountains of our kingdom and enter the city of Xi'an. In memory of the return of the aforementioned scholar, they built a temple and an especially tall tower with a height of approximately seventy metres, and today, in addition to its historical importance, this tower is counted among the highest and best places to see the landscape in all directions around the city of Xi'an. Located 40 kilometres east of the city, the shrine of that Chinese pilgrim is nestled on a happy

هیوان-تسنگ زایر چینی که بعد از مسافرت
به افغانستان و هند بامجموعه ئی از آثار
و اسناد به شهر (سیان) در چین مراجعت
کرده است.

Figure 2 This image appears in the original text between these two paragraphs. It is identified as 'Xuanzang the Chinese pilgrim who, after travelling to Afghanistan and India, returned to the city of Xi'an in China with a collection of works and documents', recounting a well-known story about the transmission of Buddhism to China.

green hill, and along the road, we observed green fields and fresh hills that comprise the natural beauty of Xian. Next to another city by the name of Luoyang, there is another historic site known as Longmen, which is a valley in which a large river passes through the middle. Along the side of the small mountain on the western banks of the river, hundreds and thousands of tunnels have been dug in the heart of the granite, just as they have in Bamyan. Here, from around the fifth century CE to the eighth, beautiful and exquisite carvings and sculptures were created, and one can see that they have hundreds of interesting points of comparison with the Buddhist statues of Bamyan which require intensive study.

The Afghan cultural delegation saw new things in the New China that indicate the awakening of a great nation and represents the work and effort of a few hundred million people under the wide-ranging plans of a single regime.[28] In the course of 4,500 years of history, China has passed through eras of majesty and glory, of warring and federal kingdoms, of imperialism, of civil war, eras of wandering, eras of hunger, and of eras dissolution; finally, in the last 9 years, for the first time in its long history, China has come under the influence of a single administrative regime.

The New China is busy with restoring what has been lost, and because of the long periods of ignorance and negligence that they have gone through, their desire for compensation for the past is all the greater. China, an agricultural country whose farmers are famous around the world for their good attitude and perseverance, is making great strides in the pursuit of industrialization. Next to every city, another city has been established by the density of factories and workshops and worker camps, and by very simple principles, through melting down some minerals in a small clay furnace, every Chinese peasant family has been tasked with participating in the increase in production of iron and steel.[29]

The People's Republic of China has activated the expansive agricultural, construction, and industrial plans of a quarter of the world's population in the expansive land of China. The power of the people in this country is extremely weighty and performs the work of heavy machinery and mechanized devices. The people of China, men and women, wear simple uniforms and are similar to one another. Chinese women do not have time to wear makeup. Among the millions of Chinese women, you will not see the least amount of makeup on the face or on the lips. It feels as though the men and women are all occupied with work and developing their country and homeland. A great nation and a well-organized mass of people in the middle of the continent of Asia have woken up, and at the front of every campaign targeting the personal, social, and national life of Chinese individuals and Chinese society, the word 'activity' can be read.

Kohzad's open letter demonstrates the rhetorical power of the combination of heritage and developmental discourse. His appeal that Afghanistan rediscover its ancient links to Asia is predicated on his belief in the contemporary success of China and Japan to modernize and industrialize. He delivers this message in an evocative way, literally rediscovering those links for himself and his audience as he walks the reader through the Forbidden Palace and describes the sense of joy and connection the group felt by experiencing the physical presence of these historical links. By emphasizing the historical and spiritual kinship between China and Afghanistan, Kohzad is making an implicit argument that Afghanistan is also capable of the same kinds of economic and industrializing success that he argues has been seen in China and Japan. He is also arguing for a particular kind of modernization, the same kind of top-down, state-sponsored projects like the ones that supported *Anjoman-e Tarikh*.

Sources like these are invaluable in adding to our understanding how different locales responded to development discourse and the challenges of modernity. Additional research is sorely needed on the history of Afghanistan's modern developmental history and its relationship with China. The combination of heritage and development continues to be a core feature of the diplomatic messaging of the Chinese state to this day, and underscores its relationship with Afghanistan and other countries in Central Asia and the Middle East. Understanding these relationships can therefore help not only to de-provincialize the history of Central Asian and Afghanistan, but also to better understand a critical set of contemporary political and economic relationships.

Notes

1 Ahmad Ali Kohzad, 'Chin [China]', Āryānā, Dey 1337, no. 192 (1958).

2 Thomas H. Johnson, and Ludwig W. Adamec, *Historical Dictionary of Afghanistan* (Lanham, MD: Rowman & Littlefield Publishers, 2021), 293–4.

3 The term was coined by Rudyard Kipling in his novel *Kim* in 1901, and the historiographical interpretation can be found throughout writing on the history of Afghanistan, from contemporaneous accounts to today. For the classic popular contemporary account, see Peter Hopkirk, *The Great Game: On Secret Service in High Asia* (New York, NY: Kodansha International, 1992).

4 Robert D. Crews, *Afghan Modern: The History of a Global Nation* (Cambridge, MA: Belknap Press, 2015); Marjan Wardaki, 'Rediscovering Afghan Fine Arts: The life of an Afghan Student in Germany, Abdul Ghafur Brechna', *Modern Asian Studies* 55, no. 5 (2021): 1544–80; Elisabeth Leake, *Afghan Crucible: The Soviet Invasion and the Making of Modern Afghanistan* (Oxford, UK: Oxford University Press, 2022).

5 Nile Green, 'The Afghan Discovery of Buddha: Civilizational History and the Nationalizing of Afghan Antiquity', *International Journal of Middle East Studies* 49, no. 1 (2017): 47–70, 48.

6 *Āryānā* is an ancient geographic term used by Greek and Roman authors to describe the inhabitants and lands of the eastern part of the Persian Achaemenid Empire, including modern Afghanistan and eastern Iran, up to the Indus River in today's Pakistan. This name itself points to Kohzad's aim to build a national consciousness in Afghanistan based on the ancient history of the region.

7 Sayyid Ali al-Dawood, 'āryānā (majale)', *Dā'erat-ol-Ma'āref-e Bozorg-e Eslāmi (Encyclopedia Islamica)* 1 (2018): 117.

8 V. P. Vaidik, 'Afghan Non-Alignment: Changing Faces', *International Studies* 20, no. 1–2 (1981): 239–55, 239.

9 Ibid.

10 Zalmai Nishat, and Hameed Hakimi. 'Pakistan-Afghanistan Relations: Emergence of New Nation States and the Search for Identity', in *Pakistan-Afghanistan Relations: Pitfalls and the Way Forward*, ed. Huma Baqai and Nausheen Wasi (Islamabad: Friedrich-Ebert-Steftung [FES], 2021).

11 The North-West Frontier Province (NWFP, now renamed as Khyber Pakhtunkhwa).

12 Thomas Barfield, *Afghanistan: A Cultural and Political History* (Princeton, NJ: Princeton University Press, 2010), 209–10.
13 Shenyu Dai, 'China and Afghanistan', *The China Quarterly* 25 (1966): 213–21, 216.
14 Ibid.
15 John Garver, *China's Quest: The History of the Foreign Relations of the People's Republic of China* (New York, NY: Oxford University Press, 2016), 92–113.
16 Ibid., 216.
17 Ibid., 217.
18 'Zhōnghuá rénmín gònghéguó zhōu'ěnlái zǒnglǐ hé āfùhàn wángguó wū dé shǒuxiàng de liánhé gōngbào. (Joint Communique between Premier Zhou Enlai of the People's Republic of China and Prime Minister Daud of the Kingdom of Afghanistan).' *Zhōnghuá rénmín gònghéguó guówùyuàn gōngbào (People's Republic of China State Council Gazette)*. No. 4, 28 January 1957. p. 64.
19 Referring to the Timurid Empire, a culturally Persian Turko-Mongol Empire that ruled over much of the Middle East and Central Asia in the early fifteenth century. Founded by the famous conqueror Timur, also called Tamerlane, its capital was originally Samarqand but moved to Herat after his death. Although Timur himself almost pursued a military campaign against the Ming Emperor Hongwu, his successors developed substantial commercial and political relations with the Ming court. See Ralph Kauz, 'Timurid Commercial Relations with China', in *Oxford Research Encyclopedia of Asian History* (Oxford, UK, 2023).
20 The First Sino-Japanese War (1894–5), in which the Meiji government of Japan, which had made reforms to its political and military system based on the European model, defeated the Qing state. After this victory, Japan was increasingly seen as an equal to Western countries, a status it cemented with its victory over Russia in the Russo-Japanese War (1904–5) a decade later.
21 Although the exact composition of this group other than Kohzad is not mentioned in the text, from context it appears that it consisted of a small group of government-affiliated academics, most likely those affiliated with Kohzad's Historical Society of Afghanistan.
22 Son of Timur and ruler of the Timurid Empire from 1405 to 1447. Under his rule, relations between the Ming and the Timurids stabilized and flourished.
23 Oldest son of Shahrukh who briefly ruled the Timurid Empire from 1447 to his assassination in 1449.
24 A Timurid prince and brother of Ulugh Beg, he held important political roles and was known for his patronage of the arts. He was especially well known as a practitioner and patron of calligraphy and Persian miniature painting. The artists and artisans he and his father, Shahrukh, sponsored in Herat are known for the presence of Chinese-style motifs in their art, likely a result of the embassies exchanged with China during this period. See Roemer, H.R. 'BĀYSONḠOR, ḠĪĀṮ-AL-DĪN' Encyclopaedia Iranica, Vol. IV, Fasc. 1 (1989): 6–9.
25 The Yongle Emperor, third emperor of the Ming who reigned from 1402 to 1424.
26 'The Rise of the Two Auspicious Constellations and the Confluence of the Two Oceans', written by Abd-al-Razzāq Samarqandī, a Persian scholar and historian at the Timurid court. He witnessed or participated in many political events, military campaigns and diplomatic missions, and his book is an important record of the affairs of the Timurid state. This work includes extensive commentary on the Timurid relationship with China, and includes the travelogue of Ghiyāth al-dīn Naqqāsh of Herat about his journey to the Ming court. See C. P. Haase, 'Abd-Al-Razzaq Samarqandi', *Encyclopædia Iranica*, Vol. I, Fasc. 2 (2011): 158–60.

27 A painter sent by Baysunghur as an envoy to the Ming. Besides his profession, which can be understood from his name (Naqāsh meaning painter), and the fact that he was ordered to record his journey by Baysunghur, little else is known about him.

28 Kohzad uses the term *rezhim* to describe China's government, which has been preserved in the translation, but it is worth nothing that it does not carry the pejorative meaning that the term has today.

29 A reference to the Great Leap Forward, in which Chinese peasants famously were mobilized to produce steel in crude backyard blast furnaces. Ironically, this process for which Kohzad expresses so much enthusiasm resulted primarily in a poor-quality product that was mostly useless, and the disruption it caused contributed to the Great Chinese Famine of 1959–61.

10

Forging the vanguard of African socialism: Nationalization, respectability and ideological struggles at Kivukoni College, Tanzania

Eric Burton

Introduction

On 12 April 1962, Julius Nyerere laid out his vision of Tanganyika's (and, after 1964, Tanzania's) future state ideology during a conference on African Socialism.[1] Appropriating the newly coined Kiswahili term *ujamaa* ('familyhood'), Nyerere defined socialism not as a system of relations of production, but as an 'attitude of mind' marked by an emphasis on mutual assistance, hard work and individual responsibility. Instead of embracing the historical path and standards of industrial society, Nyerere championed collective agricultural production in order to build a socialist and self-reliant society based on what he saw as traditional African values. As a locally inflected alternative to the dominant universalist models of the time, liberal capitalism and Marxism-Leninism, *ujamaa* became one of the world's most durable 'peripheral socialisms' in the Global South that were devised to address the challenges of colonial underdevelopment, dependency and Cold War threats to post-colonial sovereignty.[2]

The conference at which Nyerere first proclaimed his vision of *ujamaa* took place in the former Ghana Hotel, situated at a beach overlooking the harbour of Dar es Salaam, the country's capital. The hotel had just been turned into an educational institution, henceforth known as Kivukoni College. Its main task, as stipulated by the institution's executive committee in 1962, was not produce good examinees but prepare citizens 'with a will to assist in the development of their country' for the practical tasks and responsibilities of 'key posts' in public service and private business, without any examination.[3] Officially opened on 29 July 1961, five months before Tanganyika's independence, Kivukoni College trained thousands of civil servants, party functionaries, teachers, trade unionists and others who were crucial in steering and implementing visions of *ujamaa* in Tanzania. Initially modelled on Oxford's Ruskin College, the nominally autonomous institution was officially turned into a party school in 1969.[4] The emphasis on the private sector was dropped as the *ujamaa* vision of development became tied to an interventionist state.[5] By the 1970s, graduates were supposed to adhere to and 'defend the party's policies whenever necessary', bringing it closer to the model of Marxist-Leninist cadre schools.[6] Kivukoni continued to train party cadres during the first neoliberal economic reforms in the 1980s and was closed only during the transition from one-party rule to multi-party democracy in 1992.

Kivukoni College was thus both typical and highly specific for its time, when concepts of socialism and models of development were diversifying in the periphery, but ruling parties in post-colonial countries seldom institutionalized ideological education. Through Kivukoni's institutional history, this chapter asks how socialist ideological education was conceptualized, fought over and practised in the Global South. While Kivukoni College is frequently mentioned in the secondary literature as 'ideological school', detailed accounts of its history are rare.[7] Comparable socialist ideological institutions in Africa were most notably the *Winneba Ideological Institute* (1961–6, after 1962 known as *Kwame Nkrumah Institute of Economics and Political Science*) in Ghana and *Lumumba Institute* (1964–5) in Kenya.[8] In contrast to Kivukoni College, however, both were closed few years after their opening by political opponents who saw these schools as hotbeds of Marxist subversion and radicalism; in the case of Ghana, after a coup.[9] The fate of these various institutions was by no means disconnected: as will be shown below, the coup against Nkrumah influenced thoughts on cadre training in Tanzania. Much of the institution's trajectory, however, had to do with local dynamics.

This chapter argues that the ideological character of Kivukoni College only evolved gradually, growing out of a former emphasis on professionalization and soft skills. This process was shaped by the country-wide drive for nationalization and self-reliance and a reconfiguration of transnational connections. Apart from offering an insight into the institutionalization of socialist political ideological education in Africa, Kivukoni's history also illuminates how the policies of 'manpower development' and 'nationalization', key concerns in many countries of the Global South at the time, were discussed and implemented at educational institutions. Both rested on the belief that state and party institutions could plan and bring about development or, in Kiswahili, *maendeleo* – itself a contested and dynamic concept.[10]

The analysis is primarily based on documents held at the party archives in Dodoma, including correspondence between the party headquarters and the college as well as evaluations of course participants. The account also draws on interviews with party functionaries,[11] official annual manpower development reports and the college periodical *Mbioni*[12] (held at the East Africana Collection, University of Dar es Salaam), as well as archives of European organizations that entertained relations with Kivukoni College. Based on these sources, which reveal a number of social practices at this institution, the essay adds to existing accounts of ideological 'laboratories' of socialist education[13] a perspective that takes into account the gendered character and contradictions of education, including disciplinary expectations tied to tropes of respectability that were not specifically socialist, but central for the legitimacy of the one-party state.

Establishing Kivukoni College

The founding of Kivukoni College was decided upon in 1958 at the National Conference of TANU (Tanganyika African National Union), the territory's most influential nationalist party led by Nyerere. In Tanganyika as elsewhere, anti-colonial parties and colonial regimes usually shared the view that modern sovereign statehood and economic growth required a cohort of educated elites, the lack of which colonial powers conveniently used as an argument to delay independence. Efforts in planning education and 'manpower' thus highly influenced policies and debates in the 1950s in the Global South.[14] Already before independence, TANU and other parties criticized the lack of educational institutions and scholarships, particularly for higher education, and sought ways to speed up the process of 'manpower development' through a twin strategy: establishing more (and more inclusive) educational institutions in the country and sending people abroad for training. By the late 1950s, as more countries were transitioning towards independence and Cold War competition over the hearts and minds in the Global South intensified, these strategies of 'manpower development' were increasingly internationalized.[15] TANU began sending people to the UK, Liberia, Ethiopia and elsewhere where scholarships became available, including communist countries.[16] The people newly trained were then to replace colonial officers and other expatriates in the expanding state bureaucracy.

Fearing the political impact of a TANU-run school in the territory, British colonial officials initially withheld permission for the opening of Kivukoni College.[17] As independence was approaching, the party could go ahead and founded the independent Tanganyika Education Trust Fund, which became the college's organizational and financial backbone. Initial funding came mostly from within the territory. A fundraising tour through the country was organized in cooperation with Joan Wicken, Nyerere's personal assistant who had been working for the Labour Party's Commonwealth department and began cooperating with TANU in the mid-1950s. Donations came from party members, business owners, various cooperatives and numerous other individuals, including countless villagers who contributed a few coins or all kinds of small items that could be sold for cash, including nuts, maize, beans or chickens.[18]

In contrast to funds, sourced domestically, the educational concept was an import. The trustees had agreed in late 1959 that the college should be 'of a like nature to (but differing in any respect … which the trustees shall … think fit from) Ruskin College in the City of Oxford, England'.[19] It was supposed to expose committed adults with a limited level of formal education to social scientific theories, gear their minds towards nation-building and development, and enable them to implement their knowledge. Several key actors of the college's early history had ties to the socialist Fabian Society, and Nyerere knew some of them from his student years and later visits to Great Britain. Wicken was herself a graduate of Ruskin College.[20] Following interviews in Oxford, the political scientist and strong critic of settler politics Colin Leys was recruited as first principal of the college, but soon left for a post at Makerere in 1962.[21] He was succeeded by A. N. Scotney and, in 1963, by the Canadian Griffiths Cunningham, an economic historian with a practical background in cooperative work who had joined Kivukoni as a lecturer in its first year and remained principal until 1969.[22]

Forging and remaking connections

Cunningham oversaw a decade of expansion at Kivukoni, marked by contradicting trends of diversification and nationalization. The intake of long-course students increased from 39 (1961) to around 50 to 70 for several years, while the number of participants in short-term courses skyrocketed from 75 in 1964 to over 450 in 1970, fluctuating strongly in the years thereafter. Growing student numbers required more buildings, funds and qualified personnel. Remarkable for a college affiliated (albeit still loosely) with a nationalist political party, most lecturers were neither card-carrying party members nor citizens. Faculty included young Westerners and a few African political exiles who had made their way to Tanzania, including the American graduate James Lowry (1961), the British activist scholar Lionel Cliffe (1962–4), the Malawian dissident Henry Chipembere[23] or the South African economist Ethan Mayisela (1962–4), as well as annually between one and three American Peace Corps volunteers (1961–7). The overall number of lecturers rose from 5 (1961) to almost 20 (1969) and then bounced back to 13 (1971), with an increasing share of Tanzanians.

Sources of income were also temporarily diversified with a mainly Western orientation. Among the foreign supporters was the forerunner of the West German *Konrad-Adenauer-Stiftung* (the political foundation closely aligned to the conservative Christian Democratic Union party, CDU), the *Eichholz-Akademie*, contributing more than DM 300,000 between 1963 and 1967 for scholarships and other aspects.[24] The lecturer for 'Labor Economics' and 'Industrial Relations', Karl Joachim Schmidt, was also sent and paid by this West German political organization. These ties were soon severed as Tanzanian politics and concepts evolved further.

In February 1967, the ruling party adopted the Arusha Declaration as key policy document which elevated *ujamaa* from a political concept to state ideology. A central guideline for about two decades, the Arusha Declaration emphasized economic sovereignty and self-reliance through agricultural production, but also led to the nationalization of banks and major industries in the country. This signalled a shift from Nyerere's earlier definition of socialism as an 'attitude of mind' towards socialism as a socio-political formation marked by substantial state ownership and interventions in the economy, which left many Western observers concerned that Tanzania was heading towards doctrinaire Marxism-Leninism. Perceiving a growing ideological divide, the conservative West German foundation phased out its support for Kivukoni College in May 1967.[25] From funding through extraversion in the Cold War world, the college went back to its initial reliance on funds sourced within the country. By 1968, the government footed the college's bills for recurrent and capital costs.[26] The material support of the West German foundation was omitted in the college's contemporary publications as well as later hagiographic accounts, perhaps also because this dependency on foreign resources contradicted *ujamaa*'s emphasis on self-reliance.

The push for self-reliance also had an impact on the recruitment of faculty members. Expatriates were gradually replaced by Tanzanian lecturers as part of a second nationalization drive throughout the country, although the shortage of qualified academics slowed these efforts. This staffing policy preferring citizens over non-citizens had already been a major controversy in Tanzania following independence when trade unionists and TANU's more radical wing protested the slow progress of 'Africanization' in the civil service and pressed Nyerere to accept a pace of Africanization beyond his gradualist and technocratic preferences.[27] They argued that 'Africanization' (rather than just nationalization) of positions was necessary to undo the racialized hierarchies entrenched under colonial rule which had preferred Europeans and Asians (who also qualified for citizenship, and still dominated the higher and middle ranks in most sectors at the time).[28] At Kivukoni College and elsewhere in Tanzania, 'nationalization' thus often actually meant 'Africanization'.[29] Nationalization stayed on the state's agenda throughout the *ujamaa* era as the presence and influence of 'expatriates' continued to be seen as an infringement of the young nation-state's political and economic sovereignty. From the mid-1960s to the mid-1980s, official manpower reports referred to the preferred recruitment of citizens as 'localization' (rather than 'nationalization'). Paying attention to this 'ethno-qualitative aspect of manpower', in the words of an official report from 1978, would enable Tanzania to 'become independent of foreign manpower' and 'put the economy under our own control'.[30]

In addition to this push for nationalization, there were forces in TANU and the trade union that would have liked to see more communist lecturers employed at Kivukoni. In the late 1960s, the policy of non-alignment meant for many Tanzanian institutions facing manpower shortages, including in the educational sector, that the presence of Western expatriates could be counterbalanced with the recruitment of Eastern Europeans. Indeed, job interviews for new Kivukoni lecturers were conducted in Warsaw and Moscow in July 1967,[31] but anti-communism, widespread in Tanzania's elite and expatriate circles, prevented closer leanings towards Eastern Europe at the time. In contrast to Kenya's Lumumba Institute with its Soviet and Chinese lecturers or the Winneba Ideological Institute in Ghana with faculty from various Warsaw Pact countries, Kivukoni College's connections to the communist world remained loose, comprising mostly of guest lectures, delegation visits, and exhibitions. This was also due to the Cold War thinking of the remaining Western expatriates at the college who still held powerful positions. Principal Cunningham welcomed and recommended the assistance of the International Labour Office (ILO) and other international organizations espousing social democratic ideals but advised shunning any influence from communist countries. In 1969, a committee chaired by Cunningham overruled the recommendation of a NUTA (National Union of Tanganyika Workers) commission to recruit an East German for trade union courses at the College; a Swede was appointed instead.[32] Very much in line with Nyerere's attitude, this distancing seemingly applied only to countries perceived as 'hard-line' communist such as the USSR or East Germany: In the late 1960s, Branislav Vukovic from non-aligned Yugoslavia and Jiří Pleskač from Czechoslovakia joined the college as lecturers. In 1969, Israel Elinewinga, a former secondary school principal and education officer for Arusha region, took over from Cunningham and was appointed as the first Tanzanian principal.[33] From 1971 onwards, all staff members were Tanzanian citizens.[34]

In contrast to the early 1960s, the policy of non-alignment and national self-reliance outweighed not only Cold War pressures but also pragmatic material considerations. When Kivukoni was planned to expand further and open seven satellite colleges throughout the country in the mid-1970s, the *Friedrich-Ebert-Stiftung* (FES), a West German political foundation closely related to the Social Democratic Party (SPD), offered technical support and funds – on the condition that it could also place a lecturer at the college. While Nyerere encouraged a closer alignment with West German social democrats, Minister of Education Simon Chiwanga emphasized that Kivukoni College trained political leaders and thus had a special status that ruled out any external influence. The offer of the FES was snubbed, even though the expansion would suffer from a shortage of resources.[35] In terms of both personnel and funding, Kivukoni had made a nationalist turn which enabled new linkages between training and ideological content.

Professionalizing careers

Despite a change in Kivukoni's funding structure and composition of faculty from extraversion to nationalization under the impression of the Arusha Declaration, the role of the college as reflected in career aspirations of the Tanzanian course participants remained remarkably stable. Right from its establishment, Andrew Ivaska has noted, Kivukoni College was 'a proven way station for civil servants and party cadres rising through the ranks'.[36] Generally, demand exceeded supply: adults could apply for the long course on their own initiative, and the number of applications far outstripped places available. In 1961, 39 students were selected from 350 applicants; in 1972, 1,598 persons applied for 166 places.[37] The gender imbalance was a concern to the college leadership. In 1961, only 2 of 39 long-course participants were women. In 1964, Principal Cunningham still reported that female applicants were 'as rare as hen's teeth'.[38] Photos and lists suggest that women did not make up more than 10 per cent of long-course participants or faculty until the early 1970s, at least.[39]

The college promised professionalization, but opposed the widely shared understanding of education as a means to attain a higher socio-economic status. In its early years, the college offered thematically focused short courses (first one, later three months) and more general long courses (first six, later nine months) with the intention of equipping promising young leaders as well as seasoned activists who had little formal education with social scientific perspectives so that they could serve as nation-builders in various official capacities. Syllabi in the mid-1960s included technocratic hands-on administrative subjects as well as introductions to economics, politics, sociology, history (with a focus on African history), communications and English. Course participants wrote speeches, extracted information from books and practised preparing development plans for their own districts. In contrast to university students, who lived a comparatively elitist life with convenient accommodation and three-course meals,[40] 'we cut grass and we washed our dishes', a first-year participant remembered, but so did the lecturers and the principal: they 'served themselves and joined us in the sweeping'.[41] These practices and participation in daily chores as well as agricultural activities were meant to inculcate a socialist, egalitarian attitude among both staff and students and instil respect for manual labour. This was done already in the early 1960s, anticipating civic duties and ideals of 'education for self-reliance' proclaimed more widely as the decade progressed.[42]

In the early years of independence, with many positions up for grabs, a visit at Kivukoni boosted many careers and contributed to a professionalization of officials, including TANU 'veterans'.[43] Unlike the Winneba Ideological School in Ghana, which aimed to spread Nkrumah's vision of Pan-Africanism not only among citizens but also among freedom fighters and trade unionists from the whole continent (and offered special courses for them),[44] Kivukoni College principally targeted citizens as students. Of 465 long-course students until March 1967, only 15 were classified as 'refugees', which referred to political exiles from South Africa, Mozambique and other countries.[45] The most important criterion for the selection of Tanzanian candidates was a 'patriotic attitude' (*moyo wa Kitaifa*).[46] TANU leaders urged lower party bureaucrats 'to select the best people who have the feelings of the Republic at heart rather than depending on academic qualifications only'.[47] In practice, however, most grassroots activists, many of whom were women, were excluded as the language of instruction until 1972 remained English and expatriate teachers were rarely fluent in Kiswahili.[48]

Of the applicants that were selected, most were still fairly young and had some professional experience. In 1967, the average age of long-course participants was twenty-seven; many were married and already had children.[49] Among 440 participants of the long course (with a duration of thirty weeks) between 1961 and 1966, about a quarter were party officials, the rest came from other institutions and professions. Many graduates took leading positions: by the late 1960s, 14 graduates served as Regional Commissioners or Area Commissioners, 8 were members of parliament, 30 trade union functionaries, 60 civil servants, and 7 army officers; there were also, however, numerous rank-and-file members from various professional groups, for instance 20 community development assistants and 50 teachers.[50]

Most people saw personal advancement and collective gains as two sides of the same coin. One candidate who asked to switch courses wrote 'that my being prevented from attending the course will be an upset and might interfere with my future which every person looks forward [to]'.[51] Hopes to improve one's personal status and perhaps get access to a higher position in party or state institutions[52] chimed with collective trajectories in late colonial and early post-colonial Tanzania when education was the main mechanism of social mobility and the expanding ranks of the bureaucracy were filled with graduates from secondary schools, vocational colleges and universities. Many students attending Kivukoni College affirmed *ujamaa*'s egalitarian values as far as the society as a whole was concerned, but also strongly believed that a certain measure of socio-economic differentiation and scope for individual achievement, fuelled by educational merit and measured in material rewards, was desirable. In a 1966 survey, for instance, seventy-two mid-level government and party officials attending the course strongly rejected the idea that all people should receive the same salary.[53]

Without tangible rewards, the value of spending several months at Kivukoni College was not self-evident to all, however. Many graduates faced difficulties in converting their course attendance into promotions or salary increases.[54] Despite repeated protests from participants, the college only issued a certificate of attendance and not a degree or diploma, which was the relevant symbolic currency for jobs and pay scales. This had been agreed upon already in 1960 to avoid further social stratification and the transformation of Kivukoni into a breeding ground of individualist white-collar elitism and careerism.[55] In a 1963 circular letter addressed to all regional secretaries, TANU's general secretary emphasized that attending courses did *not* guarantee an employment with TANU or the government.[56] Given the 'soft' symbolic value of attending Kivukoni, course participants left if alternative educational opportunities for acquiring 'hard' degrees or diplomas opened up.[57]

Leading bureaucrats in government ministries usually also preferred to have their employees qualified at universities rather than Kivukoni College, to the chagrin of college officials. In May 1971, Principal Mwakawago complained that 'studies in Western countries (*mafunzo ya Ulaya*) which do not conform to our politics are given more importance than party education offered at Kivukoni'.[58] This might be read as a structural conflict between actors of the politico-ideological field on the one hand and the bureaucratic sphere on the other, but the party itself offered contradictory signals regarding the role of the college in the late 1960s. Although Nyerere advocated the education of high-ranking party functionaries at Kivukoni College following the Arusha Declaration, leaders there complained that neither government ministries nor the trade union or TANU provided 'a reasonable calibre of students'.[59] In a letter to party headquarters, Kivukoni College's Principal Cunningham claimed that he and Nyerere had agreed that no high-ranking party functionary should 'for long hold his job unless he had attended a full course at Kivukoni College'. Cunningham wanted to see more regional executive secretaries and other senior functionaries undergo training.[60] TANU National Executive Secretary Pius Msekwa replied that Cunningham should be satisfied with the increased number of mid-level officials that TANU had sent, claiming that these were the functionaries doing crucial grassroots work.[61]

Reporting on respectability

Officials at the local level were indeed central to the party's image and for the implementation of party policies – and Kivukoni was one of the few places where these functionaries could be disciplined. In letters to newspapers and party headquarters, many citizens raised complaints against the misbehaviour of TANU officials and government functionaries.[62] In a letter from 1972, for instance, a man from a village in Korogwe complained that TANU's area commissioner was 'killing' *ujamaa* and betraying his duty to 'bring development'. According to the letter, the TANU leader organized seminars for the party's women's wing only to seduce and dishonour 'our children' by turning them into his 'prostitutes' (*malaya*).[63] Many of these letters addressing the party leadership were written by men who described instances of how they or their kin had been offended and 'disrespected' (or literally, had had their honour 'broken', *kuvunjiwa heshima*) by state and party representatives. The complaints revolved around allegations of embezzlement, insults, witchcraft and drunkenness as well as improper sexual relations. It is possible that such letters were not only outbursts of indignation from 'ordinary citizens' against party elites, but also expressions of local power struggles. In any case, they illustrate how important tropes of respectability were in exerting and challenging authority, and how they figured in debates about development, decolonization and citizenship.[64] It is thus not surprising that this category also mattered at the college and in evaluations of course participants. Party leaders wanted to ascertain the social respectability of mid-level functionaries: They did not only have to have an understanding of development plans and the principles of the Arusha Declaration, but should also conform to norms of respectability.

Similar to what Jeffrey Ahlman has shown for the cultural politics at the Bureau of African Affairs in Ghana, Kivukoni College was a site where discipline was enforced and where students were evaluated according to standards that were themselves subject to change.[65] Evidence suggests that this was done in an unsystematic and non-transparent way. While the college did not issue degrees or certificates, it did send confidential 'Reports on the Performance' to employers and party institutions.[66] Some of the reports were addressed directly to Nyerere as the party chairman, though it is unclear if he read them himself. In 1970, the principal and 'strong disciplinarian' Israel Elinewinga[67] wrote micro-evaluations of two to ten lines based on 'confidential anecdotes and reports maintained by the College throughout the Nine Months [*sic*] of the course.'[68] His assessments thus involved prior surveillance and secret record-keeping. Filtered through the principal's eyes and categories, these 'anecdotes and reports' travelled to the party headquarters but remained hidden to the course participants themselves. It is possible that the principal's comments carried some weight for further decisions, as the person reading the evaluations in the party headquarters apparently graded the persons again. These grades followed often, though not always, Elinewinga's words.[69]

The reports were part of a non-transparent system of supervision. Elinewinga imagined Kivukoni College as a site where candidates could be screened for their fitness to lead and learn, but strangely for an institution that had just been turned officially into a party college, his reports lacked references to political views at large. Seen in context with selection practices and curricula, the evaluations suggest that the college should produce disciplined and professionalized officials rather than an ideologically homogeneous vanguard. Evaluating participation in self-reliance activities, sociability, disciplined social behaviour and academic qualities, Elinewinga described course participants as 'a very good material for further education' or 'not teachable material'. One woman participant was praised as a 'very intelligent and serious student' exhibiting 'effective qualities of reliable leadership' and a 'tremendous amount of untap[p]ed academic potentialities'; another student, a female TANU district executive secretary, as 'well informed and reliable'. Similar to other male functionaries in Tanzania at the time,[70] Elinewinga saw women with leadership qualities as 'women's leaders' or 'an asset in Women's leadership' rather than leaders per se. He associated women with feminized spheres of work, seeing them as a 'good Adult Educator especially for women' or 'asset as nurse in an ujamaa village'. This rationale diverted women's career paths to positions of minor influence and buttressed male dominance in the higher echelons of the one-party state. Women who did profit from attending Kivukoni College were usually mission-educated and from (relatively) elite backgrounds; they assumed leading positions in women's organizations.[71]

Elinewinga also resorted to categories of respectability such as honour (*heshima*) and disgrace (*aibu*), particularly when referring to the supposed transgression of social norms that could even lead to expulsions. Allegations of inappropriate levels of alcohol consumption and improper gender relations, including sexual relations, figured as criteria of dismissal. A gendered reading suggests that these criteria were not applied evenly. There were several unmarried women (recognizable through the 'Ms' added to their names) who took part in the 1970 nine-month course, two of whom received exceptionally negative evaluations. One read:

> Totally ineffective student in every way. Her main interest and perhaps the only, is MEN for whom she seemed to be stronger than Hercules. A regrettably total wastage.

Words were even harsher in another evaluation in which Elinewinga did not mention classroom performance at all:

> A lamentably [*sic*] total right-off. She is not only an alcoholic, but also a sexual disgrace and liar. Can only be recommended for psychitric [*sic*] treatment.

Such judgements, in which the principal impersonated a moralizing generational authority over course participants' sexual life and gender relations were not confined to female participants. One man, for instance, was described as '[u]ncultured, especially when it involves women'. Still, the scathing verdicts on the two unmarried women cited above stand out for their harsh and destructive tone that undermined the women's respectability and prospects of employability. Possibly, some of the students indeed participated in the 'sexual revolution' fuelled by urbanization and the escape from the control of family networks.[72] The migration of unmarried women to urban spaces and newly evolving gender constellations provoked a widespread perception of moral crisis hinging on themes such as promiscuity, prostitution and pregnancies out of wedlock.[73] Unmarried women with an independent lifestyle were seen as antithetical to *ujamaa*'s vision of self-reliance and its emphasis on African traditions.[74] Counter-reactions to this process involved verbal and physical abuse. Male members of the TANU Youth League, the party's youth wing, openly attacked young women wearing miniskirts or wigs, thereby constraining opportunities for 'female accumulation, mobility, and autonomy'.[75] This also applied to Elinewinga's evaluations.

College authorities repeatedly expulsed students prior to the completion of the course, usually justifying this with references to discipline and respectability rather than wrong ideological positions or inadequate classroom performance. Two students were 'discontinued due to gross indiscipline and hooliganic behaviour' and 'because of being unreliable and behaving as a hooligan'. The term 'hooligans' (*wahuni* in Kiswahili) was a shorthand used by both colonial and post-colonial bureaucrats to refer to young men who were usually un(der)employed (i.e. not employed in the formal economic sector), unmarried and poor. They were perceived as potential instigators of unrest and obstacles to orderly development.[76] For Elinewinga, *wahuni* could not be a part of the *ujamaa* project. In sum, Elinewinga's evaluations indicate that respectability – rather than 'correct' ideological knowledge – was crucial at Kivukoni College in 1970.

Training makada

Senior party functionaries recalled in conversations that Kivukoni had always been the party's ideological school.[77] Records evoke a much more ambivalent image, however. The 1961 application guidelines, perhaps still influenced by the political constraints of late colonialism, claimed that the college did not 'propagate any particular ideology'.[78] A North American observer noted as late as 1968 that Kivukoni College was 'a training school for party personnel, trade unionists, bureaucrats and party workers', but there existed 'no ideological school as such in the country, although party militants have been pushing for one for some time'. He went on to speculate that Nyerere had resisted this demand because of being 'suspicious of the concept' and 'aware of the unsatisfactory record of Kwame Nkrumah's Ideological School at Winneba in Ghana' – with which there had been no direct exchanges.[79] Faculty in favour of turning the college into an ideological school, such as the expatriate lecturer Belle Harris, warned that Kivukoni College might degenerate into a 'Stalinist Institution' where 'socialist education has been replaced by sloganised propaganda' serving the 'exploitative class'. As Harris argued in 1968, this was the fate that had befallen Nkrumah's college, and this was why it had failed.[80] The lesson from the Ghanaian example for Harris – but not for other Tanzanians at the college, as we will see – was that more ideology was harmful. As late as 1969, Principal Cunningham claimed that '[i]n teaching socialism at Kivukoni we have attempted to be broadminded while at the same time giving our students as clear an understanding as is possible of the confused and very very confusing world of socialism'.[81]

Establishing ideological orthodoxy was difficult, given that *ujamaa* was not a rigid ideology but rather a contested set of ideas and practices in flux. In 1963, the political scientist Peter Burke had found that Kivukoni's alumni were 'among the few who understand Ujamaa as a national theory and as a guide to action', but they interpreted it in more radical terms than Nyerere. They fused Marxist terminology and racialist approaches in which the nationalization of key industries should put an 'end to Asian domination of the economy'. Some even equated *ujamaa* with socialism à la Sovietique, with one course participant explaining how Eastern Bloc countries 'have always prospered under the methods of Ujamaa'.[82]

The 1967 Arusha Declaration reinvigorated the competition between various understandings of socialism in the party and at Kivukoni College. The politician Kingunge Ngombale-Mwiru pushed for Kivukoni's transformation into an ideological college as lecturer (1967) and as principal (1972–3). He had joined TANU as a government clerk in the month of its establishment in 1954 and quickly earned credentials as an effective mobilizer. Much of his thinking evolved through radical South-South circuits. A friend of his, returning from studies in India, introduced him to *Das Kapital*. Henceforth, creative thinking in Marxist terms shaped his political strategies. After working and studying in Liberia and Senegal from 1958 to 1966, Ngombale-Mwiru returned to Tanzania and was asked by Nyerere in 1967 to teach politics, with a focus on *ujamaa* and self-reliance, at Kivukoni College. He rose to the position of the party's main ideologue (albeit in the shadow of Nyerere) and wrote or co-authored important policy statements from the late 1960s to the 1980s, including parts of the Arusha Declaration.[83]

In 1972, Nyerere appointed Ngombale-Mwiru as principal of Kivukoni College. Ngombale-Mwiru was loyal to Nyerere, but was never shy to articulate his more radical outlook. In the college's mouthpiece *Mbioni*, he argued shortly after the Arusha Declaration that this document had some shortcomings. The building of socialism required the training of political cadres who oversaw the necessary economic and social transformations, constituted the link between the leadership and the masses, and removed all 'parasitic classes', particularly the 'parasitic politico-bureaucratic bourgeoisie, the ally of imperialism …, from political power'.[84] He recommended that socialist-minded cadres rather than neutral administrators should 'constitute the backbone of our system' and suggested the establishment of workers' councils in parastatal companies to turn 'nationalization' into true 'socialization'.[85] Perhaps for strategic reasons, Ngombale-Mwiru did not mention communist parties as blueprints for his view on ideological education. He rather relied on a Pan-African and anti-imperialist frame of understanding and bolstered his call for cadre education with a reference to the fall of Nkrumah's regime in Ghana. In contrast to the opinion of the lecturer Belle Harris cited above, Ngombale-Mwiru saw the coup in Ghana as resulting from the *lack* of political education in schools and within the party.[86] Without political cadres, and education in the hands of 'foreign and local reactionary elements', Tanzania's socialism would also fail.[87]

The college's refashioning in the early 1970s was foreshadowed by a 1967 memorandum authored by Ngombale-Mwiru and seven other Tanzanian tutors, all of whom were card-carrying TANU members.[88] The memorandum was submitted to the Executive Committee of the college and also copied to the Central Committee of the party. They suggested a shift from 'liberal education' to the training of 'socialist political cadres'. The syllabus needed 'ideological unity and … coherence which will allow the student to see the interconnectedness of what he is being taught' in a holistic course on 'politics, socialism and political economy'.[89] This resembled an initiative launched by leftist academics at the University College of Dar es Salaam for a more integrated course structure transcending disciplinary boundaries which eventually led to the establishment of the Institute of Development Studies. The memorandum by the Tanzanian Kivukoni tutors also demanded a change of the language of instruction to Kiswahili as the use of English excluded grassroots workers and consolidated colonial and careerist mindsets.[90]

These changes were implemented when Ngombale-Mwiru became principal after Tanzanian politics had made another turn to the left with the proclamation of the 1971 Party Guidelines, the *Mwongozo*. Mainly authored by Ngombale-Mwiru, the *Mwongozo* was, according to George Roberts, a 'key turning point in the history of the *ujamaa* project'.[91] It sought to mobilize the population by calling for vigilance against internal and external enemies such as the Portuguese who also threatened Tanzania, which provided assistance to Mozambican liberation fighters. Domestically, Nyerere faced mounting criticism due to an exodus of capital and rising unemployment. In contrast to the Arusha Declaration, the *Mwongozo* had a class struggle component. It encouraged workers to speak out against oppressive managers and opened up 'public debate over socialism in an unprecedentedly wide fashion, while also marking the ideological rise of its authors to make Tanzania much more of a vanguard, party-supremacist state'.[92] When Nyerere appointed Ngombale-Mwiru as regional commissioner of Coast region, he 'quickly set on forming people's militia and organizing ideological classes for workers after office hours'.[93]

In his next position as principal of Kivukoni College in 1972–3, Ngombale-Mwiru implemented the demands sketched in the 1967 memorandum. In another memorandum to the Executive Committee in 1972 – now written in Kiswahili – he discussed the college's turn from 'liberal education' to *ujamaa*-based education in the years after the Arusha Declaration.[94] Kivukoni College, he argued, was one of its kind in Africa, and many of the thousands of graduates now filled the higher echelons of the party and the government – yet still, the party was not directly involved in the selection of students. In his view, course elements such as the obligatory three-week sojourns in *ujamaa* villages had to be complemented by further instruments to 'unite theory and practice' such as visits to factories. Ngombale-Mwiru also proposed new course formats with durations reaching from two weeks for the highest party leaders to two years, all including substantial portions of 'practice' (especially living and working in villages). Achieving ideological unity was seen as a question of scale and homogeneity: Kivukoni had to branch out so that *all* party cadres could undergo training within a period of five years. In March 1973, TANU's Central Committee approved the opening of seven new satellite colleges.[95]

The new syllabus promoted anti-colonial and radical socialist views. Moving away from a structure based on sometimes ill-defined social science subjects and technocratic theories on development, the 1972 curriculum married Third Worldist revolutionary anti-imperialism with nationalism and emphasized a radical take on world history. It was to instil a sense of pride and broader historical positioning where progress was predicated on anti-colonial rather than developmentalist categories. Instead of modernization theory's teachings about an economic 'take-off', it offered partisan accounts of colonialism and past or ongoing African 'liberation wars' in Algeria, Cameroon and Kenya, African 'revolutions' of Egypt (Nasser), Congo (Lumumba), Ghana (Nkrumah), Algeria (FLN), Guinea (Sekou Touré) as well as African American struggles for emancipation. The curriculum's global outlook was also reflected in a section on workers' movements and revolutions, beginning with Haiti 1796, proceeding with Paris 1789/1871, England, Russia 1917, China 1949, Cuba 1959, and culminating in the coverage of Allende's Chile. The subject of politics included a discussion of the historical strategies of TANU and Zanzibar's ASP (thus omitting other political parties in Tanzanian history) and introduced typologies of socialism (utopian, social-democratic, scientific, African) and political parties (party of notables, mass parties, vanguard parties, fascist parties).[96] Not all of these contents and aspects of radicalism were completely new – the African American civil rights organizer

Stokely Carmichael had given a guest lecture at Kivukoni in 1967, for instance – but the reorientation towards Marxist categories, radical geographies and heroized anti-colonial histories marked a clear departure from earlier 'liberal' curricula and their emphasis on development.

The shift towards a more politicized education is also visible in how college leaders evaluated course participants. In 1972, the Acting Principal Tamilwai Thomas Lukindo (temporarily standing in for Ngombale-Mwiru) sent short assessments to Nyerere, with copies going to TANU headquarters and other senior party functionaries. Lukindo was a trained teacher with an MA degree in History from the United States who had joined the college as a lecturer in 1969.[97] Lukindo's assessments of sixty-eight participants of a three-month politics course in 1972, which included an extended stay in an *ujamaa* village, were particularly focused on students' dedication to participate in self-reliance activities in a rural environment.[98] Practical commitment rather than theoretical knowledge should be evidence of true socialist conviction. Lukindo's mostly lukewarm assessments lacked the acrimonious attacks and moralistic undertones so characteristic of Elinewinga's evaluations discussed above, but respectability remained a criterion. This became evident in judgements of 'immature' and 'childish behaviour' or chattiness. Lukindo singled out the participants who, according to the information he had received, could not bear the hardships, complained too much or showed little commitment in doing manual labour. In the case of a two-week course for district planning officers, Lukindo lauded those who had exhibited 'revolutionary thought' and a 'standpoint' (*msimamo*) that was 'firm', 'good', 'without problems' or 'correct'. He recommended a few students for leadership positions, but whoever read the assessments in the party headquarters attached importance only to the most negative ones and made a red cross next to the names concerned.

The evaluations were in line with Ngombale-Mwiru's vision of the college as a site where political leaders would receive valuable advice and mid-level cadres would be put on the right path, or 'straightened' (*kupigwa msasa*). Respectability in Ngombale-Mwiru's terms was thus closely linked to his view of vanguardist socialist cadre training: personal integrity and the readiness to defend the 'correct' path. As he wrote in 1973, those who had committed 'capitalist sins' were supposed to tremble when they faced Kivukoni's hard-line teachers.[99] 'Sin', in this sense, was a moral category not charged with sexual connotations. Ngombale-Mwiru had not been particularly fond of Youth League members' chauvinist attacks against women wearing mini-skirts and make-up. To him, focusing on cultural conflicts of this kind was a political dead end as far as the liberation and emancipation of Africa were concerned.[100]

Vanguardism, expansion and closure under neoliberalism

Ngombale-Mwiru argued that there needed to be a 'vanguard within the mass party'.[101] According to his recollection, Kivukoni's 'students were very much in favour of a vanguard system', to an extent that there was a 'revolutionary situation'.[102] Party conservatives dragged Ngombale-Mwiru to a hearing in front of the Central Committee where he was charged of turning Kivukoni College into a breeding ground of Marxism-Leninism and aiming to convert TANU into a Leninist cadre party. When Ngombale-Mwiru insisted that a politically reliable vanguard would be indispensable, it took Nyerere's personal intervention to save him from being expelled from the party.[103] He was transferred, however, to an ideologically less sensitive position as regional commissioner of Tanga region.[104]

At the college's annual opening in July 1973, Nyerere tried to placate his conservative critics. He affirmed that Kivukoni should produce '*ujamaa* cadres' (*makada wa Ujamaa*, importing the English term 'cadre') but quickly added that '[p]eople saying that one cannot build *ujamaa* without following Marxism-Leninism are misled' (wapotovu).[105] Nyerere, a devout Catholic, reiterated that TANU was anti-capitalist and secular, but not anti-religious; it was a mass party, not a vanguard party. Although Nyerere mentioned the existence of socialist (*kisoshialisti*) countries such as China and the Soviet Union as proof that the lifespan of capitalism was coming to an end, he repeated that Tanzania was not, and would not become, communist. Emphasizing this demarcation, Nyerere used the term *kisoshialisti* for communist countries, but reserved *kijamaa* (referring to *ujamaa*) for Tanzania.[106] (In the curriculum cited above, in contrast, 'scientific socialism' had been translated as '*Ujamaa wa kisayansi*'.) In sum, he affirmed the principles of cadre education and learning from other socialist models, but tried to disentangle this from communist contents, vanguard partyism and universalism. Nyerere also rebuffed the idea of Ngombale-Mwiru from 1972 to turn Kivukoni into a dynamic think tank to advance theoretical production: 'It should only *explain* TANU's policies, that's it.'[107]

With the college's role fixed in that diffusionist mode, the plan to expand ideological education was carried out, albeit constrained by a shortage of resources. The opening of three colleges (Ilonga, Uyole and Kasulu) was delayed due to financial difficulties, while the shortage of teachers, classrooms and reference books negatively affected classes at other sites.[108] The lack of resources also reduced the student intake at Kivukoni College, where buildings could actually accommodate up to 150 long-course students annually.[109] A sojourn at Kivukoni College, or one of its satellites, became a necessary rite of passage for mid-level party functionaries.[110] This increased the number of those aware of party policies and equipped more party cadres with a fairly homogenic background (while not all top-level party functionaries attended Kivukoni College, most district commissioners had done so)[111] and enabled the party to penetrate economic and social areas even more. In 1975–6, for instance, when the government tried to increase the effectiveness of parastatal companies, twenty-five 'political commissars' were delegated from Kivukoni College to the country's key industrial sites 'to be the guardians of government and party policies at the key centres of production' and 'to encourage worker exertion'.[112]

Despite these efforts, *ujamaa*'s 'hegemonic decade', as Issa Shivji has called it, was coming to an end. Western donors and Tanzanian reformers began pushing for economic liberalization in the late 1970s, while the party's old guard tried to rebrand itself as revolutionary and truly socialist. Self-criticism went along with an adherence to the vanguardist model. The 1981 Guidelines (*Mwongozo*), again authored by Ngombale-Mwiru, contained the confession 'that the Party had failed to lead the struggle with clear ideology and theoretical depth' and 'failed to inculcate in its cadres a profound grasp of the socialist theory without which it is not possible to understand society'.[113] In the 1980s, the party leadership concluded a number of cooperation agreements with Eastern European communist parties and sent cadres behind the Iron Curtain for ideological training. From 1985, Nyerere's successor, the new President Ali Hassan Mwinyi, opposed the party's left wing. He removed Ngombale-Mwiru and other members who resisted economic reforms from their cabinet positions.[114] Against the rising tide of neoliberalism, Ngombale-Mwiru still headed the party's Ideology and Education section. As late as April 1989, he led a delegation to Budapest to sign an agreement with Hungary's ruling party on exchanges with Kivukoni College.[115] With Tanzania's transition to multi-party democracy, the concept of cadre training lost its relevance and the ruling party lost its exclusive access to government funds. Kivukoni and all zonal colleges except the one in Zanzibar were closed in 1992.[116]

Conclusion

Since its opening in 1961, Kivukoni College was an ideological laboratory where socialism was not only supposed to be taught and learned, but also lived. Situated on the beach, at the site of a former hotel where Nyerere had first presented his vision of *ujamaa*, it was a microcosm for socialist political education, intended to diffuse *ujamaa*'s *doxa* and aiming to forge functionaries for the emerging one-party state in courses that emphasized self-reliance activities. College officials evaluated course participants with reference to not only classroom performance and political outlook but also tropes of respectability and a participation in manual labour.

National and transnational dimensions of 'manpower development' intersected in the history of the institution. Both Tanzanians and non-Tanzanians (from Africa, North America, Western Europe and Eastern Europe) shaped Kivukoni's first decade, weighing in on the question if it should resemble Oxford's Ruskin College, become like Nkrumah's ideological institute in Ghana or carve out a national character of its own. The college's connections to the world were recalibrated several times. Sources of funds and personnel were first diversified, then nationalized, as the institution itself came to be a demonstration of *ujamaa*'s tenet of self-reliance. The curriculum changed from a developmentalist and technocratic outlook to anti-colonial teachings of state ideology.

The transition from liberal adult education for development to party-supremacist cadre training under the banner of anti-colonial liberation between 1967 and 1972 was significant, but it was not a sudden and complete overhaul, also because a full-blown vanguardist turn as imagined by Ngombale-Mwiru and other radicals was resisted by more conservative party officials. Although its curricula covered revolutions and socialisms across the globe, the institution was geared towards spreading the ideology of *ujamaa* within the borders of Tanzania, not beyond. Across the change to an ideological school, Kivukoni College was a transit station in the career-making, professionalization, and disciplining for thousands of Tanzanian party functionaries, civil servants and various professional groups, but only few Pan-African militants and members of liberation movements from other countries.

Kivukoni's institutional trajectory over three decades helps to understand how a one-party state came about and operated in practice, how elites sought to produce officials in charge of implementing Tanzania's development drive in the context of decolonization and the Cold War, and how strategies of socialist state-building in the Global South were constantly evolving, disseminated and contested. This happened in debates over the college's role among high-ranking party officials and lecturers, everyday classroom performance, agricultural labour and gender relations. In that sense, Kivukoni College was both more and less than the term 'ideological school' suggests: it was a site of reproducing the party's political and generational authority, a place of contested social relations, and an ideological laboratory to test what *ujamaa* was and could be.

Notes

1 Priya Lal, *African Socialism in Postcolonial Tanzania: Between the Village and the World* (Cambridge: Cambridge University Press, 2015), 27.

2 Priya Lal, 'Tanzanian Ujamaa in a World of Peripheral Socialisms', in *The Routledge Handbook of the Global Sixties: Between Protest and Nation-Building*, ed. Jian Chen et al. (London, New York: Routledge, 2018), 367–80.

3 Brochure 'Kivukoni College. Aims & Objects', International Institute of Social History (henceforth: IISH), ICSDW Archives, 162. Thanks to Su Lin Lewis for sharing this material.

4 United Republic of Tanzania (henceforth: URT), *Annual Manpower Report to the President 1969* (Dar es Salaam: Government Printer, 1970), 42.

5 On the Tanzanian developmental state, see Leander Schneider, *Government of Development: Peasants and Politicians in Postcolonial Tanzania* (Bloomington: Indiana University Press, 2014).

6 URT, *Annual Manpower Report to the President 1975* (Dar es Salaam: Government Printer, 1976), 105.

7 Most comprehensive is the hagiographic account by Hamza A. K. Mwenegoha, *Pambazuko la Siasa: Historia ya Chuo cha Chama Kivukoni College* (Dar es Salaam: Tanzania Publishing House, 1977). For an examination of the college's early years, see Saida Yahya-Othman, *Development as Rebellion. A Biography of Julius Nyerere: Book One. The Making of a Philosopher Ruler* (Dar es Salaam: Mkuki na Nyota, 2020), 162–9.

8 Further examples are the *President's Citizenship College* in Zambia, revolutionary Zanzibar's *Ideological College and Party Museum* or Zimbabwe's *Chitepo School of Ideology*.

9 Gerardo Serra and Frank Gerits, 'The Politics of Socialist Education in Ghana: The Kwame Nkrumah Ideological Institute, 1961–6', *Journal of African History* 60, no. 3 (2019): 407–28; Daniel Branch, *Kenya: Between Hope and Despair, 1963–2010* (New Haven, Ann Arbor, Michigan: Yale University Press, 2011), 51.

10 Emma Hunter, 'A History of *Maendeleo*: The Concept of "Development" in Tanganyika's Late Colonial Public Sphere', in *Developing Africa. Concepts and Practices in Twentieth-Century Colonialism*, ed. Joseph M. Hodge, Gerald Hödl and Martina Kopf (Manchester: Manchester University Press, 2014), 87–107.

11 Some of these interviews are published; others were conducted by the author (in one case together with Atuswege Burton) in Dar es Salaam and Dodoma in 2014 in English and Kiswahili. All translations from Kiswahili are by the author.
12 I would like to thank Immanuel Harisch for sharing issues of *Mbioni* with me.
13 Serra and Gerrits, 'The Politics of Socialist Education'.
14 See, for instance, Valeska Huber, 'Planning Education and Manpower in the Middle East, 1950s–60s', *Journal of Contemporary History* 52, no. 1 (2017): 95–117.
15 Eric Burton, 'Decolonization, the Cold War, and Africans' Routes to Higher Education Overseas, 1957–65', *Journal of Global History* 15, no. 1 (2020): 169–91.
16 Mwenegoha, *Pambazuko*, 1.
17 Wicken to Nyerere, London, 1 October 1958; Nyerere to Kambona, 28 January 1959, both in CCMA, NP/008/A (Foreign Affairs – Europe).
18 See Mwenegoha, *Pambazuko*, 3–4; 'Meeting Minutes', 14 December 1959, Chama cha Mapinduzi Party Archives, Dodoma (henceforth: CCMA), NP/003; Wicken to Selamani Kitundu (TANU Provincial Secretary Mbeya), 9 October 1960, CCMA, GEN/217/1; Joan Wicken, 'The Beginnings of Kivukoni College', *Mbioni* V, no. 8 (1969): 7–8; Yahya-Othman, *Development as Rebellion*, 162–9.
19 'Meeting Minutes', 14 December 1959, CCMA, NP/003.
20 Andrew Ivaska, *Cultured States: Youth, Gender, and Modern Style in 1960s Dar es Salaam* (Durham, NC: Duke University Press, 2011), 56–7, 230fn68; Issa G. Shivji, 'Mwalimu and Marx in Contestation: Dialogue or Diatribe?', *Agrarian South: Journal of Political Economy* 6, no. 2 (2017): 196.
21 Yahya-Othman, *Development as Rebellion*, 167–8.
22 'Press Statement: Kivukoni College Tutor Appointed', undated, CCMA, GEN-217-1.
23 George Roberts, *Revolutionary State-Making in Dar es Salaam: African Liberation and the Global Cold War, 1961–1974* (Cambridge: Cambridge University Press, 2021), 188.
24 Archive of the Konrad-Adenauer Foundation, AF P 47 206. Thanks to Stefan Reith for sharing this document.
25 Stefan Reith, 'Präsident Kikwete eröffnet Programm zu Ethik und guter Regierungsführung', 14 May 2015, http://www.kas.de/tansania/de/publications/41333/.
26 Anon., 'Proposals for the Kivukoni College Programme of Education 1969–1974', undated [November 1968], CCMA, 1003.
27 Paul Bjerk, *Building a Peaceful Nation. Julius Nyerere and the Establishment of Sovereignty in Tanzania, 1960–1964* (Woodbridge: Boydell & Brewer, 2015), 74–83.
28 Ronald Aminzade, *Race, Nation, and Citizenship in Post-colonial Africa: The Case of Tanzania* (Cambridge: Cambridge University Press, 2013), 114–25.
29 See, for instance, Principal's Report for the Kivukoni College Executive Committee to be held on 30 April 1969, CCMA, THQ/C/C.50/17. See also Branwyn Poleykett and Peter Mangesho, 'Labour Politics and Africanization at a Tanzanian Scientific Research Institute, 1949–66', *Africa* 86, no. 1 (2016): 142–61.
30 URT, *Annual Manpower Report to the President 1976* (Dar es Salaam: Government Printer, 1978), 109.
31 Agenda Executive Committee, 8 July 1967, CCMA, THQ/C/C.50/17.
32 One functionary lobbying for the recruitment of the GDR lecturer was Rashidi Utukulu, the Director of NUTA's Educational Department. Lamprecht to FDGB, Dar es Salaam, 2 February 1969, Stiftung Archiv der Parteien und Massenorganisationen der DDR im Bundesarchiv, Berlin (SAPMO-BArch Berlin), DY 30/98133, fol. 209.

33 Ngila Mwase, 'The Life and Times of the Late Israel Elinewinga', *The Guardian*, 1 March 2016, https://www.ippmedia.com/en/columnist/life-and-times-late-israel-elinewinga.
34 Mwenegoha, *Pambazuko*, 37.
35 Volker Vinnai, 'Die Arbeit der Friedrich-Ebert-Stiftung in Tansania – 40 Jahre Zusammenarbeit mit Parteien, Gewerkschaften, Zivilgesellschaft und Regierung', in *Die Arbeit der Friedrich-Ebert-Stiftung in Indonesien, Tansania und Zentralamerika seit den 1960er Jahren*, ed. Norbert v. Hofmann, Volker Vinnai and Hermann Benzing (Bonn: Dietz, 2010), 116–17.
36 Ivaska, *Cultured States*, 57.
37 Mwenegoha, *Pambazuko*, 28; Yahya-Othman, *Development as Rebellion*, 167.
38 Cunninham to Pamela Peachey (International Council of Social Democratic Women), Dar es Salaam, 22 September 1964, ICSDW Archives, 162. Tanzania 1962–6 (Kivukoni College).
39 Mwenegoha, *Pambazuko*, 52–60.
40 Yahya-Othman, *Development as Rebellion*, 166.
41 Leonard Kawala, 'What I Gained from Kivukoni College', *Mbioni* V, no. 8 (1968): 26.
42 Yahya-Othman, *Development as Rebellion*, 166.
43 Pius Msekwa, interviewed by Eric Burton and Atuswege Burton, Dar es Salaam, 23 November 2014.
44 Matteo Grilli, *Nkrumaism and African Nationalism: Ghana's Pan-African Foreign Policy in the Age of Decolonization* (Basingstoke: Palgrave Macmillan, 2018), 234–5.
45 'The Job Distribution Break-Down of Long Course Graduates', *Mbioni* 5, no. 8 (1969): 29–30.
46 TANU AG Secretary A. F. M. Malaya to TANU Deputy Secretary General, 23 October 1962, CCMA, GEN/217/1.
47 Kisenge to TANU Coast Regional Secretary, 19 July 1963, CCMA, GEN/217/1.
48 'Information Sheet: A Residential College for Adult Education Dar es Salaam – Tanzania', 2 August 1967, CCMA, THQ/C/C.50/17.
49 Ibid.
50 G. L. Cunningham, 'Kivukoni College – Post-Arusha Declaration Period', *Mbioni* 2, no. 10 (1966): 3.
51 Community Development Assistant B.M. Mwakibinga to Community Development Division Commissioner, 3 April 1964, CCMA, GEN/217/II.
52 See, for instance, Kawala, 'What I Gained', 23–4.
53 Aminzade, *Race*, 152.
54 Kawala, 'What I Gained', 23–4; Poleykett and Mangesho, 'Labour Politics', 155.
55 Mwenegoha, *Pambazuko la Siasa*, 4.
56 Circular of TANU Secretary General E. A. Kisenge to all TANU Regional Secretaries, 18 November 1963, CCMA, GEN/217/1.
57 Elinewanga to Nyerere, 17 January 1970, CCMA, THQ/C/E.20/2/Vol. II.
58 Mwakawago to Commissioner for Rural Development, Ministry of Regional Administration & Rural Development, 18 May 1971, CCMA, THQ/C/E.20/2/Vol. II.
59 'Proposals for the Kivukoni College Programme of Education 1969–1974', undated [November 1968], CCMA, 1003.
60 Cunningham to TANU National Executive Secretary Pius Msekwa, Dar es Salaam, 8 March 1968, CCMA, 1003.
61 Msekwa to Cunningham, 23 March 1968, CCMA, 1003.

62 See, for instance, the file 'Complaints on Regional/Area Commissioners' (1967–75), CCMA, THQ/A.25/3. On complaints at the local level in the 1960s, see Emma Hunter, *Political Thought and the Public Sphere in Tanzania: Freedom, Democracy, and Citizenship in the Era of Decolonization* (New York: Cambridge University Press, 2015), 196–200.

63 Athumani Nyori to TANU Executive Secretary, 1 March 1972, CCMA, THQ/A.25/3.

64 James R. Brennan, *Taifa: Making Nation and Race in Urban Tanzania* (Athens: Ohio University Press, 2012), 17; Maria Suriano, 'Letters to the Editor and Poems: Mambo Leo and Readers Debates on Dansi, Ustaarabu, Respectability, and Modernity in Tanganyika, 1940s–1950s', *Africa Today* 57 (2011): 39–55.

65 Jeffrey S. Ahlman, 'Managing the Pan-African Workplace: Discipline, Ideology, and the Cultural Politics of the Bureau of African Affairs', *Ghana Affairs* 15/16 (2012/2013).

66 This was apparently done since the college's founding. See 'Kivukoni College. Aims & Objects. A Statement Authorized by the Executive Committee 10 November 1962', IISH, ICSDW Archives, 162. Tanzania 1962–6 (Kivukoni College).

67 For the characterization as disciplinarian, see Mwase, 'The Life and Times'.

68 Elinewanga to Nyerere, 17 January 1970, CCMA, THQ/C/E.20/2/Vol. II. The following quotes are taken from this source.

69 A reader, most likely a functionary in the party headquarters, added one, two or three stars in red ink next to most names.

70 Samwel Mhajida, 'Motherhood, Career Development and Modernization: Experiences of Early Post-colonial Tanzanian Women', *Journal of Education, Humanities and Sciences* 10, no. 2 (2021): 12.

71 For the careers of Kivukoni graduates Blandina Geugeu and Dorcas Nyangata, see Lal, *African Socialism*, 106–7; more generally on women's professional careers after independence, see Mhajida, 'Motherhood', 7.

72 Emily Callaci, *Street Archives and City Life: Popular Intellectuals in Postcolonial Tanzania* (Durham: Duke University Press, 2017), 23.

73 Marjorie Mbilinyi, 'Struggles Concerning Sexuality among Female Youth', *Journal of Eastern African Research and Development* 15 (1985): 111–23.

74 Andrew M. Ivaska, '"Anti-mini Militants Meet Modern Misses": Urban Style, Gender and the Politics of "National Culture" in 1960s Dar es Salaam, Tanzania', *Gender & History* 14, no. 3 (2002): 584–607.

75 Ivaska, 'Cultured States', 217.

76 Andrew Burton, *African Underclass: Urbanisation, Crime & Colonial Order in Dar es Salaam* (London et al.: James Currey et al., 2005), 4–6.

77 Muhammed Khatib, interviewed by Eric Burton, Dar es Salaam, 9 October 2014; John Chiligati, interviewed by Eric Burton, Dodoma, 19 November 2014.

78 Cited in Yahya-Othman, *Development as Rebellion*, 166.

79 Neville Linton, 'Nyerere's Road to Socialism', *Canadian Journal of African Studies* 2, no. 1 (1968): 4; Griffiths Cunningham, 'Kivukoni College: The First Eight Years', *Mbioni* V, no. 8 (1968): 13–14.

80 Belle Harris, 'An Ideological Institute for Tanzania?', in *Tanzania: Revolution by Education*, ed. Idrian N. Resnick (Arusha: Longmans of Tanzania, 1968), 158.

81 Cunningham, 'Kivukoni College – The First Eight Years', *Mbioni* 5, no. 8 (1969): 20–1.

82 Fred G. Burke, 'Tanganyika: The Search for Ujamaa', in *African Socialism*, ed. William H. Friedland and Carl G. Rosberg (Stanford: Stanford University Press, 1964), 199–200.

83 Kingunge Ngombale-Mwiru and Issa G. Shivji, 'Mazungumzo kati ya Kingunge Ngombale-Mwiru na Issa Shivji', *Chemchemi*, no. 2 (2009); Issa G. Shivji, *Development as Rebellion. A Biography of Julius Nyerere: Book Three. Rebellion without Rebels* (Dar es Salaam: Mkuki na Nyota, 2020), 151–2.
84 Kingunge Ngombale-Mwiru, 'The Arusha Declaration on *Ujamaa na Kujitegemea* and the Perspectives for Building Socialism in Tanzania', *Mbioni* III, no. 10 (1967): 15. See also Shivji, 'Mwalimu and Marx', 217fn10.
85 Ngombale-Mwiru, 'The Arusha Declaration', 25.
86 Ibid., 27.
87 Ibid.
88 'Memorandum on Future Role of the College', 26 August 1967, CCMA, THQ/C/C.50/17.
89 Ibid.
90 Ibid.
91 Roberts, *Revolutionary State-Making*, 237.
92 James R. Brennan, 'Debating the Guidelines: Literacy, Text and Socratic Socialism in 1970s Tanzania', Paper delivered at African Studies Workshop, University of Chicago, 6 May 2014, 8.
93 Shivji, 'Mwalimu and Marx', 209.
94 K. Ngombale-Mwiru, 'Mapendekezo ya kimsingi kuhusu jukumu jipya la Kivukoni', 1972, CCMA, 1032. The following is based on this memorandum.
95 TANU Central Committee, 'Mkutano kutayarisha muundo mpya wa Chuo cha TANU Kivukoni', Dar es Salaam, 21 March 1973, CCMA, 1032.
96 Chuo cha Kivukoni, 'Mukhtasari wa mafunzo ya siasa', 1972, CCMA, 1032.
97 See 'Maelezo Binafsi ya Mwalimu T. T. Lukindo', CCMA, THQ/C/E.20/2/Vol. II.
98 This paragraph is based on Lukindo to Nyerere, 22 March 1972, CCMA, THQ/C/E.20/2/Vol. II. The following quotes are also taken from this document.
99 '"Paradox" ya Walimu wa Chuo cha TANU Kivukoni', 31 December 1973, CCMA, THQ/C/E.20/2/Vol. III.
100 Brennan, 'Debating the Guidelines'.
101 'TANU: A Mass Party with a Vanguard', *Sunday News*, 31 December 1972, cited in Peter Meyns, *Nationale Unabhängigkeit und ländliche Entwicklung in der 3. Welt: Das Beispiel Tanzania* (Berlin: Oberbaumverlag, 1978), 238, 282.
102 Interview with Ngombale-Mwiru in 2016, cited in Jeremy Friedman, *Ripe for Revolution: Building Socialism in the Third World* (Cambridge, MA: Harvard University Press, 2021), 155.
103 Ngombale-Mwiru and Shivji, 'Mazungumzo', 71; Friedman, *Ripe for Revolution*, 155.
104 Burton, *In Diensten des Afrikanischen Sozialismus*, chapter 9.
105 'Hotuba ya Rais Nyerere', 2 July 1973, CCMA, THQ/C/E.20/2/Vol. III.
106 On the vanguard question, see Shivji, *Development as Rebellion*, 48–50 and chapter 8.
107 Ngombale-Mwiru, 'Mapendekezo' (cited above), 1972, CCMA, 1032. The quote (with my emphasis added) is from 'Ufunguzi wa Chuo cha TANU Kivukoni Tarehe 2/7/73', CCMA, THQ/C/E.20/2/Vol. III.
108 URT, *Annual Manpower Report 1975*, 105.
109 Ibid., 118–21.
110 Muhammed Khatib, interviewed by Eric Burton, Dar es Salaam, 9 October 2014.
111 Pius Msekwa, interviewed by Eric Burton and Atuswege Burton, Dar es Salaam, 23 November 2014.

112 S. S. Mushi, 'Tanzania', in *Indigenization of African Economies*, ed. Adebayo Adedeji (London: Hutchinson, 1981), 217–18.
113 Cited in Shivji, 'Mwalimu and Marx', 214–15.
114 Aminzade, *Race*, 246.
115 'Cooperation Agreement', Budapest, 9 April 1989, CCMA, CMM/OND/183/37/Vol. 2 Hungary.
116 John Chiligati, interviewed by Eric Burton, Dodoma, 19 November 2014.

11

Fish, discontent, and socialist modernities and dreams in Kwame Nkrumah's Ghana

Nana Osei-Opare

On 6 March 1957, Ghana's fight for political sovereignty from Britain was complete. Ghana's newfound existence had initiated a global revolution. The 'state of Ghana ... had struck imperialism in Africa the blow from which it would never recover', Caribbean Marxist C. L. R. James wrote impassionedly.[1] The moment birthed intense possibilities for societal and global transformation. Spearheaded by its first leader, Kwame Nkrumah, Afro-socialists in Ghana possessed 'worldmaking' and grand visions and plans about how they would transform the largely British monopolized, agrarian and non-industrialized society into a monopsony, modern, industrialized, socialist society.[2] Ghana's visionaries sought to emulate the rapid, large-scale industrialization and modernization projects undertaken by socialist and communist countries in Eastern Europe, the Soviet Union and China. In this way, the socialist project in Ghana assumed a quite different character than Julius Nyerere's socialist project across the African continent in Tanzania.[3]

Under the moniker of '*ujamaa*', Nyerere's Tanzania eschewed large-scale industrialization, nationalized certain sectors of the economy and sought a return to a quasi-romanticized 'traditional' African village habitus.[4] For Ghana's revolutionaries, however, a return to a pre-colonial, idealized or romanticized African society or the nationalization of certain sectors of the Ghanaian economy was deeply undesirable. Instead, the state created numerous state industries and corporations to compete with and eventually unseat the almost unrivalled power European firms held. Completed in 1965, a year before the Western-backed National Liberation Council instigated a military coup to overthrow Nkrumah, the Volta River Project epitomized Ghana's industrialization drive and project of economic self-determination. The task of rupturing Ghana from its current and earlier political, economic and social histories and turning it into a socialist, industrialized society was herculean and would certainly be dangerous to certain segments of society.

Indeed, Ghana's socialist visions would have particularly troubling implications for the fishing communities' political, economic and gendered relations and societal structures. Littered across Ghana's Atlantic coastline, the fishing communities constituted some of the new nation's poorest groups. They were also one of the groups most subjected to sustained public and state scrutiny and attack. Sections of the Ghanaian press and government dismissed the fishing communities' practices and tools, whose industry had sustained, shaped and spurred the domestic and international fishing industries for centuries, as 'backward' and in desperate need of modernization. Powerful figures in the state saw no overlap or connection between the local fishing community and socialist modernization and economic efficiency. With the press, they demonized and sought to delegitimize the local political economy of fishing and its ontologies. Increasingly conceived of as a singular political and social group during the Nkrumah years, the fishing community – in all its manifestations – represented the antithesis of the state's modernization dreams. For certain state figures, overhauling, or perhaps erasing, the fishing economy represented both an opportunity to remake Ghanaian society and indefinitely curtail Ghana's unfavourable expenditure of foreign currency reserves. For those in a rush to modernize or secure Ghana's economic independence (or seeking to capitalize financially on new market and state forces), the opportunity to remake the fishing political economy could not be passed over.

Thus, to modernize the fishing industry, persons with state-sanctioned power and the press turned away from local fishing ontologies and well-crafted and structured political and economic practices to create the Ghana Fishing Corporation (Corporation). State officials purchased Soviet, British, Norwegian and Japanese fishing trawlers to fanfare and arranged for Ghanaians to study fishing techniques from and in said countries. With its newly minted modern equipment and fishing techniques, the Corporation was expected to embody Ghana's new post-colonial socialist modernity and modernization dreams and spearhead Ghana's fishing revolution. To justify moving away from the very sophisticated local fishing political economy and to garner support for the new, the press and certain government officials began a campaign of demonizing the fishing communities and their practices. At times, these attacks appeared well-coordinated,

By examining the fishing communities' tussles with the Corporation and the socialist, 'backward', gendered and modernization discourses surrounding them during the Nkrumah-era (1957–66), this chapter is interested in the reactions and actions of those whom socialist modernity, development and modernization was supposed to replace or displace, and those considered its antithesis.[5] Whereas scholars have shown how cocoa became, at once, a mobilizing symbol for anti-Nkrumah forces, a symbol of Asante nationalism and an important crop for building nationalist socialist development dreams in the 1950s and 1960s, fish has not received similar attention.[6] Yet, during Ghana's early years, the political economy and distribution and consumption of fish became both a symbolic and literal manifestation of Ghana's socialist project. While there is a growing literature on the fishing industry and communities in Ghana,[7] a gap exists on how those societies and sectors confronted hegemonic and public discourses that their practices embodied backwardness and were detrimental to the nation's socialist and developmentalist utopias during the Nkrumah era.[8]

In fighting the Corporation and teleological developmentalist and modernist constructions, the chapter unpacks how the fishmongers simultaneously flipped what constituted developmental progress and modernity on its head, while seeking to maintain the gendered division of labour and gender relations of power within their communities. The fishing communities did not view themselves or their practices as outside of history, anachronistic or antithetical to Ghana's present and future but as fundamental or at the very least mutually constitutive piece of the state's modernist agenda. This chapter is constructed primarily by exploring Ghanaian government presidential reports, memoranda and cabinet agenda meeting minutes; speeches and reports by Ghanaian regional commissioners; discussions from the British colonial office; newspaper articles and editorials; trade deals between Ghana and Britain, the Soviet Union, Japan and Norway; and fishing statistics and data in Ghanaian, British, Russian and American archives.

The history of fishing and gender relations in Ghana's fishing communities

For a millennium, Africans along the West African coast have earned a living through fishing or canoe-building.[9] Carved out of felled tree trunk, the canoes' average shelf-life was roughly two to three years and exceeded eighty feet at times. Fifteenth- and sixteenth-century European accounts of local fishing communities and Anlo oral traditions reveal communities '"at home on the sea"'.[10] In some oral histories, the ancestors came from the sea,[11] highlighting their intimacy with and connectivity to the coast. Fishing communities in Ghana are mobile and migratory. Their footprint on the West African coast is noticeable. Their fishing techniques and home governing structures are replicated in contemporary modern states such as Liberia, Guinea, Côte d'Ivoire, Senegal, Benin and Nigeria.[12] In some sense, they remained 'strangers' within these communities.[13]

The political economy of fishing is instrumental to local ontologies of gender and kin, and religious and social relations.[14] It is highly stratified along gender; and there is a gendered division of labour. Eighteenth-century European accounts observed that men fished while women were 'responsible for processing and marketing fish'.[15] Besides the act of catching fish, which men bar women from due to religious, cultural and superstitious reasons,[16] women control all the other aspects of the industry.[17] Akua Opokua Britwum argues that women 'add value, distribut[e] and preserv[e] fish to ensure its availability long after the peak season'. Generally, fish makes its way from the coast to the interior, sometimes 'well over 100 or 200 miles' inland through vehicles. Women were are also responsible for 'finding markets outside their locality'[18] and accompany the trucks if it involves 'short distances'.[19] These occupations are passed down generationally and along gendered lines. Mothers teach their daughters the art of smoking, drying and processing fish while fathers show their sons how to fish.[20] Most families in fishing communities are polygamous.[21] Besides separate 'purses',[22] husbands and wives usually have independent homes and sleep apart. The '"fish smoking stoves"' are in the woman's home and if a wife is not smoking fish that evening, she sometimes dwells in her husband's house.[23] How does the wife procure said fish?

After catching the fish, husbands or male-relatives do not simply give their wives or female-kin the fish to process and sell. Wives and female-kin are forced to purchase the fish from their husbands or male relatives. While wives purchase the fish from their husbands, their husbands 'borrow money from' them to procure 'food, school fees or petrol'.[24] Esther Yeboah Danso-Wiredu argues that this practice is 'monopol[istic]' and 'safeguards the investment of … wives and friends by keeping them in business'.[25] Ragnhild Overa argues that '[t]he right of a wife to buy fish through a husband is … an important institution in the fishing community'. Yet, Britwum maintains that husbands are indifferent to whether their wives suffer losses in the market since it solely impacts the woman's purse-strings. In fact, Britwum maintains that '[b]usiness failure on the part of women is unacceptable and the communities do not tolerate it'. Instead, she argues that the process makes women vulnerable and their vulnerability is exacerbated by their degree of separation from the fishermen. Women without husbands or 'blood ties' in the fishing industry are estranged from the initial process of fish procurement.[26] They often purchase fish at a higher price from women with kin or romantic relations to the fishermen. This effectively marginalizes and estranges women out of wedlock and without male-kin. The logics of this economy may push a woman without male-kin into marriage.[27] While the system guarantees men customers, women have to continuously seek and maintain their own clientele.

The conditions surrounding the processing of fish also inform social, gender and kin relations at the most intimate level. Although women and men play 'complimentary roles', Irene Odotei argues that 'theoretically it is the male who is vested with superior authority'.[28] 'It is fishing', Britwum argues, 'that gives men control over fresh fish, which in turn gives them power over women'. 'Policy making', Britwum warns, 'fails to take these roles into account'.[29] Whereas the proponents of socialism, development and modernization justified their policies and ideas as necessary to improve the material conditions of the most vulnerable, any change to the catching, processing or marketing of fish would directly impact the power, gender and economic relations among and within the fishing communities, particularly women.

Fish and socialist national body politic

During the Nkrumah era, debates in the public and private sphere swirled about fish's importance to the national body-politics' health, and the state's socialist project and strength. Through fish, a national conversation emerged about private and public partnerships, the interconnectedness of socialist and economic development to diet and health, food distribution, and good governance and governmental authority. The relationship between fish and public health and anxieties over it had a longer history in Ghana. A few decades before independence, the British regime expressed concern about protein deficiency in the colony and hoped that the creation of the Volta River Project would produce 'ample fish' and solve the problem.[30] The issue remained germane after independence. In private and public, writers and government ministers outlined the challenges and dangers insufficient fish supply had on the health of the national body-politic. In an internal government memorandum, in August 1962, the importance of providing 'high calorific food', particularly 'protein', to 'the public' was stressed.[31] In the pages of the Ghanaian newspaper, the *Evening News*, a writer called Ba-Ghana argued that 'The nation needs a healthy, robust population and sufficient supply of fish in the diet is one of the surest ways of achieving this'.[32] 'Fish', K. Amoa-Awuah, the Deputy Minister of Agriculture, argued in April 1963: 'forms an important part of our diets. It is imperative for … us' to 'maintain our health and keep our bodies in tune … to play our part in the reconstructional programme of Ghana'.[33] The *Ashanti Pioneer*, at the heart of the anti-government opposition, argued that the ability to distribute fish, at a reasonable price 'all over the centres and provinces' represented good state governance and development. These acts would improve 'living standards' and result in 'a happy state' and 'harmony between the government and governed'.[34] Fish became the discursive text through which socialist and nationalist discourses about reconstructing new socialist persons and subjects were articulated. National conversations framed and associated 'robust', 'healthy' and fully able-bodied persons as key to the state's forward progress. As the *Ashanti Pioneer* wrote, the state's authority to govern hinged precisely on its ability to control the fishing political economy. The threat of social disorder, state upheaveal and even regime change was not lost on anyone. In 1962 and 1963, anti-government forces launched several attacks on Nkrumah's life. Moreover, bomb explosions had killed CPP supporters at rallies near the seat of state power, the Flagstaff House.[35] Across the continent, the stench of regime change filled the air. In 1963, successful coups transpired in the Republic of Dahomey (now Benin), Togo and the Republic of Congo. The president of Togo, Sylvanus Olympio, was even murdered.[36] That stench was now trying to make its way to Ghana. In both the hallways of government and in the public pages, there was an increased urgency to provide sufficient fish for national productivity and security. Its lack could spell dire consequences for the new nation's leaders.

Ghana imported most of its fish and internal demand outpaced local output. In 1961, Ghana imported about 14,057 tonnes of 'canned fish at £G2,179,338' and the population consumed about 55,000 tonnes of fish.[37] According to the government's data, fish consumption was increasing yearly, resulting in a continued widening imbalance between fish importation and cost. In 1962, the consumption of fish in Ghana increased by almost 42 per cent to approximately 78,000 tonnes.[38] A 1962 United Nations Food and Agriculture Organization survey concluded that Ghana needed 'about 100,000 tons' of 'fresh fish' a year to satisfy present and future demand. However, the Chairman of the Corporation, S. B. Ofori, reported that the local fishing communities only produced forty-thousand tonnes, leaving a sixty-thousand-tonne deficit.[39] The external report showed a huge discrepancy between the quantity of fish needed for local consumption and that produced locally. Officials noted that 'very little or no fish canning [wa]s done [in] Ghana'.[40] Ghana was almost entirely reliant on canned fish imports to fill this void. The unfavourable fish trade balance represented neocolonialism in the classical Nkrumahian sense. Nkrumah's conception of neocolonialism would appear in his 1965 book, *Neocolonialism: The Last Stage of Imperialism*. Ghana was expending its precious foreign reserves – needed to transform the country – to acquire a commodity that lay in abundance within its national boundaries. It also made the new state dependent on foreign actors to build a healthy national body politic and its socialist visions. Consequently, the new state was determined to reduce this gap for financial, political and nutritional reasons.

To curtail this increasingly deteriorating neocolonial situation, the state did not primarily seek to bolster local fishing communities' production but to replace them. Besides seeking to alleviate the lack of fish through 'intensify[ing]' its 'drive for the organization of fishing Co-operatives' and to 'introduce fish pond farming',[41] the government decided to create the Corporation. Led by Ofori, who had been selected for this position because he had operated a very successful fishing co-operative, the Corporation was intended to 'provide sufficient fish and fish-products to raise the living standards and as early as possible to displace all imports of fish and fish products; to work towards a surplus fish catch and fish-products for export'. The state acquired 'a fleet of modern fishing vessels and to motorise [n]early all canoes and small crafts'[42] to support the Corporation's efforts 'to provide sufficient fish and fish products to feed the nation and to displace all imported fish and fish products thereby maintaining our [Ghana's] foreign currency'. The government signed deals with governments and private companies from the USSR, Japan, Norway and Britain to acquire fishing vessels.[43] Further plans to purchase 'a canning factory and a fishmeal plant' from the 'Russian or Japanese' governments were 'immediately' underway.[44] In March 1963, Japanese 'industrialists expressed … [a] willingness to establish' a fishing nets factory in Ghana.[45] The following year, a Ghana-USSR contract stipulated that the Soviets would 'construct fish canning factories with an output of 20,000 cans per day, fish smoking plant with daily output of 6 tons of smoked fish, fish cookery ship to produce 1 ton of various products per day, fish meal and greet plan with output of up to 30 tons of raw products a day'.[46] Alongside purchasing machinery, the new leaders believed that educating a new generation and class of people in modern fishing techniques would overturn the neocolonial situation and increase domestic fish production.

As a result, the state's leaders sent Ghanaians abroad to learn those practices.[47] In early 1965, the Ghanaian government signed a deal with Norway. Moreover, the state sent 142 Ghanaians abroad to learn 'fishing techniques' and had further plans to send 30 Ghanaians to Britain to 'train as deck officers and engineers to help operate the Corporation's vessels and trawlers'.[48] Krobo Edusei, the then Minister of Food and Agriculture, praised these deals, insisting that they would 'contribute a great deal to the development of Ghana's fishing industry as it would provide personnel to man the country's fishing vessels'. However, the state also signed a deal with Norway in early 1965 to establish a 'fishing training centre at Tema for Ghanaian deck officers and engineers'.[49]

These deals were not without some controversy. When K. Amoa-Awuah and other Ghanaian officials travelled to the USSR in November 1962 to inspect the fishing trawlers Ghana was negotiating to purchase from the Soviets, he was prevented from inspecting them, leaving the Ghanaians incensed.[50] In a separate incident, confidential debates between the British treasury, a private British company called the Atlantic Shipbuilding Company, the British Board of Trade and the British Commonwealth Relations Office (formerly its colonial apparatus) were being had about the Atlantic Shipbuilding Company's request to sell six fish trawlers to Ghana. After much internal discussion and disagreement, the British agreed to allow the Atlantic Shipbuilding Company to pursue the aforementioned contract with the Ghanaian state in order to bring business to Newport, England, and to 'prevent the Russians from' controlling the fish trawlers market.[51] While some British officials feared that the Soviet fishing trawlers and the dock might be converted into 'minelayers or coastal ships', others ridiculed the suggestion, asking 'against whom would the mines be laid? And against whom would the trawlers be defending [against]'?[52] Some British officials framed Ghana's fishing projects as an extension of Soviet military might and imperialism – a threat to British interests in West Africa. Despite the internal disagreement, the Ghanaians and the British signed a deal for the latter to sell six trawlers to Ghana.[53] The debates surrounding the procurement of fishing trawlers and increasing fish consumption in Ghana laid bare global and domestic geopolitical and security concerns, and the power of a powerful, private British businessman to shape and compel British foreign policy in Ghana. The bizarre treatment Ghanaian officials faced in the USSR also highlighted the uneven power relations between Ghana and the world's leading industrial economies. However, the question of fish did pose a national security risk, just not in the way the British Foreign Affairs office imagined. Ghanaian officials and press saw protein deficiency as a national security risk. '[U]nhealthy' bodies could not build the self-sufficient, industrialized, socialist society necessary to ensure Ghana's complete independence from imperialism's geopolitical and economic structures. Moreover, the failure to create a healthy national body politic risked inflaming domestic instability.

Despite these international controversies, the Ghanaian state's plans to give the Corporation a strong foothold in all aspects of the fishing political economy – the fishing, processing and marketing – were forging ahead. The state lamented that present access to cold stores was racialized and 'catered for a small European population'. Cold-stores would ensure that the fish could move from the coast to the interior without spoiling. To deracialize access to cold stores, Amoa-Awuah informed the fishing community in a 1963 speech that the Corporation would build twenty-four more cold stores that year. The listeners were further informed that the government would provide the Corporation with numerous 'cold storage facilities as well as fish processing plants'.[54] Outside of the public glare and in an internal memorandum, Ofori plotted how the Corporation would seize control of the women's economic sector. He informed the Ghanaian cabinet that the Corporation intended to enter 'the four fields of fish preservation and ... conversion', which were smoking, salting, drying and canning. The amount and quantities of imported canned fish provided proof to the Corporation that there was a domestic market for it.[55] First under the cover of secrecy in 1962, then publicly in 1963, the Minister of Agriculture affirmed that the Corporation was permitted to set up 'Fish Markets' at 'strategic' coastal 'points' like 'Tema, Elmina, Miema, Mumford, Ada, and Keta'.[56] The Corporation was not acting independently of the state but with its backing to undermine the political economic sphere in which the women had control.

At a meeting with market women, Mr G. N. Ennin, the marketing officer of the Foodstuffs Division of the Ghana Agricultural Produce Marketing Board, instructed the 'women to co-operate' with the state's attempt to eliminate their economic position within the industry.[57] However, the state's intention to create cold stores and to eliminate the 'middlemen' from fish distribution was a direct assault on women's economic roles in the preparation, distribution and sale of fish. It would undermine their economic livelihoods. Thus, the actions and intentions of the Corporation and the state would further exacerbate women's inferior position in the divisions of labour and power relations between them and the fishermen.

The state and press were excited to welcome the modern fish trawlers and the motorization of canoes to its shores to increase fish yields, hopefully leading to greater fish consumption, dwindling dependence on the importation of foreign fish and the preservation of Ghana's foreign cash reserves. Discourses about the fishing industry and communities' backwardness, archaic practices and the need to modernize them began to circulate within the upper echelons of the government and the press. In a memorandum to the Ghana's Presidential Cabinet in August 1962, Ofori blasted the fishing industry as 'unplanned, archaic and capitalistic'. Ofori argued that the state's governing party, the Convention People's Party (CPP), had to 'revolutionalise' the fishing sector and 'provide an efficient and stable fishing industry based on scientific principles'.[58] In Ofori's opinion, the techniques the fishing communities used were unscientific and based on illogical and irrational sentiments. Outside government circles, economist Rowena M. Lawson argued in the 1960s that the European staff Fisheries Department followed scientific procedures and processes while the local non-fishing capitalists were 'ordinary', 'ignorant' and 'illiterate'. Lawson maintained that fishmongers were transitioning 'from a primitive to a mechanised industry'.[59] The Food and Agricultural Organization of the United Nations' Regional Fisheries Officer for Africa in Ghana, Dr A. R. N. O. Meshkat, further pushed the idea that the fishermen were 'backward' and used less sophisticated tools. In a seminar on 'Fishery, Development Planning and administration', Meshkat urged the delegates to convince the fishermen to 'replace their old nets with modern ones', 'to buy the best natural fibre' because they are more durable and caught more fish and 'to teach them (the fishermen) the modern scientific fishing techniques'. The Regional Fisheries Officer hoped that with 'gradual education things would change for the better'.[60] These sentiments were published in the Ghanaian press. The reading public were informed that the fishmongers and their techniques were outdated and backward. In addition, press reports dismissed the idea that the fishmongers could modernize on their own. Instead, it was up to the Ghanaian technocrats and foreigners to salvage the fishing industry and educate the local fishing communities, who had been fishing for centuries, about the latest scientific and modern fishing techniques.

The usage of the words 'illiterate' and 'ignorant' was not misplaced. They were part of a broader societal discourse and lexicon justifying socialism and socialist policies in Ghana. In 1962, the CPP introduced the Work and Happiness Programme, whose goals included eradicating the body-politic of illiteracy, hunger and ignorance – the evils of the colonial society. In his welcome speech to Anastas Mikoyan, First Deputy Prime Minister of the Soviet Union, on 16 January 1962, John E. Hagan, the Regional Commissioner of the Central Region and a key socialist theorist, argued that Ghana's socialism would end, amongst other things, 'ignorance, … the legacy of imperialism and colonialism'.[61] Others claimed that 'illiteracy creates ignorance and ignorance is a disease' and that socialism stood to 'eradicate' it.[62] Comrade J. J. Mensah-Kane, the Headmaster of Ghana National College in Cape Coast, summed up some of socialism's virtues: 'Freedom from disease, Freedom from ignorance, Freedom from poverty, unemployment, and tribulations.'[63] If ignorance were a disease, something capable of crippling the socialist body-politic, then it had to cured or removed. Thus, in framing the fishmongers as ignorant, individuals were implicitly calling for them to be cured or eradicated. If they refused to be cured, to take their medicine, then more severe medical procedures, acts of removal, had to be employed – voluntarily or by force. Initially, government officials tried to convince the fishmongers to take the medicine to heal their ignorance and backwardness.

Some government officials led rallies within the fishmongers' towns and communities to try and increase enthusiasm for their initiatives and to convince the fishmongers that they were not antithetical to the state's modernization efforts but part and parcel of it. In 1962, Amoa-Awuah urged the 'fishermen … to form co-operative societies to contribute towards the achievement of complete economic independence for Ghana'. Speaking to the fishing communities of Eastern Nzima, near Nkrumah's birthplace, Awuah was adamant that the 'Government was prepared to stop importing fish … but could do so only when fishermen … could adequately meet the country's demand[s]'.[64] But, as time progressed, it became apparent that Amoa-Awuah's actions were a public-relation stunt. They were not grounded in reality. Government officials had already concluded that the fishmongers could not meet the new nation's demands. Soon, rather than urge the fishmongers to take medicines to cure their 'ignorance', a corporation had been created to eliminate the fishmongers from the process.

Now, some changed tact and tried to convince the fishmongers to support the Corporation because that would improve their comrades' standard of living. At a fishmongers' rally on 9 April 1963, at Takoradi, Amoa-Awuah, who only a year prior had informed the fishmongers that they could satisfy the nation's fish consumption demands, now urged them to put their weight behind the Corporation. He told the fishmongers that it was their duty to 'co-operate with' the Corporation's officials in order to revolutionize Ghana's fishing industry and to 'raise our standard of living and to enable us to live as free, healthy and prosperous men and women in this progressive land of Ghana'. 'Comrades', Amoa-Awuah continued, 'Ghana expects to rid her fishing industry of all hardship and foreign exploitation. We must thus put an immediate stop to the importation of fish and fish products and conserve our valuable foreign exchange. Our rural population must be sufficiently fed with fish to eliminate the dread of malnutrition that now plagues the people living in those areas'. In addition, Amoah-Awuah tried to reassure the fishmongers that the Corporation was not established to compete with them or undermine their livelihood but to 'assist' them in bridging 'the gap between' Ghana's nutritional requirements' and what they produced.[65]

For the fishing communities, Amoa-Awuah's claims were somewhat hollow considering that the government did not provide them with the 'modern tools' necessary to dominate the national fishing industry. When those tools did become available, the government quickly side-stepped the fishermen as its potential users and gave it to the Corporation. This was deliberate. Discussions were held within government circles about supplying the fishmongers with motorized boats.

However, they were shot down.[66] Some officials held an arrogant attitude towards the fishmongers and were appalled by their failure to bow to the Corporation's power and march towards modernity. For these figures, if the Corporation was displacing the fishmongers livelihoods and its gendered division of labour and social relations, then it was a necessary historical movement.[67]

Towards the latter half of 1963, the press shifted from modernization critiques of the fishing industry to demonizing its entire political economy, particularly the processes that women had historically controlled. Some commentators believed that the local fishing communities were artificially raising the prices and hiding the fish and critiqued the political economy of the distribution of fish. In the *Evening News* on 22 October 1963, a writer called Ba-Ghana insisted that women in the fishing communities were hoarding fish, leading to its absence in the markets and resulting in higher prices. '"This is a horrifying"' occurrence, Ba-Ghana argued, where the fish 'vanishes into thin air with the price of fish still soaring higher and higher'. This was not due to market fluctuations, he concluded, but as a result of a deliberate plot by 'persons and others too numerous to mention are assisting heartless and cruel racketeers and profiteers to abtain [*sic*] chits for bulk supply of fish from supply depots which they in turn hand over to other middlemen and women who finally retail same to the real fishmongers from whom the housewife obtains her supply for the family meals'.[68] In the guise of protecting the housewives, Ba-Ghana called for the destruction of the political economy that protected select women in the fishing industry since it was they who largely dictated fish prices. They were the metaphorical middlemen in this process. According to Ba-Ghana, the wives' or women's exclusive or first right of refusal to purchasing fish from their husbands was a blatant act of 'patronage' and corruption.

Blaming women for the high costs of living would be replicated in 1979 and 1981 under John Jerry Rawlings's military regime. With pretenses and pretensions to combating high inflation and racketeering, security forces physically attacked women and burned down their businesses in the state's largest cities.[69] But, nearly two decades earlier, figures like Ba-Ghana urged the Corporation to 'take over the entire mechanized fishing industry in the country'. Ba-Ghana exclaimed, '"Away with racketeers"'![70] If people like Ba-Ghana had their wish, the Corporation would metaphorically burn down the entire fishing enterprise and the social structures surrounding it. The fishing communities expected this was the ultimate goal, despite government official claims to the contrary.

For the pro-and-anti-government factions, corruption and patronage were among the chief culprits of the state's deteriorating economy, the suffering of millions and the unfulfilled dreams and expectations of Black Independence and socialist modernity. Ba-Ghana continued: 'Patronage is still having its grip on Ghanaian life and people must remember the Dawn Broadcast'. Public anger against patronage and individuals enriching themselves at their fellow citizens' and state's expense were swirling. Nkrumah could not deny or dismiss these criticisms, forcing him to address them head on in his famous Dawn Broadcast speech on 8 April 1961. There, Nkrumah attacked individuals who used '"party membership and official position for personal gain or for the massing of wealth"'.[71] These individuals were stealing from the state and its people and cultivating a culture of corruption. Using the state's idioms, Ba-Ghana argued that the socialist state had to eradicate 'at all costs … the filthy fish racket which is going on now'.[72]

The fishing community responds

In response to the Corporation's creation, its activities and the press's demonization, the various fishing communities across the Ghanaian coast banded together to form a unified oppositional voice. While figures like Amoa-Awuah argued that the Corporation would eliminate malnutrition and foreign exploitation, he was silent on whether the Corporation would instigate domestic exploitation and dismantle centuries-old economic and social practices and activities. Despite the government's rhetoric and attempts to convince the fishmongers that the Corporation was intended to protect and aid their interests, the fishmongers were sceptical. As time progressed, the fishmongers' suspicions that the Corporation was ultimately designed to marginalize them – to destroy their livelihoods and to take food away from their bellies – were becoming acute realities. On 30 April 1963, the fishmongers in the Western and Central Regions held an emergency meeting at Cape Coast.[73] They discussed their 'anxieties, sufferings, inconveniences, disadvantages, bordering upon hunger' and their 'very urgent needs for means of livelihood for thousands of the poor men and women forming the Fishing Communities of Ghana, of whom we are part and parcel'. The local fishmongers complained that they had 'been struggling for daily maintenance and existence against modern foreign fishing boat trawlers and high-powered vessels'. The fishmongers noted that they worked diligently in silence, but were 'at the brink of starvation'.[74] Despite working in silence, the women were neither silent nor invisible. A few months prior, on 5 February, as shown in Figure 3, the fishmongers attended a 'big rally at Cape Coat'. Most of the attendees captured at the rally were women, underscoring their centrality to the fishing economy. They were part of the politics of dissent. Their physical presence and sheer numbers at the rally outlined their outsized growing concerns about how the state's new policies would weaken or destroy their economic and social positions, particularly the reification of male dominance in the industry and their private lives. While a January 1964 referendum cemented Ghana as a one-party state in 1964, the government remained sensitive to letters and acts of discontent from its people.[75] Thus, we might be able to read the women's presence at the rally as a physical expression of concern, displeasure or at the extreme, a public rebuke of government's fishing initiative(s). Indeed, rather than helping the local fishmongers as Amoa-Awuah had claimed, the fishmongers informed the government that the Corporation was suffocating them. They implored the minister to travel through the fishing towns and villages to witness their suffering. 'And in tears', the fishmongers concluded, 'we implore you to act … We pray and pray you fervently to act now to save us … Help! Please Help!, for we are being starved'.[76] Even prior to the Corporation's rise, some have argued that the 'coastal

Figure 3 'Fishermen's big rally at Cape Coast', *Daily Graphic*, 5 February 1963. 'Section of the fishermen who attended the rally listening attentively to the minister.'

fishing communities in Ghana were among the poorest in the country'.[77] Thus, an already vulnerable situation had been exacerbated. Furthermore, the fishmongers complained bitterly that the government was diverting 'millions of pounds' from them 'to support the "Ashanti-packed" Fishing Corporation', which they believed was 'maneuvering to usurp' their 'rights and chances'.[78]

Not only had the fishmongers framed their opposition to the Corporation in terms of financial interests, but they linked it to ethnic favouritism. Northern Ghanaians made similar accusations against the Ashantis in the government's Soviet Geological Survey Team.[79] According to the fishing communities, the socialist government was deliberately creating an asymmetrical playing field vis-à-vis itself and the Corporation in its quest to eliminate the state's need for fish importation. The fishing communities believed that if the state invested and funnelled millions of dollars into their coffers and operations that they had the know-how, connections and management to feed the nation. The fishmongers' stories highlight the complex impact state industries and enterprises had upon those whom it was supposed to serve, how they could dismantle local gender and social relations and the intersectional webs of exploitation that could arise from these processes. While Ghanaian state industries were intended to curtail foreign economic exploitation and domination of Ghanaian markets, some domestic economic actors found these institutions as harbingers of oppression. The fishmongers' call for the Ghanaian leadership to visit their villages and observe their sufferings underscored the disconnect between figures like Amoa-Awuah and the fishing communities, often comprising of very small ethnic groups.

Not all government officials overlooked the fishmongers' concerns, however. In October 1963, Nathaniel Welbeck – the parliamentary member for Cape Coast and CPP's Executive Secretary, the former Minister of Works and Housing, and Ghana's Ambassador to the Congo when Patrice Lumumba's government fell apart – backed his constituents in parliament: Welbeck yelled: 'We must not merely talk shout socialism, when we know that all the poor women fishmongers are being deprived of the opportunities for selling fish by people who have never been in the industry, and are forcing their way into it and taking it over. The Ghanaian masses who have supported Osagyefo from 1947 to 1963 in his long, dedicated and brilliant leadership deserve to be rid of all party sharks and anti-socialist tycoons. The whole world is watching us. Our attempt to build a socialist state should not be sabot-and [*sic*] eranks [*sic*] who hate the very name and aims of our socialist revolution'.[80] For Welbeck, socialism was not a merely a verbal ideology but it had to have real currency for its subjects. The destruction of local livelihoods, particularly its gendered aspects, jarred with socialism. As a matter of political allegiance and expediency, Welbeck warned Nkrumah and his fellow party members that permitting the fishing communities to suffer risked alienating their own political support base – one that had loyally followed the party against their political foes from the moment of the CPP's inception.

On 21 June, J. B. Morrison, the Regional Secretary of the Western Region, also expressed grave concerns about the fishermen's alarming state of affairs and attempted to find ways to alleviate them. Despite the 'urgency of this question', Morrison was startled that the district commissioners had done nothing significant to address the fishmongers' dire straits despite knowing about it for months. These fears went against newspaper articles that praised the fishing industry as one of the most 'exciting careers that offer[ed] a school-leaver a good chance of reaching the top by … 21'.[81] Yet, the situation had deteriorated to such an extent that Morrison called for an immediate meeting between all of the affected parties to resolve the matter.[82] Becoming an independent fishmonger did not seem so attractive anymore with strong attacks from the Corporation and press.

The district commissioners ignored Morrison's message, prompting Morrison to write to them again on 11 July expressing his dismay and horror that there was a '"Dead" silence … on the fate of the indigenous fishermen and fishmongers'.[83] In this context, indigeneity did not refer to African vis-à-vis Europeans. Instead, it was invoked to distinguish between the small ethnic groups from the Akans. Yet, the Corporation was not the only entity competing with the Ghanaian fishmongers. Frenchmen were also manning French trawlers on the Ghanaian shores.[84] The fishmongers were fighting against multiple entities – their government, the press and Asian and European capital and products. In another private memorandum to all the district commissioners on August 17, Morrison reiterated that the Corporation was intended to aid the 'indigenous fishermen and fishmongers' and not to 'usurp' their 'rights and chances' as was 'happening now'.[85] But, why had there been total silence on the matter?

Problems with the fishing corporation

The Corporation had engaged in a deliberate campaign to bifurcate the fishmongers' unity and garner the support of local public officials. The Corporation held rallies in local communities and promised the fishmongers many things, including to educate their children 'overseas', a financial and educational expenditure and aspiration that the fishmongers could only imagine. The district commissioners insisted that the Corporation was closely collaborating with the local fishmongers. Morrison ridiculed the insinuation that the Corporation was 'work[ing] hand in hand with the Co-operatives'. He noted that 'there has been no practical move made towards this objective' and characterized the Corporation's claims as 'instrument[s] of propaganda to induce the fishing communities towards support; but with the concealed intent of creating confusion in the Co-operative camps, to open a chance to displace the co-operative organization'. The Corporation was disrupting and uprooting their local rivals through sophisticated and blunt measures. Morrison chided the Corporation for manipulating public opinion with falsehoods and lamented how district commissioners were 'easy prey to the subtle plans of the Corporation'. The Corporation was 'guilty of undue conceit … of attempts' to operate 'as though Government-sponsored, but more or less private enterprise, and manoeuvring to overlap the operations of the Fishing Co-operatives'.[86] The Corporation blurred the lines between itself and the state for its benefit. Such tactics provided the Corporation with the veneer of authority, hegemony and unstoppability. Morrison was keen to dismantle this well-constructed façade. He reminded everyone that the Corporation was not the government and that it had to 'adopt the proper procedure and more constitutional method of approach, by negotiation with the regional bodies through the national body'.[87] Morrison reminded the District Officers that they had the power to reject the Corporation's permits to stage rallies in their neighbourhoods and encouraged them to do so. A failure to tease out the differences in the relationship between the government and the Corporation, Morrison alleged, would justifiably raise the fishmongers' 'suspicion of a deliberate intention by the Fishing Corporation to obstruct the operations and functions'.[88]

The modernizing vessels the Ghanaian state hoped they were purchasing turned out to be unreliable. In a February 1965 investigation and hearing into why one of the fishing vessels sank at sea, the committee concluded that there was a '"fundamental defect" due to [the] faulty construction of the boat' rather than another claim that the boat was overloaded with 'fish'.[89] The fleets entering Ghana were defective. J. N. N. Adjetey, the Chief Fisheries Officer, testified that the Corporation had to reduce its fleets from over 350 to about 14 and that several of its 'retail ships were badly sited and unprofitable and had to be closed down'. Only four out of the ten fish trawlers built in the Soviet Union were still in use.[90] By 1964, two of the six trawlers Ghana purchased from Britain had 'proved unsatisfactory' and were subsequently 'sold to Chile'.[91] By 2 February 1965, the Corporation only had 'eleven sea-going vessels'; the others were inoperative.[92] Besides suffering from defective trawlers from the capitalist and communist worlds, claims of internal mismanagement haunted the Corporation.

In 1963, the Ghanaian newspapers lamented a brewing 'fish racket' within the Corporation. As negativity began to engulf the Corporation, the press began to gender it as female. The papers singled out cabinet and parliament officials' wives and suspicious foreign trade deals with countries like Japan and the Côte d'Ivoire as part of the Corporation's misdeeds.[93] Some members of the Corporation and Soviet citizens engaged in 'irregularities', particularly with the sale and purchase of fish. Some Ghanaians 'provide[d] entertainment for the Russians while their vessel remained in port' and then would sell the fish directly to the Soviets, contrary to the government's regulations.[94] Health inspectors like E. K. Attakorah failed to account for 184 cartons of rotten fish between November 1963 and December 1965 and condemned 464 cartons of fish without issuing verifying certificates and sold them on the black market.[95]

The press echoed calls from the Minister of Justice, Mr K. A. Ofori-Atta, and Welbeck to set up 'a commission of enquiry to look into allegations of favouritism and nepotism in the award of contracts in the fishing industry which is causing unfair distribution of fish and a serious racket should be taken up at once'. The press argued that '[w]hen state functionaries and other unscrupulous party members and deputies use their offices to rob the hard working masses in socialist countries by using smart capitalist tricks and shameless effrontery, such rascals are given very severe punishment'.[96] If Ghana were to live up to its socialist ethos, it had to severely punish individuals who were stealing from the masses. The public scandal surrounding the Corporation and the political economy of fish prompted the National Liberation Council (NLC), who removed Nkrumah's government on 24 February 1966, to set up a commission to investigate the Corporation in 1967.

Conclusion

The fisherfolk would not fall into history's dustbin so easily, however. Throughout Nkrumah's presidency, the local fishermen outperformed the Corporation. The fishermen in their hand-made canoes hauled in more fish than the Corporation did with their 'experts' and '31-foot motor boats', prompting the fishermen to laugh and taunt their 'competitors'.[97] The NLC's 1967 Commission had determined that the Corporation failed to break the tide of foreign fish importation during the Nkrumah-era. The Commission dryly noted that Ghana still imported 60 per cent of its fish during the Corporation's commercial peak in 1965. Regarding fish, Nkrumah's government had been unable to disrupt the neocolonial economy. The Commission's committee even sarcastically alleged that the imported fish was of better quality and 'yielded more profit than the fish brought in by the Corporation's own vessels'.[98] Furthermore, from 1961 to 1964, canoe fisheries produced thousands of tonnes more fish than the motor fishing vessels and landing foreign vessels.[99] The unfavourable trade imbalance propelling fish consumption also symbolized spawned neocolonial fears and debates. From the available sources, it is unclear whether the Corporation had strengthened the positioning of men vis-à-vis women within the fishing communities while weakening the fishing community overall.

These early defeats were discernible blows to the Corporation's image as the embodiment of modernity, development and Ghana's socialist future. For the socialist visionaries, this episode was rather embarrassing and undercut the promises of socialist modernization. It demonstrated that older and local African forms of knowledge and political economic practices were superior to modernized equipment and teachings. The primarily uneducated fishing communities contested the imposition and visions of socialist modernities and internationalisms while throwing into doubt teleological ideas of progress and development, and Africans' place within them. Fishing, fish and the fishing communities were not peripheral conversations about socialist modernities, development and gender relations. They dominated Ghanaian public and private debates. They were powerful symbols and imagined vehicles of the reconstruction and self-fashioning of Ghana's body-politic and self-image. To some of the self-assured and acclaimed modernizers of Ghana, the fish communities' 'primitive' tactics and operations were indicative of Ghana's backward past and antithetical to its modernist future. Yet, if the past could defeat the future – what promise did black, socialist independence hold?

Notes

1 C. L. R. James, *Nkrumah and the Ghana Revolution* (Durham: Duke University Press, 2022), 5.

2 Adom Getachew, *Worldmaking after Empire: The Rise and Fall of Self-Determination* (Princeton: Princeton University Press, 2019). On monopoly capitalism in Ghana, see Gareth Austin and Chibuike Ugochukwu Uche, 'Collusion and Competition in Colonial Economies: Banking in British West Africa, 1916–1960', *Business History Review* 81, no. 1 (2011): 1–26.

3 I have discussed in more detail how Ghana's socialism, its political-economy, was situated within black Marxists readings and understandings of state-capitalism. See Nana Osei-Opare, 'Ghana and Nkrumah Revisited: Lenin, State Capitalism, and Black Marxist Orbits', *Comparative Studies in Society and History* 65, no. 2 (2023): 399–421. Moreover, in my forthcoming book, *Socialist Decolony: Black and Soviet Entanglements in Ghana's Decolonization and Cold War Projects* (New York: Cambridge University Press), I discuss the cultural and social construction of socialism in Ghana.

4 Priya Lal, *African Socialism in Postcolonial Tanzania: Between the Village and the World* (Cambridge: Cambridge University Press, 2017).

5 Abena Dove Osseo-Asare discusses the unfortunate plight of the Haatso and Kwabenya communities displaced by Ghana's atomic reactor and their estrangement from nuclear knowledge. See *Atomic Junction: Nuclear Power in Africa after Independence* (Cambridge: Cambridge University Press, 2019), 139–69. Kara Moskowitz shows how Nandi squatters in Kenya fought against the creation of the paper mill factory. See *Seeing Like a Citizen: Decolonization, Development, and the Making of Kenya, 1945–1980* (Athens: Ohio University Press, 2019), 197–221.

6 Polly Hill, *The Migrant Cocoa-Farmers of Southern Ghana* (Cambridge: Cambridge University Press, 1963); Gwendolyn Mikell, 'Filiation, Economic Crisis, and the Status of Women in Rural Ghana', *Canadian Journal of African Studies* 18, no. 1 (1984): 195–218; Jean M. Allman, *The Quills of the Porcupine: Asante Nationalism in an Emergent Ghana* (Madison: the University of Wisconsin Press, 1993), 16–83; Francis K. Danquah, 'Sustaining a West African Cocoa Economy: Agricultural Science and the Swollen Shoot Contagion in Ghana, 1936–1965', *African Economic History* 31 (2003): 43–74; Gareth Austin, *Labour, Land and Capital in Ghana: From Slavery to Free Labour in Asante, 1807–1956* (Rochester: the University of Rochester Press, 2009).

7 Irene Odotei, 'Gender and Traditional Authority in the Artisanal Marine Fishing Industry in Ghana', *Institute of African Studies Research Review* 15, no. 1 (1999): 15–38; Akua Opokua Britwum, 'The Gendered Dynamics of Production Relations in Ghanaian Coastal Fishing', *Feminist Africa* 12 (2009): 69–85; Esther Yeboah Danso-Wiredu, 'Gendered Dynamics and Reciprocity in Fishing Communities in Ghana: The Case of Penkye in Winneba', *Journal of Black Studies* 49, no. 1 (2018): 53–70; Marloes Kraan, 'More Than Income Alone: The Anlo-Ewe Beach Seine Fishery in Ghana', in *Poverty Mosaics: Realities and Prospects in Small-Scale Fisheries*, ed. Svein Jentoft and Arne Eide (London: Springer Dordrecht Heidelberg, 2011), 147–72; Ragnhild Overå, 'Institutions, Mobility, and Resilience in the Fante Migratory Fisheries in West Africa', *Transactions of the Historical Society of Ghana* 9 (2005): 103–23; Moses Adjei and Ragnhild Overå, 'Opposing discourses on the offshore coexistence of the petroleum industry and small-scale fisheries in Ghana', *The Extractive Industries and Society* 6, no. 1 (2019): 190–7.

8 The planning and implementation of one of Ghana's biggest development projects, the Akosombo Dam, around the Volta Lake displaced local fishing communities, resulting in the emigration of male fishermen and producing unintended environmental and political economic consequences, such as an increase in fish and spread of disease. See Dzodzi Tsikata, *Living in the Shadow of the Large Dams: Long Term Responses of Downstream and Lakeside Communities of Ghana's Volta River Project* (Leiden: Brill, 2006); Stephan F. Miescher, *A Dam for Africa: Akosombo Stories from Ghana* (Bloomington: Indiana University Press, 2023).

9 Edward Reynolds, *Trade and Economic Change on the Gold Coast, 1807–1874* (New York: Longman Publishing Group, 1974), 20.
10 Robert Smith, 'The Canoe in West African History', *The Journal of African History* 11, no. 4 (1970): 515–33; Robin Law, 'Between the Sea and the Lagoons: The Interaction of Maritime and Inland Navigation on the Precolonial Slave Coast', *Cahiers d' Etudes africaines* 114, no. XXIX-2 (1989): 209–37.
11 Carl Christian Reindorf, *History of the Gold Coast and Asante* (London: Forgotten Books, [1895] 2015), 5–6.
12 Overå, 'Institutions, Mobility and Resilience in the Fante Migratory Fisheries in West Africa', 106, 108, 114–16.
13 Elliott P. Skinner, 'Strangers in West African Societies', *Africa: Journal of the International African Institute* 33, no. 4 (1963): 307–20; William A. Shack and Elliott P. Skinner (ed.), *Strangers in African Societies* (Berkeley: University of California Press, 1973).
14 Odotei, 'Gender and Traditional Authority in the Artisanal Marine Fishing Industry in Ghana', 15 and 18; Moses Adjei and et al., "The Role of Socioeconomic Factors, Psychological Motivations, and Social Networks in Women's Participation in Community-Based Fishery Management in Ghana', *Coastal Management* 51 (2023): 1–20.
15 Britwum, 'The Gendered Dynamics of Production Relations in Ghanaian Coastal Fishing', 69; Odotei, 'Gender and Traditional Authority in the Artisanal Marine Fishing Industry in Ghana', 20.
16 Danso-Wiredu, 'Gendered Dynamics and Reciprocity in Fishing Communities in Ghana', 66–7.
17 Moses Adjei, 'Gendered Spaces and Entanglements: Analysis of Fisher Couples' Decision-Making and Practices in Ghana's Western Region', *Gender, Place, & Culture: A Journal of Feminist Geography* 30 (2023): 14–18.
18 Britwum, 'The Gendered Dynamics of Production Relations in Ghanaian Coastal Fishing', 69–73.
19 Odotei, 'Gender and Traditional Authority in the Artisanal Marine Fishing Industry in Ghana', 24.
20 Danso-Wiredu, 'Gendered Dynamics and Reciprocity in Fishing Communities in Ghana', 58–64.
21 Jemimah Etornam Kassah and Cephas Asare, 'Conflicts in the Artisanal Fishing Industry of Ghana: Reactions of Fishers to Regulatory Measures', in *Blue Justice: Small-Scale Fisheries in a Sustainable Ocean Economy*, ed. Svein Jentoft, Ratana Chuenpagdee, Alicia Bugeja Said, and Moenieba Isaac (Switzerland: Springer International Publishing, 2022), 104.
22 Overå, 'Institutions, Mobility and Resilience in the Fante Migratory Fisheries in West Africa', 110.
23 Danso-Wiredu, 'Gendered Dynamics and Reciprocity in Fishing Communities in Ghana', 66.
24 Overå, 'Institutions, Mobility and Resilience in the Fante Migratory Fisheries in West Africa', 110–11.
25 Danso-Wiredu, 'Gendered Dynamics and Reciprocity in Fishing Communities in Ghana', 64.
26 Britwum, 'The Gendered Dynamics of Production Relations in Ghanaian Coastal Fishing', 75.

27 There have been other instances in Colonial Ghanaian history where laws were passed to encourage single women into marriage. See Jean Allman, 'Rounding up Spinsters: Gender Chaos and Unmarried Women in Colonial Asante', *The Journal of African History* 37, no. 2 (1996): 195–214.
28 Odotei, 'Gender and Traditional Authority in the Artisanal Marine Fishing Industry in Ghana', 21.
29 Britwum, 'The Gendered Dynamics of Production Relations in Ghanaian Coastal Fishing', 73, 75 and 81.
30 Stephan F. Miescher, 'Ghana's Akosombo Dam, Volta Lake Fisheries & Climate Change', *Daedalus* 150, no. 4 (2021): 126.
31 Ghana Public Records and Archives Administration Department (PRAAD)-Accra, ADM/13/2/95, August 1962, 'Fisheries', United Ghana Farmers' Council Agricultural Development Programme (Co-Operative and Settlements Sector).
32 Ba-Ghana, 'Stop This Bad Fish Racket', *Evening News*, 22 October 1963, 5.
33 PRAAD-Sekondi WRG8/1/267, 9 April 1963, speech by K. Amoa-Awuah.
34 'Feeding the Nation', *The Ashanti Pioneer*, 13 July 1962, 2.
35 '4 Killed, 85 Injured in Nkrumah Bomb Plot', *Chicago Daily Defender*, 10 January 1963, 10; PRAAD-Accra RG17/1/211, 21 September 1962, Nikita Khrushchev to Kwame Nkrumah; 'Two Killed by Bomb at Nkrumah Palace', *The New York Times*, 10 September 1962, 1.
36 Ali A. Mazrui, 'Thoughts on Assassination in Africa', *Political Science Quarterly* 83, no. 1 (1968): 40–1; Noel Dossou-Yovo, 'The Experience of Benin', *International Journal on World Peace* 16, no. 3 (1999): 60–1; David Eaton, 'Diagnosing the Crisis in the Republic of Congo', *Africa: Journal of the International African Institute* 76, no. 1 (2006): 46.
37 PRAAD-Accra ADM/13/2/95, August 1962, 'Memorandum on Ghana Fishing Corporation', by S. B. Ofori.
38 'Fish Consumption Is Very High', *Evening News*, 17 September 1963, 1.
39 PRAAD-Accra ADM/13/2/95, August 1962, 'Memorandum on Ghana Fishing Corporation'.
40 PRAAD-Accra ADM13/2/95, August 1962, 'Fisheries', United Ghana Farmers' Council Agricultural Development Programme (Co-Operative and Settlements Sector).
41 PRAAD-Accra ADM13/2/95, August 1962, 'Fisheries'. According to Aaron Windel, the British colonial office encouraged 'native co-operatives' in 'rural Africa'. Some of these fishing cooperatives were certainly colonial holdovers. See 'Co-Operatives and the Technocrats, or "the Fabian Agony" Revisited', in *Brave New World: Imperial and Democratic Nation-Building in Britain Between the Wars*, ed. Laura Beers and Geraint Thomas (London: University of London Press, 2011), 251.
42 PRAAD-Accra ADM/13/95, August 1962, Memorandum, by the minister of agriculture.
43 PRAAD-Sekondi WRG8/1/267, 9 April 1963, speech by K. Amoa-Awuah. By May 1964, Ghana and the Soviet Union had signed multiple fishing deals. PRAAD-Accra ADM13/2/104, May 1963, 'Report of Ghana Economic Mission to Japan'; D0221.19, 3 February 1964, V.E. Davies to J.D. Hennings.
44 PRAAD-Accra ADM13/2/95, August 1962, 'Memorandum on Ghana Fishing Corporation'.
45 PRAAD-Accra ADM13/2/104, May 1963, Krobo Edusei, 'Report of Ghana Economic Mission to Japan'.

46 PRAAD-Sekondi WRG8/1/267, 17 August 1963, J. E. Morrison to all district commissioners.
47 PRAAD-Accra ADM/13/95, August 1962, Memorandum by the minister of agriculture.
48 'Corp Makes Big Profit', *Daily Graphic*, 2 February 1965, x.
49 'Centre Will Train Fishing Personnel', *Daily Graphic*, 23 January 1965, 1.
50 The Archive of Foreign Policy of the Russian Federation (AVPRF), 12 December 1962, Ghanaian embassy to Soviet Foreign Ministry.
51 The British National Archives (TNA) DO221/19, 3 February 1964, V. E. Davies to J. D. Hennings.
52 TNA DO221/19, 6 February 1964, J. Chadwick to J. D. Hennings.
53 TNA DO221/19, 12 February 1964, W. N. Wenban-Smith to J. Chadwick; Do221/19, 13 February 1964, J. Chadwick.
54 PRAAD-Sekondi WRG8/1/267, 9 April 1963, speech by K. Amoa-Awuah.
55 PRAAD-Accra ADM13/2/95, August 1962, 'Memorandum on Ghana Fishing Corporation', by S.B. Ofori.
56 PRAAD-Accra ADM13/2/95, August 1962, Memorandum by the minister of agriculture; PRAAD-Sekondi WRG8/1/267, 9 April 1963, speech by K. Amoa-Awuah.
57 'Cold Stores Will Aid Food Marketing', *The Ashanti Pioneer*, 9 July 1962.
58 PRAAD-Accra ADM13/2/95, August 1962, 'Memorandum on Ghana Fishing Corporation', by S.B. Ofori.
59 Rowena M. Lawson, 'The Transition of Ghana's Fishing from a Primitive to a Mechanised Industry', *Transactions of the Historical Society of Ghana* 9 (1968): 90–104.
60 'Don't Use Old Nets, Fishermen Advised', *Evening News*, 18 July 1963.
61 The State Archive of the Russian Federation (GARF), f. 5446, op. 120, d. 1726, A Welcome Address by Hon. J. E. Hagan, Regional Commissioner in Honour of Anastas Mikoyan, First Deputy Prime Minister of the Soviet Union, 16 January 1962.
62 Group 1, 'Seminar Report on "Nkrumaism"' (Cape Coast, Ghana: Mfantsiman Press, 1962), 13.
63 J. J. Mensah-Kane, 'The Convention People's Party', in *Seminar Report on 'Nkrumaism'* (Cape Coast, Ghana: Mfantsiman Press, 1962), 39.
64 'Asked to Form Co-Operatives', *The Ashanti Pioneer*, 9 July 1962.
65 PRAAD-Sekondi WRG8/1/267, 17 August 1963, J. E. Morrison to all district commissioners.
66 PRAAD-Accra, ADM13/2/95, August 1962, 'Notes of a Meeting Held on 18 July 1962, Agricultural Production Drive Committee'.
67 PRAAD-Sekondi WRG8/1/267, 6 August 1964, Fisheries Office (Western Region) to the secretary of the regional commissioner.
68 Ba-Ghana, 'Stop This Bad Fish Racket'.
69 Bianca Murillo, *Market Encounters: Consumer Cultures in Twentieth-Century Ghana* (Athens: Ohio University Press, 2017), 157–8; Gracia Clark, 'Price Control of Local Foodstuffs in Kumasi, Ghana, 1979', in *Traders Versus the State: Anthropological Approaches to Unofficial Economies*, ed. Gracia Clark (New York: Routledge, [1998] 2019), 57–79.
70 Ba-Ghana, 'Stop This Bad Fish Racket'.
71 Kwame Nkrumah, Dawn Broadcast speech, 8 April 1961.
72 Ba-Ghana, 'Stop This Bad Fish Racket'.
73 They met under the banner of the Ghana National Co-operative Fishing and Marketing.

74 PRAAD-Sekondi WRG8/1/267, 30 April 1963, Central and Western Branches of the Ghana National Co-operative Fishing and Marketing to the Nkrumah, N. A. Welbeck, Ayeh-Kumi, Nana Kobina Nketsia, Minister of Finance (F. K. D. Goka), general secretary of the Ghana Agriculture Co-Operatives (Martin Appiah-Danquah), and to all members of parliament, all district members, all paramount chiefs and all other important government figures.

75 See Nana Osei-Opare, '"If You Trouble A Hungry Snake, You Will Force It to Bite You": Rethinking Postcolonial Archival Pessimism, Worker Discontent, and Petition Writing in Ghana, 1957–66', *Journal of African History* 62, no. 1 (2021): 59–78.

76 PRAAD-Sekondi WRG8/1/267, 30 April 1963, Central and Western Branches of the Ghana National Co-operative Fishing and Marketing to the Nkrumah, N. A. Welbeck, Ayeh-Kumi, Nana Kobina Nketsia, Minister of Finance (F. K. D. Goka), general secretary of the Ghana Agriculture Co-Operatives (Martin Appiah-Danquah), and to all members of parliament, all district members, all paramount chiefs and all other important government figures.

77 Denis W. Aheto, Noble K. Asare, Belinda Quaynor, Emmanuel Y. Tenkorang, Cephas Asare, and Isaac Okyere, 'Profitability of Small-Scale Fisheries in Elmina, Ghana', *Sustainability* 4, no. 11 (2012): 2785–2794, 2786.

78 PRAAD-Sekondi WRG8/1/267, 1 May 1963, J. E. Morrison to J. K. Mensah.

79 I discuss this further in my forthcoming book, *Socialist Decolony*.

80 'The Fish Racket', *Evening News*, 21 October 1963, 1.

81 'Fishing Industry', *The Ashanti Pioneer*, 9 July 1962.

82 PRAAD-Sekondi WRG8/1/267, 21 June 1963, regional secretary to D. K.Mensah.

83 PRAAD-Sekondi WRG8/1/267, 11 July 1963, J. B. Morrison to all the district commissioners.

84 'Crew of Wrecked Trawler Are Safe', *The Ashanti Pioneer*, 10 July 1962, 1.

85 PRAAD-Sekondi WRG8/1/267, 17 August 1963, J. B. Morrison to all the district commissioners.

86 PRAAD-Sekondi WRG8/1/267, 5 August 1963, J. B. Morrison to all the district commissioners; PRAAD-Sekondi WRG8/1/267, 17 August 1963, J. B. Morrison to all the district commissioners.

87 PRAAD-Sekondi WRG8/1/267, 6 August 1964, Fisheries office (Western Region) to the secretary of the regional commissioner.

88 PRAAD-Sekondi WRG8/1/267, 5 August 1963, J. B. Morrison to all the district commissioners.

89 'Faulty Construction Caused Sinking of Vessel', *Daily Graphic*, 3 February 1965, 1.

90 PRAAD-Accra ADM5/3/214, 'Interim Report: Instrument of Appointment/ Commission of Enquiry (State Fishing Corporation) Instrument, 1967'.

91 DO221/19, 12 February 1964, W. N. Wenban-Smith to J. E. Chadwick.

92 'Corp Makes Big Profit'.

93 Ba-Ghana, 'Stop This Bad Fish Racket'.

94 PRAAD-Accra ADM5/3/214, 'Interim Report', 71, 72.

95 Ibid., 17.

96 'The Fish Racket'.

97 PRAD-Cape Coast RG3/5/1067, 20 December 1957, J. Atopie Christian, 'Proposals for the Establishment of Large Scale Fishing, Fish Processing, and Food Manufacture'.

98 See PRAAD-Accra ADM5/3/214, 'Interim Report', 4.

99 Stanford University, Hoover Archive, (Hoover): Donald S. Rothchild Papers, Box 144, 'Table XXV: Total Marine Fish Production 1961–1964'.

12

Indians as experts on democracy and development: South-South cooperation in the Nehru years

Taylor C. Sherman

The history of development has expanded in highly productive ways in the past three decades. Development and modernization are no longer regarded as exclusively tools of the American Cold War agenda, nor are they any longer understood as a matter of top-down imposition of ideas from the West upon the colonized or recently decolonized world.[1] Indeed, it is widely accepted that colonized countries moulded ideas about development as they interacted with people, ideas and programmes, and that the decolonizing world influenced the shape and direction of international institutions as these were being developed in the aftermath of the Second World War.[2] And yet, the locus of initiative is usually assumed to lie with Europeans and North Americans: Asians and Africans responded and shaped, but they are rarely regarded as the experts themselves. More recently, historians have begun to trace the connections across Asia and Africa between the 1930s and 1970s.[3] While Northern citizens are often part of these networks, the focus has shifted to the creativity, ingenuity and energy of leaders and citizens of the decolonizing world. In addition to the focus on large diplomatic events such as the Bandung Conference,[4] scholars have drawn our attention to regular international conferences,[5] and they have highlighted the importance of non-official actors, including non-communist socialists,[6] women,[7] literary figures[8] and artists[9] in building Afro-Asian solidarity on a broader basis. And yet, there has been very little work that traces how these exchanges influenced thinking on development and modernization.[10] This paper brings these two fields together, and in so doing contributes to historiography on the international dimensions of Indian developmentalism, on the role of UNESCO in international development and on radio broadcasting as post-colonial pedagogy.

Histories of India under its first prime minister, Jawaharlal Nehru (1947–64), have long been attentive to the international networks of experts and ideas that have shaped the country's development strategies.[11] While earlier works argued that Indian development was a foreign imposition, more recent scholarship has emphasized the ways in which Indians took in ideas from theorists and experts from the global north, but with the express understanding that those theories would have to be modified to suit Indian conditions.[12] Historiography on Ghana has moved in a similar direction.[13] New scholarship on both countries now argues that socialism was given a local meaning and was not merely imported straight from the books of Karl Marx to the fields and factories of India and Ghana.[14] In turn, the assumption that both countries pursued exclusively high-modernist, state-led projects such as building steel mills and mammoth hydro-electric dams, has been replaced by the acknowledgement that both also encouraged low-modernist, self-help centred developmentalism.[15]

However, the existing historiography has almost completely missed the fact that independent India regarded itself as an important site for the production of expert knowledge about development that could be exported to the wider developing world. Indeed, Indian policymakers understood themselves to be partaking in experiments designed to identify new universal principles of modernization and development. The country hosted innumerable international conferences, usually under the aegis of the United Nations (UN), with the express aim of spreading ideas devised in India to the decolonizing world. And it sent out Indian experts across Asia and Africa to disseminate the insights garnered from the Indian experience to other parts of the world.

In most cases, India disseminated its expertise through the UN and its agencies. In the past two decades it has become clear that the UN cannot be conceived as a set of institutions bearing the imprint of western universalism, but rather as the site of 'competing universalisms'.[16] Indeed, India, it has been demonstrated, was key to shaping everything from the missions to the everyday conduct of the UN and its various agencies.[17] Yet, India's role in shaping UNESCO has not been explored. And while historians have critically examined UNESCO's ambition to build a common sense of humanity after the horrors of the Second World War, this article takes a different approach.[18] It argues that one of the key roles UNESCO played was as a hub-and-spoke international organization. Ideas developed not entirely in isolation, but largely in one country, could be *universalized* and exported to other countries through UNESCO. Part of this process of universalization was centring the principle that every new tool of development must be adapted to local circumstances. This research explores one example of this, a UNESCO-funded programme to use radio programming to further rural development.

Existing historiography on state-produced Indian radio and film in this period tends to regard these productions as essentially top-down pedagogic exercises, deployed to inculcate proper norms of civic behaviour. The prevailing argument is that producers had a 'high-brow', and condescending attitude towards audiences, who, in turn, found official productions 'boring'.[19] While not denying the essentially didactic character of media productions, the example of farm radio forums suggests that pockets of dialogue could open up between listeners and producers which in turn impacted the larger radio landscape. Indeed, this research demonstrates the multiple possibilities of and the changing nature of state didacticism. Pedagogy was evolving rapidly in the decades after the Second World War, and this is reflected in the increasingly dialogic character of the farm radio forums.

Developing expertise

Indian freedom had been achieved in 1947 after a decades-long campaign which had centred on the fact that the British had drained the wealth of the country and left it impoverished and underdeveloped.[20] At independence, therefore, the primary imperative of the leaders of the new country was to reverse this legacy. Although scholars had for decades assumed that during this period India focused on heavy industrialization,[21] in recent years it has become apparent that they were equally focused on rural development.[22] Indeed, after the catastrophe of the Bengal Famine, which, in 1943 had seen around three million people perish of starvation, one of the central priorities of the Government of India and of state governments was to avoid another famine by growing more food.[23] At the same time, they pursued plans to develop Indian industry, by founding new state-run enterprises as well as by garnering the support of private industrialists and encouraging them to make themselves 'part of the plan'.[24]

Although India aimed at economic independence, which it defined as economic self-sufficiency, this did not mean that Indian leaders pursued this aim in isolation from the rest of the world. Indeed, international experts were a prominent feature of Indian development thinking. American engineers and town planners, who had gained experience in the final years of the British Raj, were invited to return or carry on their work after independence.[25] At the same time, India reached out to specialists in other parts of the world. By the middle of the 1950s, there was regular traffic in international experts, attending conferences and advising on everything from individual buildings to the nation-wide five-year plans.[26] Meanwhile, Indian delegations travelled the world to study programmes developed elsewhere and explore their applicability to conditions back home.[27] And civil servants and specialists from African countries toured India to do the same.[28]

So far as governments in India had a shared approach to foreign expertise, they agreed on the necessity for the experts to adapt to India. Let us take one of the most prominent examples of foreign expertise: the construction of Chandigarh as the new capital of the divided province of Punjab, under the direction of the Swiss Architect, Charles-Édouard Jeanneret, known as Le Corbusier. When the foreign expert arrived for his first meeting with India's Planning Commission in April 1952, he was told at the top of the meeting that, while they were keen to get whatever assistance they could from outside, solutions to the country's problems would 'have to be evolved in India'. The discussion continued in a similar mode, with members of the Planning Commission telling Le Corbusier that high-rise buildings, which the Swiss was famous for designing, were 'not suitable for Indian conditions'. Le Corbusier responded by commending the views of P. N. Thapar, Director of Public Works and Head of the Chandigarh Capital Project, who had told him when they had first met, 'I do not want any foreigner – except what is absolutely essential and [that] too for as little time as possible'. Far from being a tabula rasa upon which Le Corbusier could construct his utopian city,[29] it was agreed that Chandigarh would be a site for 'research' and a training ground for Indian architects.[30]

A similar pattern emerges when one examines many of the development projects initiated in the 1940s and 1950s. The word that appeared most frequently as Indian leaders described these initiatives was 'experiment'. India's new leaders regarded their country as a laboratory for the evolution of new ideas about development and modernization. They were determined to use all the tools of mid-century social science in the process. Indian governments conducted large and complex surveys, and developed statistical methods to do so, producing post-colonial knowledge about the young country.[31] They undertook pilot projects, which were then evaluated with the aim of learning from them before rolling out a scheme across a wider area. International organizations and foreign charitable foundations were often key in the early stages of a new experiment, funding small-scale projects on everything from refugee rehabilitation in Uttar Pradesh to the mechanization of fishing in what would become Tamil Nadu.[32] The Planning Commission, and in particular its Programme Evaluation Organisation, was central to the evaluation and evolution of these experiments.[33]

This laboratory for the evolution of new ideas and practices of development was not meant for the exclusive use of India. Indeed, it was widely believed that India's experience would be useful for other countries in Asia and Africa. However, this export process was nuanced, often carried out with multiple partners, especially the UN, and modelled on India's own ideals, which stressed, above all, the importance of adaptation to local conditions.

An early and prominent example of Indian experience being exported was in the area of democratic elections, where India saw itself as a world leader. Its first general elections were a mammoth task, which saw the participation of hundreds of millions of illiterate voters in one of the world's most complex democratic processes. Prepared virtually since independence, and conducted between 1951 and 1952, the elections were overseen by Sukumar Sen, India's first Chief Election Commissioner.[34] In 1953, Sen was appointed to oversee elections in the Sudan, then still governed by the British. Upon arrival in the country, Sen found that the entire machinery for the election had to be devised 'from scratch'. He oversaw the revision of laws and the drafting of rules based on India's experience.[35] Sen insisted upon the 'Sudanification' of the administrative structures, 'partly to educate the nationals in managing this important public affair' but also to keep the British out of it.[36] This pedagogical function was a central theme in many projects of the age: they were designed to teach politicians, administrators and the people of decolonizing countries the skills necessary to then carry on themselves.

Back at home, after India had completed its second general election, New Delhi hosted the Commonwealth Parliamentary Association Conference in December 1957. Inaugurating the conference and speaking to the cheers of the attendees from forty-nine delegations, President Rajendra Prasad noted that India did not need to boast about its democratic achievements, for 'encomiums have been showered us'. He ventured that, while the 'younger parliaments' could hope to learn from the conference, 'I am also vain enough to think that perhaps even the older parliaments may derive some benefit by studying the work done in the younger parliaments'.[37]

Indians were also keen to share their experience and expertise in one of the most prominent areas of development, the construction of large dams. International experts came to the subcontinent to assist in the design and construction of large and complex hydro-electric facilities. At independence India had 118 dams of all heights, but during the first and second plans more than 500 river valley schemes of all kinds, including 74 dams of over one-hundred feet in height were introduced.[38] One of the earliest and most complex of these schemes was the Damodar Valley Corporation (DVC), which had its origins in the aftermath of the Bengal famine, and was modelled on the Tennessee Valley Authority.[39]

Through these projects Indian engineers and administrators evolved their own distinct approaches to modernization projects. Focusing on two individuals helps bring this point into relief. One comes from the development economist and DVC Secretary, Sudhir Sen, and the other from Kanwair Sain, an engineer, and later the Chairman of India's Central Water and Power Commission, who also worked on the Damodar projects. The biographies of the two men were strikingly similar: both came of age during the national movement, but neither was a blind follower of Gandhi, Nehru or the Congress.[40] Both men had had contact with experts in Europe and the United States, but neither was captive to rigid theories.[41] For example, Sudhir Sen, writing much later about his experience in the USSR, recorded the way he was impressed when Soviet experts recognized that Marx's theories would not work in India. Sen derided those who blindly followed Marxist dogma, as 'non-scientists and non-experts, which is all the more reason not to surrender reason to them'.[42]

For all the similarities, the two men's approaches to dam-building could not have been more different. Sen may have believed that some principles were valid in every context, but, he argued, the models and the technology developed must be 'largely tailored to suit specific situations and frequently adjusted to changing conditions'.[43] Kanwar Sain, by contrast, comes closer to a purely technocratic approach to dam building. In an article published in 1955 on the Social Repercussions of Hydraulic Projects in his country, Sain discussed how to measure precipitation, evaporation and assess the geology of the region. But he made no mention of enquiring into working methods, land tenures or the habits of the local population. His assumption, in essence, was that as one built dams to control flooding, the people would inexorably be transformed. Describing the results of one project he declared, peasants 'who accepted the vagaries of nature, both in case of floods or drought, as their inescapable fate (kismet ka kasoor) now feel more confident of human ability to mitigate natural calamities like droughts and floods'.[44]

The Secretary and the Engineer each took their own lessons from their experience in India and brought them to other countries, often through the agencies of the UN. Sen became the UN resident advisor to the Volta River Project in Ghana in the early 1960s.[45] Sain became what he described as a 'technical ambassador' overseeing UN work on the Mekong River Basin Development in Laos, Thailand, Cambodia and Vietnam in the same period.[46]

Indeed, the UN was central to the dissemination of Indian expertise, and Indians seemed to seek roles on as many UN bodies as possible. Hansa Mehta helped draft the Universal Declaration on Human Rights, and when she departed Kamaladevi Chattopadhyay took her place. Ramaswami Mudaliar and Palamadai S Lokanathan were respectively the first President of the Economic and Social Council (ECOSOC) and the first Executive Secretary of the Economic and Social Commission for Asia and the Far East. Rajkumari Amrit Kaur represented India as a founding member of the World Health Organisation, and the physicist Homi J. Bhabha, presided over the first UN Conference on Peaceful Uses of Atomic Energy. Indians also populated the rank and file of the UN's operations: Indian experts occupied 84 out of 136 places in the UN Technical Administration by 1952. These men and women advised governments from Lebanon to the Philippines on everything from co-operatives and malaria control to training civil servants and radio operators.[47]

Indian cities also played host to innumerable UN symposiums and conferences. These covered an enormous range of topics, from community development and low-cost housing to statistics, state-run industries, the petroleum industry and the problems of rapid urbanization, to give just a few examples. These large gatherings tended to pull together experts from all over the world, but with a particular strength in amassing people from Asia, Europe and North America. They often included practical elements, such as tours to relevant Indian sites, or examples of locally engineered prototypes. A common aim of these conferences was not to develop universal blueprints that could be exported across the decolonizing world, but to articulate universal principles from which local solutions could be devised.

One result of all of these exchanges is that at least some international experts began to re-think their own practice after their experience in India. If we circle back to Chandigarh, Jane Drew, half of a husband-and-wife team who had been brought in to advise on architecture for housing, shops and quotidian public buildings, found her own ideas about her profession altered by her work in India. Reflecting on her experience with the construction of low-cost housing in Chandigarh, Drew remarked, 'I have had to conclude that the time is past when the Architect believed he had to consecrate his talents only to houses for the rich or to public and commercial buildings'. She sought to derive principles upon which such low-cost houses ought to be designed and constructed elsewhere. She argued, for example, that these one and two-room dwellings ought to be built of 'materials common to or similar to those of the houses of the rich', so as to avoid breaking up the visual harmony of a block 'in a brutal way'. She, like the Indian architects that she had worked with in the city, made the case that, aesthetically, 'the houses of the poor are as important in a city as the houses of the rich'.[48] Another result was that Indian experiences in the fields of democracy and development were regarded as useful starting points for the development of similar projects in Africa and Asia. To understand how these exchanges evolved, the next section focuses on the use of radio programming to improve agricultural production and agrarian life.

Radio broadcasting for rural development in India

Public radio broadcasting took off in the 1920s and quickly made its way round the world, including to India. By the 1930s, provincial governments in South Asia had designed some programming for rural areas, primarily in the form of digests of informative pamphlets. Seizing upon the importance of radio, after independence, All

India Radio (AIR) expanded, with new stations in regional towns and new transmitters around the country. By the end of the 1950s, AIR was broadcasting from twenty-eight stations in forty-eight dialects.[49] Governments in India had also begun to subsidize the purchase of community radio sets for use in villages. With the promise of 50 per cent funding from the Government of India, the number of new community radio sets expanded from 1,330 in 1954–5 to 13,542 in 1956–7.[50]

Radio farm forums, therefore, did not introduce Indian villagers to radio. Rather, they took a different approach to programming and listening. Like so many government initiatives in the 1940s and 1950s, radio farm forums were intended to spur villagers to improve their own village life.[51] The idea behind these forums was to develop programming in a different way to this end, because 'To broadcast programmes is one thing, to make sure that they are assimilated by the audience and acted upon is quite another'.[52] To achieve this aim, the programming developed with UNESCO was entertainment-led, and the broadcast was followed by a discussion in the local village forum. This approach had first been tried in Canada, in the aftermath of the Great Depression. When these proved highly successful, the Canadian experience was the basis upon which farm radio forums were established in France, Italy and Japan.[53] The use of radio in this way in the decolonizing world, however, was deemed to require a 'parallel' approach, which is where the Indian experiment, conducted with the help of UNESCO, comes in. Indeed, India was already experimenting to this end before the UNESCO-funded programme was launched: Radio farm forums were tried in Bombay state, in Kannada, Marathi and Gujarati, as part of the Grow More Food Programme, launched in September 1949.[54] Initially, it seems, these programmes included the discussion element, but did not focus on entertainment.[55]

As with many of the other UN Agencies, Indian ideas and initiatives had shaped UNESCO from the outset, with people and ideas flowing back and forth between India and UNESCO. Led in part by Khushwant Singh, who would later become famous for his novel about partition, *Train to Pakistan*, and other literary works, India's delegation to UNESCO pushed for UNESCO's remit regarding the spread of culture across the world to shift focus away from imperial cultures. In 1954, India's delegation argued that European and American culture 'is already known throughout the world', while the cultural productions of Asia and Africa remain 'largely unknown and frequently misunderstood'. It was, India argued, UNESCO's responsibility to 'put the balance right' and focus on popularizing literature, painting and music from Asia and Africa throughout the world.[56] India had already secured a UNESCO pledge to arrange for the exchange of feature programmes between member states,[57] and this would increase the momentum behind this push. When the Government of India struck a deal with UNESCO to experiment with radio farm forums, Khushwant Singh, by that time employed at the UNESCO secretariat, was then delegated back to India to oversee the project. This meant circumventing, at least partially, the staid leadership of B. V. Keskar, the Union Minister for Information and Broadcasting, who is said to have taken an austere, high-brow approach to programming.[58]

The UNESCO-AIR Farm Forum Project took place in 150 villages around Pune in what was then Bombay State in 1956. With a grant of $19,000, a small number of radios were provided for villages that did not yet have a community radio set, and programming was developed. The project generated twenty programmes, each of thirty minutes. A committee of ten people, including educationalists, and experts in agriculture and public health devised a list of topics for the programmes. Development and production was entrusted to a small AIR team from the region, P. L. Deshpande from Bombay and V. D. Madgulkar of Pune.

The half-hour broadcast included light music, *bhajans* (devotional songs) and folk songs as well as the featured entertainment-cum-education programming. This was then followed by Listeners' Corner, in which 'suggestions, criticisms and comments from the members of the farm forums were broadcast and discussed and questions answered'. Many segments were recorded in villages, for, 'to invite the villagers to the studios made them self-conscious and took away the genuineness of the atmosphere'.[59]

The topics covered a large span of rural life. The first programme included a dialogue on fatalism and a subsequent dialogue which was designed to impress 'the idea of "do it yourself" on the minds of listeners'.[60] This was a central message of Indian socialism of the time, which emphasized the importance of collective self-help in the face of large social and economic problems and small government budgets.[61] The second feature was a play by V. D. Madgulkar, called 'The Engagement which was Broken and Mended', in which negotiations about arranging a marriage hinged on village self-help. The main character, Patil, resident of a model village, refuses to arrange the marriage of his daughter because the groom's family, though wealthy themselves, hale from a village that is 'underdeveloped'.[62] Linking the prestige of well-off families to the productivity and sanitation of the larger village implied that it was the duty of the higher castes to guide their village towards improvements. Deploying existing hierarchies for new developmentalist ends was another central feature of Indian socialism.[63]

The remaining programmes are a run through of the issues facing rural India and official approaches to them. The third instalment was a feature on democracy called 'We are the Rulers'. A central theme of several programmes was the importance of education at all levels: broadcasts included a play on adult education, a discussion on village *balwadis* (preschools) and a dialogue between a farmer and a teacher in which the latter tried to convince the farmer that his children could receive an education that was relevant to agricultural life. Numerous programmes addressed rural production, not just food grains, but fruit, poultry, cattle, water conservation and pest eradication.

On the latter topic, Madhukar Kulkarni wrote a play in Marathi called Uncle Rat, which was written as a folk-drama. Uncle Rat opens with the different products of a village, from crops to clothes, being consumed by a plague of rats. Because the god Ganesha, or Ganpati as he is called in Marathi, has a rat as a companion, the main character, Dhondi, appeals to Ganpati, who holds a public hearing of his grievances. The rat rebuts the villager's accusations with a counter-claim, telling the deity: 'It was he who did not take proper care of his crop. The science of agriculture has made great advances. But do these people try to learn the new methods? No. They even refuse to meet the experts who are sent to teach them. People who are so careless and indifferent about their fields deserve to be ruined'.[64] Dhondi, then replies 'The rat has indeed opened our ears! It looks as if it's all our fault'. Ganpati, in turn, confesses that he sent the rats to the village 'to open the eyes of the ignorant'.[65] Dhondi returns to earth and fetches the Pest Officer, who then gives him a lecture on using poison to kill the rats, and then burying or burning their remains. Reading the script, one instantly notes the presumed necessity of enlightenment issuing from the gods, and also the tendency to frame all of rural society in terms most legible to Hindus of the dominant castes.

Radio farm forums were not just about broadcasting new programmes, but they were also specifically designed to 'stimulate lively discussion among the listeners without raising controversial political issues'.[66] Each forum had twenty to twenty-five people, who discussed the topic immediately after the broadcast. These assemblies did tend to reflect the hierarchies of village life. As the organizers reported, it had not been possible to include many women, and, though they had tried to include villagers from different castes, 'this was not always possible'. The hierarchies of village life emerged in other ways too, for in the conversations, 'village school masters tended to be the most vocal and the other village functionaries were able to dominate as a result of their authority'. Elder members of the forum had to be coached to allow younger members to express their opinions freely, and it took two or three meetings before new conventions could be established on this front.[67] Indeed, one of the primary outcomes of touted by the leaders of the project was that villagers learned to discuss their common issues together.

As was standard for any of India's mid-century 'experiments', the UNESCO project was evaluated using the latest tools of social science. A team from the Tata Institute for Social Sciences in Bombay, led Dr A. M. Lorenzo, Head of the Department of Social Research, with a visiting Fulbright Professor of Social Research, Paul Neurath, surveyed villagers and wrote a report. The survey focused on a sample of villages – just 20 out of 150 that participated – as was in line with India's development of sampling methods more broadly.[68] Not only were villages with radio farm forums subjected to surveys, but the evaluation also surveyed control villages, which did not participate in the forums, in order to 'estimate how much of the newly won knowledge could reasonably be attributed to radio farm forum and how much of it should be considered as the result of other factors'.[69] Equally, the villages were divided into those that already had access to a radio and had been part of community development projects, and those for whom these elements were new to village life. Many of those chosen to take part in the experiment were already prosperous villages, while those that ended up in the control group were 'some of the really poor villages in the district'.[70] This is typical of development programmes of the time, which tended to channel resources to areas deemed 'responsive' to the changes, which were invariably more developed already.[71]

The staff of the evaluation team comprised ten interviewers, a field supervisor, a research assistant and a typist. These interviewers included five men and five women.[72] Women were a growing part of the workforce in the 1950s, particularly in areas concerned with social welfare.[73] The data they gathered was tabulated by a chief tabulator, five further tabulators (many of whom had also been interviewers), two research assistants and a typist. Their raw material included 1600 pre- and post-broadcast questionnaires, 1600 observation questionnaires, all coordinated by Mr D. D. Jadhav, the chief organizer. While interviewers recorded their 'personal impressions' in diaries, these questionnaires aimed at 'more objective judgement' through quantifying the participation with rating numerical scales. Thus, participants were evaluated on a five-point scale, given one point for 'complete lack of participation' and five points for 'excellent participation'.[74] As was common, the defects of the rating system were also noted in the report.

At the outset, the evaluation team sought to understand whether radio farm forums and the discussion groups could be used to transmit 'new knowledge'. As the experiment proceeded, the evaluators decided on a third objective, to understand 'the role of radio farm forums as a new institution in village life and as an instrument in general village uplift'. The evaluators' report details which programmes elicited more participation, and which less; which inspired people to act, and which did not. A recurring theme of the report was the wide variation in participation between broadcasts on different topics, and between the different villages. Programmes relating to specific improvements in daily lives of farmers seemed to elicit the desired response, while those pertaining to topics outside of the purview of farmers' experience, such as an explanation of the community development programme, were generally not as well-received.

Since the objective was to understand whether new knowledge had been gained, the researchers also devised a quantitative approach to this question. The interviewers rated each person's level of knowledge before and after a broadcast on a numerical scale, combining them to create a composite score defining the 'average level of knowledge' before and after the experiment, and dividing these into groups such as agriculturalists and non-agriculturalists, men and women, literate and non-literate villagers, etc. To be fair to the evaluators, they acknowledged the somewhat arbitrary nature of their evaluation system, asking rhetorically, 'This is the way every society raises its level of knowledge; some learn the new with understanding, some heart it and can repeat it without understanding and some don't react at all. Why then devise complicated measuring devices to establish that this process had taken place once more in the forums?' They concluded that all they really needed to determine was 'whether the total level of knowledge … had been raised sufficiently to warrant the conclusion that the ordinary learning process had been set in motion' without specifying how deeply or how widely the new knowledge had been absorbed.[75]

Knowledge gained on specific issues was also calculated. Thus, it was reported that familiarity with the use of rat poison increased from 132 people to 236 people out of 254 surveyed, while the number of people who burned rat carcasses increased from 77 to 146 where there were radio farm forums.[76] In the villages without radio farm forums, sometimes villagers learned about these issues by virtue of being in the control group: the interviewers had to explain issues to them in order to make sense of the questions, and in so doing conveyed enough information for villagers to gain knowledge. The evaluators reported, 'What a balwadi (kindergarten) is, was learned by 175 people in the forums, by only 36 in the non-forums, and a good number of the latter learned it from the interviewers who had to explain the world to them'.[77]

In addition to the quantitative evaluation, the observers noted anecdotally several changes made in the aftermath of the broadcasts. The evaluators recorded that many villages decided to take action along the lines suggested in the programming. It was noted that villages often took decisions almost immediately after a broadcast, and that they were nearly identical:

> [T]o keep the village clean; to plant papaya trees … to eat more fruit; to buy rat poison and to bury or burn dead rats; to start a co-operative society; buy books for neo-literates; start compost pits; go to the doctor when ill; use cowdung [*sic*] for manure; start a *balwadi*; get good poultry; have cattle vaccinated; buy a pure-bred bull; start literacy classes.[78]

And yet, there were other villages who 'set off on new lines of thought' during the period of the experiment. In Kandhapuri, it was decided that 'the person who cuts down a tree should plant five trees', even though this had not been suggested in a broadcast. In Niwana, the village decided to 'introduce prizes in school' to encourage students to 'take more interest in studies'. In Khanapur, it was decided to read the newspaper aloud in the village 'in order to increase the knowledge of the people'. One village decided to repair a well and allow Dalits to use it, while others chose to capture monkeys (a village pest) through collective effort, experiment with dry farming or build a playground for the school.[79]

Indeed, the surprising – to the social scientists – ability of villagers to take independent initiative segues into one of the things that amazed the social scientists the most. Before the experiment it had been widely assumed that those relatively isolated in villages would have roughly the same level of knowledge. After all, 'they grow the same fruit, sow the same grains, breed the same cattle, raise the same chickens, have little opportunity to get out of their villages, and have done all of this together for generations'. However, this was, Neurath declared, 'a rather serious fallacy'. In every forum there were people who 'made contributions of concrete information, often with rather complicated details, which their neighbours did not know or suspect that the speaker knew'. He recounted the experience of a discussion on fruit gardening in which 'an old man, well above 70' spoke up. Initially, everyone laughed at him speaking, and 'he himself was amused by it'. But he spoke for twenty minutes, 'lecturing' his fellow villagers on the topic, telling them things he had known that had only come to their attention over the day's radio broadcast.[80]

The evaluation determined that the radio farm forum, far from simply transmitting knowledge to the ignorant, 'brings out a good deal of information that is latent in the villages and makes it part and parcel of general village knowledge'.[81] One member of the press who visited Nabovani Shetkari Mandal at Hivare recorded the same thing in less diplomatic language. The reporter was frankly surprised at the quality of the conversation witnessed: 'Their discussion has given us a shock as to our ideas regarding their knowledge and experience. We city people must now give up the idea that the farmers are ignorant'.[82]

The experiment in radio farm forums, it was concluded, had proven to be a 'success beyond expectation'. The increase in knowledge in the villages had been 'spectacular'. The use of discussions was judged to be a success by the evaluators, who relied on the villagers' reports that they found these conversations to be 'excellent' or at least 'good'. Indeed, the experiment revealed that the radio farm forum could be a new institution in village life. The forums functioned as a middle ground between a gram sabha (village assembly) and an elected gram panchayat (village council) – being more flexible than a meeting and less binding than the council's decisions. Thus, the forums 'became an important instrument in village democracy', enabling more people to take part in decision-making in the village. They were able to initiate voluntary action better than a formally elected panchayat could. The villagers themselves petitioned to have the forums continued (or to introduce them where they did not yet exist), and made suggestions for improvements in programming, such as including *bhajans* (devotional songs), folk music and folklore.[83]

After the experiment was concluded, farm radio forums continued in the existing areas, and also expanded. But they did not go unchanged. While women participated in the original experiment in very small numbers, groups of women in villages took the initiative to set up separate farm forums for themselves, particularly in Madras and Andhra. When asked why they established their own forums, the women explained, 'You talk about seeds and agriculture … in villages women are also dealing with seeds and agriculture. They also go to the fields during harvest. Why should they not listen and discuss? … Once we have organized the forum and got together the village-level worker pays greater attention to us'. In some places, the men and women listened together, but then separated into single-gender groups for the discussion. By 1965, there were more than 3,000 women's listening clubs, mostly in the South and East of the country, with more than one-third of those in Andhra alone. All India Radio did have rural programming for rural women, but these women established forums to listen to the radio farm forum broadcasts.[84]

A second innovation worth mentioning was in the field of programming. Producers from AIR worked to make the programmes 'attractive and effective', which, they discovered, meant involving village folk directly. It was reported: 'Villagers like to listen to their own kith and kin, they have more faith in the broadcast when they hear one of their own people talk about his experience'. Indeed, local AIR stations had begun to send teams to the forums to record sessions, and also to 'scout for talent, for prospective farmer-broadcasters among members'.[85]

Transmitting the Indian experience to Ghana

Even as the programme was being adjusted as it rolled out across India, the country's representatives at UNESCO also worked to help spread the Indian experience to other parts of the world. At a UNESCO meeting on Information Media in Asia in Bangkok in 1960, a resolution was passed that urged governments to 'encourage setting up of farm forums like those successfully carried out in India with UNESCO's cooperation'. Similar resolutions were passed at the Asian Broadcasters Conferences in Malaya and South Korea.[86] UNESCO undertook to provide technical training in the use of farm radio forums.[87]

Within a few years, another experiment was underway in West Africa. Public radio had taken off with great popularity in Ghana from 1956, when Ghanaians began to take control of broadcasting. Ghana had introduced more popular programming more quickly than India, with broadcasts covering traditional festivals and celebrations, and local music. Agricultural programming, however, still tended to be rather staid, and moreover, delivered in English by University Lecturers, and so missed their audience. With aid from Australia, the Colombo Plan and the UN, radio broadcasting expanded in the years after independence. By the first part of the 1960s, the success of farm radio forums in Canada and India had been noted, and UNESCO declared, 'We had no doubt that it would work in Ghana and elsewhere in Africa too'.[88]

The Ghanaian experiment was conducted between 1964 and 1965 and overseen by Andrew A. Opoku, who left Ghana to spend a year in Canada, studying radio farm forums, and then recruited two technical experts before the project began. Village organizers were provided with 'a slightly revised version of the All-India Radio Guide for field organization of farm forums'. As in India, twenty special broadcasts were prepared, along with materials to aid discussions of the issues. While it borrowed specific aspects of the experiment from India, the Ghana experiment also adhered to the idea, familiar in both Indian and Ghanaian thinking about development aid, that nothing should be adopted without adjusting it to local circumstances. It was stressed that 'each country needs to make adaptations consistent with its own pattern of land settlement and rural social organization'.[89]

As in India, Ghana had already organized some forum-style programming in agricultural communities before the project began. The UNESCO-funded project, like the Indian one, involved the creation of twenty special broadcasts. A subjects committee met to determine which topics the special programmes ought to cover. Participating ministries included Education, Agriculture, Social Welfare, National Council for Ghana Women, the Nutrition Board and the Institute of Ideological Studies. Sixty forums were established in forty villages in eastern Ghana, with another twenty villages acting as a control group.

Whereas in India women were either excluded altogether from the forums or had to establish their own, they seem to have been integrated more easily in Ghana. Special programming was organized for them from the start. It is implied in the UNESCO report that this was down to their social status in Ghana: 'Long before Mrs Pankhurst and her suffragettes fought and won the franchise for the Englishwoman, Ghanaian women were working and making their own way'. Referring in all likelihood to the famous anti-colonial fighter Yaa Asantewaa, the publication reminded readers that Ghanain women had long played 'leading roles as chieftains and war captains'.[90] Today, the report continued, women 'control the pulse of consumer trade' and in rural areas, 'A diligent woman has her own share of the fruits of her toil'. While amongst the Akan of Ghana, where there was a matriarchal system, 'the wife's resources return to her own family's pool, to which her offspring are heirs'.[91]

When it came to subject-matter, the Ghanaian broadcasts were quite different from those developed for India. There was, for example, more emphasis on trading agricultural produce. There were broadcasts on the Seven Year Plan and on government loans and subsidies, on education, family budgets and even the development of the nuclear family in Ghana, on employment in rural areas, as well as on marketing foodstuffs and storing perishable crops.

One broadcast took the form of a radio play, written by Ofori Debra, encouraging young people to remain in rural areas and work in agriculture. The play began with a discussion between two mothers, Peasemaka and Pe Biribi Di, with the former worried because her eleven children had all been to school, but 'They are roaming about aimlessly'. The two then exchange stories of children who run up debts, roam from city to city, are unable to make ends meet and so remain reliant upon their elders. The two are joined by a third woman, Seewaa, who has come from the fields, where crops are rotting, unharvested.

A young man, Badu, who has returned from the city, then joins the conversation, telling the women how he sleeps in petrol stations at night, and goes without food if the restaurant he is cleaning dishes in is closed. He tells them, 'Hunger is an ever-present companion', and that the young women in the cities searching for work are 'more to be pitied'. When the elder women suggest to Badu that he could stay in the village and work, he scoffs, 'But there is no amusement here, where is the cinema? You have no electricity. No pipe-borne water supply. Where can one attend a ballroom dance in this place?' Peasemaka counsels the other elders that they must take Badu's statement seriously, telling them, 'if we wish our young people to remain in the villages and work there, we have to bring some of the amenities of the city here too'. Seewaa then suggests advertising the troubles of those who migrate to cities, to reduce the drift to the cities.

The conversation then turns to what the government and the villagers can each do about this 'social evil'. One person suggests adopting 'modern methods of farming' in order to spark the interests of young people. Seewaa notes that some educated youth can work as clerks and managers on cooperative farms. Peasemaka argues that local councils should start enterprises such as poultry farming, animal husbandry and crafts, to employ the youngsters. She notes that the government is trying to stop people moving to cities, but 'we shouldn't forget that when a single tree is exposed to the wind it breaks under the strain. We have to assist the government to assist us'. Pe Biribi De then adds that some youth may go to the cities, but parents should ensure they do so only if they have secured a job in advance. Badu, the young man recently returned from the city, has the last word, saying, 'I have slaved for mere strangers. I have been pushed from pillar to post, exploited and flattened out by cruel taskmasters'. He tells the group that 'even the slightest improvement' in the village will bring all the young people 'rushing back home'.[92] The play, while directly addressing the issue of urban migration, is also a model of using community discussion to solve a shared problem. It models the ideal citizen, who does not just complain and demand government action, but finds solutions to her own problems. This reflects the self-help model of development promoted by governments in both India and Ghana at the time.

By this time, the farm radio forum was also being imagined less as a top-down enterprise and more as a chance to collaborate with the rural population in Ghana. These innovations seem to reflect at least some of the insights garnered from the Indian experience after the initial UNESCO experiment, for it was noted how responsive listeners were to the voices and opinions of their fellow village dwellers. As the report boasted, 'The quintessence of the forum method is recognition and respect for the contribution of simple village folk'.[93] Before the programme began, villagers sat and discussed the topic, exchanging ideas and looking at visual aids provided by the project team. Each programme then began with a village crier sounding the traditional gong to assemble the people and greeting the gathering. This was followed by 'crowd noises of anxious members hurrying to be at the meeting'. Rather than diving straight into the night's topic, the first part of each broadcast consisted of 'reports, comments and criticisms from the forums', which were read by a woman announcer.[94] The programmes were divided into groups of four. After three broadcasts, a 'talk-back' session took place. For these, representatives from the villages went to the city to recapitulate and react to the previous three sessions. The aim of the 'talk-back' broadcast was to review and reinforce subject-matter, and also increase local interest by featuring the voices of members from local farm forums on the radio.

The methodology of the social science research had also evolved by the middle of the 1960s, though the basic structure of the experiment, with surveys before and after the broadcasts, was retained. Compared to India, there was a more complex mix of villages chosen, including two urban areas, and the initial surveys included more information about the socio-economic status of the participants, including their marital status, level of formal education or 'planned learning' they had experienced and what crops they farmed. Additionally, the study group deployed different methods for quantifying the survey results, including numerical figures for the effectiveness of individual broadcasts, rather than all twenty together.[95] As a whole, the report on Ghana included fewer anecdotes or qualitative examples, so that the information presented was in the form of abstract statistics, when compared to the information gathered in India a decade before. For example, it reported simply the number of respondents surveyed who said they'd taken action on increasing production, crops, poultry or livestock, rather than recording the particular action taken.

Conclusions

The report, rather unsurprisingly, concluded that Farm Radio Forums were a success that ought to be brought, with necessary adjustments, to the rest of Africa. The history of the radio farm forum is not a simple story of a development idea being developed in India and disseminated to Ghana. There was a Canadian precedent, Australians on the scene and UNESCO acted as the hub and spoke organization, universalizing this development knowledge in an iterative fashion.

In the worldwide set of experiments known as development in the 1940s–70s, India was keen to be a laboratory for the development of new ideas and practices. When a pilot project undertaken in India was successful, it was rolled out across the country, and India's representatives began touting the benefits to other decolonizing states, often via UN agencies. These countries drew on the Indian experience. But the starting point for India's experiments – that programmes had to be adjusted to local conditions – was central to the export of these projects to other countries.

A post-colonial socialism, shared by India and Ghana, also seems to be at play in the content and objectives of the Farm Radio Forums. Though the state was acting in pedagogic mode, the lessons were not to be imbibed entirely passively. The programmes were designed to spur action from citizens, precisely because the state was not regarded as capable of taking a monopoly over all development initiatives. This was a matter of finances, for sure, but it was also a form of socialism that encouraged – albeit in limited ways – 'talk back' from citizens.

Notes

1 Joseph Morgan Hodge, 'Writing the History of Development (Part 2: Longer, Deeper, Wider)', *Humanity* 7, no. 1 (2016): 125–74; David C. Engerman and Corinna Unger, 'Introduction: Towards a Global History of Modernization', *Diplomatic History* 33, no. 3 (2009): 375–85.

2 An approach pioneered by Sunil Amrith, *Decolonizing International Health: India and Southeast Asia, 1930–65* (Houndmills: Palgrave Macmillan, 2006).

3 For a useful summary of this historiography, Ismay Milford, Gerard McCann, Emma Hunter and Daniel Branch, 'Another World? East Africa, Decolonisation, and the Global History of the Mid-Twentieth Century', *The Journal of African History* 62, no. 3 (2021): 394–410.

4 Amitav Acharya and See Seng Tan (eds.), *Bandung Revisited: The Legacy of the 1955 Asian-African Conference for International Order* (Singapore: National University of Singapore Press, 2008), 1–16; Christopher J. Lee, *Making a World After Empire: the Bandung Moment* (Athens: Ohio University Press, 2010); Naoko Shimazu, 'Diplomacy as Theatre: Staging the Bandung Conference of 1955', *Modern Asian Studies* 48, no. 1 (2014): 225–52.

5 Su Lin Lewis and Carolien Stolte, 'Other Bandungs, Afro-Asian Internationalisms in the Early Cold War', *Journal of World History* 30, no. 1/2 (2019): 1–20.

6 Su Lin Lewis, 'We Are Not Copyists': Socialist Networks and Non-alignment from Below in A. Philip Randolph's Asian Journey', *Journal of Social History* 53, no. 2 (2019): 402–8.

7 Francisca de Haan, 'Continuing Cold War Paradigms in Western Historiography of Transnational Women's Organisations: The Case of the Women's International Democratic Federation (WIDF)', *Women's History Review* 19, no. 4 (2010): 547–73; Paul Emiljanowicz, 'Translocality and the Future: Postcolonial Connectivities in 1960s Ghana', *Postcolonial Studies* 26, no. 1 (2023): 112–30; Su Lin Lewis, 'Women, Hospitality and the Intimate Politics of International Socialism, 1955–1965', *Past & Present* (2023), firstview.

8 Hala Halim, 'Lotus, the Afro-Asian Nexus, and Global South Comparatism', *Comparative Studies of South Asia, Africa and the Middle East* 32, no. 3 (2012): 563–83.

9 Joan Kee, *The Geographies of Afro Asia: Art Beyond Solidarities* (Berkeley: University of California Press, 2023).

10 A few exceptions: Naaborko Sackeyfio-Lenoch, 'Decolonization, Development, and Nation Building in Ghana-Asia Relations, 1957–1966', *The International Journal of African Historical Studies* 49, no. 2 (2016): 235–53; Ismay Milford and Gerard McCann, 'African Internationalisms and the Erstwhile Trajectories of Kenya Community Development: Joseph Murumbi's 1950s', *Journal of Contemporary History* 57, no. 1 (2021): 111–35.

11 Partha Chatterjee, 'Development Planning and the Indian State', in *State and Politics in India*, ed. Patha Chatterjee (Delhi: Oxford University Press, 1995), 271–97; Benjamin Zachariah, *Developing India: An Intellectual and Social History, c. 1930–50* (Delhi: Oxford University Press, 2005).

12 Vivek Chibber, *Locked in Place: State-Building and Late Industrialisation in India* (Princeton, NJ: Princeton University Press, 2008); Jason A. Kirk, *India and the World Bank: The Politics of Aid and Influence* (London: Anthem Press, 2010); David C. Engerman, *The Price of Aid: the Economic Cold War in India* (Cambridge,

MA: Harvard University Press, 2018); Nikhil Menon, *Planning Democracy: Modern India's Quest for Development* (Cambridge: Cambridge University Press, 2022).

13 Paul Emiljanoqicz, 'Tensions, Ambiguities, and Connectivity in Kwame Nkrumah: Rethinking the "National" in Postcolonial Nationalism', *Interventions* 21, no. 5 (2019): 615–34.

14 Taylor C. Sherman, '"A New Type of Revolution": Socialist Thought in India, 1940s–1960s', *Postcolonial Studies* 21, no. 4 (2018): 485–504; Jeffrey S. Ahlman, *Living with Nkrumahism: Nation, State, and Pan-Africanism in Ghana* (Athens: Ohio University Press, 2017), Chapter 4.

15 Daniel Immerwahr, *Thinking Small: The United States and the Lure of Community Development* (Cambridge, MA: Harvard University Press, 2015); Ahlman, *Living with Nkrumahism*, Chapter 3; Taylor C. Sherman, *Nehru's India: A History in Seven Myths* (Princeton: Princeton University Press, 2022), Chapter 4.

16 Sunil Amrith and Glenda Sluga, 'New Histories of the United Nations', *Journal of World History* 19, no. 3 (2008): 251–74.

17 Kirk, *India and the World Bank*; Manu Bhagavan, *The Peacemakers: India and the Quest for One World* (New Delhi: Harper Collins Publishers India, 2012); Aditya Balasubramanian, and Srinath Raghavan, 'Present at the Creation: India, the Global Economy and the Bretton Woods Conference', *Journal of World History* 29, no. 1 (2018): 65–94; Waheguru Pal Singh Sidhu, 'The Accidental Global Peacekeeper', in *India and the Cold War*, ed. Manu Bhagavan (Chapel Hill, NC: University of North Carolina Press, 2019), 79–99.

18 Glenda Sluga, 'UNESCO and the (One) World of Julian Huxley', *Journal of World History* 21, no. 3 (2010): 393–418; Paul Betts, 'Humanity's New Heritage: UNESCO and the Rewriting of World History', *Past & Present* 228 (2015): 249–85.

19 Robin Jeffrey, 'The Mahatma Didn't Like the Movies and Why It Matters: Indian Broadcasting Policy, 1920s–1990s', *Global Media and Communication* 2, no. 2 (2006): 204–24; Srirupa Roy, *Beyond Belief: India and the Politics of Postcolonial Nationalism* (New Delhi: Permanent Black, 2007), Chapter 1; Isabel Huacuja Alonso, *Radio for the Millions: Hindi-Urdu Broadcasting Across Borders* (New York: Columbia University Press, 2023), Chapter 3.

20 Bipin Chandra, *The Rise and Growth of Economic Nationalism in India* (Delhi: Anamika Publishers, 2004, reissue).

21 Chatterjee, 'Development Planning'; Zachariah, *Developing India*.

22 Immerwahr, *Thinking Small*; Engerman, *The Price of Aid*.

23 Taylor C. Sherman, 'From "Grow More Food to Miss a Meal"': Hunger, Development and the Limits of Postcolonial Nationalism in India, 1947–1957', *South Asia: Journal of South Asian Studies* 36, no. 4 (2013): 571–88; Benjamin Seigel, *Hungry Nation: Food, Famine and the Making of Modern India* (Cambridge: Cambridge University Press, 2018).

24 Sherman, *Nehru's India*, Chapter 4.

25 Daniel Klingensmith, *'One Valley and a Thousand': Dams, Nationalism, and Development* (Delhi: Oxford University Press, 2007); Annapurna Shaw, 'Town Planning in Postcolonial India, 1947–65: Chandigarh Re-Examined' *Urban Geography* 30, no. 8 (2009): 857–78.

26 David C. Engerman, 'Learning from the East: Soviet Experts and India in the Era of Competitive Coexistence', *Comparative Studies of South Asia, Africa and the Middle East* 33, no. 2 (2013): 227–38.

27 For example, Report of the Indian Agricultural Team to USSR, Poland and Czechoslovakia, September–October, 1954 (New Delhi: Ministry of Food and Agriculture, 1954); Report of the Delegation to China on Agrarian Co-Operatives (New Delhi: Planning Commission, 1957).
28 For example, United Nations Technical Assistance Programme, *Report on Local Government Study Tour of Yugoslavia and India by Senior Officials of African States* (New York: United Nations, 1964).
29 Rosemary Wakeman, *Practicing Utopia: An Intellectual History of the New Town Movement* (Chicago: University of Chicago Press, 2016), Chapter 3.
30 Minutes of the meeting of the Planning Commission to meet M Le Corbusier, 17 April 1952, Fry & Drew Papers, Royal Institute of British Architects, F&D/1/1. See also Sherman, *Nehru's India*, Chapter 7.
31 Menon, *Planning Democracy*.
32 Immerwahr, *Thinking Small*, Chapter 3; Ajantha Subramanian, *Shorelines: Space and Rights in South India* (Palo Alto: Stanford University Press, 2009), Chapter 3.
33 Sherman, *Nehru's India*, Chapter 4.
34 Ornit Shani, *How India Become Democratic: Citizenship and the Making of the Universal Franchise* (Cambridge: Cambridge University Press, 2018).
35 *Times of India*, 22 December 1953, 9.
36 *Times of India*, 6 November 1953, 1.
37 *Times of India*, 3 December 1957, 8.
38 Kanwar Sain, *Modern Trends in the Design & Construction of Dams & Power-Houses* (Delhi: Atma Ram and Sons, 1962), 7.
39 Klingensmith, *'One Valley and a Thousand'*.
40 Kanwar Sain, *Reminiscences of an Engineer* (New Delhi: Young Asia Publications, 1978), 2–6; Sudhir Sen, *Wanderings: In Search of Solutions of the Problem of Poverty* (Madras: Macmillan India, 1989), 3.
41 Sain, *Reminiscences*, 78–9.
42 Sen, *Wanderings*, 37.
43 Ibid., 104.
44 Kanwar Sain, 'The Social Repercussions of Hydraulic Projects in India', *Civilisations* 5, no. 2 (1955): 183–91, at p. 189.
45 Sen, *Wanderings*, 67–8.
46 Sain, *Reminiscences*, 379.
47 *Times of India*, 2 March 1954, 8.
48 Jane Drew, Senior Architect to the Government of Punjab, Chandigarh Project, Note on Low-Cost Housing, [undated], Fry & Drew Papers, RIBA Collections, F&D/1/1.
49 J. C. Mathur and Paul Neurath, *An Indian Experiment in Farm Radio Forums* (Paris: UNESCO, 1959), 16.
50 Mathur and Neurath, *An Indian Experiment*, 17.
51 Immerwahr, *Thinking Small*; Sherman, *Nehru's India*.
52 B.P. Bhatt, *Radio Broadcasting Serves Rural Development: I. Radio rural forums spread throughout India* (Paris: UNESCO, 1965).
53 Cassidy Foxcroft, 'Canadian Farm Radio Forum' (Ontario Institute for Studies in Education, 2018) https://wordpress.oise.utoronto.ca/librarynews/2018/05/17/canadian-farm-radio-forum/; Mathur and Neurath, *An Indian Experiment*, Preface, n.p.
54 On grow more food, see Sherman, From 'Grow More Food' to 'Miss a Meal'; Siegel, *Hungry Nation*.
55 *Times of India*, 24 September 1949, 4.

56 *Times of India*, 21 November 1954, 8.
57 *Times of India*, 15 June 1950, 10.
58 Alonso, *Radio for the Millions*, Chapter 3.
59 Mathur and Neurath, *An Indian Experiment*, 33.
60 Ibid., 34.
61 Sherman, 'A New Type of Revolution'.
62 Mathur and Neurath, *An Indian Experiment*, 34.
63 Sherman, 'A New Type of Revolution'.
64 Mathur and Neurath, *An Indian Experiment*, 47.
65 Ibid., 48.
66 Ibid., 22.
67 Ibid., 30.
68 On the importance of sampling in India and its development by P. C. Mahalanobis, see Menon, *Planning Democracy*.
69 Mathur and Neurath, *An Indian Experiment*, 61–2.
70 Ibid., 68.
71 Sherman, *Nehru's India*, Chapter 4.
72 Miss R. Gadgil, Miss S. Vinekar, Miss L. Paralkar, Miss R. Dhupkar, Mrs R. Karve, Mr S. Hombali, Mr G. M. Gawankar, Mr C. Natu, Mr P. Kulkarni and Mr K. Y. Karnik. Mathur and Neurath, *An Indian Experiment*, 62.
73 Taylor C. Sherman, 'Not Part of the Plan? Women State Feminism and Indian Socialism in the Nehru Years', *South Asia: Journal of South Asian Studies* 44, no. 2 (2021): 298–312.
74 Mathur and Neurath, *An Indian Experiment*, 69.
75 Ibid., 89–90.
76 Ibid., 97–8.
77 Ibid., 98.
78 Ibid., 82.
79 Ibid., 82–3.
80 Ibid., 100.
81 Ibid., 100–1.
82 Ibid., 41.
83 Ibid., 106.
84 UNESCO, Radio Broadcasting Serves Rural Development, 26.
85 Ibid., 23.
86 Ibid., 30.
87 Ibid.
88 UNESCO, *An African Experiment in Radio Forums for Rural Development: Ghana 1964/5* (Paris: UNESCO, 1968), 7–9.
89 UNESCO, *An African Experiment*, 22.
90 Albert Adu Boahen, 'Yaa Asantewaa in the Yaa Asantewaa War of 1900: Military Leader or Symbolic Head?' *Ghana Studies* 3 (2000): 111–35.
91 UNESCO, *An African Experiment*, 8.
92 Ibid., 17–21.
93 Ibid., 9.
94 Ibid., 12.
95 Ibid., 29–35.

13

Confronting capitalism in twentieth-century Latin America

Kevin A. Young

The violent decimation of the Latin American Left and the neoliberal counterrevolution of the late twentieth century crushed hopes for the near-term overthrow of capitalism. If in the mid-1980s there were still lively debates about the transition to socialism, thereafter most leftists scaled back their ambitions. One indication of this shift was that most 'Pink Tide' politicians of the early twenty-first century did not envision an end to capitalism within their lifetimes. Revolutionary experiments like the Zapatista autonomous zones or worker-run factories in Argentina, however inspiring, were mostly confined to the subnational level. Leftist scholars of Latin America took to cataloguing the casualties of neoliberalism or celebrating small-scale resistance. Some scorned political economy altogether, viewing economic development as an inherently insidious 'discourse' propagated by a paternalistic West.[1] The topic of development was mostly relinquished to economists unsympathetic to socialism.

This is a shame, for there are important lessons, both positive and cautionary, to be learned from socialists in twentieth-century Latin America. The region's Left has always been more creative and complex than its critics allege, including with respect to ideas about economic development. Moreover, Latin Americans have made vital contributions to the broader anti-imperialist tradition. Studying this history is important for excavating lost possibilities. It can also help clarify the challenges for which the Left has not yet found answers.

Recent years have seen a renewal of interest in Latin American socialisms and internationalisms.[2] This essay draws from existing literature, both new and old, on the theory and practice of socialism on the Latin American Left. I touch on the economics of socialist development and also related questions that preoccupied twentieth-century revolutionaries, including worker decision-making and communal autonomy, the relationship of consciousness to economic change, the need for international cooperation and how to end gender, sexual and racial hierarchies. I focus on socialists in the Marxist and anarchist sense, meaning those committed to working-class control of the economy.

* My thanks to Joanna Crow, William Figueroa, Su Lin Lewis, Marc Matera, Kelvin Ng, Nana Osei-Opare, Taylor Sherman, Diana Sierra Becerra and Matthew Shutzer for the helpful comments.

The chapter is organized into four sections. The first addresses the 1910s through 1930s. During these years Latin Americans made trenchant critiques of capitalism, empire and social hierarchies in their societies. The radicals were defeated but did contribute to notable reforms in their societies. The second section covers the early postwar period. The 1940s through the late 1950s featured state-led industrialization and modest social reforms, embodied in the developmentalist and populist regimes that held power. State repression of radicals did not prevent the creative assimilation of new ideas on the Left, for instance from Marxist feminisms and popular nationalisms. The third section deals with the early years of the Cuban Revolution, examining both its domestic economic policies and its international relationships and reverberations. This period featured rising discontent with Soviet orthodoxies, new attempts at international economic cooperation and, by the early 1970s, some important critiques of the Cuban model's own limitations. In the fourth section I look at the mixed-economy approaches to development that were attempted in Peru, Chile, Nicaragua, Venezuela and elsewhere.

I make three causal arguments. First, the distinctive timing of decolonization in Latin America had important implications for the region's Left as compared with most of Africa and Asia. Latin America's early independence and long acquaintance with de facto economic domination led to early critiques of neocolonialism, which focused on the impacts of private enterprise, foreign investment and market dependence in formally independent areas. Latin America's situation proved that ending formal colonial rule would not necessarily bring economic or social liberation. This helps explain why economic structuralism and dependency theory originated primarily in Latin America. By the 1960s decolonization in Africa and Asia had elucidated the shared predicament, as leaders of newly independent nations assailed neocolonialism and increasingly prioritized 'tricontinental' cooperation with Latin America.

Critics of neocolonialism were not all socialists, however. A second theme is the relationship between revolutionaries and reformists. I argue that the anti-capitalist Left was largely responsible for the century's progressive reforms, sometimes spearheading them directly but more often through indirect influence, as when scared elites embraced reform to neutralize the revolutionaries. This is especially apparent in the aftermath of the Cuban Revolution. It happened at both national and global levels. Multilateral projects of the 1960s and 1970s like the UN Conference on Trade and Development (UNCTAD), the G-77 and proposals for a New International Economic Order derived much of their (limited) power from the threat of socialist revolution. Conversely, the near-destruction of the Left in most places between the 1950s and 1980s doomed the prospects for meaningful social democracy.

Third, the Latin American Left was shaped by both local and global factors. This point may seem obvious, but it merits emphasis given still-common depictions of leftists as mouthpieces for the Kremlin. Local or domestic influences included movements of workers, small farmers, students, women, Indigenous people, Afrodescendants and progressive Catholics, who engaged in 'reciprocally transformative dialogues' with leftist ideology and organizations.[3] International forces that influenced the Left included the Moscow-led Communist International (1919–43), the regional spread of resource nationalism in the 1920s and 1930s, the theories of structuralism and dependency in the 1950s and 1960s, the Cuban Revolution and transnational dialogues about the role of gender, race, religion, popular participation, armed struggle and elections in revolutionary transitions. The Left was also shaped by the hostility of its enemies, to which it sometimes responded with radicalization and sometimes with attempts at conciliation.

The rise of Latin American anti-imperialism

Anti-imperialism had been present in Latin America and the Caribbean since the start of empire itself, as seen in the multifaceted Indigenous and African resistance to colonial subjugation. Neocolonialism, too, quickly came under attack after most of the region expelled the Spanish Crown in the 1820s. Already in 1829 Simón Bolívar warned that 'the United States seems destined by providence to plague Latin America with misery in the name of liberty'.[4] The intensification of US imperialism thereafter would help shape the formation of a pan-Latin American consciousness, consolidating the notion of 'Latin' America as well as later formulations like 'Indo-Hispanic America', defined in opposition to the Northern aggressor.[5]

Criticisms of empire took on a more economic focus as US and European capitalists extended their tentacles over the region. In 1896 the Argentine socialist Juan Justo wrote that 'English capital has done what its armies could not do. Today our country is a tributary to England. Each year many millions of gold pesos are sent off to the shareholders of English enterprises operating in the country.'[6] England was soon displaced by the United States as the major economic and geopolitical power in the region. US investors backed by US gunboats hungrily acquired Latin American natural resources, markets and transportation routes.

Criticisms of economic dependency intensified in the 1920s. Speaking to the Comintern Congress in Moscow in 1928, Ecuadorian Communist Ricardo Paredes called attention to the 'intermediary forms' of foreign subjugation, describing as 'dependencies' those countries 'which have been penetrated economically by imperialism but which retain a certain political independence'. Peruvian Marxist José Carlos Mariátegui wrote that Latin American countries 'function economically as colonies of European and North American industry and finance'.[7] These critiques stressed the distortions of Latin American economies caused by foreign trade and investment. Among the results were a lack of diversification and industrialization and the collaborationist nature of national bourgeoisies.

Moreover, the enrichment of neocolonial powers was accompanied by increased inequality and repression inside Latin American countries, often spearheaded by liberal oligarchies in alliance with foreign capital. Land dispossession, declining nutrition levels and the repression of organized labour were common consequences.[8] Some Marxists and anarchists stressed what would later be called internal colonialism, expressed in the particularly acute exploitation of the peasantry. Some noted the importance of anti-Indigenous and anti-Black racism in reproducing this structure and advocated the right of self-determination for Indigenous and Afro peoples. This position was influenced by the living examples of rebellion in the 1910s and 1920s, especially Indigenous revolts in Mexico and the Andes. One US Communist told the 1928 Comintern Congress that Indigenous movements were 'the greatest reserve of revolutionary energy that exists in Latin America' and therefore demanded the Left's attention.[9]

The most broadly shared basis for anti-imperialist mobilization, however, was the defence of mineral and fossil fuel wealth. Those resources were in high demand with the industrialization of the North Atlantic, the invention of the internal combustion engine and the First World War, which made governments' generous collaboration with foreign investors appear more offensive. By the 1910s and early 1920s, leftists, social democrats and nationalist capitalists all demanded policies to increase national control over subterranean resources. Nationalization, the creation of public enterprises and higher royalty rates were common programmatic goals and were reflected in new government policies in Argentina, Bolivia, Brazil, Chile, Colombia, Mexico and Uruguay. Resource nationalism was increasingly central to Latin American thinking about economic development. Nationalists argued that greater state control over resources was a prerequisite for industrialization and diversification, while progressives added that national control was also necessary for advancing social rights like good wages, public education and healthcare.[10]

The Mexican Revolution galvanized this sentiment across the region. The most heretical article of its 1917 Constitution gave the state 'the right to impose on private property such limitations as the public interest may demand'. In the 1930s the Mexican state nationalized the oil sector and redistributed tens of millions of acres of land to peasants. The notion that private property was subject to expropriation in the public interest was soon incorporated into new constitutions across Latin America. Anti-imperialists often invoked 'the healthy values of nationalist defense practiced in Mexico' in their attacks on the 'privileges established in favour of foreign capitalists' in their own countries, as Bolivian university students did in 1928.[11]

Post-revolutionary Mexico also became a meeting point for leftist organizers from around the region (and world), many having fled repressive dictatorships in their lands.[12] Several of the most important internationalist organizations of the 1920s were established in Mexico, including the Alianza Popular Revolucionaria Americana (American Popular Revolutionary Alliance, APRA) in 1924, the Liga Antiimperialista de las Américas (Anti-Imperialist League of the Americas) in 1925 and the Comité Manos Fuera de Nicaragua (Hands Off Nicaragua Committee) in 1928.[13] The Mexican government did not spearhead these solidarity efforts, and its meagre aid to the Nicaraguan guerrillas fighting US occupation made no difference in the war there. It did, however, provide some economic support for moderate nationalist forces, for example by training technical personnel for Bolivia's state oil company after 1936.[14]

Solidarity with the Nicaraguan guerrillas who fought the US Marine occupation between 1927 and 1932 was the most visible internationalist campaign of the 1920s. Latin American condemnation of the occupation, and the stubborn survival of the guerrilla campaign itself, led the US government to disavow unilateral intervention in 1933 and to opt (temporarily) for less overt means of projecting imperial power. It also led, in conjunction with anti-imperialist struggles in Haiti, Mexico and elsewhere, to the codification of the non-intervention principle in international law in the 1940s.[15]

The implications for economic development were apparent to Latin American nationalists. Although anti-intervention struggles in Nicaragua and Haiti were not centrally concerned with natural resource wealth, the fight for sovereignty had clear importance for economic policy. Both countries were subjected to customs receiverships and other measures that ensured US control of their finances. Many anti-imperialists also argued that the fundamental impetus behind US empire was economic. Staving off a capitalist crisis in the metropole required the United States to assert 'its dominance over markets, transport routes, and sites of raw materials', as José Carlos Mariátegui wrote in a 1927 essay on Nicaragua.[16]

While Mariátegui's analysis of imperial motives was broadly shared in anti-imperialist circles, the strategic and policy implications were more contentious. The main dividing line among Latin American nationalists by the late 1920s was the role of the middle classes and national bourgeoisies. How much weight, if any, should those classes be allowed to exert within the anti-imperialist movement? The debate often centred on divergent readings of Mexico, China and Russia – the first two multiclass nationalist coalitions, the third an anti-capitalist revolution. Víctor Raúl Haya de la Torre sought to make APRA the 'Guomindang of Latin America', meaning that middle-class and business interests would be allowed leadership roles. This position was based on the assumption that those classes could act independently of foreign capital and that the latter could be made 'a cooperator in national economic development' rather than a mere extractor of wealth.[17]

Radicals like Mariátegui deemed Haya de la Torre's position opportunistic and naïve. Though Mariátegui knew capitalists could not be eliminated overnight, he opposed giving them any leadership within the movement. He warned that the anti-imperialist struggle 'does not erase antagonisms between classes, it does not suppress their difference of interests'. He pointed to 'the experience of Mexico, where the petite bourgeoisie [and the large bourgeoisie] has ended up in agreement with Yankee imperialism'.[18] The Guomindang's 1927 betrayal and massacre of Communists proved to many that middle-class leaders could not be trusted, influencing the Comintern's rejection of interclass alliances between 1928 and 1934. This debate was paralleled in Mexico itself by struggles over the form revolution would take. There workers and peasants mobilized for land reform, economic security and worker control of industry in defiance of the pro-capitalist post-revolutionary regimes.[19]

If this class conflict was predictable, other barriers to anti-imperialist unity were perhaps less inevitable. Most of the prominent anti-imperialist writers and orators were white, and many of them refused to recognize the reality of racism, particularly anti-Blackness, in their countries. International solidarity with occupied Haiti was noticeably rarer than with the 'mestizo' Nicaragua.[20] While radical interethnic alliances did form in some places, they required a level of consciousness and humility that most white and mestizo leaders lacked.[21] Global unity between Latin American nations and the peoples of Africa and Asia was further undermined by disagreements about whether 'dependent' Latin America belonged in the same category as the formally colonized. The Comintern-affiliated League Against Imperialism and for National Independence, founded in 1927, implicitly prioritized struggles against formal empire.[22] Psychological barriers among anti-imperialists thus exacerbated the difficulties imposed by geographic distance.

Pro-capitalist forces triumphed everywhere in Latin America during this time, but not without incorporating some of the radicals' demands. Oil nationalizations in Bolivia (1937) and Mexico (1938) were largely the product of popular agitation, in the latter case involving mobilization for a general strike. The impressive Mexican land reform of the 1930s likewise came on the heels of militant rural action, including a strike by 20,000 cotton workers in the Laguna region. Even Fulgencio Batista in Cuba was forced to adopt a fairly progressive constitution in 1940.[23] The region's capitalist regimes bore the imprints of the defeated Left.

Orthodoxy and innovation, 1940s–1950s

The other force favouring change was the Great Depression and the popular responses it provoked. Pro-capitalist politicians were compelled to embrace changes – social democratic, developmentalist, corporatist or some mix thereof – as a way of stabilizing capitalism. The Depression pummelled Latin American export economies with harsh effects on workers and losses for many middle- and upper-class sectors as well. Falling export revenues and declining ability to import led to significant import-substitution industrialization. Increasing state intervention in support of that process was initially 'imposed by circumstances', as Argentine economist Raúl Prebisch later described the enactment of exchange controls in his country.[24] Necessity forced innovation.

The theoretical framework to justify state-supported industrialization lagged behind. Prebisch's famous manifesto appeared in 1949.[25] He challenged the reigning liberal creed of comparative advantage, which asserted that the benefits of technological progress in the industrial nations would naturally trickle down to primary-good exporters in the form of lower prices. Contrary to the doctrine, Prebisch argued that Latin America's terms of trade with the industrial world had tended to decline over time, forming a pattern of 'unequal exchange'. He described a world divided between Centre and Periphery where the commodity exporters of the Periphery faced systematic disadvantages. Prebisch and others also criticized the monetarist view of inflation, arguing that inflation derived more from structural bottlenecks than from increases in the money supply. Their prescription was state intervention to promote industrialization and diversification. Prebisch's argument formed the basis for the structuralist school of economics and the emergent subdiscipline of development economics. In 1948, structuralism and developmentalism acquired an institutional home, the UN Economic Commission for Latin America (ECLA), established under Prebisch's leadership.

Structuralist thought evolved over the 1950s and 1960s in accordance with economic research and practical experience. For example, international cooperation among Peripheral economies soon received more attention as a way to combat problems such as small domestic markets, volatile commodity prices, shortage of capital goods and lack of access to rich countries' import markets. The 1963 creation of UNCTAD, with Prebisch as inaugural director, reflected this impetus. That decade also featured the formation of new regional economic blocs like the Central American Common Market and the Andean Pact, as well as exporter coalitions like the Organization of Petroleum Exporting Countries (OPEC) that sought to stabilize prices and reduce exporters' reliance on existing export products like oil.[26]

Although structuralism helped inspire the more radical schools of dependency and world-systems theories in the 1960s and 1970s, the structuralists were not socialists. On the contrary, they thought the Periphery could benefit from global capitalism given the right fiscal, monetary and regulatory policies. They argued that policy should foster the growth of the national bourgeoisie, and they allowed only a limited role for state-owned enterprises.[27] ECLA's formation coincided with intensified repression against the Left across Latin America. Communist parties were outlawed and authoritarian regimes employed 'harsh governmental measures of repression' against labour and progressive forces, as the US State Department counselled in 1950.[28] This timing is perhaps no coincidence. Washington was initially wary of ECLA but ultimately deemed it preferable to the anti-capitalist Left. Developmentalist governments of the early postwar period could generally retain US favour if they repressed the Left, made no broad-based attack on private capital and supported US foreign policy.

Within the Left itself certain orthodoxies also came under challenge. Orthodoxy in this context meant obedience to Moscow, authoritarian party structures, 'peaceful coexistence' with capitalist regimes and the non-violent pursuit of reform. This orientation was based on the argument that Latin American economies were still largely feudal in nature and must pass through a lengthy capitalist phase before reaching socialism.[29] But while many Latin American leftists certainly embraced this thinking, others did not. A more complete picture would include a range of revolutionaries whose analysis of their societies, visions of the future and strategies often diverged from Soviet dictates.

In many places leftists developed nuanced understandings of the relationship between class structure and social identities of nation, ethnicity, race and gender. Marxists in Chile and Bolivia sought to reconcile Marxism with nationalist consciousness.[30] Ecuadorian Communists and Bolivian anarchists integrated Indigenous liberation into anti-capitalist struggle.[31] Marxist women in Guatemala, El Salvador, Cuba, Uruguay and beyond embraced feminist analysis and demands.[32] These analyses in turn informed organizing priorities and tactics. Many leftists organized in rural communities, haciendas and urban residential neighbourhoods as well as industrial workplaces. Armed movements in Mexico, Bolivia and Cuba defied Moscow's injunction against guerrilla struggle and its support for national bourgeoisies. Such innovations were intimately shaped by leftist women, Indians, Afrodescendants and peasants in addition to the traditional working class.[33] Even during the heyday of Soviet hegemony over the Latin American Left, many challengers cropped up.

Diverse international connections, not just with the Soviet Union, shaped the Left's evolution during these years. Guatemala until 1954 hosted political exiles and was an important site for transnational conversations.[34] The 1954 coup also served as a cautionary lesson about the limits of the electoral route to revolution, most famously for Che Guevara, who was in Guatemala at the time. The 1949 Chinese revolution inspired many Latin American leftists who applauded its agrarian reform, industrial policy and social welfare measures. Many visited China in person. In the 1950s many on the Mexican and Bolivian Lefts cited China as a way of criticizing the more conservative revolutions in their own countries.[35] Maoism, Trotskyism and Titoism (after Yugoslavian leader Josip Broz Tito, who advocated independence from Moscow) all found considerable support in 1950s Latin America.

The Cuban example

After 1959 the most important international reference point was Cuba. Cuban revolutionaries defied the Soviets by employing armed struggle to overthrow the Batista dictatorship. In so doing they demonstrated that leftists need not confine themselves to electoral tactics and multiclass coalitions as the Soviets urged. The Cuban victory also sharpened the Left's disillusion with the related notion, advanced by ECLA and many nationalists, that national capitalists would lead the drive toward economic development. That prediction was further undermined by Brazilian capitalists' support for the 1964 military coup against a reformist government. The Cuban Revolution, the Brazil coup and other events of the 1960s contributed to the rise of dependency theory. The *dependentistas*, particularly the Marxists among them, condemned ECLA's faith in national bourgeoisies and promoted a radical break from global capitalism.[36]

The Cuban government was also crucial, both ideologically and materially, to the spread of Third World internationalism in the 1960s and 1970s. Its own internationalist initiatives in Africa and Latin America involved medical aid projects, educational missions, covert military support for anti-colonial and anti-capitalist guerrilla forces and aid to leftist governments in places like Chile and Nicaragua. Cuba was also central to multilateral efforts designed to build Third World solidarity, namely the Non-Aligned Movement (NAM) founded in Belgrade in 1961 and the Tricontinental Conference that convened African, Asian and Latin American peoples in Havana in 1966. These organs helped consolidate the notion of the Third World – nation-states not squarely aligned with the West or the Soviet bloc – and the feeling of shared interests across the Periphery. The recent tide of decolonization in Africa and southern Asia contributed to that sense of commonality.[37]

Though not specifically economic entities, NAM and the Tricontinental both bolstered the growing emphasis on economic cooperation across the Third World. This impulse dovetailed with ECLA's promotion of regional economic integration, but socialists gave the idea a more radical inflection. Without Cubans and other revolutionaries the proposals for a New International Economic Order (NIEO) in the 1970s are unthinkable. The symbolic NIEO charter adopted by the UN General Assembly in 1974 was not anti-capitalist, yet it did advocate significant restrictions on global market forces in order to make relations between the Centre and Periphery more equitable.[38]

Cuban internationalism was motivated by values of revolutionary solidarity as well as the pragmatic imperative of cultivating alliances to protect itself. Given how states typically operate, what is surprising here is the degree to which morality shaped the Cuban leadership's decisions. The Castro government was willing to jeopardize its relationship with the Soviet Union, which often opposed Cuban solidarity initiatives, and with smaller trade partners. It also accepted the considerable drain on Cuban resources that internationalist missions entailed. Moreover, the Cubans acquired a reputation for treating their foreign partners with respect.[39]

The threat to capital and empire was obvious. US officials noted in the early 1960s that throughout Latin America the 'poor and underprivileged, stimulated by the example of the Cuban revolution, are now demanding opportunities for a decent living'.[40] Latin American ruling classes expressed similar fears of contagion. The response from the United States and its regional allies was two-pronged: minor socio-economic reforms would attenuate the misery that contributed to rebellion, while ferocious violence would be unleashed on any of the 'poor and underprivileged' who demanded more than that. John F. Kennedy's Alliance for Progress entailed the creation of death-squad apparatuses in places like Colombia, El Salvador and Guatemala to ensure what US officials called 'internal security' – the protection of upper classes and foreign investors from the poor and underprivileged.[41]

The reform part was trickier to manage. In principle, US officials recognized that Latin American economic structures needed progressive changes if revolution was to be averted. This undertaking was fraught with risks, however: Latin Americans might embrace policies that Washington and local elites could not abide. This fear helps explain why reform initiatives ultimately fizzled almost everywhere. Even pro-capitalist reformers sometimes took things beyond elites' threshold of comfort, as with Dominican president Juan Bosch and Brazilian João Goulart, overthrown in military coups in 1963 and 1964. Even some close friends of the United States ventured too far. Mexican president Luis Echeverría was a leading sponsor of the 1974 NIEO vote at the UN, which he hoped would bolster his regime's legitimacy at home while reducing Cuban influence in the Third World.[42]

The US response to the NIEO threat was 'to split the Third World', in Secretary of State Henry Kissinger's words. 'Obviously we can't accept the new economic order, but I would like to pull its teeth and divide these countries up'. His approach was to 'appear forthcoming so that we are not outside of the process' and then rally Third World reformers against the radicals. This strategy exploited pre-existing divisions. Despite the language of solidarity on the lips of numerous Third World leaders, solidarity was always fragile. As one of Kissinger's colleagues noted, 'These countries can unite behind rhetoric' but in fact 'the diversity among them is enormous'.[43] The diversity stemmed in part from differing levels of national wealth and competing short-term needs (for instance, between oil exporters and importers), tensions that contributed to the disappointing performance of many regional integration projects in the Third World.[44] On a deeper level, Third World diversity also reflected disagreements about the ideal economic system.

The reason for conflict among Third World governments is clear when we consider Cuba's domestic economic model, which was more radical than the approaches adopted elsewhere. By 1961 all large private enterprises had been expropriated, a massive agrarian reform was underway and healthcare, education, housing and childcare were all free or low-cost. Furthermore, the revolution's humanism set it apart from the Soviet system. Che Guevara, the leading economic official in the government between 1959 and 1965, criticized the Soviet model's cold economism. He envisioned a revolution that would eliminate not just material inequality but also the alienation experienced by workers under capitalism (and, implicitly, under the regimented Soviet economy). The Cuban system would foster the worker's creativity and 'full human condition'. In the process, the worker 'begins to see himself portrayed in his work', which signifies 'a contribution to the life of society in which he is reflected'.[45]

For Guevara overcoming alienation also required phasing out the use of material incentives to motivate labour. He insisted that industrialization, diversification and material redistribution must be accompanied by a cultural campaign to create 'a new man', who would be increasingly motivated by incentives 'of a moral character' to contribute to the social good. He criticized the Soviet model for its overreliance on wage differentials and other material rewards, which he warned should never be 'the primary instrument of motivation' in a socialist workplace. Cuba's new wage scale in the early 1960s set the highest salary at just three times the lowest, and by 1966 all cash bonuses for overproduction were abolished in favour of moral rewards such as social recognition.[46] Guevara also criticized the use of material incentives at the macro level. The financial autonomy of Soviet state enterprises incentivized profit maximization and tacitly pitted each workplace against others. Such structural arrangements fostered individualistic consciousness rather than solidarity. For this reason Guevara advocated a centralized financing system in which 'central administrative bodies' controlled enterprises' operations and expenditures.[47]

By some measures the new system yielded impressive results. Most notable are the world-renowned improvements in the health, education and nutritional levels of the population. Even today Cuba's health and educational indicators remain impressive, even in comparison with many wealthy countries.[48] Less known than these material gains were the improvements in workers' subjective experiences after 1959. One of the most detailed studies in the early years was by sociologist Maurice Zeitlin, who in 1962 collected a national randomized sample of over 200 private interviews in twenty-one major workplaces. Zeitlin found 'that nearly three-fourths of those dissatisfied with their work in one way or another before the nationalization of industries say nationalization positively transformed their attitudes toward their work ... [W]ith it came a fundamental change in their work and their commitment to it. Socialism provided them with a desire to work which they had not experienced before'.[49]

By other measures the Cuban model was less successful. Import substitution and export diversification were limited, a pattern reinforced by trade relations with the USSR in which Cuba exported sugar in exchange for manufactures. Low growth put major constraints on the socialist project. Some bright spots in the diversification realm did develop starting in the 1980s. The development of a biotechnology sector and the export of medical services have acted as lifelines since the Soviet collapse in 1991.[50]

The causes of Cuba's economic problems are not easily disentangled. Clearly imperialism is a leading culprit. The US blockade severely impedes trade and investment. This forced isolation raises costs and exacerbates dependence on the few who are still willing to do business, such as the USSR and more recently Russia. Yet internal factors have also played a role. Cuba has never devised a satisfactory system for motivating workers, evident in the ongoing problem of worker absenteeism. The government's recurring solution, beginning in the 1970s, has been to reintroduce market incentives. This approach has brought production gains while increasing inequality and eroding collective solidarity. Another internal problem is the lack of real economic democracy or 'self-management'. Writing in 1969, Zeitlin concluded that while workers had some input over how to implement 'the objectives of the national economic plan set for their plant, the workers have no role whatsoever, to my knowledge, in determining the plan itself'.[51] Decisions about investment allocations, consumption rights and provision of public goods were mostly out of workers' hands, and nor were workers gaining the knowledge and skills necessary to participate more directly in those decisions. The recourse to market incentives has certainly not given workers any greater control. The two problems of motivation and participation are related. Greater worker control could help incentivize work; in its absence, 'the tedium of execution without self-management will blunt revolutionary zeal', as two radical economists warned in 1981.[52] The shortage of revolutionary zeal is today especially visible among younger generations who have no personal memory of the revolutionary changes of the 1960s or of the relative economic prosperity of the 1970s and 1980s.

Mixed economies in Cuba's shadow

Cuba's experiences guided other Latin American leftists who sought to transform their economies. Cuba was perceived as a symbol of revolutionary commitment, defiance and dignity. Yet leftists were also conscious of the flaws in the Cuban model. One set of limitations was external to the revolution and perhaps inevitable: the hostile reaction of imperialists and privileged domestic sectors to any major reform. After Cuba all socialist-led governments opted for a more cautious and gradualist course. They tried to divide, co-opt or persuade, rather than eliminate, the capitalist elite and to avoid all-out hostility from Washington. This involved policies and institutional changes designed to foster mixed economies composed of private, state and cooperative sectors.

Internal weaknesses of the Cuban model reinforced the preference for mixed economies. The inefficiencies of Cuban central planning and the inadequacy of moral incentives contributed to Latin American leftists' belief that private enterprise and markets must continue to play a significant role. Many were drawn to market socialism as an alternative to central planning. The Yugoslavian model, which combined market incentives with a high degree of worker self-management within enterprises, attracted particular interest.[53]

Peru drew from the Yugoslavian example during the progressive military regime of Juan Velasco Alvarado (1968–75). A variety of reformist and libertarian socialist forces had advocated some form of worker self-management prior to Velasco's 1968 coup. After taking power Velasco announced that his goal was a 'fully participatory social democracy'. In addition to nationalizing oil, mines and some other key sectors of the economy, his government expropriated 35 per cent of Peru's agricultural land and converted the large haciendas into peasant cooperatives.[54] The 1974 Social Property Law envisioned a system where workers would collectively own their firms with any surplus distributed among them. The reality did not quite match that vision, however.

The cooperative sector comprised only a small minority of the peasantry, and the law made it 'extremely difficult to convert private firms and cooperatives into social-property firms'. Industrial workers meanwhile had little control over their enterprises. And even the self-managed sectors still operated in a market system based on the profit motive (as in Yugoslavia), which fostered insularity among different groups of workers – the reason why Che Guevara had advocated centralized financial control and a phase-out of material incentives.[55] The contradictions of the Peruvian system partly reflected the regime's lack of internal coherence. Their reform measures and discourse of participation were largely intended to deprive the revolutionary socialist Left of popular support.[56] Velasco and his colleagues may have genuinely wanted to make the economy fairer, but they also saw the mixed economy as a way to preserve capitalism. As the Peruvian example suggests, mixed economies are by no means always revolutionary.

A more radical vision of the mixed economy guided Salvador Allende's socialist administration in Chile from 1970 to 1973. The Unidad Popular (UP) coalition, which included the Socialists and Communists plus several smaller parties, pursued a more aggressive strategy of nationalizations in finance, mining and various branches of manufacturing and commerce. Those nationalized enterprises would form a new 'social property area' alongside a private sector and a 'mixed' public-private sector. The goal was to ensure public control over the core of the economy so that the private sector could no longer control domestic prices and major investment decisions.[57]

The UP's economic vision reflected important critiques of other revolutions. The Socialist Party advocated worker self-management and critiqued centralized planning models as insufficiently democratic. This vision was partly rooted in some Chilean socialists' enthusiasm, dating back to the 1940s, for Yugoslavia's model of worker self-management and political autonomy from the Soviet Union.[58] One of the UP's fledgling projects, Project Cybersyn, aimed to use principles of cybernetics to manage newly nationalized industries. The immediate priority was to maximize efficiency through a system of real-time communication and feedback mechanisms, which avoided the inefficiencies seen in other countries' central planning models and allowed the government to counter the economic sabotage of the opposition. More radically, Cybersyn technology could also have been used to facilitate workers' direct participation in national planning.[59]

The most revolutionary impetus came from the UP's working-class base. As Allende's director of national planning later recalled, growing worker participation in management 'was driven in large measure by the workers themselves'. The central labour federation in 1968 had resolved 'to fight for the direct participation of workers' in management of their enterprises 'as a first step of democratization' of the economy.[60] From 1971 to 1973 many workers occupied their factories and farms, established networks for distributing consumer goods and organized *cordones industriales* (industrial 'belts') that allowed enterprises to share materials. These autonomous initiatives were key to defeating the nationwide bosses' strike and lockout of October 1972. Moreover, workers proved they could learn to run their enterprises and even increase production levels. As the leading scholar of the worker-run factories notes, 'Competence increased with the degree of participation, and the greatest gains were made by those [workers] with the greatest responsibilities'.[61] At the time of the

September 1973 coup, the labour federation was in talks with UP leaders 'to increase the role of the workers and reduce that of the State, bringing a greater decentralization that would allow for the beginning of real self-management'.[62]

Unfortunately that goal was not shared by most UP leaders. The Communist Party advocated a slow process of change under tight control of the government, with little room for working-class offensives against capital and an unclear role for worker participation in the workplace. The logic of this approach was to reassure the Chilean middle sectors and to avoid frontal confrontation with the bourgeoisie, with the goal of expanding the UP's electoral support for the 1973 and 1976 elections. Allende came from the Socialist Party but sided with the Communists and their more conservative strategy. He never stopped trying to appease the so-called centrist Christian Democratic Party, even two years after the Party's leaders had formed an alliance with the hard-right National Party to block UP initiatives. His misplaced faith in the possibility of conciliation, and his lack of faith in his own working-class base, proved fatal. The UP's political illusions were accompanied by economic illusions, such as the assumption that capitalists would respond to price controls by increasing production rather than by hoarding and disinvesting, as they did.[63] As a result the UP had no realistic strategy for countering the capital strike, the US financial blockade and the eventual military coup of 11 September 1973. Solving the severe economic problems of 1972–3, which manifested in the form of high inflation and shortages, would have required a more radical approach than most UP leaders were willing to take.

The Chilean coup and the spread of murderous right-wing military regimes across the region deflated hopes for socialist revolution. Leftist visions of Third World economic solidarity also faltered, due both to imperial hostility and the divergence of ideology and interests among Third World leaders. By the late 1970s radicals' hopes for the Non-Aligned Movement had been dashed. Chile's domestic political conflict during the Allende years was an exaggerated microcosm of the global fault lines within the Third World: whenever the possibility of revolutionary change appeared on the horizon, Right and Centre united against Left, ultimately crushing the prospects for reform as well as revolution.

In this inauspicious context the Nicaraguan Revolution triumphed in 1979. Like Allende, the Sandinistas sought a predominant role for the public sector. Although over half the economy remained privately owned, the state did obtain monopoly control over key activities such as finance and foreign trade, which enabled it to control credit and access to foreign exchange. Capitalists were excluded from political power to a greater degree than in Chile, though they were still allowed to operate news outlets and compete in the 1984 election. However, the Sandinistas' hope that capitalists could be enticed to cooperate in the economic realm despite their exclusion from government proved misplaced. The Nicaraguan economic elite soon called upon the US government and the remnants of the National Guard to sabotage the economy and wreak terror upon the population. In addition to killing some 30,000 Nicaraguans, the Contra war imposed devastating costs on the economy and forced the government to divert resources away from social programmes and public investment. The Nicaraguan experience showed that promising capitalists continued profits is often not enough to obtain their economic cooperation.[64]

Radical visions of the mixed economy suffered a major setback thereafter. The 1990 electoral defeat of the Sandinistas, the collapse of the USSR and China's capitalist transition coincided with the most triumphal period of capitalism, as neoliberal ideologues exploited Third World indebtedness to impose radical probusiness policies. Most leftists tempered their hopes. The left-of-centre parties that won election after 1998 challenged neoliberalism in many ways but did not take aim at capitalism itself.[65]

A partial exception was Venezuela under Hugo Chávez (1999–2013). Chávez's assertion of executive control over the state oil company in 2003 allowed for major new public investments in education, healthcare, housing and anti-poverty spending. The following year Venezuela and Cuba announced the formation of the Bolivarian Alliance for the Peoples of Our America (ALBA-TCP), a regional integration project for the trade of Venezuelan oil and Cuban medical services. The most novel feature of the Venezuelan process was the communal councils and communes. As understood by their organizers, those projects involved 'building self-government' to eventually replace the central state bureaucracy with alternative systems of popular governance, production and distribution. 'We believe that popular power can't be limited to just waiting for a bag of food to arrive', said one organizer of a food cooperative.[66]

The impetus for this radical turn came from multiple sources. The notion of self-management had deep roots in Indigenous and Afro-Venezuelan communities and was reinforced by the influence of intellectuals like Hungarian Marxist István Mészáros.[67] Tens of thousands of Venezuelan organizers took advantage of the opportunity to forge new communal organizations. Another driving force was, in Marx's words, 'the whip of the counterrevolution'. A right-wing coup attempt and capitalist lockout in 2002–3 inadvertently helped radicalize what had been a very moderate process of change, leading Chávez to embrace 'twenty-first-century socialism'.[68]

Hopes for a participatory social revolution in Venezuela ebbed after Nicolás Maduro's rise to the presidency in 2013. A fall in global oil prices, combined with the government's mismanagement of monetary policy and its inability to discipline private capital, contributed to a major recession. US sanctions turned a recession into a depression of historic proportions that wiped out most of the earlier gains. Many tens of thousands of Venezuelans died as a result.[69] ALBA and other trade relationships offered only a weak lifeline. Maduro weathered several coup attempts, but did quietly bend to capitalist demands for reprivatization of many nationalized sectors. The Venezuelan experience is one more reminder of the vulnerability of Global South economies to the forces of market dependence, capitalist sabotage and imperialism. A large measure of corruption and the government's own economic mistakes further undermined Venezuela's ability to respond effectively.

Unresolved questions

The historical innovations of Latin America's Left have much to teach. They can offer both moral inspiration and strategic guidance in a world plagued by extreme economic and social hierarchies, plutocracy, militarism and environmental destruction. History will take us only so far, however. As the preceding review has suggested, the Left in

Latin America (and everywhere else) has historically fallen well short of its goals. Any large-scale attempts at building an equitable and sustainable society will need to grapple with certain problems that the Left has often recognized but never adequately resolved. How can capitalists' power to block reforms be neutralized? How can Southern nations build structures for international cooperation? How can an economy foster popular empowerment in both the workplace and at the national level? And the question that looms over everything else: how can Southerners confront a growing climate emergency for which Northern elites bear most of the responsibility? Obviously such matters are also relevant to those of us residing outside the Global South.

Venturing answers to these questions or surveying how recent Latin American leftists have tried to answer them is beyond the scope of this essay. But the well-being of humanity and other living things depends on our collective ability to find answers. Surviving, let alone thriving, on a heated planet will require learning from history's liberation movements and building the organizations that can win the changes we need.

Notes

1 For example, Arturo Escobar, *Encountering Development: The Making and Unmaking of the Third World* (Princeton, NJ: Princeton University Press, 1995).

2 Some edited volumes from the last decade: Geoffroy de Laforcade and Kirwin Shaffer, *In Defiance of Boundaries: Anarchism in Latin American History* (Gainesville: University Press of Florida, 2015); Adriana María Valobra and Mercedes Yusta Rodrigo, *Queridas camaradas: Historias iberoamericanas de mujeres comunistas* (Buenos Aires: Miño y Dávila, 2017); Santiago Aránguiz Pinto and Patricio Herrera González, *Los comunismos en América Latina: Recepciones y militancias (1917–1955)*, 2 vols (Santiago: Historia Chilena, 2018); Hernán Camarero and Martín Mangiantini, *El movimiento obrero y las izquierdas en América Latina: Experiencias de lucha, inserción y organización*, 2 vols (Chapel Hill: UNC Press/Editorial A Contracorriente, 2018); Kevin A. Young, *Making the Revolution: Histories of the Latin American Left* (New York: Cambridge University Press, 2019); Thomas C. Field, Jr., Stella Krepp and Vanni Pettinà, *Latin America and the Global Cold War* (Chapel Hill: UNC Press, 2020); Tanya Harmer and Alberto Martín Álvarez, *Toward a Global History of Latin America's Revolutionary Left* (Gainesville: University of Florida Press, 2021); Marc Becker, Margaret M. Power, Tony Wood and Jacob A. Zumoff, *Transnational Communism across the Americas* (Urbana: University of Illinois Press, 2023).

3 Omar Acha and Débora D'Antonio, 'Cartografía y perspectivas del "marxismo latinoamericano"', *A Contracorriente* 7, no. 2 (2010): 243. See also Young, ed., *Making the Revolution.*

4 Quoted in Jan Knippers Black, 'The Empire Strikes Out? Western Hemisphere Lessons in Empire-Building and Maintenance', *Journal of Developing Societies* 21, nos. 3–4 (2005): 282.

5 Michel Gobat, 'The Invention of Latin America: A Transnational History of Anti-Imperialism, Democracy, and Race', *American Historical Review* 118, no. 5 (2013): 1345–75.

6 Quoted in José Luis Romero, *Las ideas políticas en Argentina* (Mexico City: Fondo de Cultura Económica, 1946), 193–4.
7 Tony Wood, 'Semicolonials and Soviets: Latin American Communists in the USSR, 1927–1936', in *Transnational Communism*, ed. Becker, et al., 84 (Paredes quoted); Mariátegui, 'La unidad de la América indo-español' (1924), in *Temas de nuestra América* (Lima: Amauta, 1975), 15.
8 For Mexico see Moramay López-Alonso, *Measuring Up: A History of Living Standards in Mexico, 1850–1950* (Stanford, CA: Stanford University Press, 2012).
9 Quote from Bertram Wolfe in Wood, 'Semicolonials and Soviets', 87. See also Joanna Crow's chapter in this volume.
10 Michael L. Krenn, *U.S. Policy toward Economic Nationalism in Latin America, 1917–1929* (Wilmington, DE: Scholarly Resources, 1990), 21–48, 71–98; Antulio Rosales, 'Resource Nationalism: Historical Contributions from Latin America', in *Handbook of Economic Nationalism*, ed. Andreas Pickel (Cheltenham: Edward Elgar, 2022), 158–63; Greg Grandin, 'The Liberal Traditions in the Americas: Rights, Sovereignty, and the Origins of Liberal Multilateralism', *American Historical Review* 117, no. 1 (2012): 68–91.
11 Comité Ejecutivo de la Universidad Boliviana, *Convenciones nacionales universitarias, 1928–1929* (La Paz: CEUB, 1982), 46.
12 Barry Carr, 'Radicals, Revolutionaries and Exiles: Mexico City in the 1920s', *Berkeley Review of Latin American Studies* (Fall 2010): 26–30; Christina Heatherton, *Arise! Global Radicalism in the Era of the Mexican Revolution* (Berkeley: University of California Press, 2022), 47–71.
13 Daniel Kersffeld, *Contra el imperio: Historia de la Liga Antiimperialista de las Américas* (Mexico City: Siglo Veintiuno, 2011); Michael Goebel, 'Forging a Proto-Third World? Latin America and the League Against Imperialism', in *The League Against Imperialism: Lives and Afterlives*, ed. Michele Louro, Carolien Stolte, Heather Streets-Salter and Sana Tannoury-Karam (Leiden: Leiden University Press, 2020), 53–78; Anne Garland Mahler, 'Global Solidarity before the Tricontinental Conference: Latin America and the League against Imperialism', in *The Tricontinental Revolution: Third World Radicalism and the Cold War*, ed. R. Joseph Parrott and Mark Atwood Lawrence (Cambridge: Cambridge University Press, 2022), 43–68.
14 Alan L. McPherson, *The Invaded: How Latin Americans and Their Allies Fought and Ended U.S. Occupations* (New York: Oxford University Press, 2014), 226; Juan José Anaya Giorgis, *Estado y petróleo en Bolivia (siglos XX–XXI)* (Cochabamba: ASDI/UMSS, 2018), 124–9.
15 Greg Grandin, *Empire's Workshop: Latin America, the United States, and the Rise of the New Imperialism* (New York: Metropolitan, 2006), 11–51.
16 'El imperialismo yanqui en Nicaragua', in *Temas de nuestra América*, 146.
17 Quoted in Goebel, 'Forging a Proto-Third World?' 59, and Eric Helleiner and Antulio Rosales, 'Toward Global IPE: The Overlooked Significance of the Haya-Mariátegui Debate', *International Studies Review* 19 (2017): 673.
18 José Carlos Mariátegui, 'Punto de vista anti-imperialista' (1929), in *Ideología y política* (Lima: Amauta, 1981), 90. See also Helleiner and Rosales, 'Toward Global IPE', and, for parallel debates in southern Asia, Kelvin Ng's chapter in this volume.
19 Barry Carr, 'The Mexican Communist Party and Agrarian Mobilization in the Laguna, 1920–1940: A Worker-Peasant Alliance?' *Hispanic American Historical Review* 67, no. 3 (1987): 371–404; Myrna Santiago, *The Ecology of Oil: Environment,*

Labor, and the Mexican Revolution, 1900–1938 (Cambridge: Cambridge University Press, 2007), esp. 290–341; Miles V. Rodríguez, *Movements after Revolution: A History of People's Struggles in Mexico* (New York: Oxford University Press, 2022).

20 Goebel, 'Forging a Proto-Third World?' 64–8; Wood, 'Semicolonials and Soviets', 85–6. Much of the solidarity with Haiti was US-based, led by Black organizers and non-Black Communists. See Margaret Stevens, '"Hands off Haiti!" Self-determination, Anti-imperialism, and the Communist Movement in the United States, 1925–1929', *The Black Scholar* 37, no. 4 (2008): 61–70; McPherson, *The Invaded*, 169–81.

21 For important exceptions see Forrest Hylton, 'Common Ground: *Caciques*, Artisans, and Radical Intellectuals in the Chayanta Rebellion of 1927', and Barry Carr, 'Identity, Class, and Nation: Black Immigrant Workers, Cuban Communism, and the Sugar Insurgency, 1925–1934', in *Making the Revolution*, ed. Young, 19–76.

22 Goebel, 'Forging a Proto-Third World?' 61, 69–72.

23 Kevin A. Young, 'Smoothing the Contradictions: The Political History of Fossil Fuels', in *The Struggle for Natural Resources: Findings from Bolivian History*, ed. Carmen Soliz and Rossana Barragán (Albuquerque: University of New Mexico Press, 2024), 174–8; Santiago, *Ecology of Oil*, 290–341; Carr, 'The Mexican Communist Party'; Ariel Mae Lambe, *No Barrier Can Contain It: Cuban Antifascism and the Spanish Civil War* (Chapel Hill: UNC Press, 2019), 185–206.

24 Quoted in Joseph L. Love, 'Raúl Prebisch and the Origins of the Doctrine of Unequal Exchange', *Latin American Research Review* 15, no. 3 (1980): 48.

25 Prebisch, 'El desarrollo económico de la América Latina y algunos de sus principales problemas', *El Trimestre Económico* 16, no. 63 (1949): 347–431.

26 OPEC's key architect, Venezuelan official Juan Pablo Pérez Alfonzo, envisioned it as a way to 'free the country from excessive dependence on a single nonrenewable resource'. Doing so required conservation, not perpetual extraction – suggesting that OPEC's early history holds lessons for curtailing fossil fuel extraction today. Pérez Alfonzo, *El pentágono petrolero* (Caracas: Ediciones Revista Política, 1967), title page (quote). See also Michael Dobson, 'Revisiting OPEC's Democratic Roots in the Age of Climate Emergency', *E-International Relations*, 17 January 2020.

27 Though some moved leftward in later decades. On state-owned enterprises see Victor Bulmer-Thomas, *The Economic History of Latin America since Independence*, 2nd edn (Cambridge: Cambridge University Press, 2003), 339–46.

28 George Kennan to Secretary of State, 29 March 1950, Doc. 330 in *Foreign Relations of the United States* [hereafter *FRUS*], *1950* (Washington, D.C.: USGPO, 1976), 2: 607. See also Leslie Bethell and Ian Roxborough (eds.), *Latin America between the Second World War and the Cold War, 1944–1948* (Cambridge: Cambridge University Press, 1992).

29 See for instance José Aricó, 'Marxismo latinoamericano' (1982), in *José Aricó: Dilemas del marxismo en América Latina: Antología esencial*, ed. Martín Cortés (Buenos Aires: CLACSO, 2020), 636–40, though Aricó does acknowledge some heterodox Marxist thinkers of the period. Heterodoxy gets more emphasis in Acha and D'Antonio, 'Cartografía y perspectivas', 220–1.

30 An influential tract from a Chilean Socialist was Oscar Waiss, *Nacionalismo y socialismo en América Latina* (Santiago: Prensa Latinoamericana, 1954). See also Joaquín Fernández Abara, 'Nacionalismo y marxismo en el Partido Socialista Popular (1948–1957)', *Izquierdas* 34 (2017): 26–49; Kevin A. Young, *Blood of the*

Earth: Resource Nationalism, Revolution, and Empire in Bolivia (Austin: University of Texas Press, 2017).

31 Marc Becker, *Indians and Leftists in the Making of Ecuador's Modern Indigenous Movements* (Durham, NC: Duke University Press, 2008); Kevin A. Young, 'Total Subversion: Interethnic Radicalism in La Paz, Bolivia, 1946–1947', in *Making the Revolution*, ed. Young, 129–55.

32 Valobra and Yusta, eds., *Queridas camaradas*; Patricia Harms, 'Breaking the Silence: Communist Women, Transnationalism, and the Alianza Femenina Guatemalteca, 1947–1954', in *Transnational Communism*, ed. Becker, et al., 169–88; Equipo Maíz, *Tula Alvarenga, obrera y militante del movimiento popular de El Salvador de 1940 a 1970* (San Salvador: Equipo Maíz, 2016), 67–83; Michelle Chase, *Revolution within the Revolution: Women and Gender Politics in the Cuban Revolution, 1952–1962* (Chapel Hill: UNC Press, 2015).

33 See sources in notes 30–32 plus Tanalís Padilla, *Rural Resistance in the Land of Zapata: The Jaramillista Movement and the Myth of the Pax Priísta, 1940–1962* (Durham, NC: Duke University Press, 2008); Stephen Cushion, *A Hidden History of the Cuban Revolution: How the Working Class Shaped the Guerrillas' Victory* (New York: Monthly Review, 2016); Sara Kozameh, 'Black, Radical, and *Campesino* in Revolutionary Cuba', *Souls* 21, no. 4 (2019): 288–311; Tiffany Sippial, *Celia Sánchez Manduley: The Life and Legacy of a Cuban Revolutionary* (Chapel Hill: UNC Press, 2020).

34 Harms, 'Breaking the Silence', 172.

35 Matthew D. Rothwell, *Transpacific Revolutionaries: The Chinese Revolution in Latin America* (New York: Routledge, 2013).

36 For a review of recent studies of Marxism and dependency see Steve Ellner, 'Dependency Theory and Its Revival in the Twenty-first Century', *Latin American Research Review*, Published online, 2 April 2024. doi:10.1017/lar.2024.12.

37 Goebel, 'Forging a Proto-Third World?' 69–72.

38 On the NIEO see the 2015 special issue of the journal *Humanity* (6, no. 1).

39 Piero Gleijeses, *Conflicting Missions: Havana, Washington, and Africa, 1959–1976* (Chapel Hill: UNC Press, 2002); Dirk Kruijt, *Cuba and Revolutionary Latin America: An Oral History* (London: Zed, 2017). See also Unfried and Martínez, this volume.

40 Daniel Braddock, 'Summary Guidelines Paper', 3 July 1961, Doc. 15, in *FRUS, 1961–1963* (Washington, D.C.: USGPO, 1996), 12: 33.

41 Michael McClintock, *Instruments of Statecraft: U.S. Guerilla Warfare, Counterinsurgency, and Counterterrorism, 1940–1990* (New York: Pantheon, 1992), 230–57.

42 Christy Thornton, *Revolution in Development: Mexico and the Governance of the Global Economy* (Berkeley: University of California Press, 2021), 166–89.

43 Kissinger and Labor Secretary John Dunlop in 'Memorandum of Conversation', 26 May 1975, Doc. 294, and 'Editorial Note', Doc. 295, in *FRUS, 1969–1976* (Washington, D.C.: USGPO, 2011), 31: 1012–14.

44 Bulmer-Thomas, *Economic History*, 288–98; Franklin Tugwell, *The Politics of Oil in Venezuela* (Stanford, CA: Stanford University Press, 1975), 60–7, 131.

45 Guevara, 'Man and Socialism in Cuba' (1965), trans. Margarita Zimmermann, in *Man and Socialism in Cuba: The Great Debate*, ed. Bertram Silverman (New York: Atheneum, 1971), 346.

46 Ibid., 343; Guevara, 'On the Budgetary Finance System' (1964), trans. Stuart Borden, in *Man and Socialism*, ed. Silverman, 134. On wages see Helen Yaffe, *Che Guevara: The Economics of Revolution* (New York: Palgrave Macmillan, 2009), 97, 204.

47 Guevara, 'On the Budgetary Finance System', 134.
48 For example, Juan José Cabello, et al., 'An Approach to Sustainable Development: The Case of Cuba', *Environment, Development and Sustainability* 14 (2012): 573–91.
49 Maurice Zeitlin, *Revolutionary Politics and the Cuban Working Class* (New York: Harper & Row, 1970), 13, 23, 199 (quote). Zeitlin's interview findings are usually ignored in scholarship on early revolutionary Cuba.
50 Helen Yaffe, *We Are Cuba! How a Revolutionary People Have Survived in a Post-Soviet World* (New Haven, CT: Yale University Press, 2020), 120–74.
51 *Revolutionary Politics*, xl.
52 Michael Albert and Robin Hahnel, *Socialism Today and Tomorrow* (Boston, MA: South End Press, 1981), 197.
53 US-based economist Jaroslav Vaněk's interpretation of Yugoslavia was very influential. His key work appeared in Spanish in 1974 as *La economía de participación: Hipótesis de evolución y estrategia para el desarrollo* (Buenos Aires: Amorrortu). Vaněk visited Peru as an adviser in the early 1970s. See Peter T. Knight, 'New Forms of Economic Organization in Peru: Toward Workers' Self-management', in *The Peruvian Experiment: Continuity and Change under Military Rule*, ed. Abraham F. Lowenthal and Cynthia McClintock (Princeton, NJ: Princeton University Press, 1976), 377–9.
54 Cynthia McClintock, *Peasant Cooperatives and Political Change in Peru* (Princeton, NJ: Princeton University Press, 1981), 3 (Velasco quoted), 33, 60, 62.
55 Knight, 'New Forms', 362, 364–5, 381 (quote); McClintock, *Peasant Cooperatives*, 17, 38.
56 McClintock, *Peasant Cooperatives*, 49; Knight, 'New Forms', 373–4.
57 Ian Roxborough, Philip O'Brien and Jackie Roddick, *Chile: The State and Revolution* (New York: Holmes & Meier, 1977), esp. 71–101.
58 Oscar Waiss, *Amanecer en Belgrado* (Santiago: Prensa Latinoamericana, 1956); Fernández Abara, 'Nacionalismo y marxismo'; Johanna Bockman, 'Democratic Socialism in Chile and Peru: Revisiting the "Chicago Boys" as the Origin of Neoliberalism', *Comparative Studies in Society and History* 61, no. 3 (2019): 661–6.
59 Eden Medina, *Cybernetic Revolutionaries: Technology and Politics in Allende's Chile* (Cambridge, MA: MIT Press, 2011), esp. 141–69.
60 Gonzalo Martner, *El gobierno del Presidente Salvador Allende, 1970–1973: Una evaluación* (Concepción: LAR, 1988), 139 (latter quotes from the Central Única de Trabajadores).
61 Peter Winn, 'Workers into Managers: Worker Participation in the Chilean Textile Industry', in *Popular Participation in Social Change*, ed. Nash, et al., 588. See also Winn's *Weavers of Revolution: The Yarur Workers and Chile's Road to Socialism* (New York: Oxford University Press, 1986), 209–26.
62 Martner, *El gobierno del Presidente Salvador Allende*, 150.
63 Roxborough, et al., *Chile*, 79.
64 Rose J. Spalding (ed.), *The Political Economy of Revolutionary Nicaragua* (Boston, MA: Allen & Unwin, 1987), especially the chapter by John Weeks, 'The Mixed Economy in Nicaragua: The Economic Battlefield', 43–60.
65 Claudio Katz, *Neoliberalismo, neodesarrollismo, socialismo* (Buenos Aires: Batalla de Ideas, 2016).
66 Quotes from Marta Grajales in the 2019 film *Venezuelans under Siege* (dir. Atenea Jiménez and Kevin Young), https://venezuelansundersiege.com/.
67 Chris Gilbert, 'Mészáros and Chávez: The Philosopher and the Llanero', *Monthly Review* (June 2022): 13–25; Jorge A. Giordani C., *La transición venezolana al socialismo* (Caracas: Vadell, 2009).

68 Marx's phrase quoted by Chávez in 2005, in Steve Ellner, 'Does the Process of Change in Venezuela Resemble a "Permanent Revolution"?' *Dialectical Anthropology* 35, no. 3 (2011): 251.

69 Francisco R. Rodríguez, *The Human Consequences of Economic Sanctions* (Washington, D.C.: CEPR, May 2023).

Afterword: Rethinking socialist developmentalisms in the 'Third World'

David C. Engerman

In the early 1970s, as increasing numbers of activists around the world celebrated solidarities within what was then called the Third World, political theorist Hannah Arendt looked on with scepticism. In her 1970 essay 'On Violence', Arendt questioned those promoting 'The Unity of the Third World'. The Third World, Arendt rebutted, is 'not a reality but an ideology'.[1] Asked later to elaborate on this claim by an incredulous interviewer, Arendt doubled down: 'I believe that the Third World is exactly what I said, an ideology or an illusion.' She mocked Third Worldists for adhering to a slogan of 'natives [*sic*] of all colonies, or all former colonies, or of all underdeveloped countries, unite!' – a phrase, she complained, 'is even crazier than the old one from which it is copied'.[2] Decades later, the historian Vijay Prashad offered a different formulation in service of a radically different agenda. The Third World, Prashad wrote in his rousing 'people's history,' was 'not a place [but] … a project'.[3]

In spite of the dramatically different valences that Arendt and Prashad invested in the category 'Third World', the two are, in a way, making the same point. Solidarities would be hard-won across the wide swaths of the globe that were neither in the First World of industrial capitalism nor in the Second World of the socialist bloc; they did not come naturally.

The Third World, in much of the usage in the 1970s and 1980s, ended up being either a residual category or a misleading ranking system; in both cases, the Third World was a product of the Cold War. That these senses of the phrase diverge from the original meaning of French demographer Alfred Sauvy is perhaps beside the point. In coining the phrase, Sauvy, like many a French intellectual, invoked the French Revolution of 1789 in order to understand the present. Sauvy's Third World, like the Third Estate of the eighteenth century, was a source of revolutionary change: 'ignored, exploited, and scorned like the Third Estate, [the Third World] will likely become something'.[4]

The rich chapters in *Socialism, Internationalism, and Development in the Third World* constitute, in a way, a road map of how different parts of the Third World sought to 'become something'. It would be a challenging assignment indeed to draw a single set of conclusions from these wide-ranging essays. Instead, let me point to some of the lessons we might take from these works for future scholarship on the Global South in the latter half of the twentieth century.

The essays in this volume intersect with this commentary on the nature, even the ontology, of the Third World.[5] A number of them, those oriented towards explorations of socialist internationalism, deal directly with the efforts to build the Third World 'project' (as Prashad had it) or to give meaning to ideology (in Arendt's dismissive formulation). They look at efforts to make the Third World into a meaningful political category. These efforts occasionally operated through previously existing, mostly European, organizations like the Moscow-based Communist International or UN agencies but more often took place in a welter of new organizations called into being in the decades after the Second World War. These new organizations could purport to encompass the whole Third World – for instance, the Group of 77 that emerged out of discussions at the UN Conference on Trade and Development. But they also could be topically or regionally defined bodies. Prime examples of the latter appear in Marc Mater's astute analysis of the 'federal moment' of decolonization in Africa, which underscores that the nation was not the only possible instrument for socialist hopes.[6] Indeed, some of the essays, like Su Lin Lewis and Wildan Sena Utama's account of socialist women's organizations, are structured around a succession of confabulations bringing together representatives from different but overlapping permutations of colonies, former colonies and long-independent nations.

These chapters rightly draw our attention to the ubiquity of solidarity conferences across the Global South. At conferences starting with the Asian Relations Conference in Delhi in 1947 then reaching its stride with the Afro-Asian Conference at Bandung, Indonesia in 1955, and accelerating after that, Third World solidarity was not just discussed but enacted.[7] The frequency and structure of these conferences invite closer analysis of the genre of the solidarity conference. Naoko Shimazu offers one approach in her close ethnographic reading of Bandung, which she considers a moment for the performance of Third World solidarity.[8] And a recent piece by Durba Mitra on Third-World feminism offers an analogous example by looking at the genre of the 'state of women' report.[9] A similarly keen analysis of the structure and the process of 'the Third World conference' could prove insightful.

Other chapters in the volume examine the workings of socialism, broadly defined, within a national context. These seek to narrate the history of the Third World in its own terms, not solely in relation to the Cold War superpowers or their former colonizers. Leading political figures, intellectuals and bureaucrats from across this Third World sought to enact one or another vision (or at least version) of socialist internationalism.

It is worth noting here that for all the talk of socialism in these essays, the Second World – once called the Socialist (or the Soviet) Bloc – makes only a few appearances, and many of those are fleeting. To be sure Joanna Crow's eye-opening account of revolutionary socialists in post-First World War Latin America includes a number of representatives from outside the continent – but mostly to show how they were criticized as exporting ideas of race that did not speak to local conditions. Of course Berthold Unfried and Claudia Martinez's essay on 'Cuban Internacionalismo' deals with a socialist state as it attempted to forge its own path of international contacts without routing everything through the self-declared leader of world socialism. And the Soviet Union and some of the European People's Republics appear as potential or actual donors to development projects ranging from Ghanaian fishing to Indian oil. This approach to understanding Third World socialisms complements the impressive efforts by those writing from the perspective of the socialist metropoles (if you will), of the USSR and the People's Republic of China.[10] Yet as many chapters show, relations between the 'socialist South' and the socialist states of Eastern Europe contained tensions. Disagreements over the specifics of what the Soviets called 'economic cooperation' were one source; differences in what constituted socialism were another. Some anti-colonial movements and post-colonial states drew close to the Soviet Union before becoming disillusioned; others were never 'illusioned' in the first place.

One of the many virtues of the essays in this volume is the embrace of pluralism. The collection points not to a singular history of development in the Global South but multiple histories. And similarly there is not a singular socialism (despite frequent assertations to the contrary); ditto for internationalism and development. A handful of essays hypothesize some of the reasons for this variation. As Kelvin Ng describes in his incisive comparison of Indian and Indonesian ideas, Third World socialism was built not just on Marxist ideas but also on Indigenous intellectual traditions as well as current economic and political circumstances. No history of these ideas would be complete without engaging the ways that Global South thinkers drew on Marxian ideas. But nor could they be complete without considering longstanding discussions Indian and Indonesian debates, many of which had little to do with Marx, or with the current conditions that writers like M. N. Roy and Tan Malaka confronted. And as Matthew Shutzer's impressive essay on Indian socialism suggests, pluralist studies of socialism entailed not just looking at different programmes or plans or critiques – but different ways that socialism was instantiated. His three logics of Indian socialism range from a popular language to an economic program ('petrosocialism') to a paradoxical political moment in the 1970s that Shutzer aptly terms 'socialism without socialists'. That socialism could be each of those, even in just one country over the course of a quarter-century, suggests the difficulty of containing socialism within a single standard definition.

Because socialism could be so many things, scholars analysing socialism in the Global South need to build on local knowledge. It is increasingly clear that doing global history requires going local, which in turn requires knowing the local. The essays in this volume offer excellent examples of how deeply rooted local knowledge sheds light on global histories. Pradito Niwandhono's incisive exploration of varieties of Indonesian socialism shows the benefits of deep immersion in the intellectual and political histories of the country. And by the same token Eric Burton's insightful analysis of the internal and external politics of Tanzania's Kivukoni College is possible only because of his knowledge of the institutions and streams of thought there. These global histories, then, gain their analytical purchase from working locally. Ditto for Tehyun Ma's clear-eyed analysis of the Chinese Nationalist Party's invocation of 'The People's Livelihood', which engaged socialism as part of an effort to sideline communism. This dynamic shares interesting resonances with Kevin Young's account of the Left in Latin America, where he sees radical politics as a spectre that allowed the passage of moderate reforms. In both cases, a real or imagined actions from the left opened up space for centrist projects.

Yet it will be no surprise to readers of this volume that our understanding of 'the global' does not draw on or reflect all experiences equally. Arendt, of course, put this more sharply: the countries in the Third World had little in common: Africa, Asia and Latin America, she wrote could be considered 'underdeveloped'. But, she continued, this categorization overlooks 'the innumerable things they do *not* have in common, and the fact that what they do have in common is only a contrast' with Europe and the United States.[11] Without endorsing Arendt's jaundiced view, it is possible, indeed necessary, to examine the many and varied obstacles to Third World solidarity.

The issues were not solely economic; political circumstances also mattered. Chronology played an important role here: the bulk of the Central and South America – excepting the much of the Caribbean – had earned independence more than a century before post-Second World War decolonization began. African nations were a decade or more behind the initial wave. Nor was everything over in one fell swoop. While the Year of Africa in 1960 is rightly heralded as a point of inflection in the continent's history, it was hardly the end of colonial rule. Portuguese colonies' struggles for independence took another dozen years or more. So it is no wonder that African historians, in particular, have long pointed out the unevenness of our imaginative geographies.[12]

Chronology was hardly the sole source of unevenness within the Third World. Examinations of the growing connections across the Third World need to remain just as attuned to missed or blocked connections. The spate of conferences, for instance, worked well for those with funds and/or official imprimatur – but of course excluded those unable to attend. As we turn to valuable 'international social histories', we need to engage the mechanisms of disconnection as well as those of connection.[13]

Such complexities and fissures are visible in this volume. The two essays centred on Latin America, by Joanna Crow and Kevin Young, admirably show how solidarity worked within the region – but their analyses sit somewhat outside the concerns and the timelines of the other historians. Berthold Unfried and Claudia Martinez's examination of Cuban internationalism focuses squarely on efforts to build solidarity across continents; the Tri-Continental, announced in Havana in 1966, adverts this aspiration in its very name. These essays show that the Third World was not a given category, but one that took different forms at different times and on different topics.

If 'underdevelopment' (in Arendt's use, common at the time) was what held the Third World together, then how would efforts to overcome that condition – development – fit into building solidarities within and beyond the Third World? Even more than socialism, development brought together much of the Third World – which, as Arendt noted, was so often defined in terms of a lack relative to the industrial economies of the North Atlantic. Indeed, development might even be the Third World's demiurge, the pursuit that called the Third World into being. As such, development dominated not just the economies but also the politics and policies of the Global South. All kinds of political claims – many antithetical to each other – invoked development.

Take, for instance, the two essays most centred on development. In her essay, Taylor Sherman identifies one channel of development that could tie together disparate elements of the Third World, what would come to be called South-South Cooperation. India, Sherman rightly notes, was long interested in providing assistance to other countries, including small-scale development programmes in Bhutan, a steady flow of mathematicians, economists and planners passing through Calcutta's famed Indian Statistical Institute, election experts helping in Sudan, or Sherman's main subject: a Ghanaian program of agricultural instruction by radio based on experiments of All-India Radio sponsored by the UN Education, Scientific, and Cultural Organization.[14]

The Soviet Union and Eastern European socialist states also sought to build tight connections to the Third World on the basis of their joint position against capitalism. Thus the state Ghana Fishing Corporation sought outside help to modernize its fleet, reaching out to the Soviet Union as well as major fishing powers in the Cold War West. Yet as Nana Osei-Opare makes clear in his thoughtful analysis of archival materials, even this seemingly modest form of development had losers as well as winners; fishing communities would be squeezed by the entrance of new ships, new processing plants, etc. Fortunately for them, modern fishing in Ghana proved to be one fiasco after another; foreign trawlers, both Soviet and British, had an abysmal operating record in Ghana. Yet such failures did little to dent the interest in development.[15] Development, as a *raison d'etat* and perhaps even a *raison d'être*, justified all kinds of efforts. Both Osei-Opare's and Sherman's essays invite interrogation of what made the respective projects (radio and fishing) qualify as developmental or socialist. That such projects could be readily understood as forms of socialism suggests how much power and resonance the term had in its time.

The essays admirably assembled here by Su Lin Lewis and Nana Osei-Opare, then, offer not just a chance to reflect on the antinomies of the Third World but also to plot a way forward. Together with much other scholarship in the past decade, these essays demonstrate that the second half of the twentieth century is no longer simply the 'Cold War Era' in which traditional European empires happened to meet their demise; instead it was an era of liberation from colonial rule during which American-Soviet geopolitical conflict occurred. These essays both exemplify and point the way to future scholarship that will illuminate the second half of the twentieth century in new ways, one that takes the visions, efforts, ideas and actions of the majority of the world's population in the Global South as driving forces of a new global history.

Notes

1 Hannah Arendt, *On Violence* (New York: Harcourt, Brace, Jovanovich, 1970), 21.
2 Arendt, 'Thoughts on Politics and Revolution' (1970), in Hannah Arendt, *Crises of the Republic* (New York: Harcourt Brace Jovanovich, 1972), 210.
3 Vijay Prashad, *The Darker Nations: A People's History of the Third World* (New York: The New Press, 2008), xv.
4 Alfred Sauvy, 'Trois mondes, une planète', *L'Observateur*, 14 August 1952, 5; Marcin Wojciech Solarz, '"Third World": The 60th Anniversary of a Concept That Changed History', *Third World Quarterly* 33, no. 9 (October 2012): 1562–3.
5 While I will use the term 'Third World' without quotation marks in this essay, I hope the foregoing discussion highlights the ways in which I see the phrase as an essential actors' category, one that shaped efforts to build solidarity across what we know

call the Global South. Using this term also emphasizes the overarching geopolitical circumstances – the Cold War – which most of these essays explore.

6 See also Adom Getachew, *Worldmaking after Empire: The Rise and Fall of Self-Determination* (Princeton: Princeton University Press, 2019); Manu Goswami, 'Imaginary Futures and Colonial Internationalisms', *American Historical Review* 117, no. 5 (December 2012): 1461–85.

7 On the Asian Relations Conference, see especially Vineet Thakur, 'An Asian Drama: The Asian Relations Conference, 1947', *The International History Review* 41, no. 3 (May 2019): 673–95.

8 Naoko Shimazu, 'Diplomacy As Theatre: Staging the Bandung Conference of 1955', *Modern Asian Studies* 48, no. 1 (January 2014): 225–52.

9 Durba Mitra, 'The Report, or, Whatever Happened to Third World Feminist Theory?', *Signs: Journal of Women in Culture and Society* 48, no. 3 (March 2023): 557–84.

10 For instance, Jeremy Friedman, *Ripe for Revolution: Building Socialism in the Third World* (Cambridge, MA: Harvard University Press, 2021) is perhaps the highest stage of socialism studies; it builds on the landmark work of Odd Arne Westad, *The Global Cold War: Third World Interventions and the Making of Our Times* (Cambridge: Cambridge University Press, 2005).

11 Arendt, 'Thoughts on Politics and Revolution' (1970), in Arendt, *Crises of the Republic*, 209–10.

12 For one prominent example, Frederick Cooper, 'What Is the Concept of Globalization Good for? An African Historian's Perspective', *African Affairs* 100, no. 399 (April 2001): 189–213.

13 I take the term 'international social history' from a neglected but prescient brief article: Charles R. Lilley and Michael H. Hunt, 'On Social History, the State, and Foreign Relations: Commentary on "The Cosmopolitan Connection"', *Diplomatic History* 11, no. 2 (Winter 1987): 243–50.

14 On ISI, see Nikhil Menon, *Planning Democracy: Modern India's Quest for Development* (Cambridge: Cambridge University Press, 2022), chap. 2. On elections, see Ornit Shani, 'A Complete Stranger to the Country: Sukumar Sen and the Sudan Election, 1953', forthcoming. On the flow of Indian economic experts through South and Southeast Asia, see Sandeep Bhardwaj, 'India and the Making of Political and Economic Order in Southeast Asia, 1919–1961' (Ph.D. Diss, Ashoka University, in process).

15 In a germinal work on development, now over three decades old, anthropologist James Ferguson showed how the failures of development usually led to calls for more development – James Ferguson, *The Anti-Politics Machine: 'Development,' Depoliticization, and Bureaucratic Power in Lesotho* (Cambridge: Cambridge University Press, 1990).

Index

www.ingramcontent.com/pod-product-compliance
Ingram Content Group UK Ltd.
Pitfield, Milton Keynes, MK11 3LW, UK
UKHW020220041026
15470UKWH00012B/681

9 781350 41343